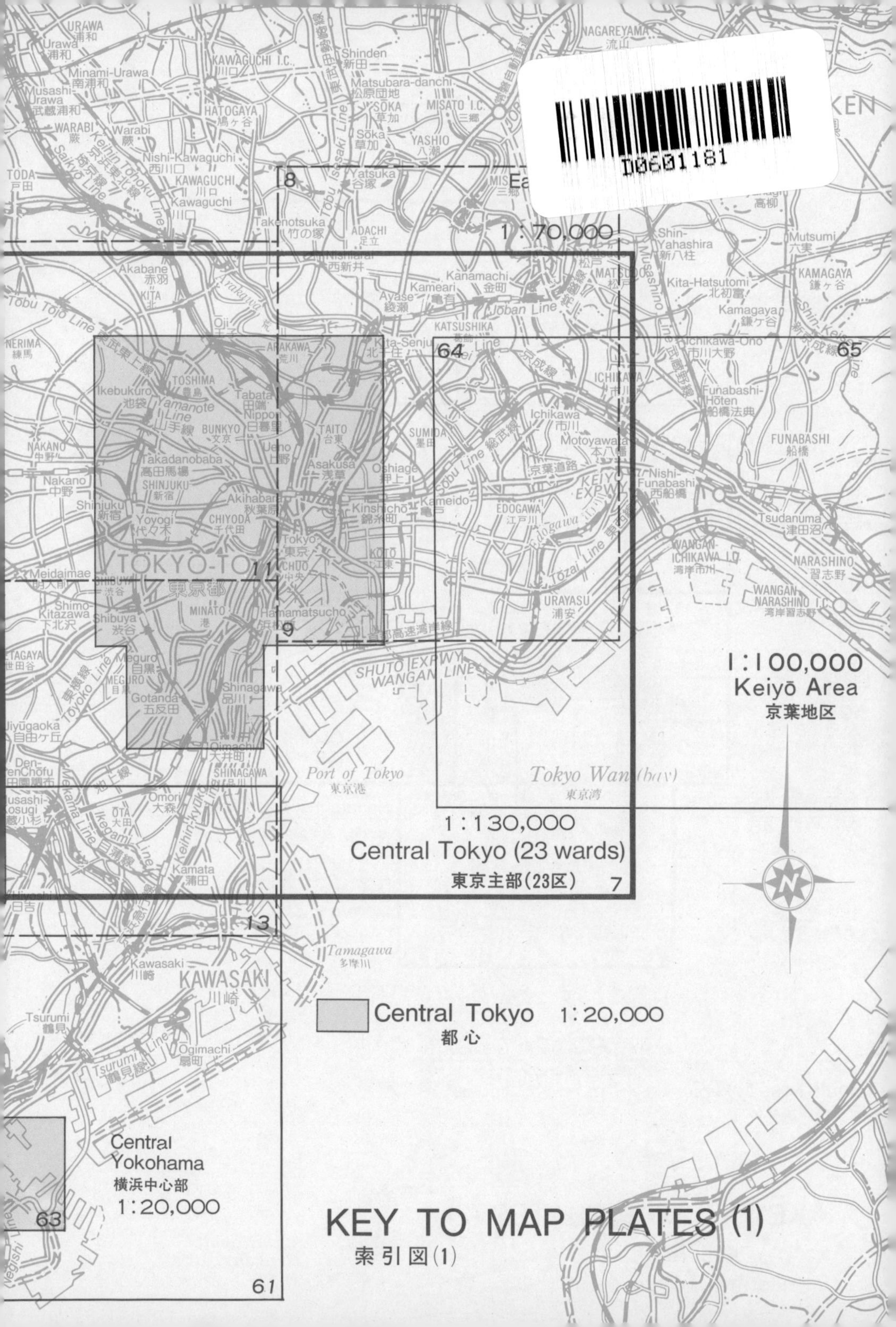

D0601181
1:70,000
8
9
11
1:130,000
Central Tokyo (23 wards)
東京主部(23区)
7
13
64
65
1:100,000
Keiyō Area
京葉地区
Tokyo Wan (bay)
東京湾
Port of Tokyo
東京港
Central Tokyo 1:20,000
都心
Central
Yokohama
横浜中心部
1:20,000
63
61
TOKYO-TO
東京都
KAWASAKI
川崎
Tamagawa
多摩川
SHUTO EXPWY
WANGAN LINE
KEY TO MAP PLATES (1)
索引図(1)

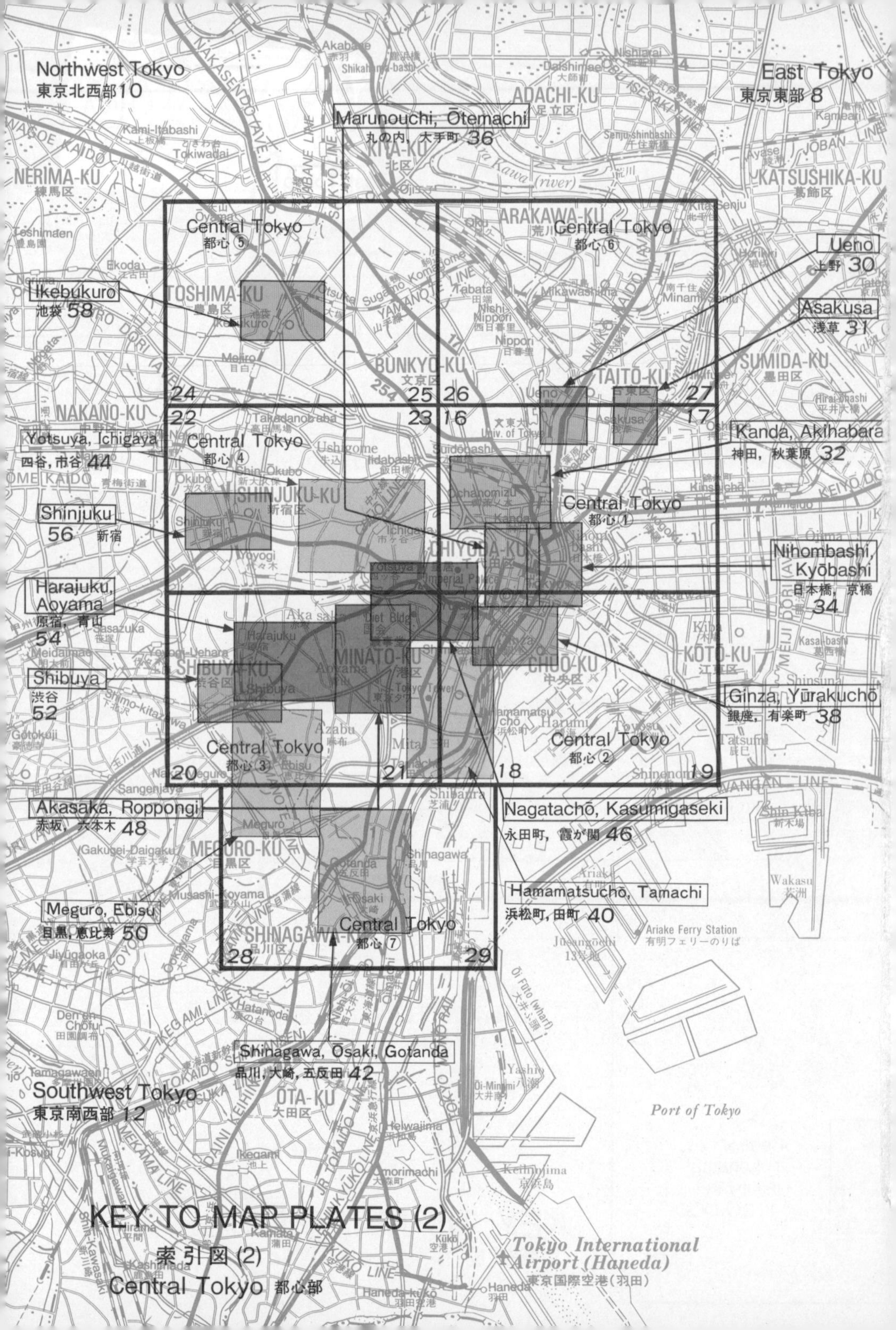

KEY TO MAP PLATES (2)

索引図 (2)

Central Tokyo 都心部

THE NEW TOKYO
Bilingual Atlas

新東京二ヵ国語地図

講談社
KODANSHA

KEY　地域図凡例

Prefectural Boundary　都県界
City *(-shi)* Boundary　市町界
Ward *(-ku)* Boundary　区界
Town *(-machi/-chō)* Boundary　町界
J.R. Line　JR線
Other Railway　その他の鉄道
Subway　地下鉄
Expressway　高速道路
Ramp　高速道路ランプ
(1) (2) (3) *Chōme* Number　丁目番号
Underground Arcade　地下街
Shopping Area　ショッピング街
Park 公園 Garden 庭園 Cemetery 霊園
Government Office　官公庁
Embassy　外国公館

Tourist Spot or Place of Historic Interest　名所旧跡
Shintō Shrine (Shr.) *(Jinja)*　神社
Buddhist Temple *(-ji,-in)*　寺院
Church, Cathedral　教会
City Office　市役所
Ward Office　区役所
Police Station (P.S.)　警察署
Fire Station　消防署
Post Office (P.O.)　郵便局
Telephone Office　NTT(支社、営業所)
Bank　金融機関
Hospital (Hosp.)　病院
School (Sch.)　学校
Factory　工場
Power Plant　発電所
Hotel, Inn　ホテル、旅館
Cinema　映画館

Published by Kodansha Ltd., 12-21, Otowa 2-chome,
Bunkyo-ku, Tokyo 112, Japan.

Printed in Japan.
First edition, 1993,

Note: While every effort has been made by the Publisher to ensure accuracy in this publication at the time of going to press, the Publisher cannot be held responsible for any loss, damage or delay that may ensue as a consequence of reference to this book. The Publisher is interested in your comments, criticisms and suggestions, especially if you find inaccuracies.

ISBN 4-06-206590-8

目次 CONTENTS

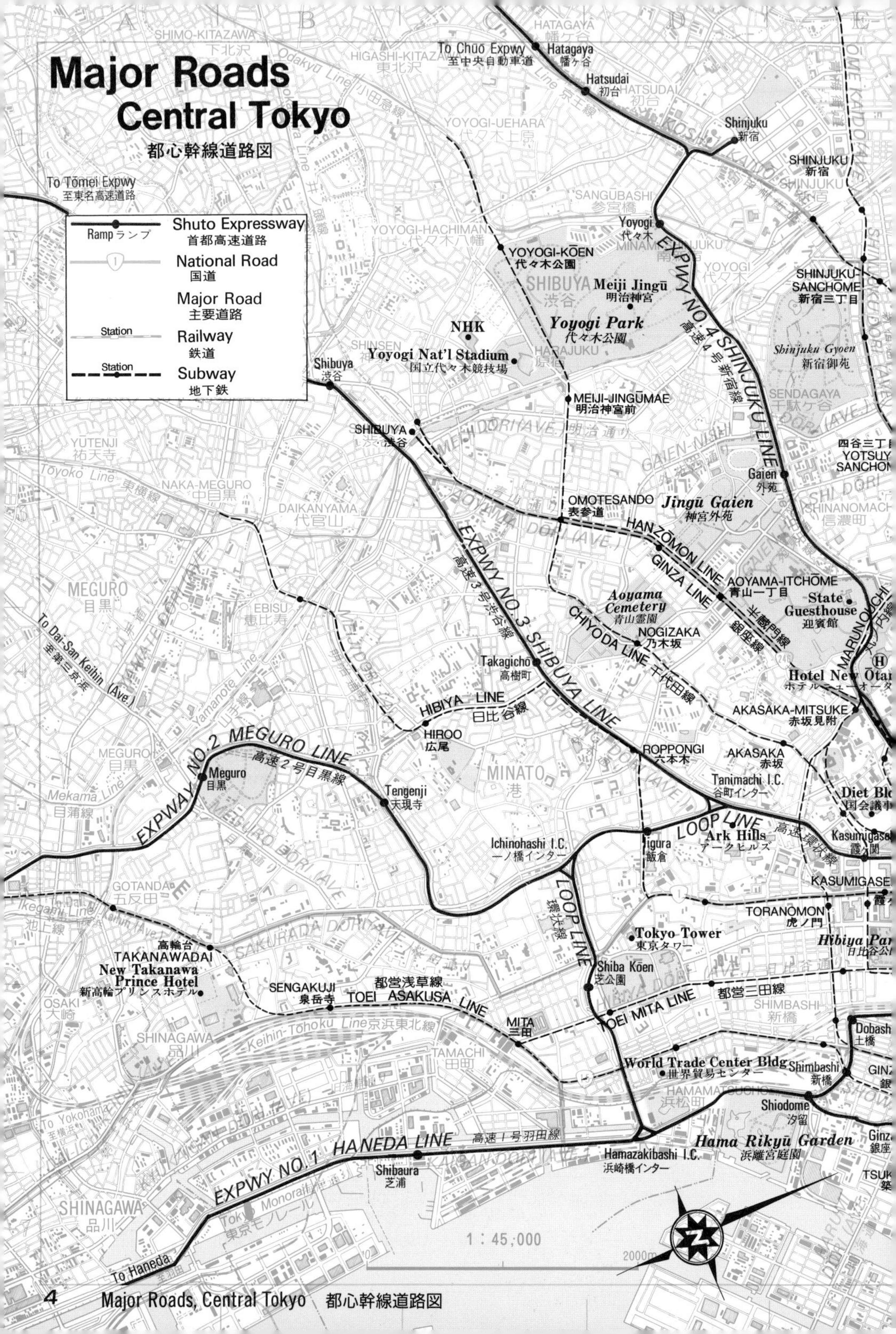
Major Roads
Central Tokyo
都心幹線道路図
Shuto Expressway
Ramp ランプ
首都高速道路
National Road
国道
Major Road
主要道路
Station
Railway
鉄道
Station
Subway
地下鉄
To Tōmei Expwy
至東名高速道路
To Chūō Expwy
至中央自動車道
Hatagaya
幡ケ谷
Hatsudai
初台
Shinjuku
新宿
Yoyogi
代々木
YOYOGI-KŌEN
代々木公園
Meiji Jingū
明治神宮
Yoyogi Park
代々木公園
NHK
Yoyogi Nat'l Stadium
国立代々木競技場
Shibuya
渋谷
MEIJI-JINGŪMAE
明治神宮前
EXPWY NO.4 SHINJUKU LINE
高速4号新宿線
SHINJUKU-SANCHŌME
新宿三丁目
Shinjuku Gyoen
新宿御苑
Gaien
外苑
OMOTESANDO
表参道
Jingū Gaien
神宮外苑
HANZŌMON LINE
GINZA LINE
AOYAMA-ITCHŌME
青山一丁目
State Guesthouse
迎賓館
Aoyama Cemetery
青山霊園
NOGIZAKA
乃木坂
CHIYODA LINE 千代田線
EXPWY NO.3 SHIBUYA LINE
高速3号渋谷線
Takagichō
高樹町
Hotel New Otani
ホテルニューオータニ
AKASAKA-MITSUKE
赤坂見附
HIBIYA LINE
日比谷線
HIROO
広尾
ROPPONGI
六本木
AKASAKA
赤坂
Tanimachi I.C.
谷町インター
EXPWY NO.2 MEGURO LINE
高速2号目黒線
Meguro
目黒
Tengenji
天現寺
MINATO
港
Diet Bldg
国会議事堂
Ark Hills
アークヒルズ
LOOP LINE
Iigura
飯倉
Ichinohashi I.C.
一ノ橋インター
Kasumigaseki
霞ケ関
TORANOMON
虎ノ門
To Dai-San Keihin (Ave.)
至第三京浜
Tokyo Tower
東京タワー
LOOP LINE
環状線
Hibiya Park
日比谷公園
高輪台
TAKANAWADAI
New Takanawa Prince Hotel
新高輪プリンスホテル
SENGAKUJI
泉岳寺
都営浅草線
TOEI ASAKUSA LINE
Shiba Kōen
芝公園
TOEI MITA LINE
都営三田線
MITA
三田
World Trade Center Bldg
世界貿易センター
Shimbashi
新橋
Shiodome
汐留
To Yokohama
至横浜
EXPWY NO.1 HANEDA LINE
高速1号羽田線
Shibaura
芝浦
Hamazakibashi I.C.
浜崎橋インター
Hama Rikyū Garden
浜離宮庭園
SHINAGAWA
品川
1 : 45,000
2000m
To Haneda

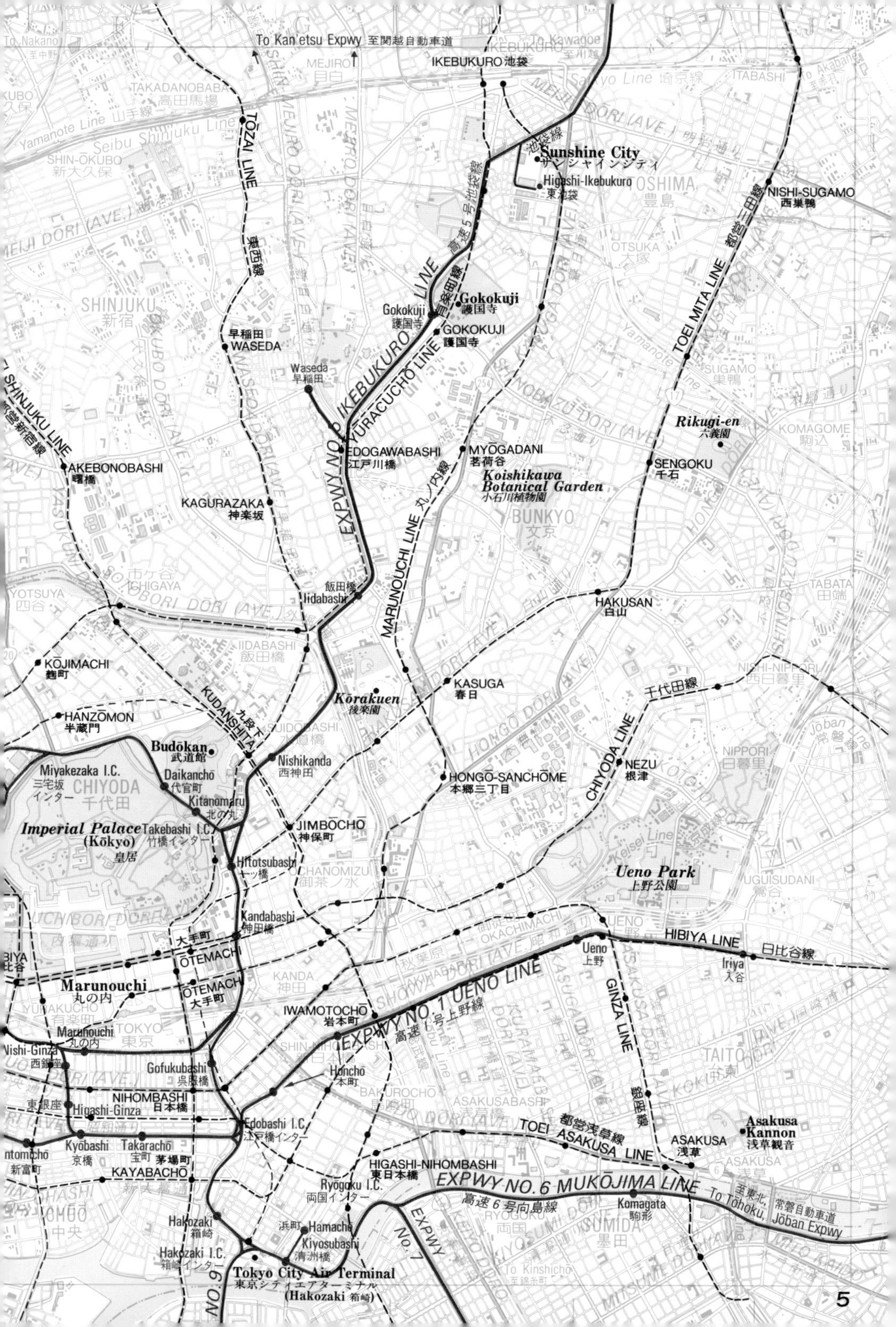
To Kan'etsu Expwy 至関越自動車道
IKEBUKURO 池袋
Sunshine City
サンシャインシティ
Higashi-Ikebukuro
東池袋
NISHI-SUGAMO
西巣鴨
TŌZAI LINE
東西線
Gokokuji
護国寺
GOKOKUJI
護国寺
早稲田
WASEDA
Waseda
早稲田
EXPWY NO.5 IKEBUKURO LINE
高速5号池袋線
YURACUCHO LINE
有楽町線
TOEI MITA LINE
都営三田線
Rikugi-en
六義園
EDOGAWABASHI
江戸川橋
MYŌGADANI
茗荷谷
Koishikawa Botanical Garden
小石川植物園
SENGOKU
千石
AKEBONOBASHI
曙橋
KAGURAZAKA
神楽坂
MARUNOUCHI LINE 丸ノ内線
飯田橋
Iidabashi
HAKUSAN
白山
KŌJIMACHI
麹町
KASUGA
春日
Kōrakuen
後楽園
千代田線
HANZŌMON
半蔵門
KUDANSHITA
九段下
Budōkan
武道館
Nishikanda
西神田
CHIYODA LINE
NEZU
根津
Miyakezaka I.C.
三宅坂インター
Daikanchō
代官町
Kitanomaru
北の丸
HONGŌ-SANCHŌME
本郷三丁目
Imperial Palace (Kōkyo)
皇居
Takebashi I.C.
竹橋インター
JIMBŌCHŌ
神保町
Hitotsubashi
一ツ橋
Ueno Park
上野公園
Kandabashi
神田橋
大手町
OTEMACHI
HIBIYA LINE
日比谷線
Ueno
上野
Iriya
入谷
Marunouchi
丸の内
EXPWY NO.1 UENO LINE
高速1号上野線
GINZA LINE
銀座線
IWAMOTOCHŌ
岩本町
Maruruouchi
丸の内
Nishi-Ginza
西銀座
Gofukubashi
呉服橋
Honchō
本町
NIHOMBASHI
日本橋
東銀座
Higashi-Ginza
Edobashi I.C.
江戸橋インター
都営浅草線
TOEI ASAKUSA LINE
ASAKUSA
浅草
Asakusa Kannon
浅草観音
Kyōbashi
京橋
Takarachō
宝町
茅場町
KAYABACHŌ
HIGASHI-NIHOMBASHI
東日本橋
Ryogoku I.C.
両国インター
EXPWY NO.6 MUKŌJIMA LINE
高速6号向島線
Komagata
駒形
To Tōhoku, Jōban Expwy
至東北、常磐自動車道
浜町
Hamachō
Kiyosubashi
清洲橋
Hakozaki
箱崎
Hakozaki I.C.
箱崎インター
Tokyo City Air Terminal
東京シティエアターミナル
(Hakozaki 箱崎)
EXPWY No.7
NO.9
To Kinshichō

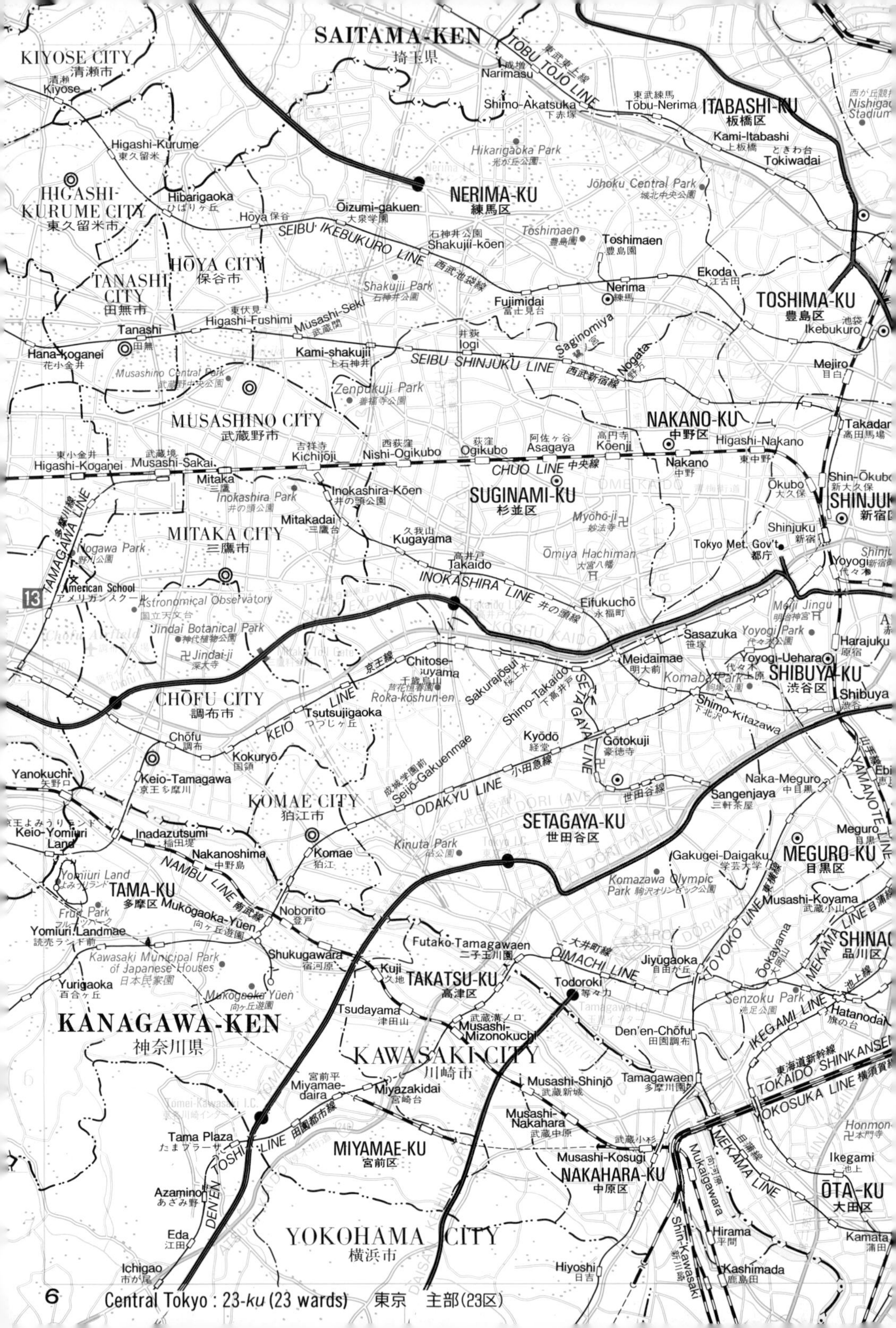

Central Tokyo : 23-*ku* (23 wards)　東京　主部(23区)

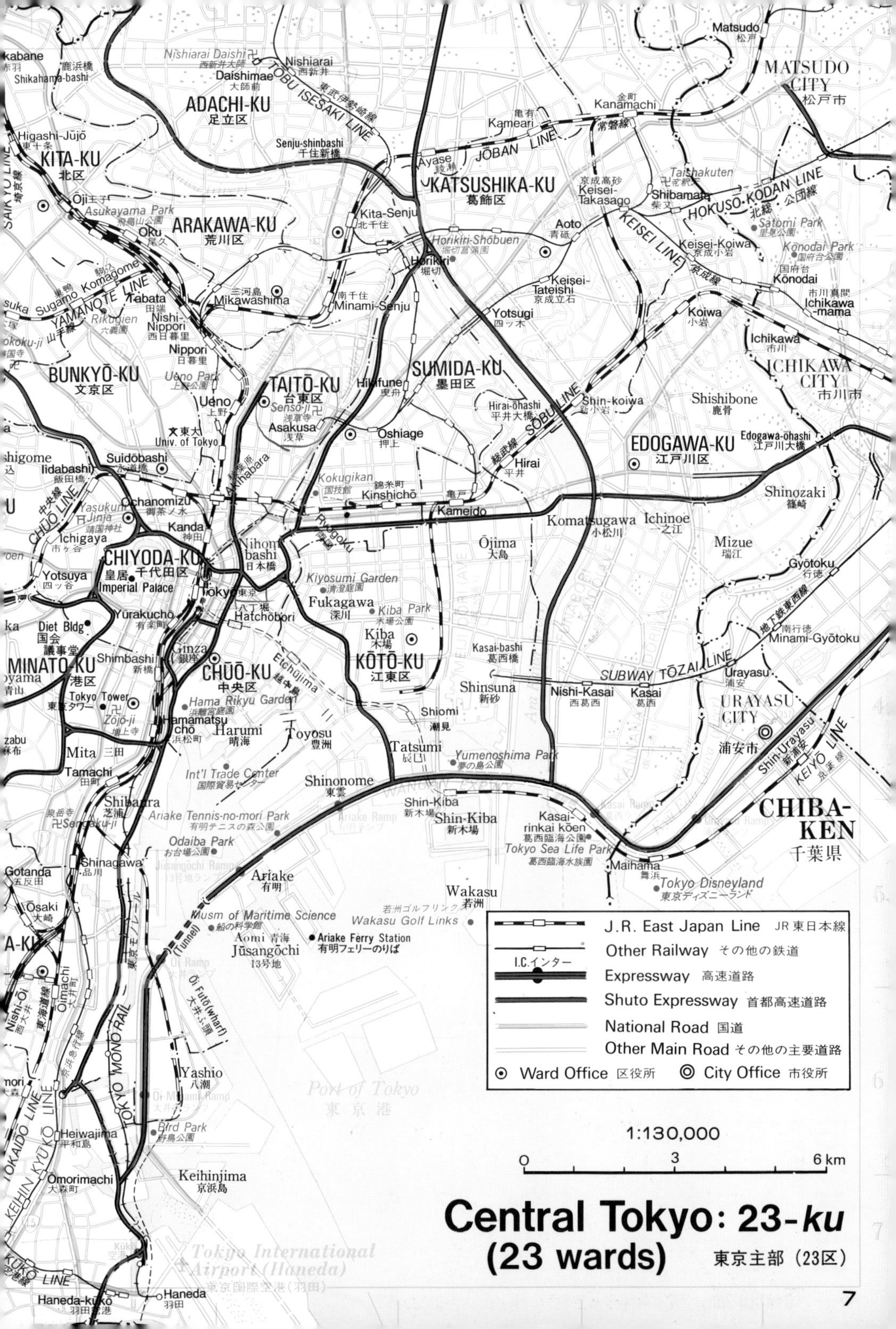

Central Tokyo: 23-*ku*
(23 wards)
東京主部（23区）
1:130,000
0 3 6 km
J.R. East Japan Line JR東日本線
Other Railway その他の鉄道
I.C.インター
Expressway 高速道路
Shuto Expressway 首都高速道路
National Road 国道
Other Main Road その他の主要道路
Ward Office 区役所
City Office 市役所
ADACHI-KU
足立区
KITA-KU
北区
ARAKAWA-KU
荒川区
KATSUSHIKA-KU
葛飾区
BUNKYŌ-KU
文京区
TAITŌ-KU
台東区
SUMIDA-KU
墨田区
EDOGAWA-KU
江戸川区
CHIYODA-KU
千代田区
CHŪŌ-KU
中央区
KŌTŌ-KU
江東区
MINATO-KU
港区
MATSUDO CITY
松戸市
ICHIKAWA CITY
市川市
URAYASU CITY
浦安市
CHIBA-KEN
千葉県
Matsudo
松戸
Kanamachi
金町
Kameari
亀有
Ayase
綾瀬
JŌBAN LINE
常磐線
Taishakuten
Keisei-Takasago
京成高砂
Shibamata
柴又
HOKUSŌ·KŌDAN LINE
北総・公団線
Satomi Park
里見公園
Kōnodai Park
国府台公園
Kōnodai
国府台
Ichikawa-mama
市川真間
Ichikawa
市川
KEISEI LINE
京成線
Keisei-Koiwa
京成小岩
Aoto
青砥
Horikiri-Shōbuen
堀切菖蒲園
Horikiri
堀切
Keisei-Tateishi
京成立石
Koiwa
小岩
Yotsugi
四ツ木
Shin-koiwa
新小岩
SŌBU LINE
総武線
Hirai-ōhashi
平井大橋
Hirai
平井
Shishibone
鹿骨
Edogawa-ōhashi
江戸川大橋
Shinozaki
篠崎
Komatsugawa
小松川
Ichinoe
一之江
Mizue
瑞江
Ōjima
大島
Gyōtoku
行徳
Minami-Gyōtoku
南行徳
SUBWAY TŌZAI LINE
地下鉄東西線
Urayasu
浦安
Kasai-bashi
葛西橋
Nishi-Kasai
西葛西
Kasai
葛西
Shinsuna
新砂
Shin-Urayasu
新浦安
KEIYŌ LINE
京葉線
Kasai-rinkai kōen
葛西臨海公園
Tokyo Sea Life Park
葛西臨海水族園
Maihama
舞浜
Tokyo Disneyland
東京ディズニーランド
Wakasu
若洲
若洲ゴルフリンクス
Wakasu Golf Links
Nishiarai Daishi
西新井大師
Nishiarai
西新井
Daishimae
大師前
TOBU ISESAKI LINE
東武伊勢崎線
Senju-shinbashi
千住新橋
Kita-Senju
北千住
Minami-Senju
南千住
Mikawashima
三河島
Hikifune
曳舟
Oshiage
押上
Kinshichō
錦糸町
Kameido
亀戸
Kokugikan
国技館
Ryōgoku
両国
Sensō-ji
浅草寺
Asakusa
浅草
Ueno
上野
Ueno Park
上野公園
Univ. of Tokyo
東大
Akihabara
秋葉原
Nishi-Nippori
西日暮里
Nippori
日暮里
Tabata
田端
Sugamo
巣鴨
Komagome
駒込
YAMANOTE LINE
山手線
Rikugien
六義園
Higashi-Jūjō
東十条
Ōji
王子
Asukayama Park
飛鳥山公園
Oku
尾久
Shikahama-bashi
鹿浜橋
Suidōbashi
水道橋
Iidabashi
飯田橋
Ochanomizu
御茶ノ水
Yasukuni Jinja
靖国神社
Kanda
神田
Ichigaya
市ケ谷
Yotsuya
四ツ谷
CHŪŌ LINE
中央線
Imperial Palace
皇居
Tokyo
東京
Nihombashi
日本橋
Yūrakuchō
有楽町
Diet Bldg
国会議事堂
Hatchōbori
八丁堀
Kiyosumi Garden
清澄庭園
Fukagawa
深川
Kiba Park
木場公園
Kiba
木場
Shimbashi
新橋
Ginza
銀座
Etchūjima
越中島
Tokyo Tower
東京タワー
Zōjō-ji
増上寺
Hama Rikyu Garden
浜離宮庭園
Hamamatsuchō
浜松町
Harumi
晴海
Toyosu
豊洲
Shiomi
潮見
Tatsumi
辰巳
Yumenoshima Park
夢の島公園
Mita
三田
Tamachi
田町
Int'l Trade Center
国際貿易センター
Shinonome
東雲
Shin-Kiba
新木場
Shibaura
芝浦
Ariake Tennis-no-mori Park
有明テニスの森公園
Sengaku-ji
泉岳寺
Odaiba Park
お台場公園
Shinagawa
品川
Ariake
有明
Gotanda
五反田
Ōsaki
大崎
Musm of Maritime Science
船の科学館
Aomi
青海
Ariake Ferry Station
有明フェリーのりば
Jūsangōchi
13号地
Ōi Futō (wharf)
大井ふ頭
Ōimachi
大井町
Nishi-Ōi
西大井
TOKYO MONORAIL
東京モノレール
Yashio
八潮
Port of Tokyo
東京港
Bird Park
野鳥公園
Heiwajima
平和島
Omorimachi
大森町
Keihinjima
京浜島
KEIHIN KYŪKŌ LINE
TOKAIDŌ LINE
Tokyo International Airport (Haneda)
東京国際空港（羽田）
Haneda
羽田
Haneda-kūkō
羽田空港
KŪKŌ LINE

East Tokyo 東京東部

Sumida-ku, Kōtō-ku, Adachi-ku, Katsushika-ku, Edogawa-ku
墨田区 江東区 足立区 葛飾区 江戸川区

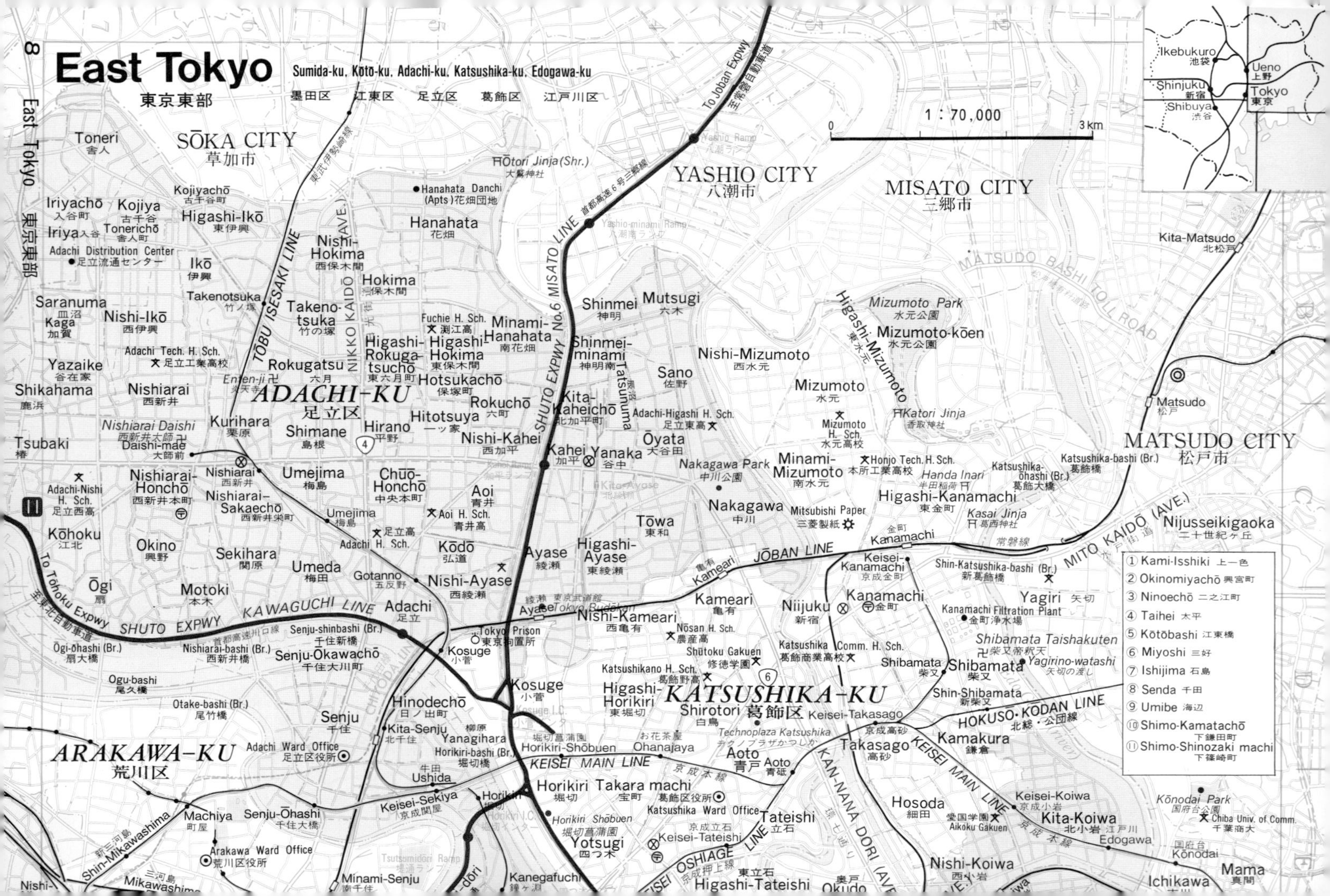

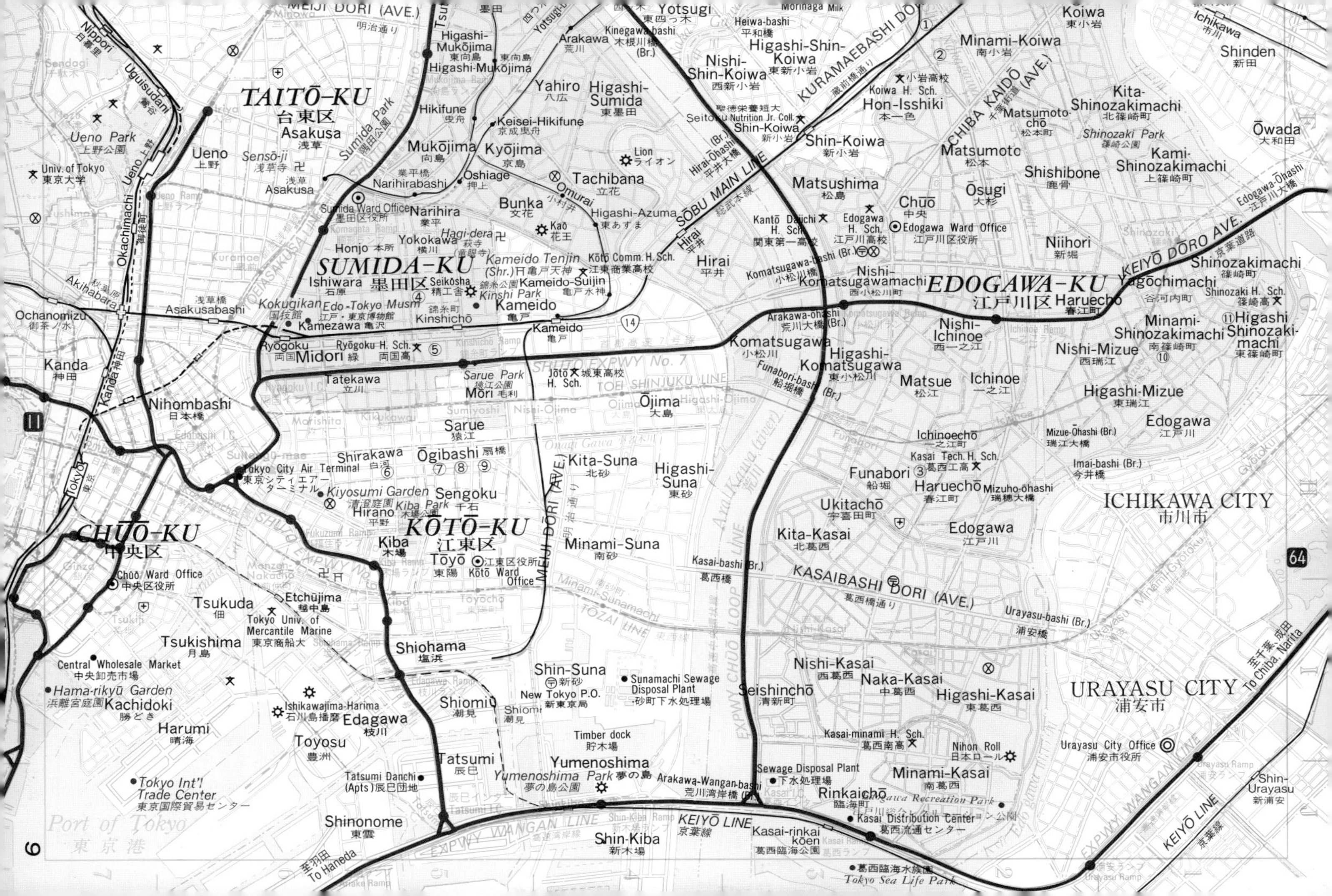

TAITŌ-KU 台東区
SUMIDA-KU 墨田区
KŌTŌ-KU 江東区
CHŪŌ-KU 中央区
EDOGAWA-KU 江戸川区
ICHIKAWA CITY 市川市
URAYASU CITY 浦安市
Ueno 上野
Ueno Park 上野公園
Univ. of Tokyo 東京大学
Nippori 日暮里
Uguisudani 鶯谷
Okachimachi 御徒町
Akihabara 秋葉原
Ochanomizu 御茶ノ水
Kanda 神田
Nihombashi 日本橋
Tokyo 東京
Asakusa 浅草
Sensō-ji 浅草寺
Asakusabashi 浅草橋
Sumida Park 隅田公園
Sumida Ward Office 墨田区役所
Honjo 本所
Ishiwara 石原
Kokugikan 国技館
Edo-Tokyo Musm 江戸・東京博物館
Kamezawa 亀沢
Ryōgoku 両国
Midori 緑
Ryōgoku H. Sch. 両国高
Kinshichō 錦糸町
Kinshi Park 錦糸公園
Seikōsha 精工舎
Kameido 亀戸
Kameido Tenjin (Shr.) 亀戸天神
Kameido-Suijin 亀戸水神
Yokokawa 横川
Hagi-dera 萩寺
Narihira 業平
Narihirabashi 業平橋
Oshiage 押上
Mukōjima 向島
Hikifune 曳舟
Higashi-Mukōjima 東向島
Keisei-Hikifune 京成曳舟
Kyōjima 京島
Yahiro 八広
Higashi-Sumida 東墨田
Bunka 文花
Kaō 花王
Tachibana 立花
Omurai 小村井
Higashi-Azuma 東あずま
Lion ライオン
Arakawa 荒川
Kinegawa-bashi 木根川橋 (Br.)
Yotsugi 東四つ木
Heiwa-bashi 平和橋
Nishi-Shin-Koiwa 西新小岩
Higashi-Shin-Koiwa 東新小岩
Shin-Koiwa 新小岩
Seitoku Nutrition Jr. Coll.
Hirai 平井
Hirai-Ōhashi 平井大橋 (Br.)
SŌBU MAIN LINE 総武本線
KURAMAEBASHI DORI
Kōtō Comm. H. Sch. 江東商業高校
Kantō Daiichi H. Sch. 関東第一高校
Komatsugawa-bashi (Br.) 小松川橋
Nishi-Komatsugawamachi 西小松川町
Matsushima 松島
Chūō 中央
Edogawa H. Sch. 江戸川高校
Edogawa Ward Office 江戸川区役所
Koiwa 東小岩
Minami-Koiwa 南小岩
Koiwa H. Sch. 小岩高校
Hon-Isshiki 本一色
CHIBA KAIDŌ (AVE.)
Matsumoto 松本
Matsumoto-chō 松本町
Ōsugi 大杉
Shishibone 鹿骨
Niihori 新堀
Kita-Shinozakimachi 北篠崎町
Shinozaki Park 篠崎公園
Kami-Shinozakimachi 上篠崎町
Shinden 新田
Ōwada 大和田
Ichikawa 市川
Edogawa-Ōhashi 江戸川大橋
KEIYŌ DŌRO AVE. 京葉道路
Shinozakimachi 篠崎町
Shinozaki H. Sch. 篠崎高
Higashi-Shinozaki-machi 東篠崎町
Minami-Shinozakimachi 南篠崎町
Yagōchimachi 谷河内町
Haruechō 春江町
Nishi-Ichinoe 西一之江
Ichinoe 一之江
Nishi-Mizue 西瑞江
Higashi-Mizue 東瑞江
Edogawa 江戸川
Matsue 松江
Higashi-Komatsugawa 東小松川
Komatsugawa 小松川
Arakawa-ōhashi 荒川大橋 (Br.)
Funabori-bashi 船堀橋 (Br.)
Ichinoechō 一之江町
Kasai Tech. H. Sch. 葛西工高
Funabori 船堀
Mizuho-ōhashi 瑞穂大橋
Mizue-Ōhashi (Br.) 瑞江大橋
Imai-bashi (Br.) 今井橋
Ukitachō 宇喜田町
Kita-Kasai 北葛西
Kasai-bashi (Br.) 葛西橋
KASAIBASHI DORI (AVE.) 葛西橋通り
Urayasu-bashi (Br.) 浦安橋
Nishi-Kasai 西葛西
Naka-Kasai 中葛西
Higashi-Kasai 東葛西
Seishinchō 清新町
Kasai-minami H. Sch. 葛西南高
Nihon Roll 日本ロール
Minami-Kasai 南葛西
Rinkaichō 臨海町
Kasai Distribution Center 葛西流通センター
Sewage Disposal Plant 下水処理場
Kasai-rinkai kōen 葛西臨海公園
葛西臨海水族園 Tokyo Sea Life Park
Urayasu City Office 浦安市役所
To Chiba, Narita 至千葉、成田
Shin-Urayasu 新浦安
KEIYŌ LINE 京葉線
EXPWY WANGAN LINE
Tatekawa 立川
Sarue Park 猿江公園
Mōri 毛利
Jōtō H. Sch. 城東高校
SHUTO EXPWY No. 7
TOEI SHINJUKU LINE
Ōjima 大島
Sarue 猿江
Shirakawa 白河
Ōgibashi 扇橋
Tokyo City Air Terminal 東京シティエアーターミナル
Kiyosumi Garden 清澄庭園
Kiba Park 木場公園
Sengoku 千石
Hirano 平野
Kiba 木場
Tōyō 東陽
Kōtō Ward Office 江東区役所
MEIJI DORI (AVE.) 明治通り
Kita-Suna 北砂
Higashi-Suna 東砂
Minami-Suna 南砂
TOZAI LINE
Chūō Ward Office 中央区役所
Tsukuda 佃
Etchūjima 越中島
Tokyo Univ. of Mercantile Marine 東京商船大
Tsukishima 月島
Central Wholesale Market 中央卸売市場
Hama-rikyū Garden 浜離宮庭園
Kachidoki 勝どき
Harumi 晴海
Ishikawajima-Harima 石川島播磨
Edagawa 枝川
Toyosu 豊洲
Shiohama 塩浜
Shiomi 潮見
Shin-Suna 新砂
New Tokyo P.O. 新東京局
Sunamachi Sewage Disposal Plant 砂町下水処理場
Timber dock 貯木場
Yumenoshima 夢の島
Yumenoshima Park 夢の島公園
Arakawa-Wangan-bashi 荒川湾岸橋
Tatsumi 辰巳
Tatsumi Danchi (Apts) 辰巳団地
Tokyo Int'l Trade Center 東京国際貿易センター
Port of Tokyo 東京港
Shinonome 東雲
Shin-Kiba 新木場
To Haneda 至羽田
64
9

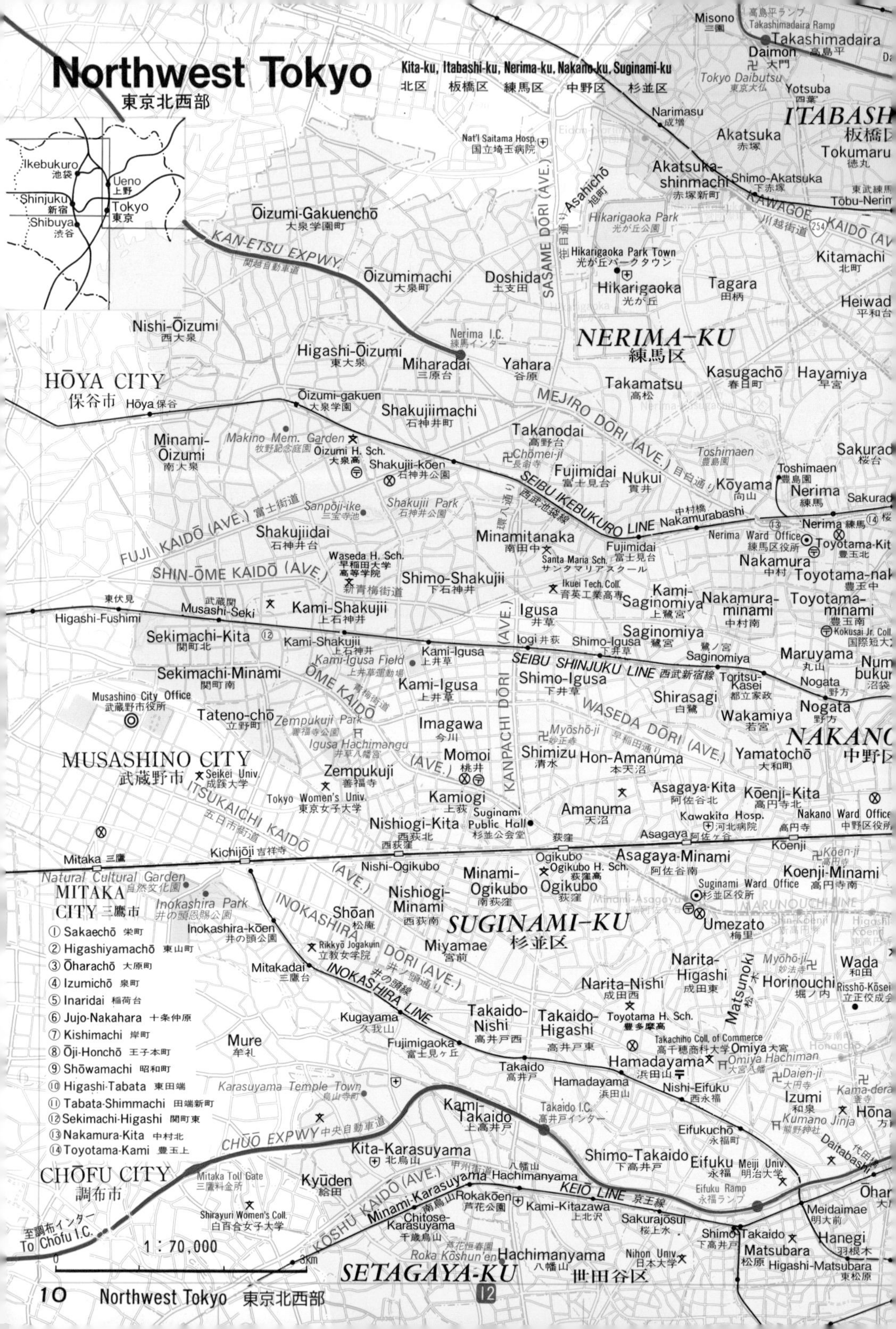
Northwest Tokyo
東京北西部
Kita-ku, Itabashi-ku, Nerima-ku, Nakano-ku, Suginami-ku
北区 板橋区 練馬区 中野区 杉並区
Ikebukuro
池袋
Ueno
上野
Shinjuku
新宿
Tokyo
東京
Shibuya
渋谷
Misono
三園
高島平ランプ
Takashimadaira Ramp
Takashimadaira
Daimon
大門
高島平
Tokyo Daibutsu
東京大仏
Yotsuba
四葉
ITABASHI
板橋区
Narimasu
成増
Nat'l Saitama Hosp.
国立埼玉病院
Akatsuka
赤塚
Tokumaru
徳丸
Akatsuka-shinmachi
赤塚新町
Shimo-Akatsuka
下赤塚
東武練馬
Tōbu-Nerima
Asahichō
旭町
SASAME DŌRI (AVE.)
笹目通り
Hikarigaoka Park
光が丘公園
KAWAGOE KAIDŌ (AVE.)
川越街道
254
Ōizumi-Gakuenchō
大泉学園町
KAN-ETSU EXPWY.
関越自動車道
Hikarigaoka Park Town
光が丘パークタウン
Kitamachi
北町
Ōizumimachi
大泉町
Doshida
土支田
Hikarigaoka
光が丘
Tagara
田柄
Heiwadai
平和台
Nishi-Ōizumi
西大泉
Nerima I.C.
練馬インター
NERIMA-KU
練馬区
Higashi-Ōizumi
東大泉
Miharadai
三原台
Yahara
谷原
Kasugachō
春日町
Hayamiya
早宮
HŌYA CITY
保谷市
Hōya
保谷
Ōizumi-gakuen
大泉学園
Takamatsu
高松
Shakujiimachi
石神井町
MEJIRO DŌRI (AVE.)
目白通り
Takanodai
高野台
Minami-Ōizumi
南大泉
Makino Mem. Garden
牧野記念庭園
Ōizumi H. Sch.
大泉高
Chōmei-ji
長命寺
Toshimaen
豊島園
Sakuradai
桜台
Shakujii-kōen
石神井公園
Fujimidai
富士見台
Nukui
貫井
Kōyama
向山
Toshimaen
豊島園
Nerima
練馬
SEIBU IKEBUKURO LINE
西武池袋線
環八通り
Sanpōji-ike
三宝寺池
Shakujii Park
石神井公園
中村橋
Nakamurabashi
FUJI KAIDŌ (AVE.)
富士街道
Shakujiidai
石神井台
Minamitanaka
南田中
Fujimidai
富士見台
Nerima Ward Office
練馬区役所
Toyotama-Kita
豊玉北
Waseda H. Sch.
早稲田大学高等学院
Santa Maria Sch.
サンタマリアスクール
Nakamura
中村
Toyotama-naka
豊玉中
SHIN-ŌME KAIDŌ (AVE.)
新青梅街道
Shimo-Shakujii
下石神井
Ikuei Tech. Coll.
育英工業高専
東伏見
Higashi-Fushimi
武蔵関
Musashi-Seki
Kami-Shakujii
上石神井
Kami-Saginomiya
上鷺宮
Nakamura-minami
中村南
Toyotama-minami
豊玉南
Igusa
井草
Sekimachi-Kita
関町北
Kami-Shakujii
上石神井
Ogi
井荻
Shimo-Igusa
下井草
Saginomiya
鷺宮
Kokusai Jr. Coll.
国際短大
Kami-Igusa
上井草
Kami-Igusa Field
上井草運動場
SEIBU SHINJUKU LINE
西武新宿線
Saginomiya
鷺ノ宮
Maruyama
丸山
Numabukuro
沼袋
Sekimachi-Minami
関町南
ŌME KAIDŌ
青梅街道
Kami-Igusa
上井草
Shimo-Igusa
下井草
Toritsu-Kasei
都立家政
Nogata
野方
Musashino City Office
武蔵野市役所
KANPACHI DŌRI (AVE.)
Shirasagi
白鷺
Nogata
野方
Tateno-chō
立野町
Zempukuji Park
善福寺公園
Imagawa
今川
WASEDA DŌRI (AVE.)
早稲田通り
Wakamiya
若宮
NAKANO
中野区
Myōshō-ji
妙正寺
Igusa Hachimangu
井草八幡宮
MUSASHINO CITY
武蔵野市
Momoi
桃井
Shimizu
清水
Hon-Amanuma
本天沼
Yamatochō
大和町
Seikei Univ.
成蹊大学
Zempukuji
善福寺
Asagaya-Kita
阿佐谷北
Kōenji-Kita
高円寺北
ITSUKAICHI KAIDŌ
五日市街道
Tokyo Women's Univ.
東京女子大学
Kamiogi
上荻
Amanuma
天沼
Kawakita Hosp.
河北病院
Nakano Ward Office
中野区役所
Suginami Public Hall
杉並公会堂
Nishiogi-Kita
西荻北
高円寺
Asagaya
阿佐ケ谷
荻窪
西荻窪
Mitaka
三鷹
Kichijōji
吉祥寺
Koenji
Kōen-ji
高円寺
Nishi-Ogikubo
Ogikubo
Ogikubo H. Sch.
荻窪高
Asagaya-Minami
阿佐谷南
Koenji-Minami
高円寺南
Natural Cultural Garden
自然文化園
Minami-Ogikubo
南荻窪
Ogikubo
荻窪
Suginami Ward Office
杉並区役所
MITAKA CITY
三鷹市
Inokashira Park
井の頭恩賜公園
Nishiogi-Minami
西荻南
Minami-Asagaya
MARUNOUCHI LINE
Shōan
松庵
SUGINAMI-KU
杉並区
Umezato
梅里
Higashi-Kōenji
① Sakaechō 栄町
② Higashiyamachō 東山町
③ Ōharachō 大原町
④ Izumichō 泉町
⑤ Inaridai 稲荷台
⑥ Jujo-Nakahara 十条仲原
⑦ Kishimachi 岸町
⑧ Ōji-Honchō 王子本町
⑨ Shōwamachi 昭和町
⑩ Higashi-Tabata 東田端
⑪ Tabata-Shimmachi 田端新町
⑫ Sekimachi-Higashi 関町東
⑬ Nakamura-Kita 中村北
⑭ Toyotama-Kami 豊玉上
Inokashira-kōen
井の頭公園
INOKASHIRA DŌRI (AVE.)
井ノ頭通り
Rikkyō Jogakuin
立教女学院
Miyamae
宮前
Narita-Higashi
成田東
Wada
和田
Mitakadai
三鷹台
Myōhō-ji
妙法寺
Matsunoki
松ノ木
Horinouchi
堀ノ内
Risshō-Kōseikai
立正佼成会
INOKASHIRA LINE
井の頭線
Narita-Nishi
成田西
Kugayama
久我山
Takaido-Nishi
高井戸西
Takaido-Higashi
高井戸東
Toyotama H. Sch.
豊多摩高
Mure
牟礼
Fujimigaoka
富士見ヶ丘
Takachiho Coll. of Commerce
高千穂商科大学
Omiya
大宮
Hamadayama
Omiya Hachiman
大宮八幡
Honanchō
Takaido
高井戸
Hamadayama
浜田山
Nishi-Eifuku
西永福
Daien-ji
大円寺
Kama-dera
釜寺
Karasuyama Temple Town
烏山寺町
Kami-Takaido
上高井戸
Takaido I.C.
高井戸インター
Izumi
和泉
Hōnan
方南
Kumano Jinja
熊野神社
CHŪŌ EXPWY
中央自動車道
Eifukuchō
永福町
Daitabashi
代田橋
Kita-Karasuyama
北烏山
Shimo-Takaido
下高井戸
Eifuku
永福
Meiji Univ.
明治大学
甲州街道
八幡山
CHŌFU CITY
調布市
Mitaka Toll Gate
三鷹料金所
Kyūden
給田
Hachimanyama
Ōhara
大原
KŌSHŪ KAIDŌ (AVE.)
Minami-Karasuyama
南烏山
Rokakōen
芦花公園
KEIŌ LINE
京王線
Eifuku Ramp
永福ランプ
Meidaimae
明大前
至調布インター
To Chōfu I.C.
Shirayuri Women's Coll.
白百合女子大学
Chitose-Karasuyama
千歳烏山
Kami-Kitazawa
上北沢
Sakurajōsui
桜上水
Shimo-Takaido
下高井戸
Matsubara
松原
Hanegi
羽根木
1 : 70,000
0
3km
芦花恒春園
Roka Kōshun'en
Hachimanyama
八幡山
Nihon Univ.
日本大学
Higashi-Matsubara
東松原
SETAGAYA-KU
世田谷区
12

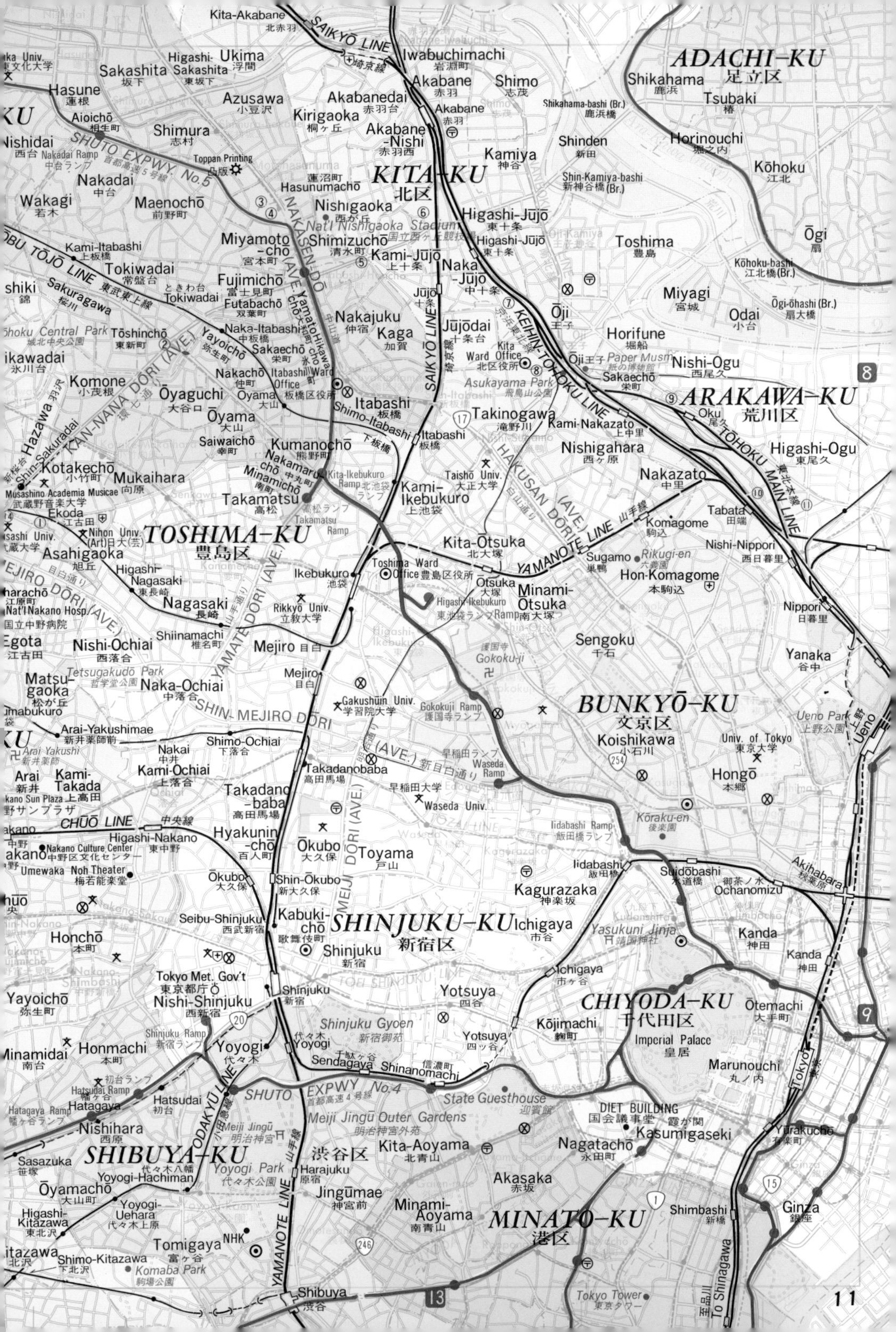

ADACHI-KU
足立区
KITA-KU
北区
ARAKAWA-KU
荒川区
TOSHIMA-KU
豊島区
BUNKYŌ-KU
文京区
SHINJUKU-KU
新宿区
CHIYODA-KU
千代田区
SHIBUYA-KU
渋谷区
MINATO-KU
港区
Kita-Akabane
北赤羽
SAIKYŌ LINE
埼京線
Iwabuchimachi
岩淵町
Akabane
赤羽
Akabanedai
赤羽台
Kirigaoka
桐ヶ丘
Akabane-Nishi
赤羽西
Shimo
志茂
Shikahama
鹿浜
Tsubaki
椿
Shikahama-bashi (Br.)
鹿浜橋
Shinden
新田
Horinouchi
堀之内
Kōhoku
江北
Kamiya
神谷
Shin-Kamiya-bashi (Br.)
新神谷橋(Br.)
Ukima
浮間
Higashi-Sakashita
東坂下
Sakashita
坂下
Hasune
蓮根
Azusawa
小豆沢
Aioichō
相生町
Shimura
志村
Nishidai
西台
Nakadai Ramp
中台ランプ
SHUTO EXPWY. No.5
首都高速5号線
Toppan Printing
凸版
Nakadai
中台
Wakagi
若木
Maenochō
前野町
蓮沼町
Hasunumachō
Nishigaoka
西が丘
Nat'l Nishigaoka Stadium
国立西が丘競技場
Higashi-Jūjō
東十条
Toshima
豊島
Ōgi
扇
Miyamoto-chō
宮本町
Shimizuchō
清水町
Kami-Jūjō
上十条
Naka-Jūjō
中十条
Kōhoku-bashi
江北橋(Br.)
Kami-Itabashi
上板橋
TŌBU TŌJŌ LINE
東武東上線
Tokiwadai
常盤台
ときわ台
Tokiwadai
Fujimichō
富士見町
Futabachō
双葉町
Jūjō
十条
Ōji
王子
Miyagi
宮城
Odai
小台
Ōgi-ōhashi (Br.)
扇大橋
Sakuragawa
桜川
NAKASEN-DŌ
Yamatochō
Nakajuku
仲宿
Kaga
加賀
Jūjōdai
十条台
KEIHIN-TŌHOKU LINE
京浜東北線
Horifune
堀船
Johoku Central Park
城北中央公園
Tōshinchō
東新町
Naka-Itabashi
中板橋
Yayoichō
弥生町
Sakaechō
栄町
Kita Ward Office
北区役所
Paper Musm.
紙の博物館
Nishi-Ogu
西尾久
Hikawadai
氷川台
Komone
小茂根
Nakachō
仲町
Itabashi Ward Office
板橋区役所
Itabashi
板橋
Asukayama Park
飛鳥山公園
Sakaechō
栄町
Oku
尾久
Ōyaguchi
大谷口
Ōyama
大山
KAN-NANA DŌRI (AVE.)
環七通
Shimo-Itabashi
下板橋
Takinogawa
滝野川
Kami-Nakazato
上中里
TŌHOKU MAIN LINE
東北本線
Higashi-Ogu
東尾久
Hazawa
羽沢
Shin-Sakuradai
新桜台
Saiwaichō
幸町
Kumanochō
熊野町
Itabashi
板橋
Nishigahara
西ヶ原
Kotakechō
小竹町
Mukaihara
向原
Nakamaruchō
中丸町
Minamichō
南町
Kita-Ikebukuro Ramp
北池袋ランプ
Kami-Ikebukuro
上池袋
Taishō Univ.
大正大学
HAKUSAN DŌRI (AVE.)
白山通り
Nakazato
中里
Musashino Academia Musicae
武蔵野音楽大学
Takamatsu
高松
Takamatsu Ramp
高松ランプ
Ekoda
江古田
Nihon Univ. (Art)
日大(芸)
Musashi Univ.
武蔵大学
Komagome
駒込
Tabata
田端
Asahigaoka
旭丘
YAMANOTE LINE
山手線
Kita-Ōtsuka
北大塚
Sugamo
巣鴨
Rikugi-en
六義園
Nishi-Nippori
西日暮里
Higashi-Nagasaki
東長崎
Ikebukuro
池袋
Toshima Ward Office
豊島区役所
Ōtsuka
大塚
Minami-Ōtsuka
南大塚
Hon-Komagome
本駒込
MEJIRO DŌRI (AVE.)
目白通り
Nagasaki
長崎
Rikkyō Univ.
立教大学
Higashi-Ikebukuro Ramp
東池袋ランプ
Nippori
日暮里
Nat'l Nakano Hosp.
国立中野病院
Egota
江古田
Nishi-Ochiai
西落合
Shiinamachi
椎名町
YAMATE DŌRI (AVE.)
Mejiro
目白
Sengoku
千石
Gokoku-ji
護国寺
Yanaka
谷中
Tetsugakudō Park
哲学堂公園
Matsugaoka
松が丘
Naka-Ochiai
中落合
Gakushūin Univ.
学習院大学
Gokokuji Ramp
護国寺ランプ
Ueno Park
上野公園
Ueno
上野
SHIN-MEJIRO DŌRI
Koishikawa
小石川
Univ. of Tokyo
東京大学
Arai-Yakushimae
新井薬師前
Arai Yakushi
新井薬師
Shimo-Ochiai
下落合
Nakai
中井
Kami-Ochiai
上落合
MEIJI DŌRI (AVE.)
新目白通り
早稲田ランプ
Waseda Ramp
Hongō
本郷
Arai
新井
Kami-Takada
上高田
Nakano Sun Plaza
中野サンプラザ
Takadanobaba
高田馬場
早稲田大学
Waseda Univ.
Kōraku-en
後楽園
CHŪŌ LINE
中央線
Higashi-Nakano
東中野
Hyakunin-chō
百人町
Iidabashi Ramp
飯田橋ランプ
Nakano Culture Center
中野区文化センター
Umewaka Noh Theater
梅若能楽堂
Ōkubo
大久保
Toyama
戸山
Iidabashi
飯田橋
Suidōbashi
水道橋
御茶ノ水
Ochanomizu
Akihabara
秋葉原
Shin-Ōkubo
新大久保
Kagurazaka
神楽坂
Seibu-Shinjuku
西武新宿
Kabuki-chō
歌舞伎町
Ichigaya
市谷
Yasukuni Jinja
靖国神社
Kanda
神田
Honchō
本町
Shinjuku
新宿
Tokyo Met. Gov't
東京都庁
Nishi-Shinjuku
西新宿
Yotsuya
四谷
Ōtemachi
大手町
Yayoichō
弥生町
Shinjuku Gyoen
新宿御苑
Kōjimachi
麹町
Imperial Palace
皇居
Minamidai
南台
Honmachi
本町
Shinjuku Ramp
新宿ランプ
Yoyogi
代々木
Yotsuya
四ッ谷
Sendagaya
千駄ヶ谷
Shinanomachi
信濃町
Marunouchi
丸ノ内
Hatsudai Ramp
初台ランプ
Hatagaya Ramp
幡ヶ谷ランプ
Hatagaya
幡ヶ谷
Hatsudai
初台
ODAKYŪ LINE
小田急線
SHUTO EXPWY. No.4
首都高速4号線
State Guesthouse
迎賓館
Tokyo
東京
Meiji Jingū
明治神宮
Meiji Jingū Outer Gardens
明治神宮外苑
DIET BUILDING
国会議事堂
霞が関
Kasumigaseki
Yūrakuchō
有楽町
Nishihara
西原
Sasazuka
笹塚
Yoyogi-Hachiman
代々木八幡
Yoyogi Park
代々木公園
Harajuku
原宿
Kita-Aoyama
北青山
Nagatachō
永田町
Ōyamachō
大山町
Yoyogi-Uehara
代々木上原
Jingūmae
神宮前
Akasaka
赤坂
Higashi-Kitazawa
東北沢
Minami-Aoyama
南青山
Shimbashi
新橋
Ginza
銀座
NHK
Tomigaya
富ヶ谷
Kitazawa
北沢
Shimo-Kitazawa
下北沢
Komaba Park
駒場公園
YAMANOTE LINE
Shibuya
渋谷
Tokyo Tower
東京タワー
To Shinagawa
至品川

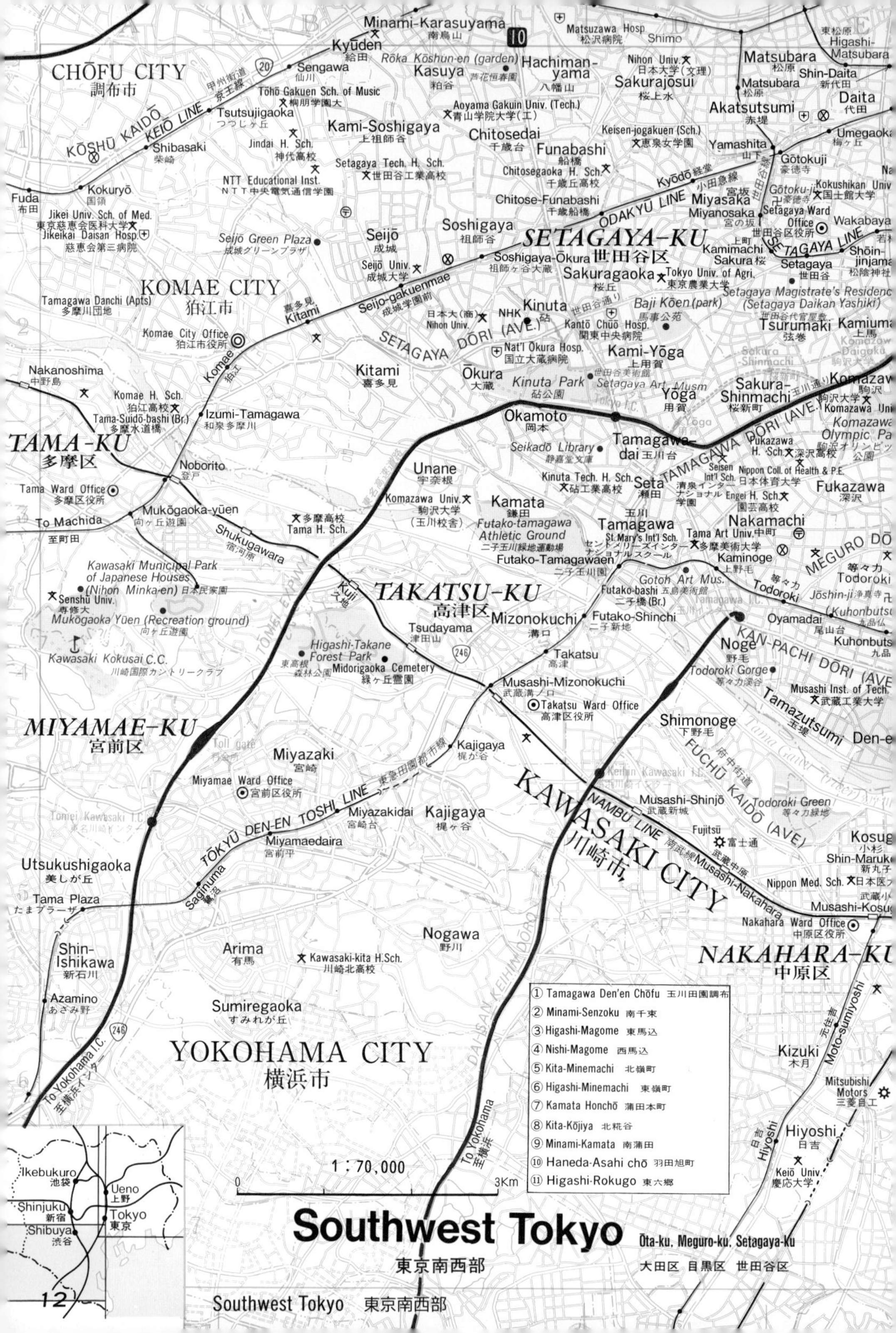
Southwest Tokyo
東京南西部
Ōta-ku, Meguro-ku, Setagaya-Ku
大田区 目黒区 世田谷区
1：70,000
0
3Km
① Tamagawa Den'en Chōfu 玉川田園調布
② Minami-Senzoku 南千束
③ Higashi-Magome 東馬込
④ Nishi-Magome 西馬込
⑤ Kita-Minemachi 北嶺町
⑥ Higashi-Minemachi 東嶺町
⑦ Kamata Honchō 蒲田本町
⑧ Kita-Kōjiya 北糀谷
⑨ Minami-Kamata 南蒲田
⑩ Haneda-Asahi chō 羽田旭町
⑪ Higashi-Rokugo 東六郷
CHŌFU CITY
調布市
KOMAE CITY
狛江市
TAMA-KU
多摩区
MIYAMAE-KU
宮前区
TAKATSU-KU
高津区
SETAGAYA-KU
世田谷区
KAWASAKI CITY
川崎市
NAKAHARA-KU
中原区
YOKOHAMA CITY
横浜市
KŌSHŪ KAIDŌ
KEIŌ LINE 京王線
ODAKYU LINE
SETAGAYA LINE
SETAGAYA DŌRI (AVE.)
TAMAGAWA DŌRI (AVE.)
MEGURO DŌRI
KAN-PACHI DŌRI (AVE.)
FUCHŪ KAIDŌ (AVE.)
NAMBU LINE
TŌKYŪ DEN-EN TOSHI LINE
TŌMEI EXPWY
DAI-SAN KEIHIN DŌRO
Minami-Karasuyama 南烏山
Kyūden 給田
Sengawa 仙川
Rōka Kōshun-en (garden) 芦花恒春園
Kasuya 粕谷
Hachiman-yama 八幡山
Matsuzawa Hosp 松沢病院
Shimo
Nihon Univ. 日本大学(文理)
Sakurajōsui 桜上水
Matsubara 松原
Higashi-Matsubara 東松原
Shin-Daita 新代田
Daita 代田
Akatsutsumi 赤堤
Tōhō Gakuen Sch. of Music 桐朋学園大
Tsutsujigaoka つつじヶ丘
Aoyama Gakuin Univ. (Tech.) 青山学院大学(工)
Kami-Soshigaya 上祖師谷
Chitosedai 千歳台
Funabashi 船橋
Keisen-jogakuen (Sch.) 恵泉女学園
Yamashita
Gōtokuji 豪徳寺
Umegaoka 梅ヶ丘
Shibasaki 柴崎
Jindai H. Sch. 神代高校
Setagaya Tech. H. Sch. 世田谷工業高校
Chitosegaoka H. Sch. 千歳丘高校
Kokuryō 国領
NTT Educational Inst. NTT中央電気通信学園
Chitose-Funabashi 千歳船橋
Kyōdō 経堂
Miyasaka 宮坂
Miyanosaka 宮の坂
Kokushikan Univ 国士舘大学
Setagaya Ward Office 世田谷区役所
Wakabayashi
Fuda 布田
Jikei Univ. Sch. of Med. 東京慈恵会医科大学
Jikeikai Daisan Hosp. 慈恵会第三病院
Seijō Green Plaza 成城グリーンプラザ
Seijō 成城
Soshigaya 祖師谷
Seijō Univ. 成城大学
Soshigaya-Ōkura 祖師ヶ谷大蔵
Kamimachi 上町
Sakura 桜
Setagaya 世田谷
Shōin-jinjama 松陰神社
Sakuragaoka 桜丘
Tokyo Univ. of Agri. 東京農業大学
Setagaya Magistrate's Residence (Setagaya Daikan Yashiki)
Tamagawa Danchi (Apts) 多摩川団地
Seijo-gakuenmae 成城学園前
Kitami 喜多見
Kinuta 砧
NHK
Nihon Univ.
Kantō Chūō Hosp. 関東中央病院
Baji Kōen (park) 馬事公苑
Tsurumaki 弦巻
Kamiuma 上馬
Komae City Office 狛江市役所
Nat'l Ōkura Hosp. 国立大蔵病院
Kami-Yōga 上用賀
Nakanoshima 中野島
Komae 狛江
Ōkura 大蔵
Kinuta Park 砧公園
Setagaya Art Musm 世田谷美術館
Yōga 用賀
Sakura-Shinmachi 桜新町
Komazawa 駒沢
Komazawa Univ. 駒沢大学
Komazawa Olympic Park 駒沢オリンピック公園
Komae H. Sch. 狛江高校
Tama-Suidō-bashi (Br.) 多摩水道橋
Izumi-Tamagawa 和泉多摩川
Okamoto 岡本
Seikadō Library 静嘉堂文庫
Tamagawa-dai 玉川台
Fukazawa H. Sch. 深沢高校
Noborito 登戸
Unane 宇奈根
Tama Ward Office 多摩区役所
Kinuta Tech. H. Sch. 砧工業高校
Seta 瀬田
Seisen Int'l Sch. 清泉インターナショナル学園
Nippon Coll. of Health & P.E. 日本体育大学
Engei H. Sch. 園芸高校
Fukazawa 深沢
Mukōgaoka-yūen 向ヶ丘遊園
Komazawa Univ. 駒沢大学 (玉川校舎)
Kamata 鎌田
To Machida 至町田
Tama H. Sch. 多摩高校
Futako-tamagawa Athletic Ground 二子玉川緑地運動場
Tamagawa 玉川
St. Mary's Int'l Sch. セントメリーズインターナショナルスクール
Tama Art Univ. 多摩美術大学
Nakamachi 中町
Shukugawara 宿河原
Futako-Tamagawaen 二子玉川園
Kaminoge 上野毛
Todoroki 等々力
Kawasaki Municipal Park of Japanese Houses (Nihon Minka-en) 日本民家園
Gotoh Art Mus. 五島美術館
Jōshin-ji 浄真寺
Senshū Univ. 専修大
Kuji 久地
Futako-bashi (Br.) 二子橋
Mukōgaoka Yūen (Recreation ground) 向ヶ丘遊園
Mizonokuchi 溝口
Futako-Shinchi 二子新地
Oyamadai 尾山台
Kuhonbutsu 九品仏
Tsudayama 津田山
Noge 野毛
Kawasaki Kokusai C.C. 川崎国際カントリークラブ
Higashi-Takane Forest Park 東高根森林公園
Midorigaoka Cemetery 緑ヶ丘霊園
Takatsu 高津
Todoroki Gorge 等々力渓谷
Musashi-Mizonokuchi 武蔵溝ノ口
Musashi Inst. of Tech. 武蔵工業大学
Takatsu Ward Office 高津区役所
Tamazutsumi 玉堤
Shimonoge 下野毛
Den-en
Toll gate
Miyazaki 宮崎
Kajigaya 梶ガ谷
Miyamae Ward Office 宮前区役所
Keihin Kawasaki I.C.
Musashi-Shinjō 武蔵新城
Todoroki Green 等々力緑地
Tomei Kawasaki I.C.
Miyazakidai 宮崎台
Kajigaya 梶ヶ谷
Fujitsū 富士通
Kosugi 小杉
Miyamaedaira 宮前平
Shin-Maruko
Utsukushigaoka 美しが丘
Musashi-Nakahara 武蔵中原
Nippon Med. Sch. 日本医大
Saginuma 鷺沼
Tama Plaza たまプラーザ
Musashi-Kosugi
Nakahara Ward Office 中原区役所
Shin-Ishikawa 新石川
Arima 有馬
Kawasaki-kita H.Sch. 川崎北高校
Nogawa 野川
Azamino あざみ野
Sumiregaoka すみれが丘
Moto-sumiyoshi 元住吉
Kizuki 木月
To Yokohama I.C. 至横浜インター
To Yokohama 至横浜
Mitsubishi Motors 三菱自工
Hiyoshi 日吉
Keiō Univ. 慶応大学
Ikebukuro 池袋
Ueno 上野
Shinjuku 新宿
Tokyo 東京
Shibuya 渋谷

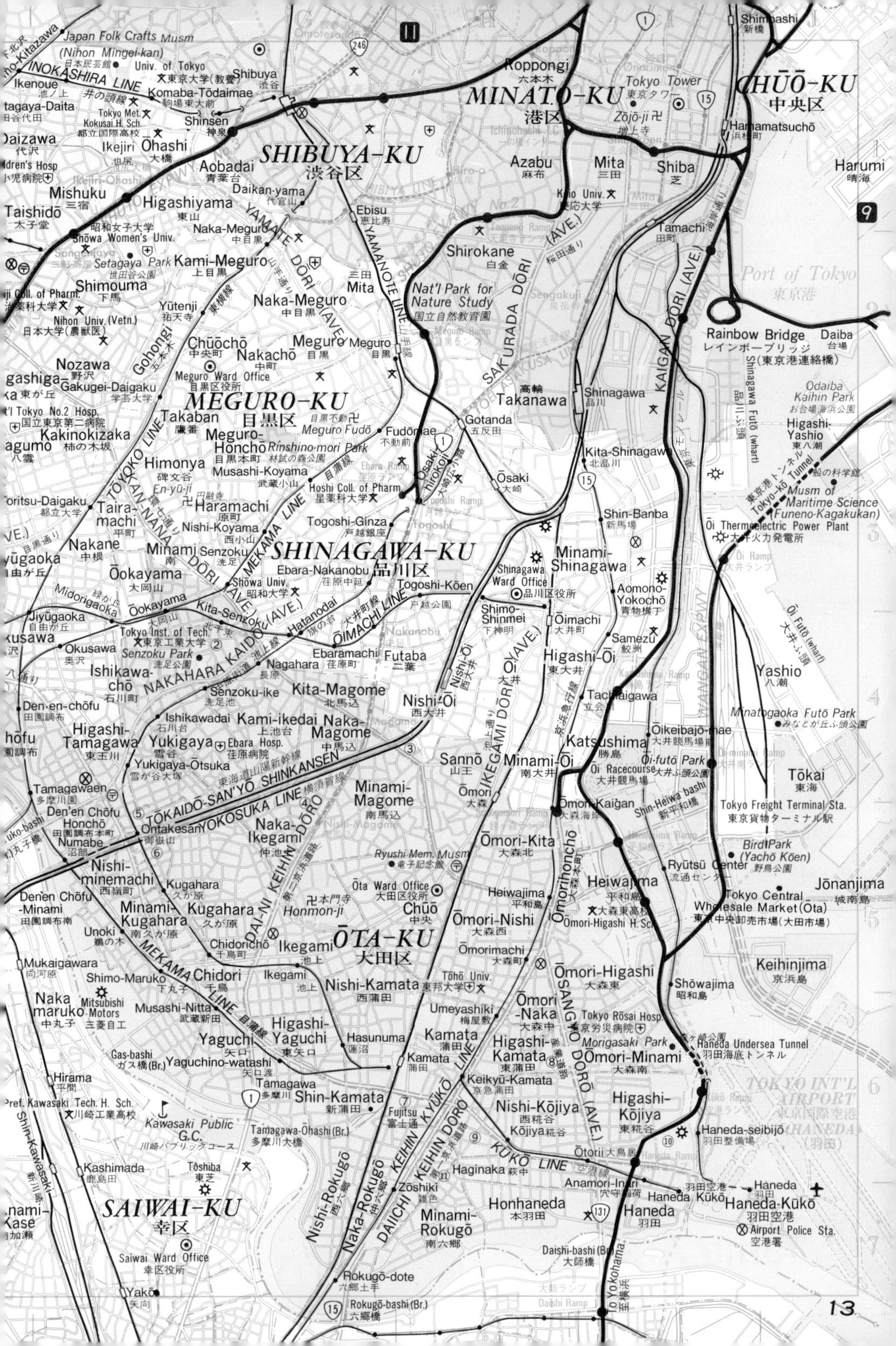

11
Japan Folk Crafts Musm
(Nihon Mingei-kan)
日本民芸館
INOKASHIRA LINE
井の頭線
Ikenoue
池ノ上
Univ. of Tokyo
東京大学(教養)
Komaba-Tōdaimae
駒場東大前
Tokyo Met. Kokusai H. Sch.
都立国際高校
Shibuya
渋谷
Shinsen
神泉
Ikejiri Ōhashi
池尻 大橋
Aobadai
青葉台
SHIBUYA-KU
渋谷区
Daikan-yama
代官山
Mishuku
三宿
Higashiyama
東山
Taishidō
太子堂
昭和女子大学
Shōwa Women's Univ.
Naka-Meguro
中目黒
Setagaya Park
世田谷公園
Kami-Meguro
上目黒
Shimouma
下馬
Yūtenji
祐天寺
Nihon Univ. (Vetn.)
日本大学(農獣医)
Nozawa
野沢
Gakugei-Daigaku
学芸大学
Gohongi
五本木
Chūōchō
中央町
Meguro Ward Office
目黒区役所
Nakachō
中町
Meguro
目黒
MEGURO-KU
目黒区
Takaban
鷹番
Meguro-Honchō
目黒本町
Kakinokizaka
柿の木坂
Himonya
碑文谷
En-yū-ji
円融寺
Rinshino-mori Park
林試の森公園
Musashi-Koyama
武蔵小山
Meguro Fudō
目黒不動
Fudōmae
不動前
Hoshi Coll. of Pharm.
星薬科大学
Tairamachi
平町
Haramachi
原町
Nishi-Koyama
西小山
Nakane
中根
Minami
南
Senzoku
洗足
Ōokayama
大岡山
TOYOKO LINE
KAN-NANA DŌRI (AVE.)
MEKAMA LINE
目蒲線
SHINAGAWA-KU
品川区
Ebara-Nakanobu
荏原中延
Togoshi-Ginza
戸越銀座
Togoshi-Kōen
戸越公園
Shōwa Univ.
昭和大学
Midorigaoka
緑が丘
Jiyūgaoka
自由が丘
Tokyo Inst. of Tech.
東京工業大学
Kita-Senzoku
北千束
Hatanodai
旗の台
ŌIMACHI LINE
大井町線
Okusawa
奥沢
Senzoku Park
洗足公園
Ebaramachi
荏原町
Futaba
二葉
NAKAHARA KAIDŌ
池上線
Nagahara
長原
Ishikawa-chō
石川町
Senzoku-ike
洗足池
Kita-Magome
北馬込
Den-en-chōfu
田園調布
Ishikawadai
石川台
Kami-ikedai
上池台
Naka-Magome
中馬込
Nishi-Ōi
西大井
Higashi-Tamagawa
東玉川
Yukigaya
雪谷
Ebara Hosp.
荏原病院
Yukigaya-Ōtsuka
雪が谷大塚
TŌKAIDŌ-SAN'YŌ SHINKANSEN
東海道山陽新幹線
YOKOSUKA LINE
横須賀線
Tamagawaen
多摩川園
Den'en Chōfu Honchō
田園調布本町
Ontakesan
御嶽山
Numabe
沼部
Naka-Ikegami
仲池上
DAI-NI KEIHIN DŌRO
第二京浜道路
Minami-Magome
南馬込
Ryushi Mem. Musm
竜子記念館
Ōta Ward Office
大田区役所
Chūō
中央
Honmon-ji
本門寺
Nishi-minemachi
西嶺町
Kugahara
久が原
Minami-Kugahara
南久が原
Den'en Chōfu -Minami
田園調布南
Unoki
鵜の木
Chidorichō
千鳥町
Ikegami
池上
ŌTA-KU
大田区
Mukaigawara
向河原
Shimo-Maruko
下丸子
Chidori
千鳥
Nishi-Kamata
西蒲田
Naka maruko
中丸子
Mitsubishi Motors
三菱自工
Musashi-Nitta
武蔵新田
Higashi-Yaguchi
東矢口
Hasunuma
蓮沼
Yaguchi
矢口
Gas-bashi
ガス橋(Br.)
Yaguchino-watashi
矢口渡
Tamagawa
多摩川
Shin-Kamata
新蒲田
Hirama
平間
Pref. Kawasaki Tech. H. Sch.
川崎工業高校
Kawasaki Public G.C.
川崎パブリックコース
Tamagawa-Ōhashi (Br.)
多摩川大橋
Kashimada
鹿島田
Tōshiba
東芝
SAIWAI-KU
幸区
Saiwai Ward Office
幸区役所
Yakō
矢向
Shin-Kawasaki
新川崎
Nishi-Rokugō
西六郷
Naka-Rokugō
仲六郷
DAIICHI KEIHIN DŌRO
第一京浜道路
Zōshiki
雑色
Minami-Rokugō
南六郷
Rokugō-dote
六郷土手
Rokugō-bashi (Br.)
六郷橋
Roppongi
六本木
MINATO-KU
港区
Tokyo Tower
東京タワー
Zōjō-ji
増上寺
Azabu
麻布
Mita
三田
Shiba
芝
Keio Univ.
慶応大学
Ebisu
恵比寿
YAMANOTE LINE
山手線
Shirokane
白金
Nat'l Park for Nature Study
国立自然教育園
SAKURADA DŌRI (AVE.)
桜田通り
Gotanda
五反田
Takanawa
高輪
Shinagawa
品川
Ōsaki
大崎
Kita-Shinagawa
北品川
Shin-Banba
新馬場
Minami-Shinagawa
南品川
Shinagawa Ward Office
品川区役所
Aomono-Yokochō
青物横丁
Shimo-Shinmei
下神明
Ōimachi
大井町
Samezu
鮫洲
Higashi-Ōi
東大井
Ōi
大井
IKEGAMI DŌRI (AVE.)
Tachiaigawa
立会川
Katsushima
勝島
Sannō
山王
Minami-Ōi
南大井
Ōmori
大森
Ōi Racecourse
大井競馬場
Ōikeibajō-mae
大井競馬場前
Ōi-futō Park
大井ふ頭公園
Ōmori-Kaigan
大森海岸
Shin-Heiwa bashi
新平和橋
Ōmori-Kita
大森北
Omorihonchō
大森本町
Heiwajima
平和島
Ryūtsū Center
流通センター
Ōmori-Nishi
大森西
Omori-Higashi H. Sch.
大森東高校
Ōmorimachi
大森町
Ōmori-Higashi
大森東
Tōhō Univ.
東邦大学
Umeyashiki
梅屋敷
Ōmori-Naka
大森中
Tokyo Rōsai Hosp.
東京労災病院
Morigasaki Park
森ヶ崎公園
Kamata
蒲田
Higashi-Kamata
東蒲田
Ōmori-Minami
大森南
Keikyū-Kamata
京急蒲田
Nishi-Kōjiya
西糀谷
Kōjiya
糀谷
SANGŌ DŌRO (AVE.)
産業道路
Higashi-Kōjiya
東糀谷
Fujitsu
富士通
KEIHIN KYŪKŌ LINE
KŪKŌ LINE
空港線
Haginaka
萩中
Ōtorii
大鳥居
Anamori-Inari
穴守稲荷
Honhaneda
本羽田
Haneda
羽田
Haneda Kūkō
羽田空港
Daishi-bashi (Br.)
大師橋
To Yokohama
至横浜
Shimbashi
新橋
CHŪŌ-KU
中央区
Hamamatsuchō
浜松町
Harumi
晴海
Tamachi
田町
9
Port of Tokyo
東京港
KAIGAN DŌRI (AVE.)
Rainbow Bridge
レインボーブリッジ
(東京港連絡橋)
Daiba
台場
Odaiba Kaihin Park
お台場海浜公園
Shinagawa Futō (wharf)
品川ふ頭
Higashi-Yashio
東八潮
Tokyo-kō Tunnel
東京港トンネル
Musm of Maritime Science
(Funeno-Kagakukan)
船の科学館
Ōi Thermoelectric Power Plant
大井火力発電所
Ōi Ramp
大井ランプ
Ōi Futō (wharf)
大井ふ頭
Yashio
八潮
Minatogaoka Futō Park
みなとが丘ふ頭公園
Tōkai
東海
Tokyo Freight Terminal Sta.
東京貨物ターミナル駅
Bird Park
(Yachō Kōen)
野鳥公園
Jōnanjima
城南島
Tokyo Central Wholesale Market (Ota)
東京中央卸売市場(大田市場)
Keihinjima
京浜島
Shōwajima
昭和島
Haneda Undersea Tunnel
羽田海底トンネル
TOKYO INT'L AIRPORT
東京国際空港
(HANEDA)
(羽田)
Haneda-seibijō
羽田整備場
Haneda
Haneda-Kūkō
羽田空港
Airport Police Sta.
空港署
13

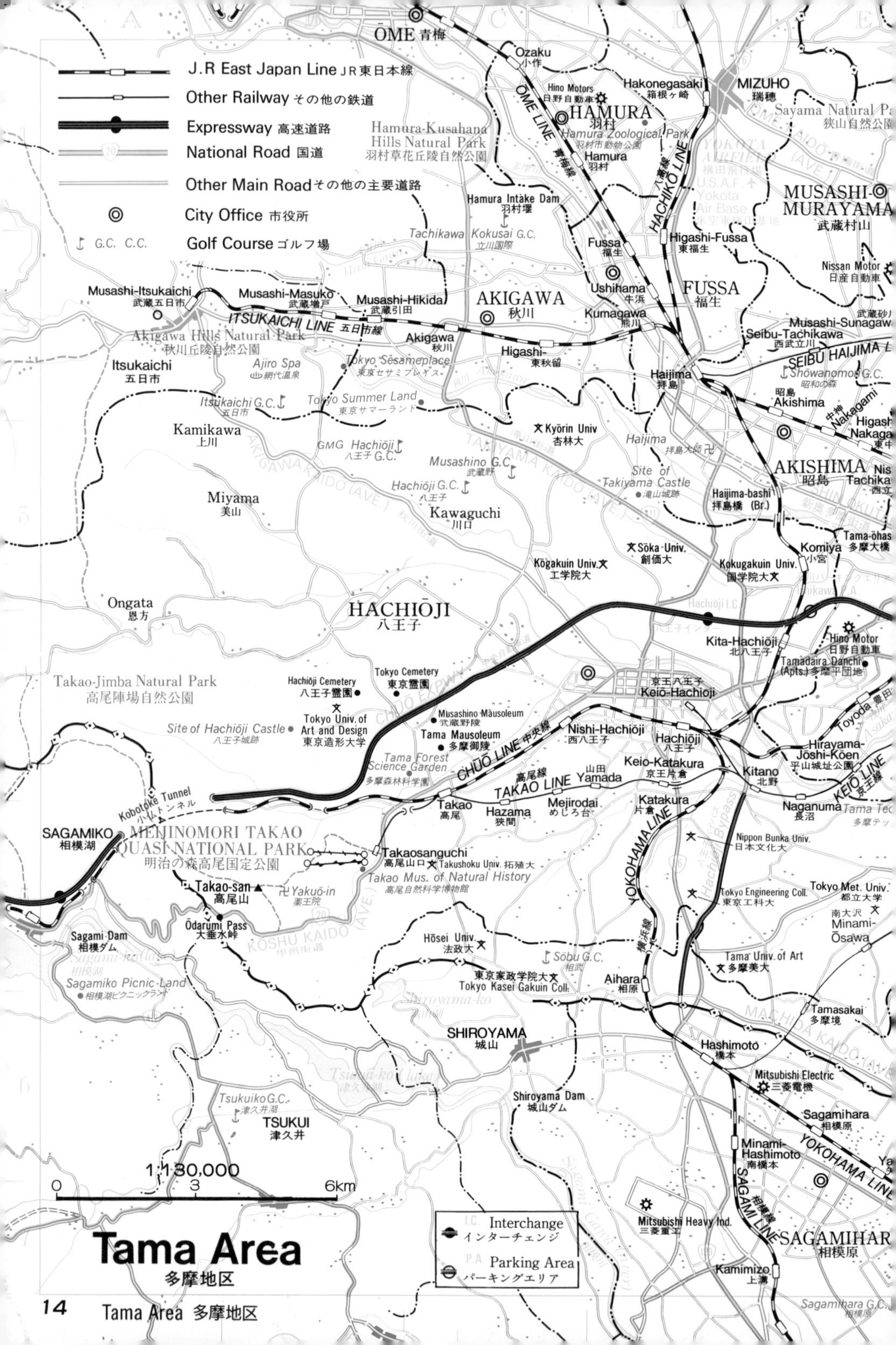
Tama Area
多摩地区
J.R East Japan Line JR東日本線
Other Railway その他の鉄道
Expressway 高速道路
National Road 国道
Other Main Road その他の主要道路
City Office 市役所
G.C. C.C.
Golf Course ゴルフ場
Interchange インターチェンジ
Parking Area パーキングエリア
1:130,000
0
3
6km
OME 青梅
Ozaku 小作
OME LINE 青梅線
Hino Motors 日野自動車
HAMURA 羽村
Hamura Zoological Park 羽村市動物公園
Hamura 羽村
Hakonegasaki 箱根ヶ崎
MIZUHO 瑞穂
HACHIKO LINE 八高線
Sayama Natural Park 狭山自然公園
YOKOTA AIRFIELD 横田飛行場
U.S.A.F. Yokota Air Base 米空軍横田基地
MUSASHI-MURAYAMA 武蔵村山
Hamura-Kusahana Hills Natural Park 羽村草花丘陵自然公園
Hamura Intake Dam 羽村堰
Tachikawa Kokusai G.C. 立川国際
Fussa 福生
Higashi-Fussa 東福生
Ushihama 牛浜
FUSSA 福生
Kumagawa 熊川
Nissan Motor 日産自動車
Musashi-Itsukaichi 武蔵五日市
Musashi-Masuko 武蔵増戸
Musashi-Hikida 武蔵引田
AKIGAWA 秋川
ITSUKAICHI LINE 五日市線
Akigawa Hills Natural Park 秋川丘陵自然公園
Akigawa 秋川
Higashi-Akiru 東秋留
Musashi-Sunagawa 武蔵砂川
Seibu-Tachikawa 西武立川
SEIBU HAIJIMA LINE
Itsukaichi 五日市
Ajiro Spa 網代温泉
Tokyo Sesameplace 東京セサミプレイス
Haijima 拝島
Showanomori G.C. 昭和の森
Akishima 昭島
Nakagami 中神
Itsukaichi G.C. 五日市
Tokyo Summer Land 東京サマーランド
Kamikawa 上川
Kyōrin Univ 杏林大
Haijima 拝島大師
AKISHIMA 昭島
GMG Hachiōji 八王子 G.C.
Musashino G.C. 武蔵野
AKIGAWA KAIDO (AVE.) 秋川街道
TAKIYAMA KAIDO (AVE.)
Site of Takiyama Castle 滝山城跡
Hachiōji G.C. 八王子
Miyama 美山
Kawaguchi 川口
Haijima-bashi 拝島橋 (Br.)
SHIN OKUTAMA KAIDO 新奥多摩街道
Sōka Univ. 創価大
Komiya 小宮
Tama-ōhashi 多摩大橋
Kōgakuin Univ. 工学院大
Kokugakuin Univ. 国学院大
Ongata 恩方
HACHIŌJI 八王子
Hachiōji I.C. 八王子インター
Kita-Hachiōji 北八王子
Hino Motor 日野自動車
Takao-Jimba Natural Park 高尾陣場自然公園
Hachiōji Cemetery 八王子霊園
Tokyo Cemetery 東京霊園
CHŪŌ EXPWY
Tamadaira Danchi (Apts.) 多摩平団地
京王八王子 Keiō-Hachiōji
Toyoda 豊田
Site of Hachiōji Castle 八王子城跡
Tokyo Univ. of Art and Design 東京造形大学
Musashino Mausoleum 武蔵野陵
Tama Mausoleum 多摩御陵
Nishi-Hachiōji 西八王子
Hachiōji 八王子
Hirayama-Jōshi-Kōen 平山城址公園
CHŪŌ LINE 中央線
Tama Forest Science Garden 多摩森林科学園
Keio-Katakura 京王片倉
Kitano 北野
KEIŌ LINE 京王線
高尾線 TAKAO LINE
山田 Yamada
Kobotoke Tunnel 小仏トンネル
Takao 高尾
Hazama 狭間
Mejirodai めじろ台
Katakura 片倉
Naganuma 長沼
SAGAMIKO 相模湖
MEIJINOMORI TAKAO QUASI NATIONAL PARK 明治の森高尾国定公園
Takaosanguchi 高尾山口
Takushoku Univ. 拓殖大
Takao Mus. of Natural History 高尾自然科学博物館
Nippon Bunka Univ. 日本文化大
YOKOHAMA LINE 横浜線
Hachiōji Bypass
Takao-san 高尾山
Yakuō-in 薬王院
Tokyo Engineering Coll. 東京工科大
Tokyo Met. Univ. 都立大学
南大沢 Minami-Ōsawa
Ōdarumi Pass 大垂水峠
Sagami Dam 相模ダム
KŌSHU KAIDO (AVE.) 甲州街道
Hōsei Univ. 法政大
Sōbu G.C. 相武
Tama Univ. of Art 多摩美大
Sagami-ko (lake) 相模湖
Sagamiko Picnic Land 相模湖ピクニックランド
東京家政学院大 Tokyo Kasei Gakuin Coll.
Aihara 相原
Shiroyama-ko
Tamasakai 多摩境
MACHIDA KAIDO (AVE.)
SHIROYAMA 城山
Hashimoto 橋本
Tsukui-ko (lake) 津久井湖
Mitsubishi Electric 三菱電機
Tsukuiko G.C. 津久井湖
Shiroyama Dam 城山ダム
Sagamihara 相模原
TSUKUI 津久井
Minami-Hashimoto 南橋本
YOKOHAMA LINE
SAGAMI LINE 相模線
Mitsubishi Heavy Ind. 三菱重工
SAGAMIHARA 相模原
Kamimizo 上溝
Sagamihara G.C. 相模原

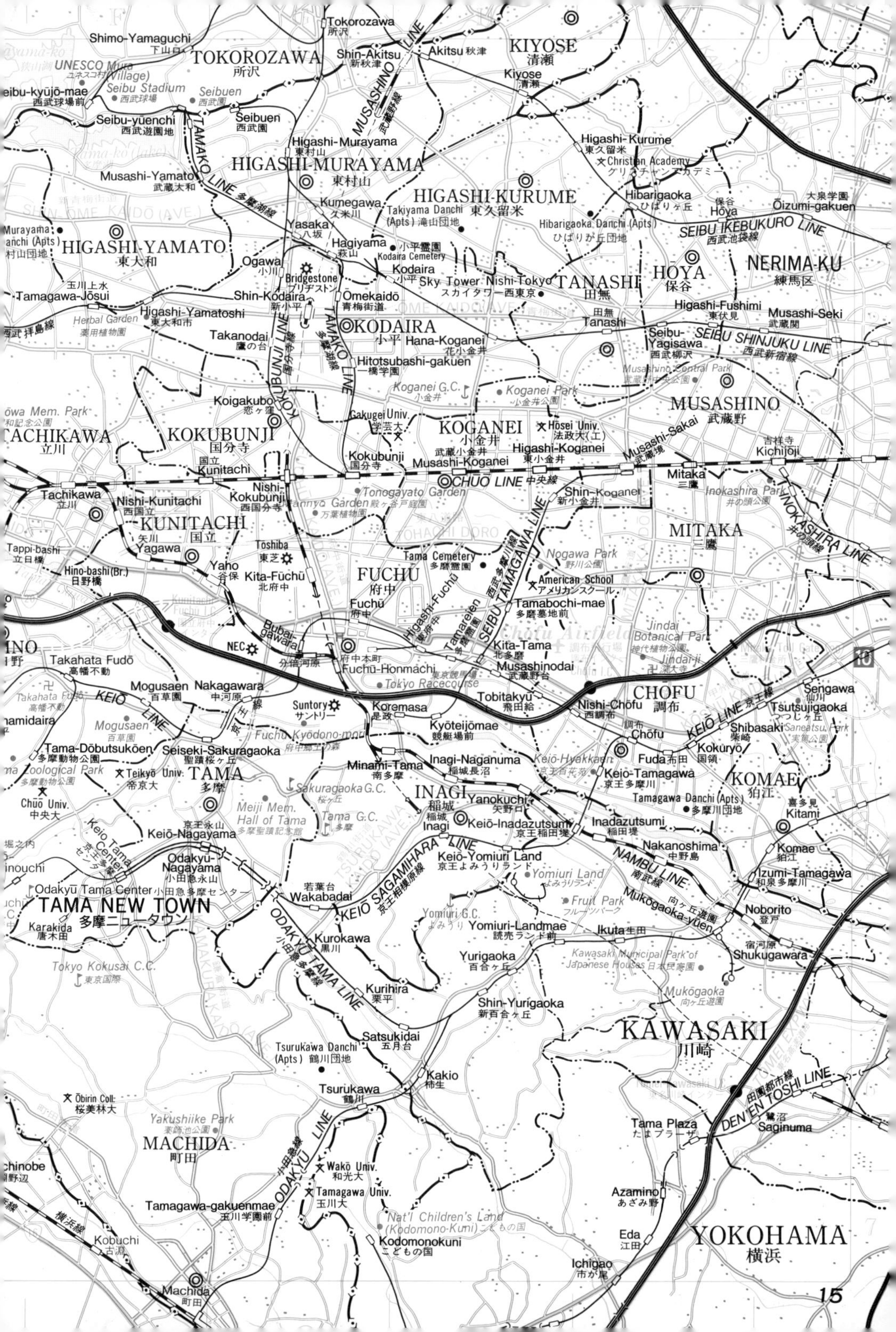
Tokorozawa
所沢
Shimo-Yamaguchi
下山口
TOKOROZAWA
所沢
Shin-Akitsu
新秋津
Akitsu 秋津
MUSASHINO LINE
武蔵野線
KIYOSE
清瀬
Kiyose
清瀬
UNESCO Mura
ユネスコ村(Village)
Seibu Stadium
西武球場
Seibuen
西武園
Seibu-kyūjō-mae
西武球場前
Seibu-yūenchi
西武遊園地
Seibuen
西武園
TAMAKO LINE
多摩湖線
Higashi-Murayama
東村山
HIGASHI-MURAYAMA
東村山
Musashi-Yamato
武蔵大和
SHIN-OME KAIDO (AVE.)
Higashi-Kurume
東久留米
Christian Academy
クリスチャンアカデミー
HIGASHI-KURUME
東久留米
Kumegawa
久米川
Takiyama Danchi (Apts)
滝山団地
Hibarigaoka
ひばりヶ丘
Hibarigaoka Danchi (Apts)
ひばりが丘団地
Hōya
保谷
Ōizumi-gakuen
大泉学園
SEIBU IKEBUKURO LINE
西武池袋線
Murayama Danchi (Apts)
村山団地
HIGASHI-YAMATO
東大和
Yasaka
八坂
Hagiyama
萩山
小平霊園
Kodaira Cemetery
Ogawa
小川
Bridgestone
ブリヂストン
Kodaira
小平
Sky Tower Nishi-Tokyo
スカイタワー西東京
TANASHI
田無
HOYA
保谷
NERIMA-KU
練馬区
玉川上水
Tamagawa-Jōsui
Shin-Kodaira
新小平
Ōmekaidō
青梅街道
OME KAIDO (AVE.)
青梅街道
Higashi-Yamatoshi
東大和市
Herbal Garden
薬用植物園
西武拝島線
KODAIRA
小平
田無
Tanashi
Higashi-Fushimi
東伏見
Musashi-Seki
武蔵関
Seibu-Yagisawa
西武柳沢
SEIBU SHINJUKU LINE
西武新宿線
Takanodai
鷹の台
Hana-Koganei
花小金井
Hitotsubashi-gakuen
一橋学園
KOKUBUNJI LINE
国分寺線
TAMAKO LINE
多摩湖線
Musashino Central Park
武蔵野中央公園
Koganei G.C.
小金井
Koganei Park
小金井公園
MUSASHINO
武蔵野
Showa Mem. Park
昭和記念公園
Koigakubo
恋ヶ窪
Gakugei Univ.
学芸大
KOGANEI
小金井
Hōsei Univ.
法政大(工)
TACHIKAWA
立川
KOKUBUNJI
国分寺
武蔵小金井
Higashi-Koganei
東小金井
Musashi-Sakai
武蔵境
吉祥寺
Kichijōji
国立
Kunitachi
Kokubunji
国分寺
Musashi-Koganei
CHUO LINE 中央線
Mitaka
三鷹
Tachikawa
立川
Nishi-Kunitachi
西国立
Nishi-Kokubunji
西国分寺
Tonogayato Garden
殿ヶ谷戸庭園
万葉植物園
Shin-Koganei
新小金井
Inokashira Park
井の頭公園
INOKASHIRA LINE
井の頭線
KUNITACHI
矢川 国立
Yagawa
TOHACHI DORO
Tama Cemetery
多磨霊園
MITAKA
三鷹
Tappi-bashi
立日橋
Toshiba
東芝
Nogawa Park
野川公園
Hino-bashi (Br.)
日野橋
Yaho
谷保
Kita-Fūchū
北府中
FUCHU
府中
American School
アメリカンスクール
SEIBU TAMAGAWA LINE
西武多摩川線
Fuchū
府中
Higashi-Fuchū
東府中
Tamareien
多磨霊園
Tamabochi-mae
多磨墓地前
Chofu Airfield
調布飛行場
Jindai Botanical Park
神代植物公園
Bubai-gawara
分倍河原
NEC
Fuchū-Honmachi
府中本町
Kita-Tama
北多摩
Musashinodai
武蔵野台
Jindai-ji
深大寺
HINO
日野
Takahata Fudō
高幡不動
Tokyo Racecourse
Mogusaen
百草園
Nakagawara
中河原
KEIŌ LINE
京王線
Suntory
サントリー
Koremasa
是政
Tobitakyū
飛田給
Nishi-Chōfu
西調布
CHOFU
調布
Sengawa
仙川
Tsutsujigaoka
つつじヶ丘
Takahata Fudō
高幡不動
Mogusaen
百草園
Kyōteijōmae
競艇場前
調布
Chōfu
KEIŌ LINE 京王線
Shibasaki
柴崎
Saneatsu Park
実篤公園
Tama-Dōbutsukōen
多摩動物公園
Seiseki-Sakuragaoka
聖蹟桜ヶ丘
Fuchū Kyōdono-mori
府中郷土の森
Minami-Tama
南多摩
Inagi-Naganuma
稲城長沼
Keiō-Hyakkaen
京王百花苑
Fuda 布田
Kokuryō
国領
Tama Zoological Park
多摩動物公園
Teikyō Univ.
帝京大
TAMA
多摩
Sakuragaoka G.C.
桜ヶ丘
INAGI
稲城
Yanokuchi
矢野口
Keiō-Tamagawa
京王多摩川
KOMAE
狛江
Chūō Univ.
中央大
Meiji Mem. Hall of Tama
多摩聖蹟記念館
Tama G.C.
多摩
Tamagawa Danchi (Apts)
多摩川団地
Kitami
喜多見
Inagi
稲城
Keiō-Inadazutsumi
京王稲田堤
Inadazutsumi
稲田堤
京王永山
Keiō-Nagayama
Keio Tama Center
京王多摩センター
Odakyū-Nagayama
小田急永山
KEIŌ SAGAMIHARA LINE
京王相模原線
Keiō-Yomiuri Land
京王よみうりランド
Yomiuri Land
よみうりランド
Nakanoshima
中野島
NAMBU LINE
南武線
Komae
狛江
Izumi-Tamagawa
和泉多摩川
Odakyū Tama Center
小田急多摩センター
若葉台
Wakabadai
Fruit Park
フルーツパーク
向ヶ丘遊園
Mukōgaoka-yūen
Noborito
登戸
TAMA NEW TOWN
多摩ニュータウン
Karakida
唐木田
Yomiuri G.C.
よみうり
Yomiuri-Landmae
読売ランド前
Ikuta 生田
Kurokawa
黒川
ODAKYŪ TAMA LINE
小田急多摩線
Yurigaoka
百合ヶ丘
宿河原
Shukugawara
Kawasaki Municipal Park of Japanese Houses
日本民家園
Tokyo Kokusai C.C.
東京国際
Kurihira
栗平
Shin-Yurigaoka
新百合ヶ丘
Mukōgaoka
向ヶ丘遊園
KAWASAKI
川崎
Satsukidai
五月台
Tsurukawa Danchi (Apts)
鶴川団地
Kakio
柿生
TOMEI EXPWY.
Tsurukawa
鶴川
Ōbirin Coll.
桜美林大
DEN'EN TOSHI LINE
田園都市線
Yakushiike Park
薬師池公園
Tama Plaza
たまプラーザ
鷺沼
Saginuma
MACHIDA
町田
Fuchinobe
淵野辺
Wakō Univ.
和光大
ODAKYU LINE
小田急線
Tamagawa Univ.
玉川大
Azamino
あざみ野
Tamagawa-gakuenmae
玉川学園前
横浜線
Nat'l Children's Land
(Kodomono-Kuni) こどもの国
Kodomonokuni
こどもの国
Eda
江田
YOKOHAMA
横浜
Kobuchi
古淵
Ichigao
市が尾
Machida
町田
10

BUNKYŌ-KU
文京区
CHIYODA-KU
千代田区
NTT Koishikawa
NTT小石川
Koishikawa
小石川
Nishikata
西片
Jiai Hosp.
慈愛病院
Hongō Dōri (Ave.)
本郷通り
Yayoi Art Mus.
弥生美術館
Yasuda Hall
安田講堂
Hongō P.O.
本郷局
Univ. of Tokyo
(Tokyo Daigaku) 東京大学
Univ. of Tokyo Hosp.
東大病院
Akamon (Red Gate)
赤門
Legal Training Research Inst.
(Shihō Kenshujo) 司法研修所
Ikenohata
Shinobazu Dōri (Ave.)
Tōshōgū
東照宮
Aquarium
水族館
Nat'l Mus. of Western Art
国立西洋美術館
Tokyo Met. Festival Hall
(Tokyo Bunka Kaikan)
東京文化会館
Japan Art Academy
日本芸術院
Ueno Park
上野公園
Benten-dō
弁天堂
Keisei-Ueno
京成上野
Ueno
上野
Ueno Ranpu
Takara Hotel
Okachimachi
御徒町
Shuto Expwy No.1
首都高速1号線
Hongō
本郷
Bunkyō Musm
文京ふるさと歴史館
Tax Office
税務署
Chūō Univ. (Sci. & Engn.)
中央大学(理工)
Bunkyō Ward Office
文京区役所
Kasuga
春日
Kōdōkan
講道館
Marunouchi Line
丸ノ内線
Motofuji Police Sta.
本富士署
Bunkyō Gym
文京総合体育館
Yushima Jinja
湯島神社
Chūō Ch.
中央教会
Kōrakuen Amusement Park
後楽園ゆうえんち
Koishikawa-Kōrakuen
小石川後楽園
Tokyo Dome
東京ドーム
(Big Egg ビッグエッグ)
Tōyō Women's Jr. Coll.
東洋女子短大
Nippon Shinpan
日本信販
Yushima
湯島
Kōrakuen Hall
後楽園ホール
Yellow Bldg
黄色いビル
Kōraku
後楽
Noh Theater
能楽堂
Ōin
桜蔭
Kyūsuisho Park
給水所公苑
Hitachi Hosp.
日立病院
Polyteck H. Sch.
工芸高校
Shōwa
昭和
Juntendo Univ.
順天堂大学
Kanda Myōjin
神田明神
Tokyo Med. & Dent. Univ.
東京医科歯科大学
Soto-Kanda
外神田
Toppan
凸版印刷
Chiyoda Line
Yamanote Line 山手線
Keihin-Tohoku Line 京浜東北線
Suidōbashi
水道橋
Chūō Line
中央線
Iidabashi
飯田橋
Mejiro Dōri
Edmont
エドモン
Misakichō
三崎町
Saru-gakuchō
猿楽町
Shuto Expwy No.5
Nihon Univ.
日本大学(法)
Surugadai
駿河台
Ochanomizu
御茶ノ水
Yushima Seidō
湯島聖堂
Izumichō
和泉町
Mitsui Hosp.
三井病院
Nishi-Kanda
西神田
Nishi-Kanda Ramp
西神田ランプ
Nikorai-dō
ニコライ堂
Meiji Univ.
明治大学
Nihon Univ.
日本大学
Manseibashi Police Sta.
万世橋署
Akihabara
秋葉原
Transportation Mus.
交通博物館
Sakumachō
佐久間町
Hotel Grand Palace
ホテルグランドパレス
Jimbōchō
神保町
Senshū Univ.
専修大学
Awajichō
淡路町
Sudachō
須田町
Shōwa Dōri (Ave.)
Kanda-Sakumagashi
神田佐久間河岸
Yasukuni Dōri (Ave.)
靖国通り
Ogawamachi
小川町
Kudan P.O.
九段局
Kudan-Minami
Tayasu-mon
田安門
Kudan Kaikan
九段会館
Chiyoda Ward Office
千代田区役所
Hitotsubashi
一ツ橋
Nishiki-chō
錦町
KANDA
神田
Tsukasa-machi
司町
Tachō
多町
Iwamotochō
岩本町
Nippon Budōkan
日本武道館
Shimizu-mon
清水門
Kyōritsu Gakuen
共立学園
Tax Office
税務署
YMCA
Kanda Police Sta.
神田署
Mitoshiro-chō
Shinkansen
Takebashi I.C.
竹橋インター
Kitanomaru Park
北の丸公園
Science Mus.
科学技術館
Hitotsubashi Ramp
一橋ランプ
Honchō Ramp
本町ランプ
Kitanomaru-kōen
北の丸公園
Tokyo Nat'l Mus. of Modern Art
東京国立近代美術館
Mainichi
毎日新聞
Uchi-Kanda
内神田
Kajichō
鍛冶町
Kodenmachō
小伝馬町
Kitanomaru Ramp
北の丸ランプ
Meteorological Agency
気象庁
Kandabashi Ramp
神田橋ランプ
Honchō
本町
Daikanchō Ramp
代官町ランプ
East Imperial Garden
(Kōkyo Higashi Gyoen)
皇居東御苑
Shin-Nihombashi
新日本橋
Hongokuchō
本石町
Muromachi
室町
Kobunechō
小舟町
Yomiuri
読売
Sankei
Kokusai P.O.
国際局
Ōtemachi
大手町
Bank of Japan
日本銀行
Mitsukoshi
三越
Mitsukoshi-mae
三越前
Chiyoda
千代田
Ōtemon
大手門
Imperial Guard H. Q.
皇宮警察本部
Palace Hotel
パレスホテル
Nippon Bldg
日本ビル
Eitai Dōri (Ave.)
永代通り
Gofukubashi Ramp
呉服橋ランプ
Imperial Household Agency
(Kunaichō) 宮内庁
JTB
Marunouchi
丸の内
Nihombashi
日本橋
Tōkyū Dept Store
東急デパート
Imperial Palace (Kōkyo)
皇居
Sakashitamon
坂下門
Shin Marunouchi Bldg
新丸ビル
Tekkō Bldg
鉄鋼ビル
Kokusai Kankō Kaikan
国際観光会館
Tokyo
東京
Kōkyo-gaien
皇居外苑
丸ビル
Marunouchi Bldg
Yaesu
八重洲
Daimal Dept Store
大丸デパート
Kabutochō
兜町
Nijūbashi
二重橋

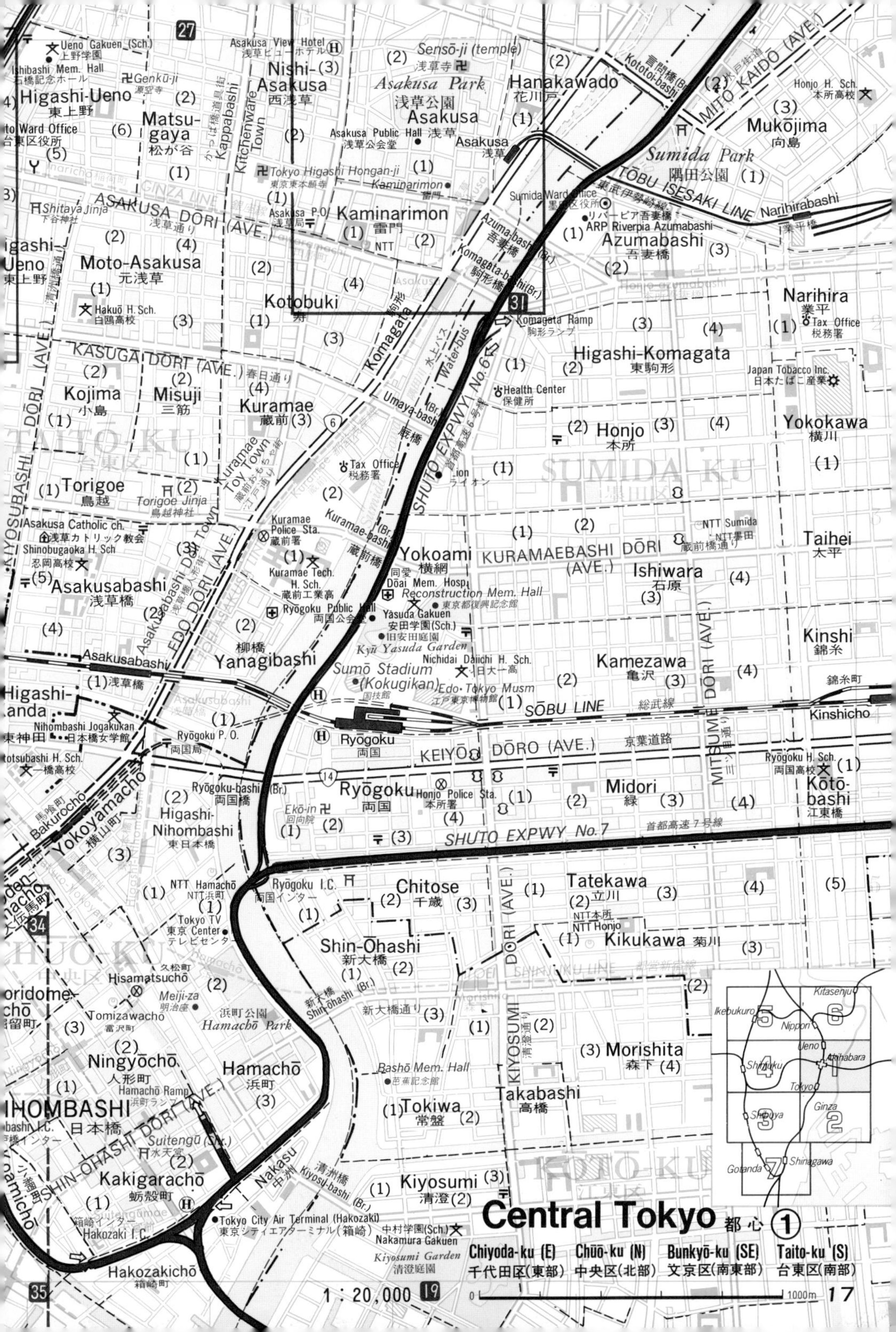

Ueno Gakuen (Sch.)
上野学園
Ishibashi Mem. Hall
石橋記念ホール
Genkū-ji
源空寺
Higashi-Ueno
東上野
Taito Ward Office
台東区役所
Matsu-gaya
松が谷
Kappabashi
かっぱ橋道具街
Kitchenware Town
Asakusa View Hotel
浅草ビューホテル
Nishi-Asakusa
西浅草
Sensō-ji (temple)
浅草寺
Asakusa Park
浅草公園
Asakusa
Asakusa Public Hall
浅草公会堂
Hanakawado
花川戸
Kototoi-bashi
言問橋
MITO KAIDŌ (AVE.)
Honjo H. Sch.
本所高校
Mukōjima
向島
Sumida Park
隅田公園
TŌBU ISESAKI LINE
東武伊勢崎線
Narihirabashi
Sumida Ward Office
墨田区役所
ARP Riverpia Azumabashi
リバーピア吾妻橋
Azumabashi
吾妻橋
Tokyo Higashi Hongan-ji
東京東本願寺
Kaminarimon
雷門
Shitaya Jinja
下谷神社
ASAKUSA DŌRI (AVE.)
浅草通り
Asakusa P.O.
浅草局
NTT
Azuma-bashi (Br.)
Komagata-bashi (Br.)
駒形橋
Higashi-Ueno
東上野
Moto-Asakusa
元浅草
Hakuō H. Sch.
白鷗高校
Kotobuki
寿
Komagata
Komagata Ramp
駒形ランプ
Narihira
業平
Tax Office
税務署
KASUGA DŌRI (AVE.)
春日通り
Higashi-Komagata
東駒形
Japan Tobacco Inc.
日本たばこ産業
Kojima
小島
Misuji
三筋
Kuramae
蔵前
Water-bus
水上バス
Health Center
保健所
Umaya-bashi (Br.)
厩橋
SHUTO EXPWY No.6
首都高速6号線
Honjo
本所
Yokokawa
横川
TAITO-KU
台東区
Kuramae Toy Town
蔵前おもちゃ街
江戸通り
Tax Office
税務署
Lion
ライオン
SUMIDA-KU
墨田区
Torigoe
鳥越
Torigoe Jinja
鳥越神社
KIYOSUBASHI DŌRI (AVE.)
Asakusa Catholic ch.
浅草カトリック教会
Shinobugaoka H. Sch.
忍岡高校
Kuramae Police Sta.
蔵前署
Kuramae-bashi (Br.)
蔵前橋
Yokoami
横網
KURAMAEBASHI DŌRI (AVE.)
NTT Sumida
NTT墨田
蔵前橋通り
Taihei
太平
Kuramae Tech. H. Sch.
蔵前工業高
Asakusabashi
浅草橋
Doll Town
EDO DŌRI (AVE.)
Dōai Mem. Hosp.
同愛
Reconstruction Mem. Hall
東京都復興記念館
Ishiwara
石原
Ryōgoku Public Hall
両国公会堂
Yasuda Gakuen
安田学園(Sch.)
旧安田庭園
Kyū Yasuda Garden
Kinshi
錦糸
Yanagibashi
柳橋
Nichidai Daiichi H. Sch.
日大一高
Sumō Stadium (Kokugikan)
国技館
Kamezawa
亀沢
Edo-Tokyo Musm
江戸東京博物館
MITSUME DŌRI (AVE.)
三ツ目通り
錦糸町
SŌBU LINE
総武線
Kinshicho
Higashi-Kanda
東神田
Nihombashi Jogakukan
日本橋女学館
Ryōgoku P.O.
両国局
Ryōgoku
両国
KEIYŌ DŌRO (AVE.)
京葉道路
Kotsubashi H. Sch.
一橋高校
Ryōgoku H. Sch.
両国高校
Kōtō-bashi
江東橋
Bakurocho
馬喰町
Yokoyamacho
横山町
Ryōgoku-bashi (Br.)
両国橋
Honjo Police Sta.
本所署
Midori
緑
Higashi-Nihombashi
東日本橋
Ekō-in
回向院
SHUTO EXPWY No.7
首都高速7号線
NTT Hamachō
NTT浜町
Ryōgoku I.C.
両国インター
Chitose
千歳
Tatekawa
立川
NTT本所
NTT Honjo
Kikukawa
菊川
Tokyo TV Center
東京テレビセンター
CHUO-KU
中央区
Shin-Ōhashi
新大橋
Shin-ōhashi (Br.)
SHINJUKU LINE
都営新宿線
Hisamatsuchō
久松町
Meiji-za
明治座
浜町公園
Hamachō Park
新大橋通り
KIYOSUMI DŌRI (AVE.)
清澄通り
Tomizawacho
富沢町
Morishita
森下
Ningyōchō
人形町
Hamachō
浜町
Bashō Mem. Hall
芭蕉記念館
Hamachō Ramp
浜町ランプ
NIHOMBASHI
日本橋
Tokiwa
常盤
Takabashi
高橋
SHIN-OHASHI DŌRI (AVE.)
Suitengū (Shr.)
水天宮
Nakasu
中洲
Kiyosu-bashi (Br.)
清洲橋
Kakigarachō
蛎殻町
Kiyosumi
清澄
KOTO-KU
江東区
Tokyo City Air Terminal (Hakozaki)
東京シティエアターミナル(箱崎)
中村学園(Sch.)
Nakamura Gakuen
箱崎インター
Hakozaki I.C.
Kiyosumi Garden
清澄庭園
Hakozakichō
箱崎町
Kitasenju
Ikebukuro
Nippori
Ueno
Akihabara
Shinjuku
Tokyo
Shibuya
Ginza
Gotanda
Shinagawa
Central Tokyo 都心 ①
Chiyoda-ku (E) 千代田区(東部)
Chūō-ku (N) 中央区(北部)
Bunkyō-ku (SE) 文京区(南東部)
Taito-ku (S) 台東区(南部)
1 : 20,000
0 1000m

Imperial Palace (Kōkyo) 皇居
Kōkyo-gaien 皇居外苑
CHIYODA-KU 千代田区
Sakuradamon 桜田門
Tokyo Central P.O. 東京中央局
Marunouchi 丸の内
Yaesu 八重洲
Chūō Police Sta. 中央署
Kabutochō 兜町
Takaracho Ramp 宝町ランプ
Kyōbashi 京橋
Marunouchi Ramp 丸の内ランプ
Tokyo Int'l Forum 東京国際フォーラム (Under construction) (工事中)
Metropolitan Police Dept H.Q.(Keishicho) 警視庁
Ministry of Justice (Hōmu-shō) 法務省
Kasumigaseki 霞が関
Kasumigaseki Gov't Offices 霞が関官庁街
Hibiya Park 日比谷公園
Hatchōbori 八丁堀
Yūrakuchō 有楽町
Yūrakuchō Mullion 有楽町マリオン
Ginza Ch. 銀座教会
Kyobashi Ramp 京橋ランプ
Shintomi 新富
Hibiya-Kōen 日比谷公園
Hibiya Public Hall 日比谷公会堂
Hibiya Chanter 日比谷シャンテ
Imperial Hotel 帝国ホテル
Dai-Ichi Kangyo Bank 第一勧銀
Hankyū 阪急
Matsuya 松屋
Mitsukoshi 三越
Chūō Ward Office 中央区役所
Tsukiji Police Sta. 築地署
NTT Tsukiji NTT築地
Hibiya City 日比谷シティ
Uchisaiwaichō 内幸町
Ginza 銀座
Matsuzakaya 松坂屋
Kabuki-za 歌舞伎座
Akashichō 明石町
Tsukiji Maternity Hosp. 築地産院
St. Luke's Hosp. (Sei Roka Byōin) 聖路加病院
Toranomon 虎ノ門
SAKURADA DŌRI (AVE.)
Nishi-Shimbashi 西新橋
HIBIYA DŌRI (AVE.)
Hakuhinkan 博品館
Higashi-Ginza 東銀座
Tōkyū Hotel 東急ホテル
Ginza Ramp 銀座ランプ
日産 Nissan
Shimbashi Enbujō 新橋演舞場
Kyōbashi P.O. 京橋局
Nishi-Hongan-ji (Tsukiji Branch) 西本願寺(築地別院)
Akatsuki Park あかつき公園
CHŪŌ DŌRI (AVE.)
SHŌWA DŌRI (AVE.)
SHIN-OHASHI DORI (AVE.)
Irifune 入船
MINATO-KU 港区
Shimbashi 新橋
SHINKANSEN 新幹線
Nat'l Cancer Center 国立がんセンター
Hydrographic Dept 海上保安庁水路部
Tsukiji 築地
IBM
NHK Broadcast Mus. NHK放送博物館
Atago 愛宕
Minato Tech. H.Sch. 港工高
Jikei Univ. Hosp. 慈恵医大病院
Seishōji 青松寺
Shiba P.O. 芝局
Jikei Med. Univ. 東京慈恵医大
Shiodome Ramp 汐留ランプ
Hamarikyū Asahi Hall 浜離宮朝日ホール
Asahi Newspapers (Tokyo H.O.) 朝日新聞
Nichirei ニチレイ
Higashi-Shimbashi 東新橋
Namiyoke Jinja 波除神社
Tokyo Central Wholesale Market (Tsukiji Ichiba) 築地市場 東京中央卸売市場
Kachidoki-bashi (Br.) 勝鬨橋
HARUMI DŌRI
Atago Police Sta. 愛宕署
Japan Red Cross (Nippon Sekijujisha) 日本赤十字社
Tokyo Prince Hotel 東京プリンスホテル
Hama Detached Palace Garden (Hama Rikyū Teien) 浜離宮恩賜庭園
Kyōritsu Coll. of Pharm. 共立薬科大
Shiba-Kōen 芝公園
Minato Ward Office 港区役所
Hamamatsu-chō 浜松町
KEIHIN-TOHOKU LINE 京浜東北線
TOKAIDO LINE 東海道線
Kachidoki 勝どき
Zōjō-ji 増上寺
Shiba Daijingu 芝大神宮
Shiba Daimon 芝大門
Shiba Park 芝公園
Tōkai District Fishery Research Laboratory 水産庁東海区水産研究所
Reimei-bashi 黎明橋
Shiba Comm.H.Sch. 芝商業高校
World Trade Center Bldg 世界貿易センタービル
Hamamatsuchō 浜松町
Kyū-Shibarikyū Garden 旧芝離宮恩賜庭園
Tokyo Trade Center 東京産業貿易会館
Tsukishima Police Sta. 月島署
Takeshiba Passenger Terminal 竹芝客船ターミナル
Toyomichō 豊海町
Furniture M 家具の博物
Int'l Trade Center Secretariat 国際見本市事務局
Shibakōen Ramp 芝公園ランプ
Shiba 芝
DAIICHI KEIHIN
YAMANOTE LINE 山手線
Hamazakibashi I.C. 浜崎橋インター
Tōshiba Bldg. 東芝ビル
Kaigan 海岸
Int'l Trade Center (Kokusai Bōeki Center) 東京国際貿易センター
NEC 日本電気
Seavans シーバンス
SHUTO EXPWY No.1 首都高速1号線
Hinode Sanbashi (pier) 日の出桟橋
Harumi Ground
Harumi Futō Park 晴海ふ頭公園
Harumi Passenger Terminal 晴海客船ターミナル
Harumi Futō (wharf) 晴海ふ頭
Tamachi 田町
TOKYO MONORAIL 東京モノレール
Shibaura 芝浦
Port of Tokyo (Tokyo-ko) 東京港
Minato-Ward Sports Center 港区スポーツセンター

Central Tokyo 都心②

Chiyoda-ku (S) Chūō-ku (S) Minato-ku (E)
千代田区(南部) 中央区(南部) 港区(東部)

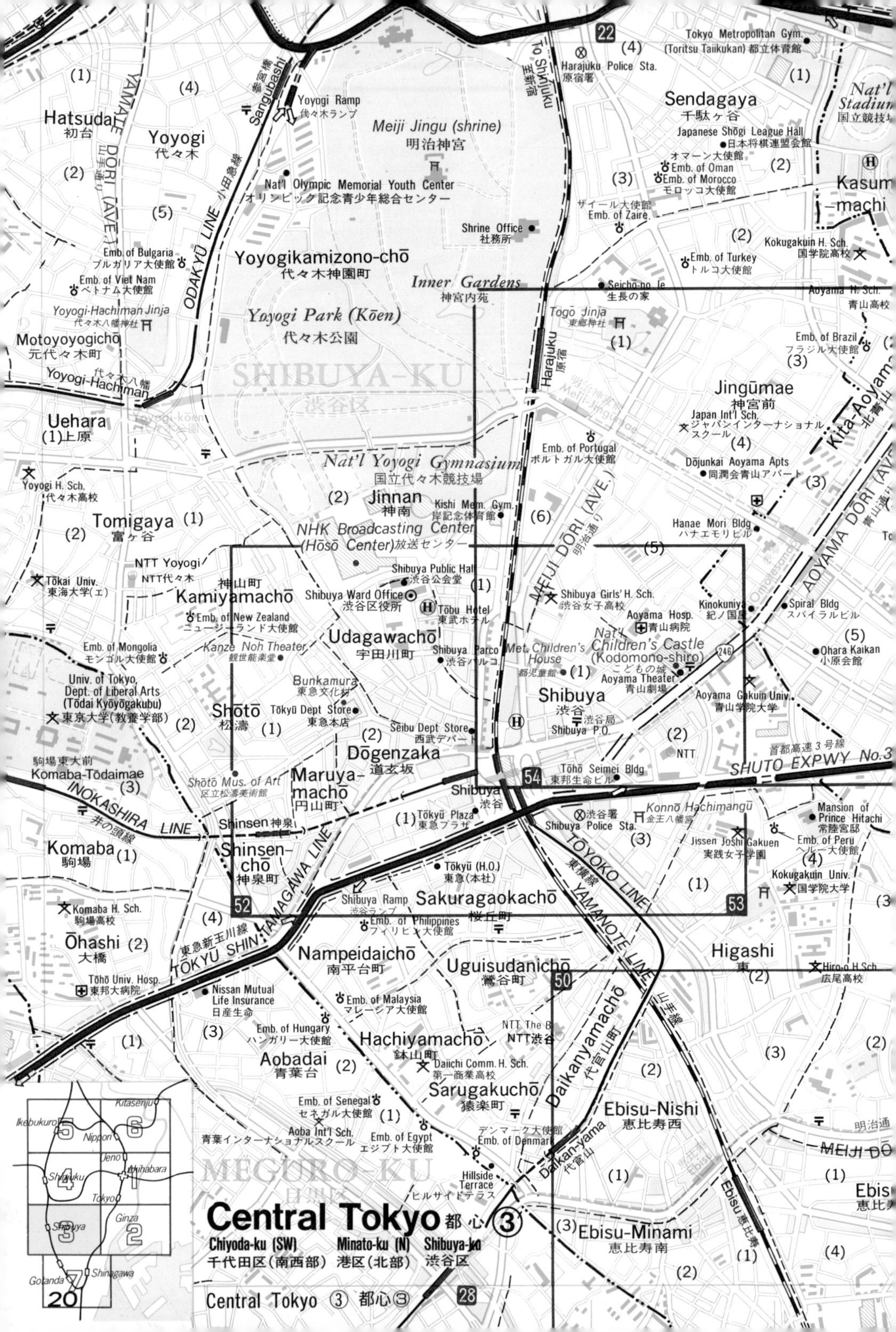
Central Tokyo 都心③
Chiyoda-ku (SW) 千代田区(南西部)
Minato-ku (N) 港区(北部)
Shibuya-ku 渋谷区
Central Tokyo ③ 都心③
Hatsudai 初台
Yoyogi 代々木
Sangubashi 参宮橋
Yoyogi Ramp 代々木ランプ
Meiji Jingu (shrine) 明治神宮
Nat'l Olympic Memorial Youth Center
オリンピック記念青少年総合センター
Shrine Office 社務所
Yoyogikamizono-chō 代々木神園町
Inner Gardens 神宮内苑
Yoyogi Park (Kōen) 代々木公園
SHIBUYA-KU 渋谷区
Emb. of Bulgaria ブルガリア大使館
Emb. of Viet Nam ベトナム大使館
Yoyogi-Hachiman Jinja 代々木八幡神社
Motoyoyogichō 元代々木町
Yoyogi-Hachiman 代々木八幡
Uehara 上原
Yoyogi-kōen 代々木公園
YAMATE DŌRI (AVE.) 山手通り
ODAKYŪ LINE 小田急線
To Shinjuku 至新宿
Harajuku 原宿
Tokyo Metropolitan Gym. (Toritsu Taiikukan) 都立体育館
Harajuku Police Sta. 原宿署
Sendagaya 千駄ヶ谷
Nat'l Stadium 国立競技場
Japanese Shōgi League Hall 日本将棋連盟会館
Emb. of Oman オマーン大使館
Emb. of Morocco モロッコ大使館
Emb. of Zaire ザイール大使館
Kasumigaoka-machi
Kokugakuin H. Sch. 国学院高校
Emb. of Turkey トルコ大使館
Seichō-no Ie 生長の家
Aoyama H. Sch. 青山高校
Tōgō Jinja 東郷神社
Emb. of Brazil ブラジル大使館
Jingūmae 神宮前
Japan Int'l Sch. ジャパンインターナショナルスクール
Meiji-jingūmae 明治神宮前
Emb. of Portugal ポルトガル大使館
Dōjunkai Aoyama Apts 同潤会青山アパート
Kita-Aoyama 北青山
AOYAMA DŌRI 青山通り
Hanae Mori Bldg ハナエモリビル
Omotesando 表参道
Nat'l Yoyogi Gymnasium 国立代々木競技場
Jinnan 神南
Kishi Mem. Gym. 岸記念体育館
MEIJI DŌRI (AVE.) 明治通り
Yoyogi H. Sch. 代々木高校
Tomigaya 富ヶ谷
NHK Broadcasting Center (Hōsō Center) 放送センター
NTT Yoyogi NTT代々木
Tōkai Univ. 東海大学(エ)
Kamiyamachō 神山町
Shibuya Public Hall 渋谷公会堂
Shibuya Ward Office 渋谷区役所
Tōbu Hotel 東武ホテル
Shibuya Girls' H. Sch. 渋谷女子高校
Kinokuniya 紀ノ国屋
Spiral Bldg スパイラルビル
Emb. of New Zealand ニュージーランド大使館
Aoyama Hosp. 青山病院
Emb. of Mongolia モンゴル大使館
Kanze Noh Theater 観世能楽堂
Udagawachō 宇田川町
Shibuya Parco 渋谷パルコ
Met. Children's House 都児童館
Nat'l Children's Castle (Kodomono-shiro) こどもの城
Aoyama Theater 青山劇場
Ohara Kaikan 小原会館
Univ. of Tokyo, Dept. of Liberal Arts (Tōdai Kyōyōgakubu) 東京大学(教養学部)
Bunkamura 東急文化村
Tōkyū Dept Store 東急本店
Shibuya 渋谷
Shibuya P.O. 渋谷局
Aoyama Gakuin Univ. 青山学院大学
Shōtō 松濤
Seibu Dept Store 西武デパート
NTT
首都高速3号線 SHUTO EXPWY No.3
Komaba-Tōdaimae 駒場東大前
Dōgenzaka 道玄坂
Shōtō Mus. of Art 区立松濤美術館
Maruyamachō 円山町
Tōhō Seimei Bldg 東邦生命ビル
INOKASHIRA LINE 井の頭線
Shinsen 神泉
Tōkyū Plaza 東急プラザ
Shibuya Police Sta. 渋谷署
Konnō Hachimangū 金王八幡宮
Mansion of Prince Hitachi 常陸宮邸
Emb. of Peru ペルー大使館
Komaba 駒場
Shinsen-chō 神泉町
Tōkyū (H.O.) 東急(本社)
Jissen Joshi Gakuen 実践女子学園
Kokugakuin Univ. 国学院大学
TŌYOKO LINE 東横線
YAMANOTE LINE 山手線
Komaba H. Sch. 駒場高校
Shibuya Ramp 渋谷ランプ
Sakuragaokachō 桜丘町
Emb. of Philippines フィリピン大使館
TAMAGAWA LINE
TŌKYŪ SHIN-TAMAGAWA LINE 東急新玉川線
Ōhashi 大橋
Nampeidaichō 南平台町
Uguisudanichō 鶯谷町
Higashi 東
Hiro-o H.Sch. 広尾高校
Tōhō Univ. Hosp. 東邦大病院
Nissan Mutual Life Insurance 日産生命
Emb. of Malaysia マレーシア大使館
Emb. of Hungary ハンガリー大使館
Hachiyamachō 鉢山町
NTT The B NTT渋谷
Daikanyamachō 代官山町
Aobadai 青葉台
Daiichi Comm. H. Sch. 第一商業高校
Sarugakuchō 猿楽町
Emb. of Senegal セネガル大使館
Aoba Int'l Sch. 青葉インターナショナルスクール
Emb. of Egypt エジプト大使館
デンマーク大使館 Emb. of Denmark
Daikan-yama 代官山
Ebisu-Nishi 恵比寿西
MEIJI DŌRI 明治通
Ebisu 恵比寿
MEGURO-KU 目黒区
Hillside Terrace ヒルサイドテラス
Ebisu-Minami 恵比寿南
Kitasenju
Ikebukuro
Nippori
Ueno
Shinjuku
Akihabara
Tokyo
Shibuya
Ginza
Gotanda
Shinagawa
22 54 52 53 50 28 20

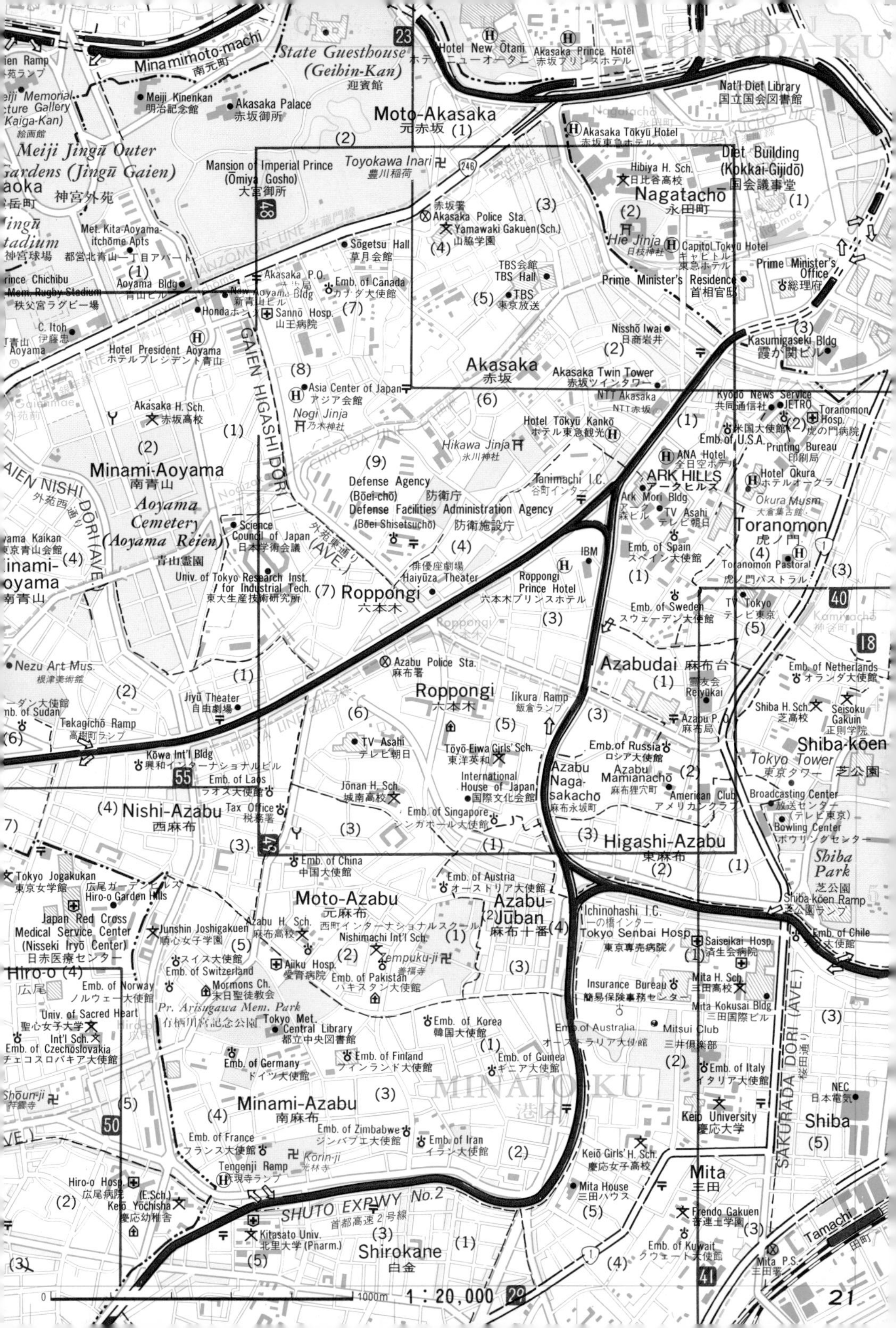

CHIYODA-KU
State Guesthouse
(Geihin-Kan)
迎賓館
Minamimoto-machi
南元町
Hotel New Otani
ホテルニューオータニ
Akasaka Prince Hotel
赤坂プリンスホテル
Nat'l Diet Library
国立国会図書館
Meiji Kinenkan
明治記念館
Akasaka Palace
赤坂御所
Meiji Memorial
Picture Gallery
(Kaiga-Kan)
絵画館
Moto-Akasaka
元赤坂
Meiji Jingū Outer
Gardens (Jingū Gaien)
神宮外苑
Mansion of Imperial Prince
(Ōmiya Gosho)
大宮御所
Toyokawa Inari
豊川稲荷
Akasaka Tōkyū Hotel
赤坂東急ホテル
Diet Building
(Kokkai-Gijidō)
国会議事堂
Hibiya H. Sch.
日比谷高校
Nagatachō
永田町
赤坂署
Akasaka Police Sta.
Yamawaki Gakuen (Sch.)
山脇学園
Hie Jinja
日枝神社
Capitol Tōkyū Hotel
キャピトル東急ホテル
Met. Kita-Aoyama-
itchōme Apts
都営北青山一丁目アパート
Sōgetsu Hall
草月会館
TBS会館
TBS Hall
Prime Minister's Residence
首相官邸
Prime Minister's
Office
総理府
Prince Chichibu
Mem. Rugby Stadium
秩父宮ラグビー場
Aoyama Bldg
青山ビル
Akasaka P.O.
赤坂局
New Aoyama Bldg
新青山ビル
Emb. of Canada
カナダ大使館
TBS
東京放送
Honda
Sannō Hosp.
山王病院
C. Itoh
伊藤忠
Hotel President Aoyama
ホテルプレジデント青山
GAIEN HIGASHI DORI
Nisshō Iwai
日商岩井
Kasumigaseki Bldg
霞が関ビル
Akasaka
赤坂
Akasaka Twin Tower
赤坂ツインタワー
Asia Center of Japan
アジア会館
NTT Akasaka
NTT赤坂
Kyodo News Service
共同通信社
JETRO
Toranomon Hosp.
虎の門病院
Akasaka H. Sch.
赤坂高校
Nogi Jinja
乃木神社
Hotel Tōkyū Kankō
ホテル東急観光
Emb. of U.S.A.
米国大使館
Printing Bureau
印刷局
Minami-Aoyama
南青山
Aoyama Cemetery
(Aoyama Reien)
青山霊園
Hikawa Jinja
氷川神社
ANA Hotel
全日空ホテル
ARK HILLS
アークヒルズ
Hotel Ōkura
ホテルオークラ
Defense Agency
(Bōei-chō)
防衛庁
Defense Facilities Administration Agency
(Bōei Shisetsuchō)
防衛施設庁
Tanimachi I.C.
谷町インター
Ark Mori Bldg
アーク森ビル
TV Asahi
テレビ朝日
Okura Musm
大倉集古館
Toranomon
虎ノ門
GAIEN NISHI DORI (AVE.)
外苑西通り
Science Council of Japan
日本学術会議
外苑東通り (AVE.)
Emb. of Spain
スペイン大使館
Toranomon Pastoral
虎ノ門パストラル
Univ. of Tokyo Research Inst.
for Industrial Tech.
東大生産技術研究所
俳優座劇場
Haiyūza Theater
Roppongi
六本木
IBM
Roppongi Prince Hotel
六本木プリンスホテル
Emb. of Sweden
スウェーデン大使館
TV Tokyo
テレビ東京
Nezu Art Mus.
根津美術館
Azabu Police Sta.
麻布署
Azabudai
麻布台
Reiyūkai
霊友会
Emb. of Netherlands
オランダ大使館
Emb. of Sudan
スーダン大使館
Jiyū Theater
自由劇場
Iikura Ramp
飯倉ランプ
Shiba H. Sch.
芝高校
Seisoku Gakuin
正則学院
Takagichō Ramp
高樹町ランプ
TV Asahi
テレビ朝日
Tōyō-Eiwa Girls' Sch.
東洋英和
Azabu P.O.
麻布局
Emb. of Russia
ロシア大使館
Shiba-kōen
Kōwa Int'l Bldg
興和インターナショナルビル
Tokyo Tower
東京タワー
芝公園
Emb. of Laos
ラオス大使館
International House of Japan
国際文化会館
Azabu Nagasakachō
麻布永坂町
Azabu Mamianachō
麻布狸穴町
American Club
アメリカンクラブ
Broadcasting Center
放送センター
(テレビ東京)
Bowling Center
ボウリングセンター
Nishi-Azabu
西麻布
Tax Office
税務署
Jōnan H. Sch.
城南高校
Emb. of Singapore
シンガポール大使館
Higashi-Azabu
東麻布
Shiba Park
芝公園
Emb. of China
中国大使館
Tokyo Jogakukan
東京女学館
Hiro-o Garden Hills
Emb. of Austria
オーストリア大使館
Moto-Azabu
元麻布
Azabu-Jūban
麻布十番
Ichinohashi I.C.
一の橋インター
Shiba-kōen Ramp
芝公園ランプ
Japan Red Cross
Medical Service Center
(Nisseki Iryō Center)
日赤医療センター
Junshin Joshigakuen
順心女子学園
Azabu H. Sch.
麻布高校
西町インターナショナルスクール
Nishimachi Int'l Sch.
Tokyo Senbai Hosp.
東京専売病院
Saiseikai Hosp.
済生会病院
Emb. of Chile
チリ大使館
Hiro-o
広尾
スイス大使館
Emb. of Switzerland
Aiiku Hosp.
愛育病院
Zempuku-ji
善福寺
Mita H. Sch.
三田高校
Emb. of Norway
ノルウェー大使館
Mormons Ch.
末日聖徒教会
Emb. of Pakistan
パキスタン大使館
Insurance Bureau
簡易保険事務センター
Mita Kokusai Bldg
三田国際ビル
Univ. of Sacred Heart
聖心女子大学
Int'l Sch.
Pr. Arisugawa Mem. Park
有栖川宮記念公園
Tokyo Met. Central Library
都立中央図書館
Emb. of Korea
韓国大使館
Emb. of Australia
オーストラリア大使館
Mitsui Club
三井倶楽部
Emb. of Czechoslovakia
チェコスロバキア大使館
Emb. of Germany
ドイツ大使館
Emb. of Finland
フィンランド大使館
Emb. of Guinea
ギニア大使館
Emb. of Italy
イタリア大使館
SAKURADA DORI (AVE.)
桜田通り
NEC
日本電気
Shōun-ji
祥雲寺
Minami-Azabu
南麻布
MINATO-KU
港区
Keiō University
慶応大学
Shiba
Emb. of France
フランス大使館
Emb. of Zimbabwe
ジンバブエ大使館
Emb. of Iran
イラン大使館
Kōrin-ji
光林寺
Keiō Girls' H. Sch.
慶応女子高校
Tengenji Ramp
天現寺ランプ
Mita
三田
Hiro-o Hosp.
広尾病院
Keiō Yōchisha
(E.Sch.)
慶応幼稚舎
Mita House
三田ハウス
SHUTO EXPWY No.2
首都高速2号線
Kitasato Univ.
北里大学 (Pharm.)
Friendo Gakuen
普連土学園
Tamachi
田町
Shirokane
白金
Emb. of Kuwait
クウェート大使館
Mita P.S.
三田署
0
1000m
1 : 20,000

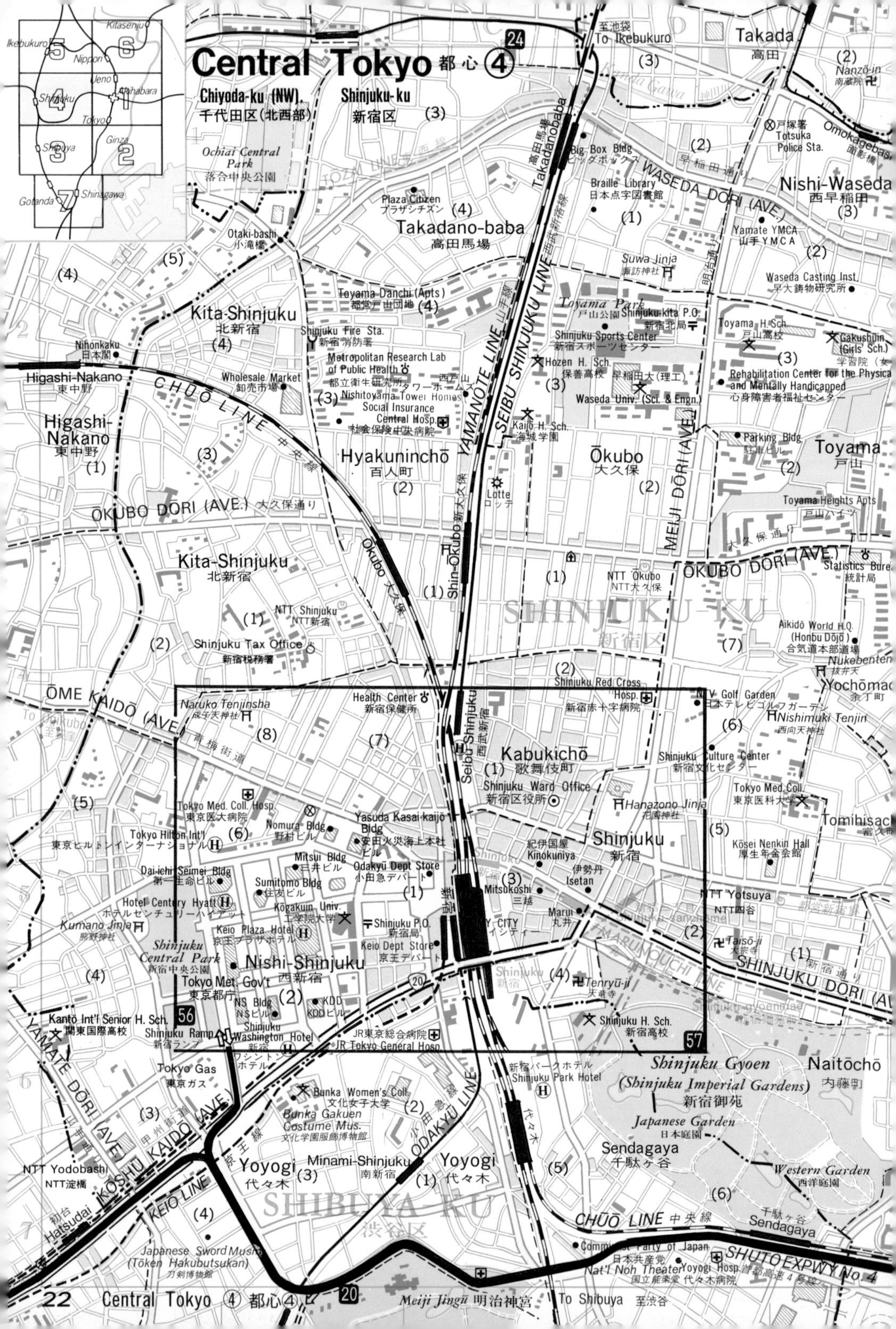

Central Tokyo 都心④
Chiyoda-ku (NW)
千代田区(北西部)
Shinjuku-ku
新宿区
Ikebukuro
Kitasenju
Nippori
Ueno
Shinjuku
Akihabara
Tokyo
Shibuya
Ginza
Shinagawa
Gotanda
To Ikebukuro
至池袋
Takada
高田
Nanzō-in
南蔵院
Totsuka Police Sta.
戸塚署
Omokagebashi
Ochiai Central Park
落合中央公園
Big Box Bldg
ビッグボックス
Takadanobaba
高田馬場
WASEDA DORI (AVE.)
早稲田通り
Nishi-Waseda
西早稲田
Braille Library
日本点字図書館
Plaza Citizen
プラザシチズン
Takadano-baba
高田馬場
Otaki-bashi
小滝橋
Yamate YMCA
山手YMCA
Suwa Jinja
諏訪神社
Waseda Casting Inst.
早大鋳物研究所
Toyama Danchi (Apts)
都営戸山団地
Toyama Park
戸山公園
Shinjuku-kita P.O.
新宿北局
Kita-Shinjuku
北新宿
Shinjuku Fire Sta.
新宿消防署
Shinjuku Sports Center
新宿スポーツセンター
Toyama H. Sch.
戸山高校
Gakushuin (Girls' Sch.)
学習院(女
Nihonkaku
日本閣
Metropolitan Research Lab of Public Health
都立衛生研究所
Hozen H. Sch.
保善高校
Waseda Univ. (Sci. & Engn.)
早稲田大(理工)
Rehabilitation Center for the Physically and Mentally Handicapped
心身障害者福祉センター
Higashi-Nakano
東中野
Wholesale Market
卸売市場
Nishitoyama Tower Homes
西戸山タワーホームズ
Social Insurance Central Hosp.
社会保険中央病院
Kaijō H. Sch.
海城学園
CHŪŌ LINE 中央線
YAMANOTE LINE 山手線
SEIBU SHINJUKU LINE 西武新宿線
Parking Bldg
駐車ビル
Toyama
戸山
Hyakuninchō
百人町
Ōkubo
大久保
Lotte
ロッテ
MEIJI DŌRI (AVE.)
Toyama Heights Apts
戸山ハイツ
ŌKUBO DŌRI (AVE.) 大久保通り
Shin-Ōkubo 新大久保
Ōkubo 大久保
NTT Ōkubo
NTT大久保
Statistics Bureau
統計局
NTT Shinjuku
NTT新宿
SHINJUKU-KU
新宿区
Aikidō World H.Q. (Honbu Dōjō)
合気道本部道場
Shinjuku Tax Office
新宿税務署
Nukebenten
抜弁天
Shinjuku Red Cross Hosp.
新宿赤十字病院
Yochōmachi
余丁町
ŌME KAIDŌ (AVE.) 青梅街道
To Ogikubo
至荻窪
Naruko Tenjinsha
成子天神社
Health Center
新宿保健所
NTV Golf Garden
日本テレビゴルフガーデン
Nishimuki Tenjin
西向天神社
Seibu-Shinjuku
西武新宿
Kabukichō
歌舞伎町
Shinjuku Culture Center
新宿文化センター
Shinjuku Ward Office
新宿区役所
Tokyo Med. Coll. Hosp.
東京医大病院
Tokyo Med. Coll.
東京医科大学
Tomihisacho
Tokyo Hilton Int'l
東京ヒルトンインターナショナル
Nomura Bldg
野村ビル
Yasuda Kasai-kaijō Bldg
安田火災海上本社ビル
Hanazono Jinja
花園神社
Kinokuniya
紀伊国屋
Shinjuku
新宿
Kōsei Nenkin Hall
厚生年金会館
Mitsui Bldg
三井ビル
Odakyū Dept Store
小田急デパート
Isetan
伊勢丹
Dai-ichi Seimei Bldg
第一生命ビル
Sumitomo Bldg
住友ビル
Mitsukoshi
三越
NTT Yotsuya
NTT四谷
Hotel Century Hyatt
ホテルセンチュリーハイアット
Kōgakuin Univ.
工学院大学
Maru
丸井
Kumano Jinja
熊野神社
Keio Plaza Hotel
京王プラザホテル
Shinjuku P.O.
新宿局
Taisō-ji
太宗寺
Shinjuku Central Park
新宿中央公園
Keio Dept Store
京王デパート
MARUNOUCHI LINE
SHINJUKU DORI (AVE.)
新宿通り
Nishi-Shinjuku
西新宿
Tenryū-ji
天竜寺
Tokyo Met. Gov't
東京都庁
NS Bldg
NSビル
KDD
KDDビル
Kantō Int'l Senior H. Sch.
関東国際高校
Shinjuku Ramp
新宿ランプ
Shinjuku Washington Hotel
新宿ワシントンホテル
JR Tokyo General Hosp.
JR東京総合病院
Shinjuku H. Sch.
新宿高校
Tokyo Gas
東京ガス
新宿パークホテル
Shinjuku Park Hotel
Shinjuku Gyoen (Shinjuku Imperial Gardens)
新宿御苑
Naitōchō
内藤町
Bunka Women's Coll.
文化女子大学
Bunka Gakuen Costume Mus.
文化学園服飾博物館
Japanese Garden
日本庭園
YAMATE DORI (AVE.)
KOSHU KAIDO (AVE.)
甲州街道
ODAKYU LINE 小田急線
Sendagaya
千駄ヶ谷
NTT Yodobashi
NTT淀橋
Yoyogi
代々木
Minami-Shinjuku
南新宿
Western Garden
西洋庭園
Hatsudai
初台
KEIO LINE
SHIBUYA-KU
渋谷区
CHŪŌ LINE 中央線
Sendagaya
千駄ヶ谷
Japanese Sword Mus. (Tōken Hakubutsukan)
刀剣博物館
Communist Party of Japan
日本共産党
Nat'l Noh Theater
国立能楽堂
Yoyogi Hosp.
代々木病院
SHUTO EXPWY No.4
首都高速4号線
Meiji Jingū 明治神宮
To Shibuya 至渋谷

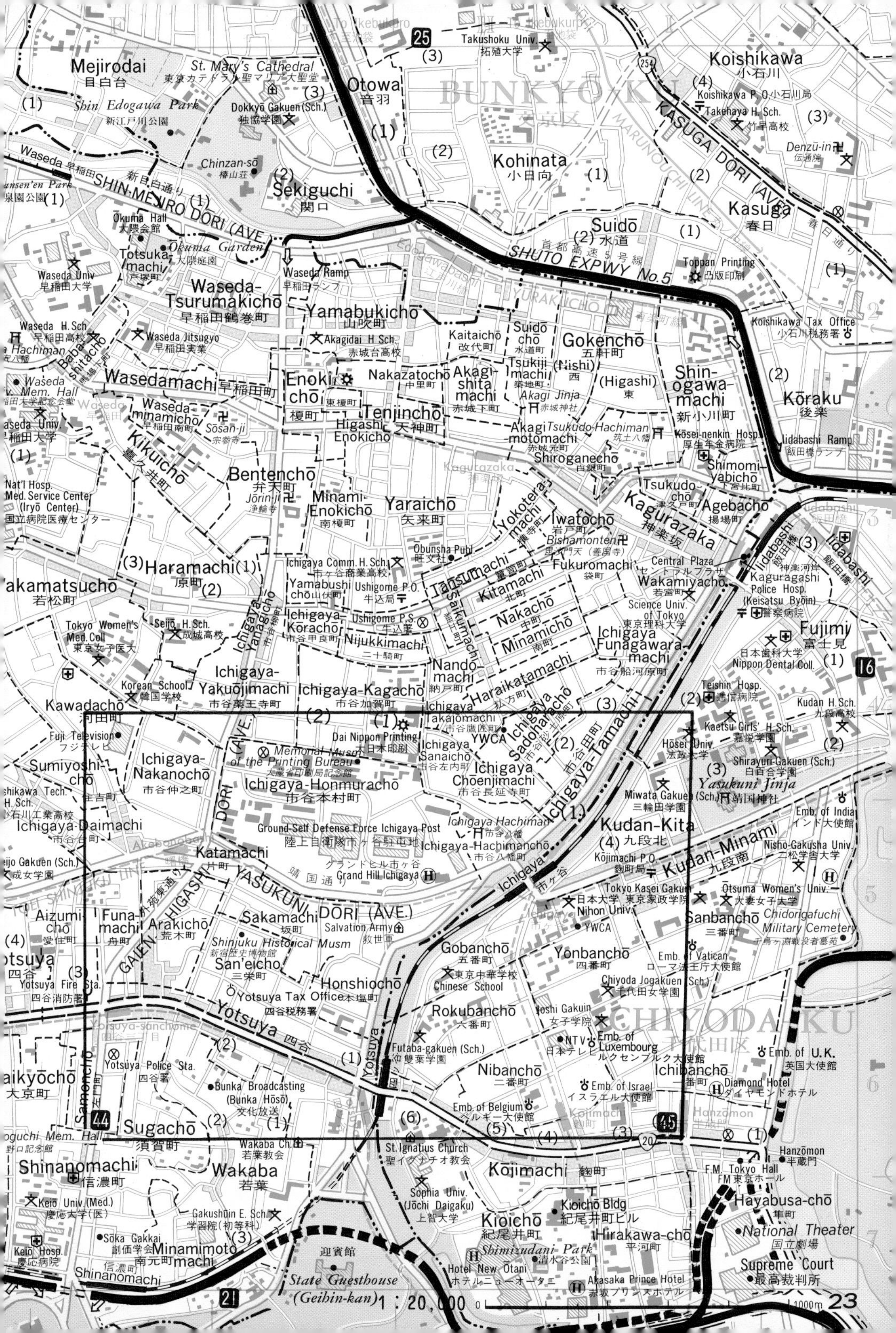

To Ikebukuro
池袋
25
Takushoku Univ.
拓殖大学
BUNKYO-KU
文京区
Koishikawa
小石川
Koishikawa P.O.小石川局
Takehaya H. Sch.
竹早高校
Denzū-in
伝通院
Mejirodai
目白台
St. Mary's Cathedral
東京カテドラル聖マリア大聖堂
Dokkyō Gakuen (Sch.)
独協学園
Otowa
音羽
Shin Edogawa Park
新江戸川公園
Chinzan-sō
椿山荘
Sekiguchi
関口
Kohinata
小日向
KASUGA DORI (AVE.)
MARUNOUCHI LINE
Kasuga
春日
春日通り
Waseda 早稲田
SHIN-MEJIRO DORI (AVE.)
新目白通り
Okuma Hall
大隈会館
Okuma Garden
大隈庭園
Totsuka-machi
戸塚町
Waseda Univ.
早稲田大学
Waseda Ramp
早稲田ランプ
Edogawabashi
江戸川橋
Suidō
水道
首都高速5号線
SHUTO EXPWY No.5
Toppan Printing
凸版印刷
YURAKUCHO LINE
有楽町線
Waseda-Tsurumakichō
早稲田鶴巻町
Yamabukichō
山吹町
Waseda H.Sch.
早稲田高校
Waseda Jitsugyo
早稲田実業
Akagidai H.Sch.
赤城台高校
Kaitaichō
改代町
Suidō chō
水道町
Gokenchō
五軒町
Koishikawa Tax Office
小石川税務署
Baba-shitachō
馬場下町
Wasedamachi 早稲田町
Enoki chō
榎町
Nakazatochō
中里町
Akagi-shita machi
赤城下町
Tsukiji machi
築地町
(Nishi)
西
(Higashi)
東
Shin-ogawa-machi
新小川町
Kōraku
後楽
Waseda-minamichō
早稲田南町
Sōsan-ji
宗参寺
Tenjinchō
天神町
Higashi Enokichō
Akagi Jinja
赤城神社
Akagi-motomachi
赤城元町
Tsukudo-Hachiman
筑土八幡
Kōsei-nenkin Hosp.
厚生年金病院
Iidabashi Ramp
飯田橋ランプ
Kikuichō
喜久井町
Bentenchō
弁天町
Jōrin-ji
浄輪寺
Kagurazaka
神楽坂
Shiroganechō
白銀町
Shimomiyabichō
下宮比町
Nat'l Hosp. Med. Service Center (Iryō Center)
国立病院医療センター
Minami-Enokichō
南榎町
Yaraichō
矢来町
Yokotera machi
横寺町
Iwatochō
岩戸町
Tsukudo-chō
津久戸町
Agebachō
揚場町
Iidabashi
飯田橋
Bishamonten
毘沙門天(善国寺)
Obunsha Publ.
旺文社
Ichigaya Comm. H. Sch.
市ケ谷商業高校
Tansumachi
箪笥町
Fukuromachi
袋町
Central Plaza
セントラルプラザ
Kagurazaka Police Hosp. (Keisatsu Byōin)
警察病院
Haramachi
原町
Wakamatsuchō
若松町
Yamabushi chō
山伏町
Ushigome P.O.
牛込局
Kitamachi
北町
Wakamiyachō
若宮町
Science Univ. of Tokyo
東京理科大学
Ushigome P.S.
牛込署
Nakachō
中町
Minamichō
南町
Fujimi
富士見
Tokyo Women's Med. Coll.
東京女子医大
Seijō H.Sch.
成城高校
Ichigaya Yanagichō
市谷柳町
Ichigaya Kōrachō
市谷甲良町
Nijukkimachi
二十騎町
Sakumachi
佐内町
Ichigaya Funagawara-machi
市谷船河原町
日本歯科大学
Nippon Dental Coll.
Nandomachi
納戸町
Haraikatamachi
払方町
16
Ichigaya-Yakuōjimachi
市谷薬王寺町
Ichigaya-Kagachō
市谷加賀町
Teishin Hosp.
逓信病院
Korean School
韓国学校
Kawadachō
河田町
Ichigaya Takajōmachi
市谷鷹匠町
Ichigaya Sadoharachō
市谷砂土原町
Kudan H.Sch.
九段高校
Dai Nippon Printing
大日本印刷
Kaetsu Girls' H.Sch.
嘉悦学園
Fuji Television
フジテレビ
YWCA
Ichigaya-Tamachi
市谷田町
Hōsei Univ.
法政大学
Ichigaya-Nakanochō
市谷仲之町
Memorial Musm of the Printing Bureau
大蔵省印刷局記念館
Ichigaya Sanaichō
市谷左内町
Shirayuri-Gakuen (Sch.)
白百合学園
Sumiyoshi-chō
住吉町
Ichigaya-Honmurachō
市谷本村町
Ichigaya Chōenjimachi
市谷長延寺町
Yasukuni Jinja
靖国神社
Miwata Gakuen (Sch.)
三輪田学園
Ichigaya-Daimachi
市谷台町
Ground Self Defense Force Ichigaya Post
陸上自衛隊市ヶ谷駐屯地
Ichigaya Hachiman
市谷八幡
Ichigaya-Hachimanchō
市谷八幡町
Kudan-Kita
九段北
Emb. of India
インド大使館
Katamachi
片町
グランドヒル市ヶ谷
Grand Hill Ichigaya
靖国通り
Kōjimachi P.O.
麹町局
Kudan-Minami
九段南
Nisho-Gakusha Univ.
二松学舎大学
Ichigaya
市ヶ谷
Tokyo Kasei Gakuin
東京家政学院
Ōtsuma Women's Univ.
大妻女子大学
YASUKUNI DŌRI (AVE.)
GAIEN-HIGASHI
外苑東通り
Aizumi-chō
愛住町
Funa-machi
舟町
Arakichō
荒木町
Sakamachi
坂町
Salvation Army
救世軍
日本大学
Nihon Univ.
Sanbanchō
三番町
Chidorigafuchi Military Cemetery
千鳥ヶ淵戦没者墓苑
Yotsuya
四谷
Shinjuku Historical Musm
新宿歴史博物館
San'eichō
三栄町
Gobanchō
五番町
東京中華学校
Chinese School
Yonbanchō
四番町
Emb. of Vatican
ローマ法王庁大使館
Yotsuya Fire Sta.
四谷消防署
Honshiochō
本塩町
Yotsuya Tax Office
四谷税務署
Chiyoda Jogakuen (Sch.)
千代田女学園
Rokubanchō
六番町
Joshi Gakuin
女子学院
CHIYODA-KU
千代田区
NTV
日本テレビ
Emb. of Luxembourg
ルクセンブルク大使館
Futaba-gakuen (Sch.)
雙葉学園
Emb. of U.K.
英国大使館
Yotsuya Police Sta.
四谷署
Bunka Broadcasting (Bunka Hōsō)
文化放送
Nibanchō
二番町
Ichibanchō
一番町
Emb. of Israel
イスラエル大使館
Diamond Hotel
ダイヤモンドホテル
Daikyōchō
大京町
Samonchō
左門町
Emb. of Belgium
ベルギー大使館
44
Sugachō
須賀町
Kōjimachi
麹町
Hanzōmon
45
20
Noguchi Mem. Hall
野口記念館
Wakaba Ch.
若葉教会
St. Ignatius Church
聖イグナチオ教会
Hanzōmon
半蔵門
Shinanomachi
信濃町
Wakaba
若葉
Kōjimachi 麹町
F.M. Tokyo Hall
FM東京ホール
Keiō Univ. (Med.)
慶応大学(医)
Sophia Univ. (Jōchi Daigaku)
上智大学
Kioichō Bldg
紀尾井町ビル
Hayabusa-chō
隼町
Gakushūin E. Sch.
学習院(初等科)
Kioichō
紀尾井町
Hirakawa-chō
平河町
National Theater
国立劇場
Sōka Gakkai
創価学会
Minamimoto machi
南元町
Keiō Hosp.
慶応病院
迎賓館
Shimizudani Park
清水谷公園
Supreme Court
最高裁判所
Shinanomachi
信濃町
State Guesthouse (Geihin-kan)
Hotel New Otani
ホテルニューオータニ
Akasaka Prince Hotel
赤坂プリンスホテル
21
1 : 20,000
0
1000m

Central Tokyo 都心⑤
Toshima-ku
豊島区
Bunkyō-ku (W)
文京区(西部)
Ōyaguchi-Kamichō
大谷口上町
Ōyama-Nishichō
大山西町
Ōyamachō
大山町
Ōyama-Kanaichō
大山金井町
Ōyama-Higashichō
大山東町
Tokyo Met. Geriatric Hosp.
東京都老人医療センター
Itabashi Ward Office
板橋区役所
Itabashi Police Sta.
板橋署
Kitazono H. Sch.
北園高校
Itabashi P.O.
板橋局
NTT Itabashi
NTT板橋
TŌBU TŌJŌ LINE
東武東上線
KAWAGOE KAIDŌ (AVE.)
川越街道
ITABASHI-KU
板橋区
Shimo-Itabashi
下板橋
Mukai-hara
向原
Ōyaguchi
大谷口
Saiwaichō
幸町
NTT Minami-Itabashi
NTT南板橋
Kumanochō
熊野町
Naka-maruchō
中丸町
Ikebukuro-honchō
池袋本町
Kumano Jinja
熊野神社
Itabashi H. Sch.
板橋高校
Hōnan H. Sch.
豊南高校
Minamichō
南町
Kita-Ikebukuro Ramp
北池袋ランプ
Toshima Jitsugyo H. Sch.
豊島実業高校
Tokyo Kōtsu Jr. Coll.
東京交通短大
Shōwa Railway H. Sch.
昭和鉄道高校
Kita-Ikebukuro
北池袋
Senkawachō
千川町
Toshima Ward Gym.
豊島区立体育館
Takamatsu
高松
Hata Sports Plaza
ハタスポーツプラザ
Takamatsu Ramp
高松ランプ
TOSHIMA-KU
豊島区
Fujimi-bashi
富士見橋
Ushigome Comm. H.Sch.
牛込商業高校
Kanamechō
要町
Ikebukuro
池袋
Ikebukuro-ōhashi
池袋大橋
Ikebukuro Skating Center
池袋スケートセンター
Kumagai Morikazu Art Musm.
熊谷守一美術館
Chihaya
千早
Toshima Ward Office
豊島区役所
Toshima Public Hall
豊島公会堂
Jōsai Gakuin (Sch.)
城西学院
Rikkyō Univ
立教大学
Marui
丸井
Tōbu Dept. Store
東武デパート
Parco
パルコ
Mitsukoshi
三越
Toshima Tax Office
豊島税務署
Tokyo Met. Art Space
東京芸術劇場
Nagasaki
長崎
Toshima Catholic Ch.
カトリック豊島教会
Nishi-Ikebukuro
西池袋
Metropolitan Plaza
メトロポリタンプラザ
Seibu Dept Store
西武デパート
Kinka-dō
キンカ堂
Labor Welfare Hall
勤労福祉会館
Hotel Metropolitan
ホテルメトロポリタン
YAMATE DŌRI (AVE.)
山手通り
To Tokorozawa
至所沢
Shiinamachi
椎名町
SEIBU IKEBUKURO LINE
西武池袋線
Jiyū Gakuen
自由学園
Seibu-Ikebukuro
西武池袋
Minami-Ikebukuro Park
南池袋公園
Tōbu Store
東武ストア
Minami-Nagasaki
南長崎
Minami-Ikebukuro
南池袋
Mejiro
目白
Mejiro Garden
目白庭園
NTT Ochiai
NTT落合
Tokyo Music Col.
東京音楽大学
Mejiro Hosp.
目白病院
Kishimojin-dō
鬼子母神堂
MEJIRO DŌRI (AVE.)
目白通り
Kawamura-Gakuen
川村学園
Seibo Jr. Coll. of Nursing
聖母女子短大
Naka-Ochiai
中落合
Holy Mother Hosp. (Seibo Byōin)
聖母病院
Shimo-Ochiai Ch.
下落合教会
Shimo-Ochiai
下落合
Mejiro Police Sta.
目白署
SHIN-MEJIRO DŌRI (AVE.)
新目白通り
Mejirogaoka Ch.
目白ヶ丘教会
Gakushūin Univ.
学習院大学
YAMANOTE LINE
山手線
TODEN ARAKAWA LINE
SHINJUKU-KU
新宿区
Otomeyama Park
おとめ山公園
Nakai
中井
日本造船技術センター
Shipbuilding Research Center of Japan
Chitose-bashi (Br.)
千登世橋
Gakushuinshita
学習院下
SEIBU SHINJUKU LINE
西武新宿線
Takada
高田
Mejiro Fudō
目白不動
To Waseda
至早稲田
至新宿
To Shinjuku

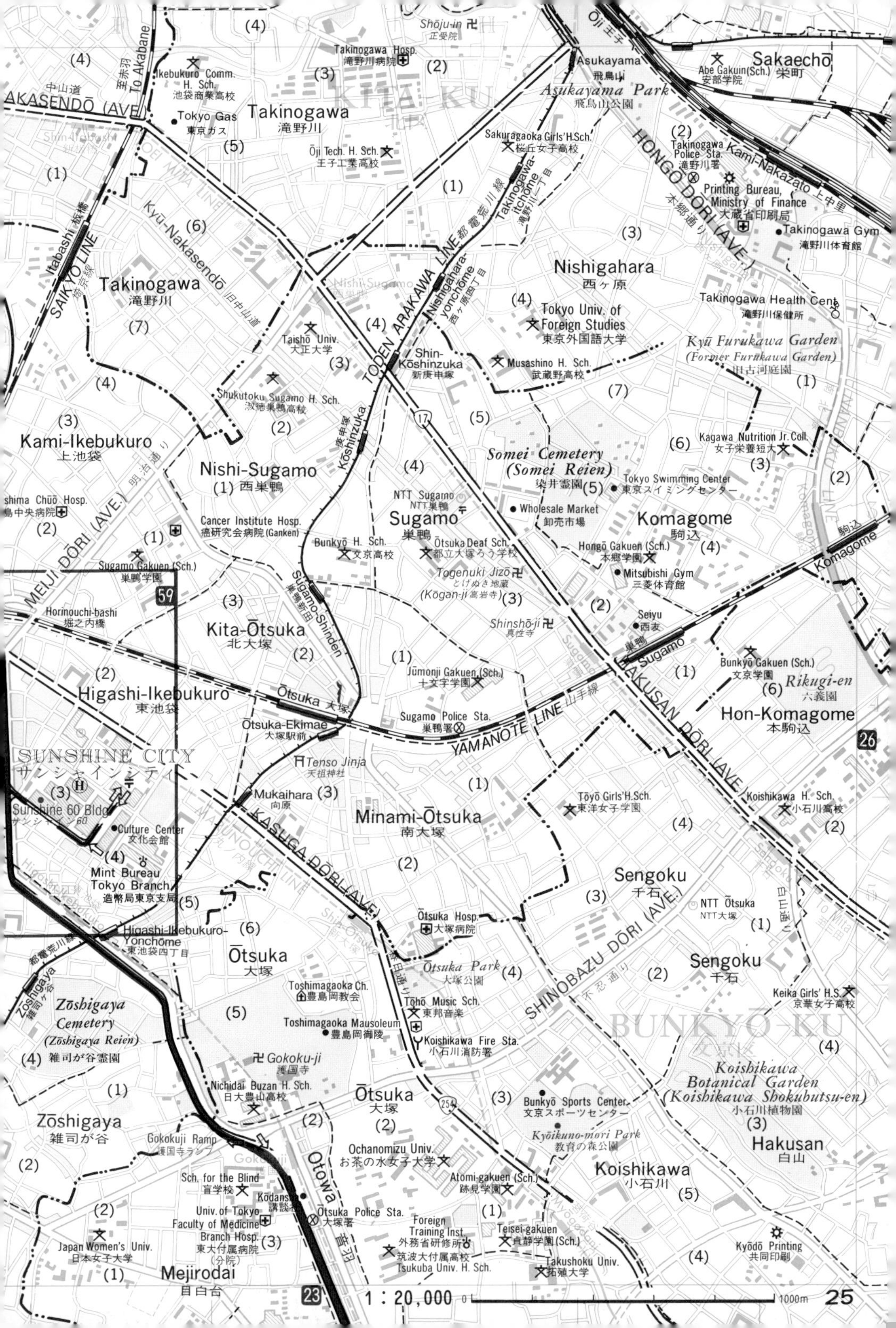

Takinogawa
滝野川
Nishigahara
西ヶ原
Sugamo
巣鴨
Komagome
駒込
Kami-Ikebukuro
上池袋
Nishi-Sugamo
西巣鴨
Kita-Ōtsuka
北大塚
Higashi-Ikebukuro
東池袋
Minami-Ōtsuka
南大塚
Ōtsuka
大塚
Sengoku
千石
Hon-Komagome
本駒込
Hakusan
白山
Koishikawa
小石川
Zōshigaya
雑司が谷
Mejirodai
目白台
Sakaechō
栄町
Asukayama Park
飛鳥山公園
Somei Cemetery (Somei Reien)
染井霊園
Kyū Furukawa Garden (Former Furukawa Garden)
旧古河庭園
Rikugi-en
六義園
Koishikawa Botanical Garden (Koishikawa Shokubutsu-en)
小石川植物園
Zōshigaya Cemetery (Zōshigaya Reien)
雑司が谷霊園
SUNSHINE CITY
サンシャインシティ
KITA-KU
BUNKYŌ-KU
YAMANOTE LINE
SAIKYŌ LINE
TODEN ARAKAWA LINE
HONGŌ DŌRI (AVE.)
HAKUSAN DŌRI (AVE.)
SHINOBAZU DŌRI (AVE.)
KASUGA DŌRI (AVE.)
MEIJI DŌRI (AVE.)
NAKASENDŌ (AVE.)
Kyū-Nakasendō
Tokyo Univ. of Foreign Studies
東京外国語大学
Ochanomizu Univ.
お茶の水女子大学
Takushoku Univ.
拓殖大学
Japan Women's Univ.
日本女子大学
Taishō Univ.
大正大学
Gokoku-ji
護国寺
Togenuki Jizō
とげぬき地蔵
Ōtsuka Police Sta.
大塚署
Sugamo Police Sta.
巣鴨署
Printing Bureau, Ministry of Finance
大蔵省印刷局
Mint Bureau Tokyo Branch
造幣局東京支局
Sunshine 60 Bldg.
Kyōdō Printing
共同印刷
1 : 20,000
1000m

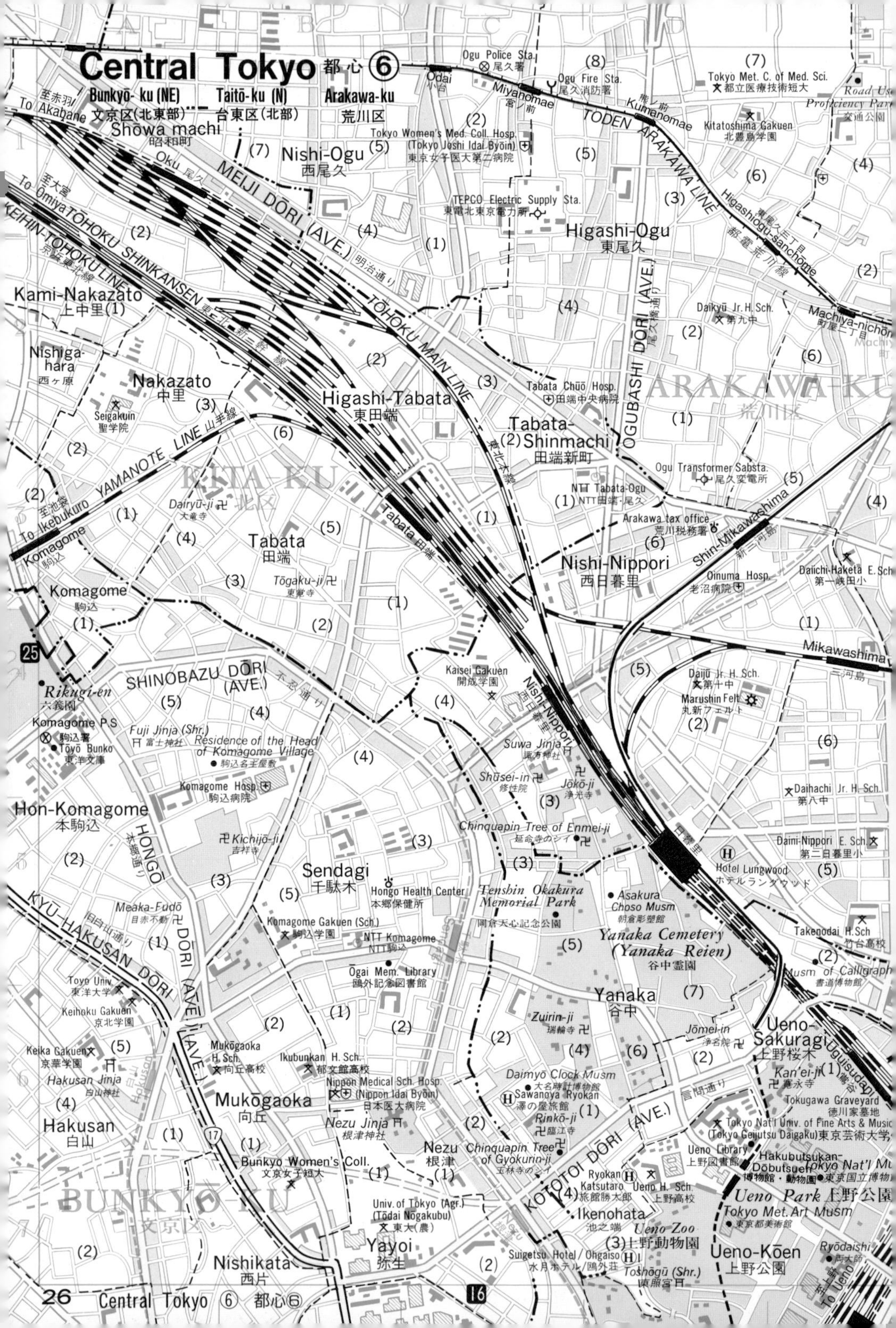
Central Tokyo 都心⑥
Bunkyō-ku (NE) 文京区(北東部)
Taitō-ku (N) 台東区(北部)
Arakawa-ku 荒川区
Shōwa machi 昭和町
Nishi-Ogu 西尾久
Higashi-Ogu 東尾久
Kami-Nakazato 上中里
Nishigahara 西ヶ原
Nakazato 中里
Higashi-Tabata 東田端
Tabata-Shinmachi 田端新町
Nishi-Nippori 西日暮里
Tabata 田端
Komagome 駒込
Hon-Komagome 本駒込
Sendagi 千駄木
Yanaka 谷中
Ueno-Sakuragi 上野桜木
Mukōgaoka 向丘
Hakusan 白山
Nezu 根津
Ikenohata 池之端
Yayoi 弥生
Nishikata 西片
Ueno-Kōen 上野公園
MEIJI DŌRI (AVE.) 明治通り
TŌHOKU MAIN LINE
TŌHOKU SHINKANSEN
KEIHIN-TŌHOKU LINE 京浜東北線
YAMANOTE LINE 山手線
TODEN ARAKAWA LINE
OGUBASHI DŌRI (AVE.)
SHINOBAZU DŌRI (AVE.) 不忍通り
HONGŌ DŌRI (AVE.) 本郷通り
KYŪ-HAKUSAN DŌRI
KOTOTOI DŌRI (AVE.) 言問通り
Yanaka Cemetery (Yanaka Reien) 谷中霊園
Tenshin Okakura Memorial Park 岡倉天心記念公園
Ueno Park 上野公園
Ueno Zoo 上野動物園
Rikugi-en 六義園
ARAKAWA-KU 荒川区
KITA-KU 北区
BUNKYŌ-KU 文京区
26 Central Tokyo ⑥ 都心⑥

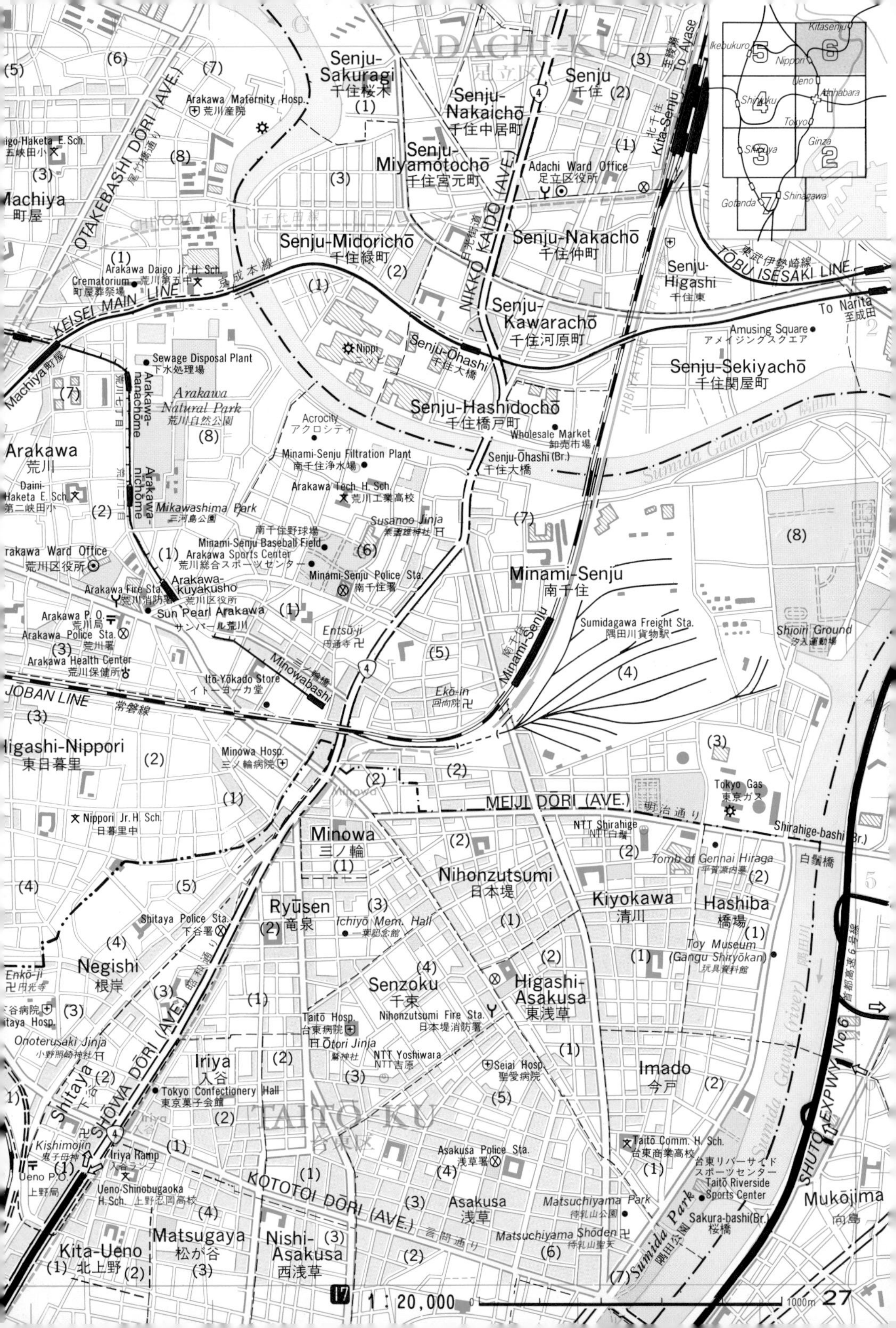

ADACHI-KU
足立区
Senju-Sakuragi
千住桜木
Senju-Nakaichō
千住中居町
Senju
千住
To Ayase
Kita-Senju
北千住
Arakawa Maternity Hosp.
荒川産院
OTAKEBASHI DŌRI (AVE.)
尾竹橋通り
Daigo-Haketa E. Sch.
五峡田小
Machiya
町屋
Senju-Miyamotochō
千住宮元町
Adachi Ward Office
足立区役所
CHIYODA LINE
千代田線
Senju-Midorichō
千住緑町
NIKKO KAIDO (AVE.)
日光街道
Senju-Nakachō
千住仲町
Arakawa Daigo Jr. H. Sch.
荒川第五中
Crematorium
町屋葬祭場
KEISEI MAIN LINE
京成本線
Senju-Higashi
千住東
TOBU ISESAKI LINE
東武伊勢崎線
Senju-Kawarachō
千住河原町
To Narita
至成田
Machiya
町屋
Amusing Square
アメイジングスクエア
Nippi
ニッピ
Senju-Ōhashi
千住大橋
Sewage Disposal Plant
下水処理場
Arakawa-nanachōme
荒川七丁目
Arakawa Natural Park
荒川自然公園
Senju-Sekiyachō
千住関屋町
Senju-Hashidochō
千住橋戸町
Acrocity
アクロシティ
HIBIYA LINE
Wholesale Market
卸売市場
Arakawa
荒川
Minami-Senju Filtration Plant
南千住浄水場
Senju-Ōhashi (Br.)
千住大橋
Sumida Gawa (river)
隅田川
Daini-Haketa E. Sch.
第二峡田小
Arakawa-itchōme
荒川一丁目
Arakawa Tech. H. Sch.
荒川工業高校
Mikawashima Park
三河島公園
Susanoo Jinja
素盞雄神社
南千住野球場
Minami-Senju Baseball Field
Arakawa Sports Center
荒川総合スポーツセンター
Arakawa Ward Office
荒川区役所
Minami-Senju Police Sta.
南千住署
Minami-Senju
南千住
Arakawa Fire Sta.
荒川消防署
Arakawa-kuyakusho
荒川区役所
Sun Pearl Arakawa
サンパール荒川
Arakawa P. O.
荒川局
Arakawa Police Sta.
荒川署
Arakawa Health Center
荒川保健所
Entsū-ji
円通寺
Minowabashi
三ノ輪橋
Sumidagawa Freight Sta.
隅田川貨物駅
Shioiri Ground
汐入運動場
JOBAN LINE
常磐線
Itō-Yōkado Store
イトーヨーカ堂
Ekō-in
回向院
Higashi-Nippori
東日暮里
Minowa Hosp.
三ノ輪病院
Tokyo Gas
東京ガス
MEIJI DŌRI (AVE.)
明治通り
Nippori Jr. H. Sch.
日暮里中
Minowa
三ノ輪
NTT Shirahige
NTT白鬚
Shirahige-bashi (Br.)
白鬚橋
Tomb of Gennai Hiraga
平賀源内墓
Nihonzutsumi
日本堤
Kiyokawa
清川
Hashiba
橋場
Ryūsen
竜泉
Ichiyō Mem. Hall
一葉記念館
Shitaya Police Sta.
下谷署
Toy Museum
(Gangu Shiryōkan)
玩具資料館
Negishi
根岸
Senzoku
千束
Higashi-Asakusa
東浅草
Enkō-ji
円光寺
Shitaya Hosp.
Taitō Hosp.
台東病院
Nihonzutsumi Fire Sta.
日本堤消防署
Ōtori Jinja
鷲神社
Onoterusaki Jinja
小野照崎神社
NTT Yoshiwara
NTT吉原
Seiai Hosp.
聖愛病院
Iriya
入谷
Imado
今戸
SHUTO EXPWY. No.6
首都高速6号線
Shitaya
下谷
SHOWA DŌRI (AVE.)
昭和通り
Tokyo Confectionery Hall
東京菓子会館
TAITŌ-KU
台東区
Kishimojin
鬼子母神
Iriya Ramp
入谷ランプ
Asakusa Police Sta.
浅草署
Taitō Comm. H. Sch.
台東商業高校
台東リバーサイドスポーツセンター
Taitō Riverside Sports Center
Ueno P. O.
上野局
Ueno-Shinobugaoka H. Sch.
上野忍岡高校
Matsuchiyama Park
待乳山公園
Sumida Park
隅田公園
Mukōjima
向島
KOTOTOI DŌRI (AVE.)
言問通り
Asakusa
浅草
Sakura-bashi (Br.)
桜橋
Matsuchiyama Shōden
待乳山聖天
Matsugaya
松が谷
Nishi-Asakusa
西浅草
Kita-Ueno
北上野
Ikebukuro
Nippori
Kitasenju
Ueno
Akihabara
Shinjuku
Tokyo
Shibuya
Ginza
Gotanda
Shinagawa
17
1 : 20,000
0
1000m

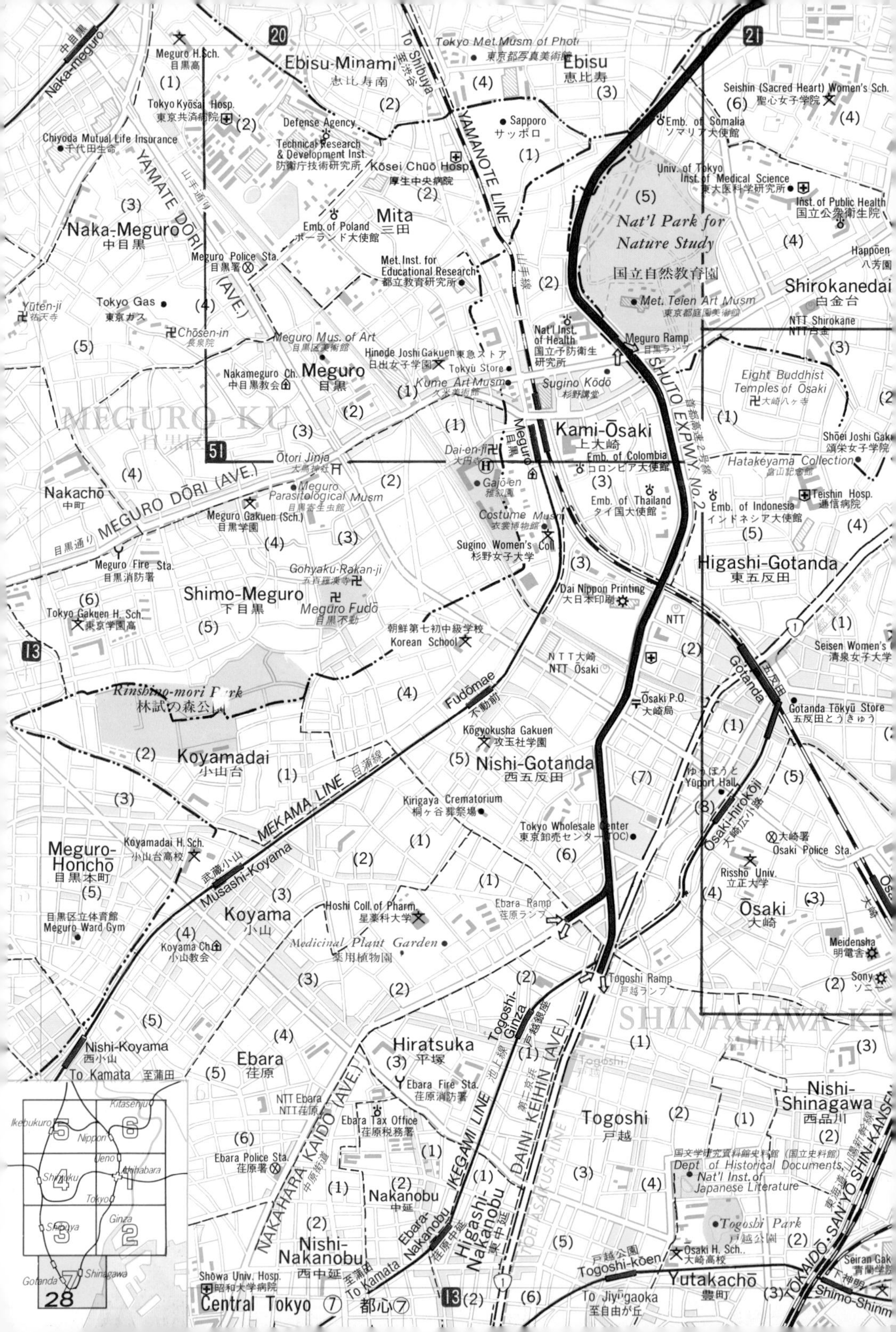

Ebisu-Minami
恵比寿南
Ebisu
恵比寿
Tokyo Met. Musm of Photo
東京都写真美術館
Meguro H. Sch.
目黒高
Tokyo Kyōsai Hosp.
東京共済病院
Defense Agency
Technical Research & Development Inst.
防衛庁技術研究所
Kōsei Chūō Hosp.
厚生中央病院
Sapporo
サッポロ
Emb. of Somalia
ソマリア大使館
Seishin (Sacred Heart) Women's Sch.
聖心女子学院
Chiyoda Mutual Life Insurance
千代田生命
YAMATE DŌRI (AVE.)
山手通り
YAMANOTE LINE
山手線
To Shibuya
至渋谷
Naka-meguro
中目黒
Naka-Meguro
中目黒
Emb. of Poland
ポーランド大使館
Mita
三田
Univ. of Tokyo Inst. of Medical Science
東大医科学研究所
Inst. of Public Health
国立公衆衛生院
Nat'l Park for Nature Study
国立自然教育園
Happōen
八芳園
Meguro Police Sta.
目黒署
Met. Inst. for Educational Research
都立教育研究所
Met. Teien Art Musm
東京都庭園美術館
Shirokanedai
白金台
Yūten-ji
祐天寺
Tokyo Gas
東京ガス
Chōsen-in
長泉院
Nat'l Inst. of Health
国立予防衛生研究所
NTT Shirokane
NTT白金
Meguro Mus. of Art
目黒区美術館
Hinode Joshi Gakuen
日出女子学園
東急ストア
Tokyū Store
Meguro Ramp
目黒ランプ
Nakameguro Ch.
中目黒教会
Meguro
目黒
Kume Art Musm
久米美術館
Sugino Kōdō
杉野講堂
Eight Buddhist Temples of Ōsaki
大崎八ヶ寺
MEGURO-KU
目黒区
Kami-Ōsaki
上大崎
Shōei Joshi Gakuin
頌栄女子学院
Ōtori Jinja
大鳥神社
Dai-en-ji
大円寺
Emb. of Colombia
コロンビア大使館
Hatakeyama Collection
畠山記念館
Nakachō
中町
MEGURO DŌRI (AVE.)
目黒通り
Meguro Parasitological Musm
目黒寄生虫館
Gajō-en
雅叙園
Emb. of Thailand
タイ国大使館
Emb. of Indonesia
インドネシア大使館
Teishin Hosp.
逓信病院
Meguro Gakuen (Sch.)
目黒学園
Costume Musm
衣裳博物館
SHUTO EXPWY. No. 2
首都高速2号線
Sugino Women's Coll.
杉野女子大学
Higashi-Gotanda
東五反田
Meguro Fire Sta.
目黒消防署
Gohyaku-Rakan-ji
五百羅漢寺
Shimo-Meguro
下目黒
Meguro Fudō
目黒不動
Dai Nippon Printing
大日本印刷
Tokyo Gakuen H. Sch.
東京学園高
朝鮮第七初中級学校
Korean School
NTT
NTT大崎
NTT Ōsaki
Seisen Women's
清泉女子大学
Gotanda
五反田
Rinshino-mori Park
林試の森公園
Fudōmae
不動前
Ōsaki P.O.
大崎局
Gotanda Tōkyū Store
五反田とうきゅう
Kōgyokusha Gakuen
攻玉社学園
Koyamadai
小山台
Nishi-Gotanda
西五反田
ゆうぽうと
Yūport Hall
MEKAMA LINE
目蒲線
Kirigaya Crematorium
桐ヶ谷葬祭場
Ōsaki-hirokōji
大崎広小路
Meguro-Honchō
目黒本町
Koyamadai H. Sch.
小山台高校
Tokyo Wholesale Center
東京卸売センター(TOC)
大崎署
Ōsaki Police Sta.
武蔵小山
Musashi-Koyama
Risshō Univ.
立正大学
目黒区立体育館
Meguro Ward Gym
Koyama
小山
Hoshi Coll. of Pharm.
星薬科大学
Ebara Ramp
荏原ランプ
Ōsaki
大崎
Koyama Ch.
小山教会
Medicinal Plant Garden
薬用植物園
Meidensha
明電舎
Togoshi Ramp
戸越ランプ
Sony
ソニー
SHINAGAWA-KU
品川区
Togoshi-Ginza
戸越銀座
Nishi-Koyama
西小山
To Kamata 至蒲田
Ebara
荏原
Hiratsuka
平塚
Ebara Fire Sta.
荏原消防署
Nishi-Shinagawa
西品川
NTT Ebara
NTT荏原
Ebara Tax Office
荏原税務署
Togoshi
戸越
Ebara Police Sta.
荏原署
NAKAHARA KAIDŌ (AVE.)
中原街道
IKEGAMI LINE
池上線
DAINI KEIHIN (AVE.)
第二京浜
TOEI ASAKUSA LINE
国文学研究資料館史料館(国立史料館)
Dept. of Historical Documents, Nat'l Inst. of Japanese Literature
TŌKAIDŌ·SANYŌ SHIN-KANSEN
東海道・山陽新幹線
Nakanobu
中延
Ebara-Nakanobu
荏原中延
Higashi-Nakanobu
東中延
Togoshi Park
戸越公園
Nishi-Nakanobu
西中延
Osaki H. Sch.
大崎高校
Togoshi-kōen
戸越公園
Seiran Gak.
青蘭学院
Shōwa Univ. Hosp.
昭和大学病院
To Kamata
至蒲田
Yutakachō
豊町
Shimo-Shinmei
下神明
To Jiyūgaoka
至自由が丘
Central Tokyo ⑦ 都心⑦
Ikebukuro
Kitasenju
Nippori
Ueno
Akihabara
Shinjuku
Tokyo
Shibuya
Ginza
Gotanda
Shinagawa

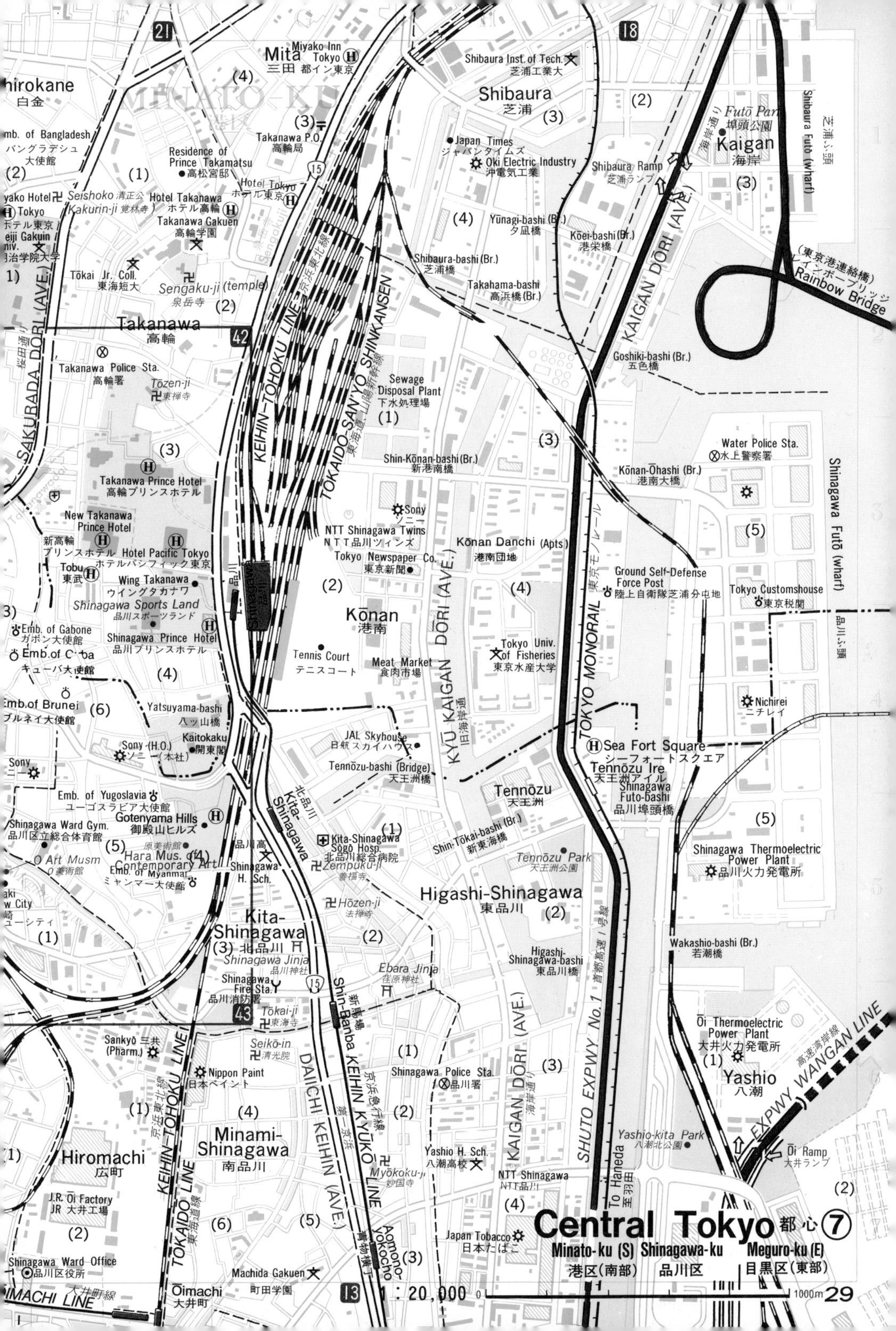

Central Tokyo 都心⑦
Minato-ku (S) Shinagawa-ku Meguro-ku (E)
港区(南部) 品川区 目黒区(東部)

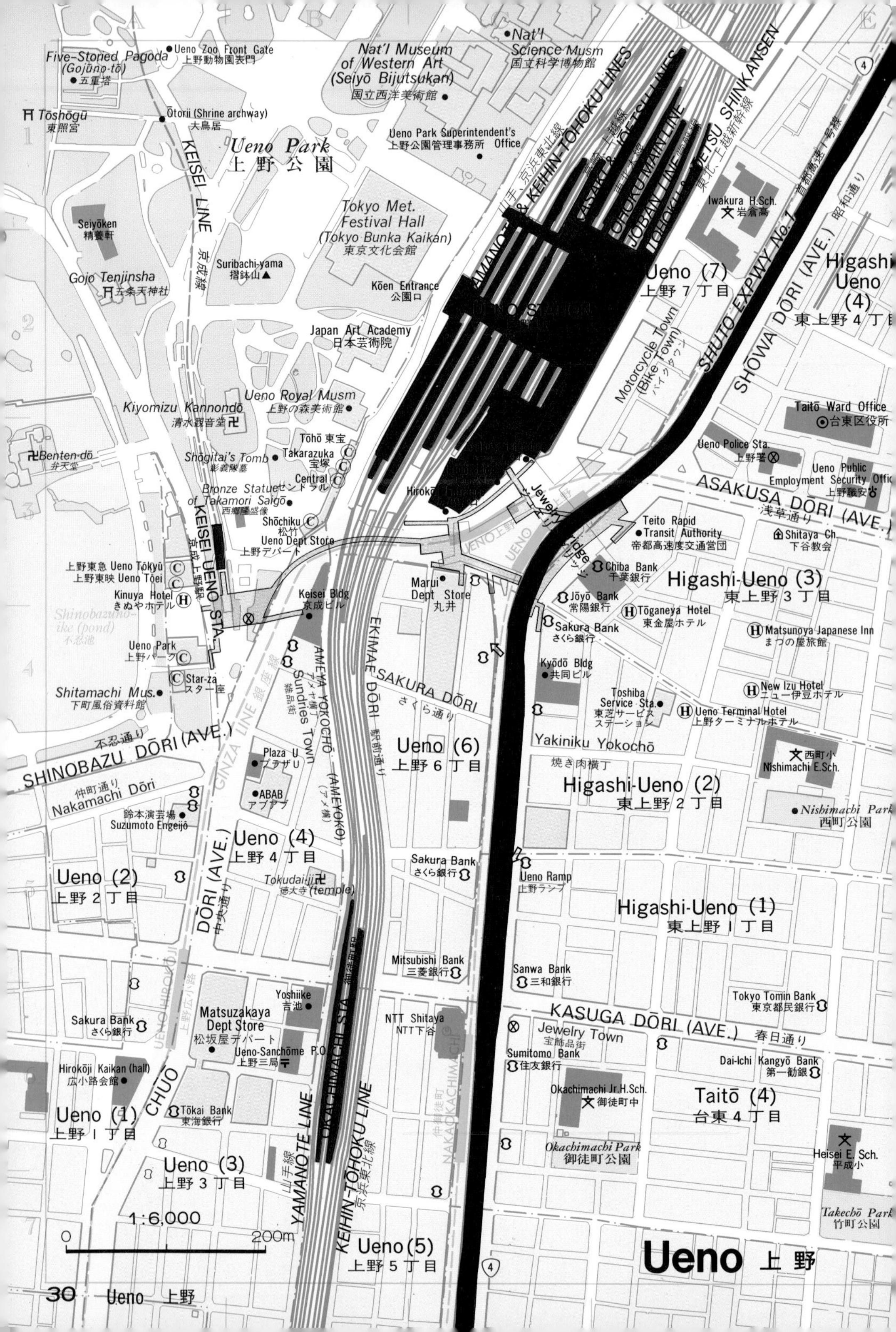

Ueno Zoo Front Gate
上野動物園表門
Five-Storied Pagoda
(Gojūno-tō)
五重塔
Nat'l Museum
of Western Art
(Seiyō Bijutsukan)
国立西洋美術館
Nat'l
Science Musm
国立科学博物館
Tōshōgū
東照宮
Ōtorii (Shrine archway)
大鳥居
Ueno Park
上野公園
Ueno Park Superintendent's Office
上野公園管理事務所
KEISEI LINE
京成線
Seiyōken
精養軒
Tokyo Met.
Festival Hall
(Tokyo Bunka Kaikan)
東京文化会館
Suribachi-yama
摺鉢山
Gojo Tenjinsha
五条天神社
Kōen Entrance
公園口
Japan Art Academy
日本芸術院
Ueno Royal Musm
上野の森美術館
Kiyomizu Kannondō
清水観音堂
Benten-dō
弁天堂
Tōhō 東宝
Takarazuka
宝塚
Central
セントラル
Shōgitai's Tomb
彰義隊墓
Bronze Statue
of Takamori Saigō
西郷隆盛像
Shōchiku
松竹
Ueno Dept Store
上野デパート
KEISEI UENO STA.
京成上野駅
上野東急 Ueno Tōkyū
上野東映 Ueno Tōei
Kinuya Hotel
きぬやホテル
Shinobazuno-ike (pond)
不忍池
Ueno Park
上野パーク
Star-za
スター座
Shitamachi Mus.
下町風俗資料館
Keisei Bldg
京成ビル
Marui
Dept Store
丸井
YAMANOTE & KEIHIN-TOHOKU LINES
山手、京浜東北線
ASAKUSA JOETSU LINES
TOHOKU MAIN LINE
JOBAN LINE
TOHOKU & JOETSU SHINKANSEN
東北、上越新幹線
UENO STATION
Hirokōji
Jewelry Bridge
UENO
Iwakura H.Sch.
岩倉高
Ueno (7)
上野 7 丁目
Higashi
Ueno
(4)
東上野 4 丁目
Motorcycle Town
(Bike Town)
バイクタウン
SHUTO EXPWY No.1
首都高速1号線
SHOWA DŌRI (AVE.)
昭和通り
Taitō Ward Office
台東区役所
Ueno Police Sta.
上野署
Ueno Public
Employment Security Office
上野職安
ASAKUSA DŌRI (AVE.)
浅草通り
Teito Rapid
Transit Authority
帝都高速度交通営団
Shitaya Ch.
下谷教会
Chiba Bank
千葉銀行
Higashi-Ueno (3)
東上野 3 丁目
Jōyō Bank
常陽銀行
Tōganeya Hotel
東金屋ホテル
Sakura Bank
さくら銀行
Matsunoya Japanese Inn
まつの屋旅館
Kyōdō Bldg
共同ビル
Toshiba
Service Sta.
東芝サービス
ステーション
New Izu Hotel
ニュー伊豆ホテル
Ueno Terminal Hotel
上野ターミナルホテル
Yakiniku Yokochō
焼き肉横丁
西町小
Nishimachi E.Sch.
Higashi-Ueno (2)
東上野 2 丁目
Nishimachi Park
西町公園
GINZA LINE
銀座線
AMEYA YOKOCHŌ
アメヤ横丁
Sundries Town
雑品街
EKIMAE DŌRI
駅前通り
SAKURA DŌRI
さくら通り
Ueno (6)
上野 6 丁目
(AMEYOKO)
(アメ横)
不忍通り
SHINOBAZU DŌRI (AVE.)
Plaza U
プラザU
ABAB
アブアブ
仲町通り
Nakamachi Dōri
鈴本演芸場
Suzumoto Engeijō
Ueno (4)
上野 4 丁目
DŌRI (AVE.)
中央通り
Ueno (2)
上野 2 丁目
Tokudai-ji
徳大寺 (temple)
Sakura Bank
さくら銀行
Ueno Ramp
上野ランプ
Higashi-Ueno (1)
東上野 1 丁目
UENO HIROKŌJI
上野広小路
Mitsubishi Bank
三菱銀行
Sanwa Bank
三和銀行
Tokyo Tomin Bank
東京都民銀行
Sakura Bank
さくら銀行
Matsuzakaya
Dept Store
松坂屋デパート
Yoshiike
吉池
Ueno-Sanchōme P.O.
上野三局
OKACHIMACHI STA.
御徒町駅
NTT Shitaya
NTT下谷
KASUGA DŌRI (AVE.)
春日通り
Jewelry Town
宝飾品街
Sumitomo Bank
住友銀行
Dai-Ichi Kangyō Bank
第一勧銀
Hirokōji Kaikan (hall)
広小路会館
CHŪŌ
Tōkai Bank
東海銀行
Ueno (1)
上野 1 丁目
YAMANOTE LINE
山手線
OKACHIMACHI LINE
KEIHIN-TOHOKU LINE
京浜東北線
NAKAOKACHIMACHI
仲御徒町
Okachimachi Jr.H.Sch.
御徒町中
Taitō (4)
台東 4 丁目
Okachimachi Park
御徒町公園
Heisei E. Sch.
平成小
Ueno (3)
上野 3 丁目
1:6,000
0
200m
Takechō Park
竹町公園
Ueno (5)
上野 5 丁目
Ueno 上野

Asakusa 浅草
1:6,000
0
200m
Senzoku (1)
千束1丁目
SENZOKU DŌRI
千束通り
Dai-Ichi Kangyō Bank
第一勧銀
Fuji Bank
富士銀行
Asakusa (3)
浅草3丁目
KOTOTOI DŌRI (AVE.)
言問通り
Taitō Traditional Crafts Musm
台東区伝統工芸展示館
Kaminari Gorogoro Kaikan
雷5656会館
Asakusa (6)
浅草6丁目
Banryu-ji
万隆寺
Nishi-Asakusa (3)
西浅草3丁目
HISAGO DŌRI
ひさご通り
Lions Mansion
ライオンズマンション
Sensō-ji Hosp.
浅草寺病院
Asahi Shinkin Bank
朝日信金
Asakusa View Hotel
浅草ビューホテル
Asakusa Tōei
浅草東映
Hanayashiki Amusement Park
花やしき遊園地
Asakusa (2)
浅草2丁目
Asakusa Jinja (Shr.)
浅草神社
Hanakawado (2)
花川戸2丁目
KOKUSAI DŌRI (AVE.)
国際通り
Asakusa Shingekijō
浅草新劇場
Tengaku-in
天嶽院
Nichirin-ji
日輪寺
WINS Asakusa
ウインズ浅草
Awashima-dō
淡島堂
Asakusa Kannondō
浅草観音堂
Asakusa Chūei
浅草中映
Nishi Sandō 西参道
Yakushi-dō
薬師堂
Mokuba-kan
木馬館
Asakusa Musm
浅草風俗歴史館
Sensō-ji (temple) 浅草寺
Niten-mon
二天門
馬道通り
Taitō Ward Hall
台東区民会館
Tokyo Trade Center (Taitō Hall) (台東館)
都立産業貿易センタ
Asakusa Ch.
浅草教会
Asakusa Tōhō
浅草東宝
Five-Storied Pagoda
(Gojūno-tō)
五重塔
Rock-za Kaikan
ロック座会館
Asakusa Bowl
浅草ボウル
Hōzō-mon
宝蔵門
Hanakawado Park
花川戸公園
Asakusa Handicrafts Musm (Asakusa Kōgei-kan)
浅草巧芸館
Denbōin Garden
伝法院庭園
Asakusa Park
浅草公園
Asakusa E.Sch.
浅草小
Footwear, Shoe Town
履物街
Asakusa Engei Hall
浅草演芸ホール
Denbōin
伝法院
Sensōji Kindergarten
浅草寺幼稚園
Sukeroku
助六
Kimuraya
木村屋
Benten-dō
弁天堂
UMAMICHI DŌRI (AVE.)
Hanakawado (1)
花川戸1丁目
Nishi-Asakusa (2)
西浅草2丁目
Rox Bldg
ロックスビル
Tokyo Club
東京クラブ
DENBŌIN DŌRI 伝法院通り
Asakusa Shōchiku
浅草松竹
Asakusa Public Hall
浅草公会堂
SHIN NAKAMISE DŌRI
新仲見世通り
Ryokan Mikawaya Bekkan
三河屋別館
TOBU ASAKUSA STA.
Sakura Bank
さくら銀行
Drum Musm
太鼓館
SUSHIYA DŌRI
すしや通り
Asakusa (1)
浅草1丁目
ORANGE DŌRI
オレンジ通り
CHINYOKO DŌRI
ちん横通り
NAKAMISE DŌRI
仲見世通り
KANNON DŌRI
観音通り
Matsuya Dept. Store
Sumida Park
隅田公園
Mitsubishi Bank
三菱銀行
ASAKUSA DŌRI (AVE.)
浅草通り
Nishi-Asakusa (1)
西浅草1丁目
Religious Goods Town
神仏具店街
Tōkai Bank
東海銀行
Kaminari-mon
雷門
Kamiya Bar
神谷バー
Fuji Bank
富士銀行
Sumitomo Bank
住友銀行
Waterbus Station
水上バスのりば
Kaminarimon (1)
雷門1丁目
Tokyo Sōwa Bank
東京相和
Asakusa Tourist Information Center
浅草文化観光センター
Asakusa P.O.
浅草局
Tawara E.Sch.
田原小
Kaminarimon (2)
雷門2丁目
Azuma-bashi (Br.)
吾妻橋
Metropolitan Tax Office
台東都税事務所
TAWARAMACHI
田原町
GINZA LINE 銀座線
NTT Asakusa
NTT浅草
Kaminarimon P.O.
雷門局
TOEI ASAKUSA LINE
都営浅草線
EDO DŌRI (AVE.)
江戸通り
Kinryū-ji
金竜寺
(2)
Tokyo Toyota
東京トヨタ
Kaminarimon Skymansion
雷門スカイマンション
Mugitoro むぎとろ
Komagata-dō
駒形堂
Sumida Gawa (river)
隅田川
(4)
Kotobuki
寿
(3)
(1)
東京銀行
Bank of Tokyo
Komagata
駒形
Sanwa Bank
三和銀行
World Bags Musm
世界のカバン館
(2)
Kurofune Jinja
黒船神社
Komagata-bashi (Br.)
駒形橋
(1)
Azumabashi
吾妻橋

Big Egg Plaza
ビッグエッグプラザ
Kōrakuen Hall
後楽園ホール
Yellow Bldg
黄色いビル
Ice Palace
アイスパレス
Kōraku (1)
後楽
Tokyo Green Hotel Kōrakuen
東京グリーンホテル後楽園
SUIDŌBASHI STATION
水道橋駅
Kotohiragu
金刀比羅宮
(1)
Hōshō Noh Theater
宝生能楽堂
Hotel Satōh
ホテルサトー
Met. Polytech. H.Sch.
都立工芸高
Ōin Gakuen (Sch.)
桜蔭学園
Hongō
本郷
Motomachi E.Sch.
元町小
Shōwa Daiichi H.Sch.
昭和第一高
BUNKYŌ-KU
文京区
Kyūsuijo Park
給水所公苑
Hongō Water Sta.
本郷給水所
(2)
Water Supply Control Center
配水コントロールセンター
17
Motomachi Park
元町公園
Century Tower
センチュリータワー
Juntendō Univ. (Med.)
順天堂大（医）
Juntendō Hosp.
順天堂医院
SOTOBORI DŌRI (AVE.)
外堀通り
CHUŌ LINE
中央線
Kanda Gawa
Misaki Inari Jinja
三崎稲荷神社
Tokyo Dental Coll.
東京歯科大
Tōyō H.Sch.
東洋高
Misakichō
三崎町
(2)
(3)
No.3 Bldg
3号館
(1)
白山通り
Athénée Français
アテネフランセ
Shufunotomo
主婦の友社
Maison Franco-Japonaise
(Nichi-Futsu Kaikan)
日仏会館
Tokyo Green Hotel Suidōbashi
東京グリーンホテル水道橋
Geidai H. Sch.
芸大付属音楽高
Ikenobō Gakuen (Sch.)
池坊学園
Nichirei (H.O.)
ニチレイ（本社）
Nihon Univ. (Law)
日本大（法）
Nihon Univ. (Econ.)
日本大（経済）
Sanraku Hosp.
三楽病院
Hamada Hosp.
浜田病院
SHUTO EXPWY NO.5
Paper Distribution Center
紙流通センター
Administrative Bldg
本館
No.2 Bldg
2号館
HAKUSAN DŌRI (AVE.)
TOEI MITA LINE
都営三田線
(2)
YMCA
Meiji H.Sch.
明治高
Kanda Jogakuen (Sch.)
神田女学園
(2)
Bunka Gakuin (Sch.)
文化学院
Tokyo Met. Cancer Detection Center
東京都がん検診センター
Kensū Gakkan
研数学館
(2)
(1)
Sarugakuchō
猿楽町
Kanda-Surugadai
神田駿河台
Nishi-Kanda 西神田
Ohara Bookkeeping Sch.
大原簿記学校
(3)
(1)
Meiji Univ.
明治大
Hilltop Hotel
山の上ホテル
Nishikanda Ramp
西神田ランプ
Kitajinbōchō P.O.
北神保町局
YWCA
Nihon Kōgyō Newspaper
日刊工業新聞
Meiji Univ. Administrative Bldg
明治大学（本部）
Ochanomizu E. Sch.
お茶の水小
Kudan-Kita
九段北
Kanda-Jimbōchō (2)
神田神保町 2 丁目
Kanda-Jimbōchō (1)
神田神保町 1 丁目
(1)
Ochanomizu Square
お茶の水スクエア
Casals Hall
カザルスホール
Senshū Univ.
専修大
Kusei Kaikan
区政会館
KUDANSHITA
Fuji Bank
富士銀行
KANDA BOOKSHOPS AREA
神田書店街
JIMBŌCHŌ
神保町
TOEI SHINJUKU LINE
Ogawamachi P.O.
小川町局
(3)
靖国通り
YASUKUNI DŌRI (AVE.)
Iwanami Hall
岩波ホール
Tuttle Books
タトル
Sanseidō
三省堂
SUZURAN DŌRI
すずらん通り
Kanda-Jimbōchō (3)
神田神保町 3 丁目
SAKURA DŌRI
さくら通り
Kudan P.O.
九段局
Taiheiyō Bank
太平洋銀行
SPORTING GOODS
スポーツ用具店
Kyōritsu Women's Univ.
共立女子大
Hotel Hitotsubashi
ホテルヒトツバシ
CHIYODA-KU
千代田区
Mizuno
美津濃
Sakura Bank (H.O.)
さくら銀行本店
首都高速5号線
Kyōiku Kaikan
教育会館
Hitotsubashi Jr.H.Sch
一橋中
Shogakukan
小学館
Kudan Kaikan
九段会館
Hitotsubashi Hall
Hitotsubashi
一ッ橋
Kudan-Minami
九段南
(1)
Kudan Common Gov't Bldg
九段合同庁舎
(2)
Chiyoda Ward Office
千代田区役所
Chiyoda Public Hall
千代田公会堂
Tokyo Electrical Eng. Coll.
東京電機大
Kyōritsu Joshigakuen (Sch.)
共立女子学園
Gakushi Kaikan
学士会館
Hakuhōdō
博報堂
Kanda Health Center
神田保健所
Public Security Investigation Agency
公安調査庁
Kyōritsu Kōdō (hall)
共立講堂
Seisoku Gakuen
正則学園
Kanda Police
神田
Shimizu-mon
清水門
TŌZAI LINE
Hitotsubashi Kōdō
一ッ橋講堂
Kanda Tax Office
神田税務署
Kinjō Gakuen
錦城学園
(3)
Kitanomaru Park
北の丸公園
Sumitomo Corp.
住友商事
Josui Kaikan
如水会館
Kōwa Hitotsubashi Bldg
興和一橋ビル
Shin Tokyo Hotel
新東京ホテル
(2)
Takebashi I.C.
竹橋インター
(1)
NTT
Kanda-Nishikichō
神田錦町
Science Museum (Kagaku Gijutsukan)
科学技術館
EXPWY LOOP LINE
Palace Side Bldg
パレスサイドビル
Tokyo Gas
東京ガス
Mainichi Newspapers
毎日新聞
Hitotsubashi Ramp
一ッ橋ランプ
高速環状線
Tokyo Nat'l Musm of Modern Art
東京国立近代美術館
Takebashi
竹橋
Marubeni (H.O.)
丸紅（本社）
TAKEBASHI
Nat'l Archives
国立公文書館
Takebashi Kaikan
竹橋会館

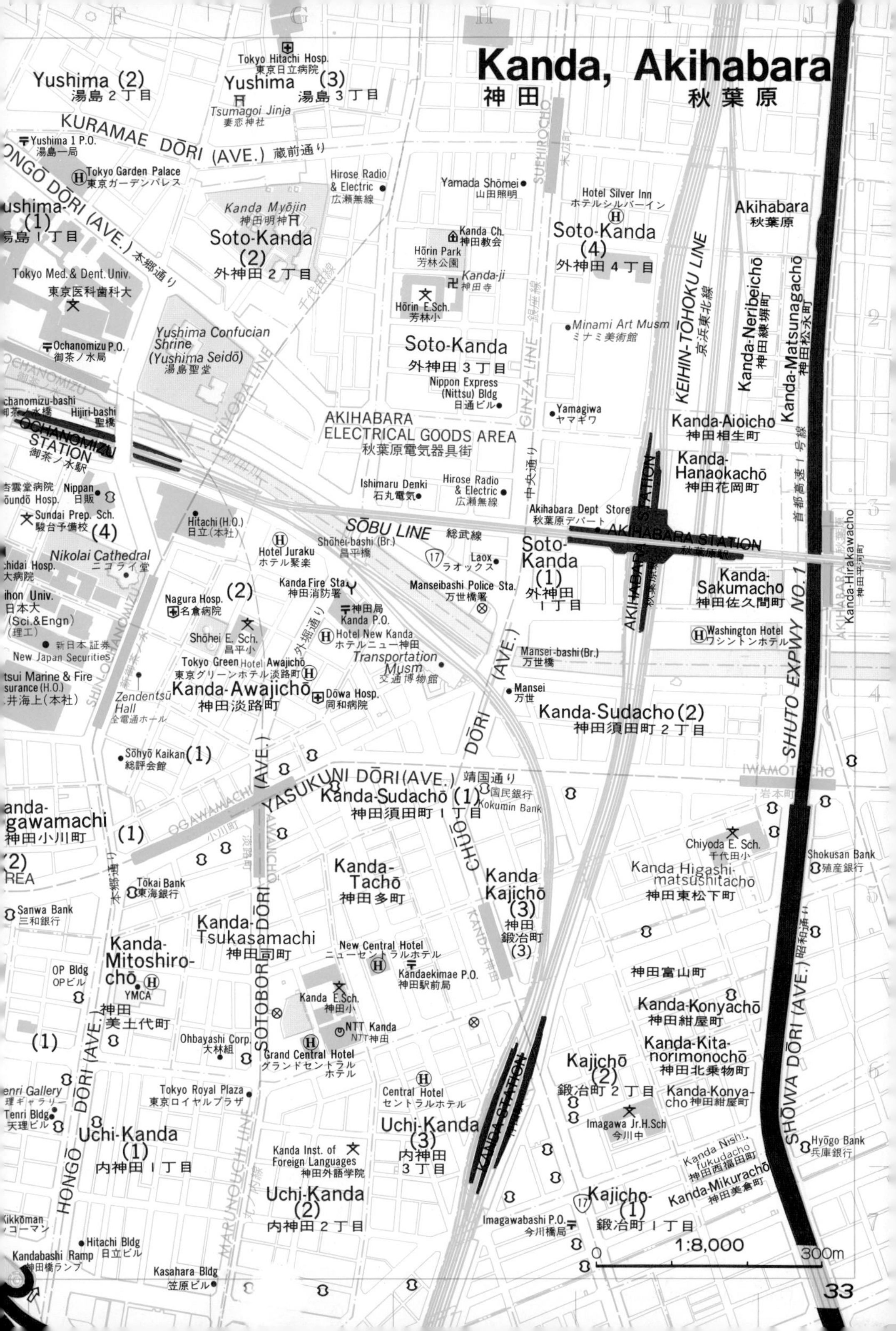
Kanda, Akihabara
神田
秋葉原
Tokyo Hitachi Hosp.
東京日立病院
Yushima (2)
湯島2丁目
Yushima (3)
湯島3丁目
Tsumagoi Jinja
妻恋神社
KURAMAE DŌRI (AVE.)
蔵前通り
Yushima 1 P.O.
湯島一局
HONGŌ DŌRI (AVE.)
本郷通り
Tokyo Garden Palace
東京ガーデンパレス
Hirose Radio & Electric
広瀬無線
Yamada Shōmei
山田照明
SUEHIROCHO
末広町
Hotel Silver Inn
ホテルシルバーイン
Akihabara
秋葉原
Yushima (1)
湯島1丁目
Kanda Myōjin
神田明神
Soto-Kanda (2)
外神田2丁目
Kanda Ch.
神田教会
Hōrin Park
芳林公園
Kanda-ji
神田寺
Soto-Kanda (4)
外神田4丁目
KEIHIN-TŌHOKU LINE
京浜東北線
Tokyo Med. & Dent. Univ.
東京医科歯科大
Hōrin E.Sch.
芳林小
千代田線
銀座線
Kanda-Neribeichō
神田練塀町
Kanda-Matsunagachō
神田松永町
Minami Art Musm
ミナミ美術館
Yushima Confucian Shrine (Yushima Seidō)
湯島聖堂
Ochanomizu P.O.
御茶ノ水局
Soto-Kanda
外神田3丁目
CHIYODA LINE
GINZA LINE
Nippon Express (Nittsu) Bldg
日通ビル
OCHANOMIZU
御茶ノ水
Ochanomizu-bashi
御茶ノ水橋
Hijiri-bashi
聖橋
OCHANOMIZU STATION
御茶ノ水駅
AKIHABARA ELECTRICAL GOODS AREA
秋葉原電気器具街
Yamagiwa
ヤマギワ
Kanda-Aioicho
神田相生町
Kanda-Hanaokachō
神田花岡町
首都高速1号線
Ishimaru Denki
石丸電気
Hirose Radio & Electric
広瀬無線
中央通り
杏雲堂病院
Kyoundō Hosp.
Nippan
日販
Sundai Prep. Sch.
駿台予備校
(4)
Hitachi (H.O.)
日立(本社)
SŌBU LINE
総武線
Akihabara Dept Store
秋葉原デパート
AKIHABARA STATION
秋葉原駅
Hotel Juraku
ホテル聚楽
Shōhei-bashi (Br.)
昌平橋
17
Laox
ラオックス
Soto-Kanda (1)
外神田1丁目
Nikolai Cathedral
ニコライ堂
Kanda-Sakumacho
神田佐久間町
AKIHABARA
秋葉原
Kanda-Hirakawacho
神田平河町
Nichidai Hosp.
日大病院
Nihon Univ. (Sci.&Engn)
日本大(理工)
Kanda Fire Sta.
神田消防署
Manseibashi Police Sta.
万世橋署
Nagura Hosp.
名倉病院
(2)
神田局
Kanda P.O.
外堀通り
Hotel New Kanda
ホテルニュー神田
Washington Hotel
ワシントンホテル
Shōhei E. Sch.
昌平小
新日本証券
New Japan Securities
Tokyo Green Hotel Awajichō
東京グリーンホテル淡路町
Transportation Musm
交通博物館
Mansei-bashi (Br.)
万世橋
Mitsui Marine & Fire Insurance (H.O.)
三井海上(本社)
Kanda-Awajichō
神田淡路町
Dōwa Hosp.
同和病院
Mansei
万世
SHUTO EXPWY NO.1
SHIN-OCHANOMIZU
新御茶ノ水
Zendentsū Hall
全電通ホール
Kanda-Sudacho (2)
神田須田町2丁目
CHŪŌ DŌRI (AVE.)
Sōhyō Kaikan
総評会館
(1)
IWAMOTOCHO
岩本町
YASUKUNI DŌRI (AVE.)
靖国通り
Kanda-Sudachō (1)
神田須田町1丁目
国民銀行
Kokumin Bank
OGAWAMACHI
小川町
AWAJICHO
淡路町
Kanda-Ogawamachi
神田小川町
(1)
(2)
AREA
Chiyoda E. Sch.
千代田小
Shokusan Bank
殖産銀行
Tōkai Bank
東海銀行
Kanda-Tachō
神田多町
Kanda Higashi-matsushitachō
神田東松下町
Kanda Kajichō (3)
神田鍛冶町(3)
KANDA
神田
Sanwa Bank
三和銀行
本郷通り
Kanda-Tsukasamachi
神田司町
SOTOBORI DŌRI (AVE.)
Kanda-Mitoshirochō
神田美土代町
New Central Hotel
ニューセントラルホテル
Kandaekimae P.O.
神田駅前局
神田富山町
OP Bldg
OPビル
YMCA
Kanda E.Sch.
神田小
Kanda-Konyachō
神田紺屋町
SHŌWA DŌRI (AVE.)
昭和通り
(1)
Ohbayashi Corp.
大林組
NTT Kanda
NTT神田
Grand Central Hotel
グランドセントラルホテル
Kanda-Kita-norimonochō
神田北乗物町
Kajichō (2)
鍛冶町2丁目
Tenri Gallery
天理ギャラリー
Tenri Bldg
天理ビル
Tokyo Royal Plaza
東京ロイヤルプラザ
Central Hotel
セントラルホテル
Kanda-Konya-cho
神田紺屋町
KANDA STATION
神田駅
Imagawa Jr.H.Sch
今川中
Uchi-Kanda (1)
内神田1丁目
Uchi-Kanda (3)
内神田3丁目
Hyōgo Bank
兵庫銀行
HONGŌ DŌRI (AVE.)
Kanda Inst. of Foreign Languages
神田外語学院
Kanda Nishi-fukudacho
神田西福田町
MARUNOUCHI LINE
丸ノ内線
Kanda-Mikurachō
神田美倉町
Uchi-Kanda (2)
内神田2丁目
Kajicho (1)
鍛冶町1丁目
Kikkoman
キッコーマン
Imagawabashi P.O.
今川橋局
Hitachi Bldg
日立ビル
1:8,000
0
300m
Kandabashi Ramp
神田橋ランプ
Kasahara Bldg
笠原ビル
F
G
H
I
J
1
2
3
4
5
6
7

Nihombashi, Kyōbashi 日本橋 京橋

Nihombashi (1)
日本橋1丁目
Nihombashi (2)
日本橋2丁目
Nihombashi (3)
日本橋3丁目
Nihombashi-Kabutochō
日本橋兜町
Nihombashi-Kayabachō (1)
日本橋茅場町1丁目
Nihombashi Kayabachō (2)
日本橋茅場町2丁目
Nihombashi-Kayabachō (3)
日本橋茅場町3丁目
Yaesu (1)
八重洲1丁目
Yaesu (2)
八重洲2丁目
Kyōbashi (1)
京橋1丁目
Kyōbashi (2)
京橋2丁目
Hatchōbori
八丁堀
Shinkawa
新川
Tokyo Stock Exchange
(Tokyo Shōken Torihikijo)
東京証券取引所
Yamaichi Securities
山一証券
Tokyo Shōken Hall
東京証券会館
Kaō (H.O.)
花王(本社)
Koami P.O.
小網局
Nihombashi P.O.
Daiwa Bank
大和銀行
Nishikawa
西川
Tōkyū Dept Store
東急デパート
Bank of Hiroshima
広島銀行
Sakura Bank
さくら銀行
Sumitomo Bank
住友銀行
Sanwa Bank
三和銀行
Bank of Yokohama
横浜銀行
Fuji Bank
富士銀行
Takashimaya Dept Store
高島屋デパート
Nakajima Hosp.
中島病院
Yamatane Mus. of Art
山種美術館
Momijigawa H. Sch.
紅葉川高
Tokyo Tomin Bank
東京都民銀行
Nihombashi Fire Sta.
日本橋消防署
Sakamotochō Park
坂本町公園
Sakamoto E. Sch.
阪本小
Tanaka Kikinzoku
田中貴金属
Center Hotel Tokyo
センターホテル東京
Seifun Kaikan Hall
製粉会館
Hotel Universe
ホテルユニバース
Reigan-bashi (Br.)
霊岸橋
Takeda Chemical
武田薬品
Chūō Police Sta.
中央署
Taiyo Mutual Life Insurance
太陽生命
Nihombashidōri P.O.
日本橋通局
Bank of Tokyo
東京銀行
Dōwa Bldg
同和ビル
Higashi Nippon Bank (H.O.)
東日本銀行(本店)
Dai-Ichi Kangyō Bank
第一勧銀
Mitsubishi Bank
三菱銀行
Takarachō Ramp
宝町ランプ
Tekko Kaikan
鉄鋼会館
Hon Yaesu Bldg
本八重洲ビル
Tokyo Kensetsu Kaikan
東京建設会館
Matsuda Yaesu Bldg
マツダ八重洲ビル
Empire Bldg
エンパイヤビル
Holiday Inn Tokyo
ホリデーイン東京
Hatchōbori P.O.
八丁堀局
Shin-Kameshima-bashi (Br.)
新亀島橋
Industrial Bank of Japan
Hokkaidō Takushoku Bank
北海道拓銀
Dai-ichi Tekkō Bldg
第一鉄鋼ビル
Ryūmeikan
竜名館
Sumitomo Marine & Fire Insurance
住友海上
Fukuoka City Bank
福岡シティ銀行
Yanagiya Bldg
柳屋ビル
Tōyō Trust
東洋信託
Dai-ni Tekkō Bldg
第二鉄鋼ビル
Bank of Ōsaka
大阪銀行
Gunma Bank
群馬銀行
Nippon Fire & Marine Insurance Bldg
日本火災ビル
Kokusai Kankō Kaikan
国際観光会館
Yaesu North Entrance
八重洲北口
Nihombashi Plaza Bldg
日本橋プラザビル
Maruzen
丸善
Daimaru Dept Store
大丸デパート
Yaesuguchi Kaikan (hall)
八重洲口会館
Yaesu Central Entrance
八重洲中央口
Dai-Ichi Kangyō Bank
第一勧銀
Nippon Trust (H.O.)
日本信託(本社)
Tokyo Sōwa Bank
東京相和銀行
Tokyo Tatemono Bldg
東京建物ビル
YAESU UNDERGROUND ARCADE
八重洲地下街
Yanmer Bldg
ヤンマービル
Yaesu Dai Bldg
八重洲ダイビル
Yaesu Bldg
八重洲ビル
Jōtō E. Sch.
城東小
Sumitomo Trust (H.O.)
住友信託(本部)
Bridgestone Mus. of Art
ブリヂストン美術館
Asahi Bank
あさひ銀行
Chiba Kogyo Bank
千葉興業銀行
Chuo Trust (H.O.)
中央信託(本店)
Shin Yaesu Bldg
新八重洲ビル
Yaesu Book Center
八重洲ブックセンター
Ajinomoto (H.O.)
味の素(本社)
Kyōbashi Chiyoda Bldg
京橋千代田ビル
Nichimen
ニチメン
Uchida Yōkō
内田洋行
Ōita Bank
大分銀行
Meijiya Store
明治屋
Chuokoron-sha
中央公論社
Ajinomoto Bldg
味の素ビル
Yamagataya Laver Shop
山形屋のり店
Nurihiko Bldg
ぬ利彦ビル
(No.1)
(No.2)
Meiji Seika
明治製菓
Kyōbashi Dai-ichi Seimei Bldg
京橋第一生命ビル
Shimizu Corp
清水建設
Pilot
パイロット
Katakura Bldg
片倉ビル
Dai-Ichi Seimei Sōgokan
第一生命相互館
Kanematsu Corp.
兼松江商
TOKYO STATION
東京駅
EITAI DŌRI (AVE.)
永代通り
CHŪŌ DŌRI (AVE.)
中央通り
SHŌWA DŌRI (AVE.)
昭和通り
SHIN ŌHASHI DŌRI (AVE.)
新大橋通り
SHUTO EXPWY
首都高速6号線
No.6
SHUTO EXPWY LOOP LINE
TOEI ASAKUSA LINE
都営浅草線
HIBIYA LINE
日比谷線
KAYABACHŌ
KYŌBASHI
TAKARACHŌ
37
15
1:6,000
0
300m

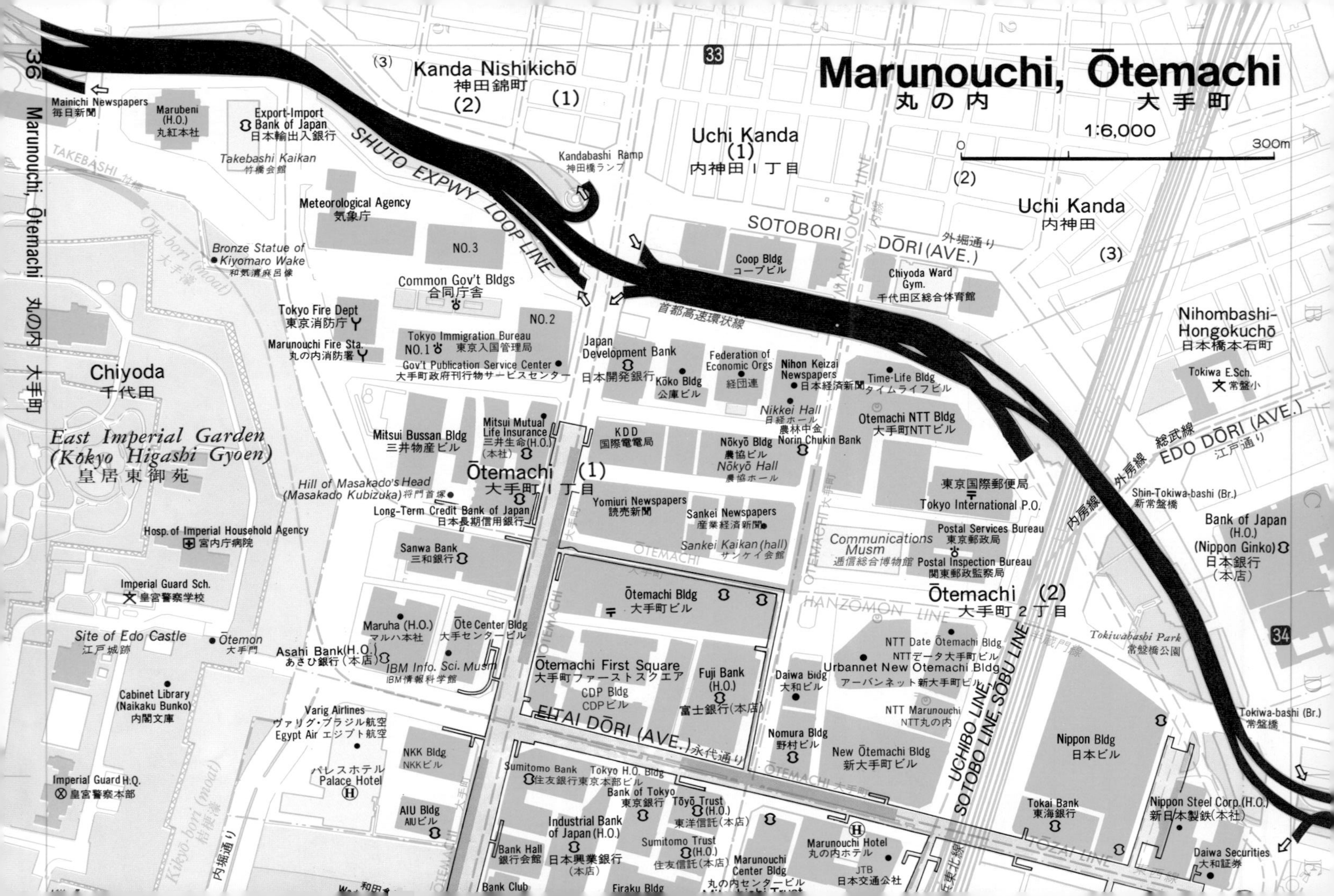

Marunouchi, Ōtemachi
丸の内 大手町
1:6,000
0
300m
33
34
Kanda Nishikichō
神田錦町
(1)
(2)
(3)
Uchi Kanda (1)
内神田1丁目
Uchi Kanda
内神田
Kandabashi Ramp
神田橋ランプ
SHUTO EXPWY LOOP LINE
首都高速環状線
SOTOBORI DŌRI (AVE.)
外堀通り
MARUNOUCHI LINE
Coop Bldg
コープビル
Chiyoda Ward Gym.
千代田区総合体育館
Nihombashi-Hongokuchō
日本橋本石町
Tokiwa E.Sch.
常盤小
EDO DŌRI (AVE.)
江戸通り
総武線
外房線
内房線
Shin-Tokiwa-bashi (Br.)
新常盤橋
Bank of Japan (H.O.) (Nippon Ginko)
日本銀行（本店）
Tokiwabashi Park
常盤橋公園
Tokiwa-bashi (Br.)
常盤橋
Mainichi Newspapers
毎日新聞
Marubeni (H.O.)
丸紅本社
Export-Import Bank of Japan
日本輸出入銀行
Takebashi Kaikan
竹橋会館
TAKEBASHI
Meteorological Agency
気象庁
NO.3
NO.2
NO.1
Bronze Statue of Kiyomaro Wake
和気清麻呂像
Ōte-bori (moat)
大手濠
Common Gov't Bldgs
合同庁舎
Tokyo Fire Dept
東京消防庁
Marunouchi Fire Sta.
丸の内消防署
Tokyo Immigration Bureau
東京入国管理局
Gov't Publication Service Center
大手町政府刊行物サービスセンター
Japan Development Bank
日本開発銀行
Kōko Bldg
公庫ビル
Federation of Economic Orgs
経団連
Nihon Keizai Newspapers
日本経済新聞
Time-Life Bldg
タイムライフビル
Otemachi NTT Bldg
大手町NTTビル
Chiyoda
千代田
East Imperial Garden (Kōkyo Higashi Gyoen)
皇居東御苑
Mitsui Bussan Bldg
三井物産ビル
Mitsui Mutual Life Insurance (H.O.)
三井生命（本社）
KDD
国際電電局
Nikkei Hall
日経ホール
農林中金
Norin Chukin Bank
Nōkyō Bldg
農協ビル
Nōkyō Hall
農協ホール
Ōtemachi (1)
大手町1丁目
Hill of Masakado's Head (Masakado Kubizuka)
将門首塚
Long-Term Credit Bank of Japan
日本長期信用銀行
Yomiuri Newspapers
読売新聞
Sankei Newspapers
産業経済新聞
Sankei Kaikan (hall)
サンケイ会館
東京国際郵便局
Tokyo International P.O.
Postal Services Bureau
東京郵政局
Communications Musm
逓信総合博物館
Postal Inspection Bureau
関東郵政監察局
Hosp. of Imperial Household Agency
宮内庁病院
Sanwa Bank
三和銀行
OTEMACHI
Ōtemachi Bldg
大手町ビル
HANZŌMON LINE
Ōtemachi (2)
大手町2丁目
Imperial Guard Sch.
皇宮警察学校
Site of Edo Castle
江戸城跡
Ōtemon
大手門
Maruha (H.O.)
マルハ本社
Ōte Center Bldg
大手センタービル
Asahi Bank (H.O.)
あさひ銀行（本店）
IBM Info. Sci. Musm
IBM情報科学館
Ōtemachi First Square
大手町ファーストスクエア
CDP Bldg
CDPビル
Fuji Bank (H.O.)
富士銀行（本店）
Daiwa bldg
大和ビル
NTT Date Ōtemachi Bldg
NTTデータ大手町ビル
Urbannet New Ōtemachi Bldg
アーバンネット新大手町ビル
NTT Marunouchi
NTT丸の内
UCHIBO LINE, SOTOBO LINE, SOBU LINE
Cabinet Library (Naikaku Bunko)
内閣文庫
Varig Airlines
ヴァリグ・ブラジル航空
Egypt Air エジプト航空
EITAI DŌRI (AVE.)
永代通り
Nomura Bldg
野村ビル
New Ōtemachi Bldg
新大手町ビル
Nippon Bldg
日本ビル
NKK Bldg
NKKビル
パレスホテル
Palace Hotel
Sumitomo Bank
住友銀行東京本部ビル
Tokyo H.O. Bldg
Bank of Tokyo
東京銀行
Tōyō Trust (H.O.)
東洋信託（本店）
Imperial Guard H.Q.
皇宮警察本部
Kikyō-bori (moat)
桔梗濠
内堀通り
AIU Bldg
AIUビル
Industrial Bank of Japan (H.O.)
日本興業銀行（本店）
Sumitomo Trust (H.O.)
住友信託（本店）
Marunouchi Hotel
丸の内ホテル
Tokai Bank
東海銀行
Nippon Steel Corp. (H.O.)
新日本製鉄（本社）
Bank Hall
銀行会館
Bank Club
Marunouchi Center Bldg
丸の内センタービル
Firaku Bldg
JTB
日本交通公社
TOZAI LINE
Daiwa Securities
大和証券

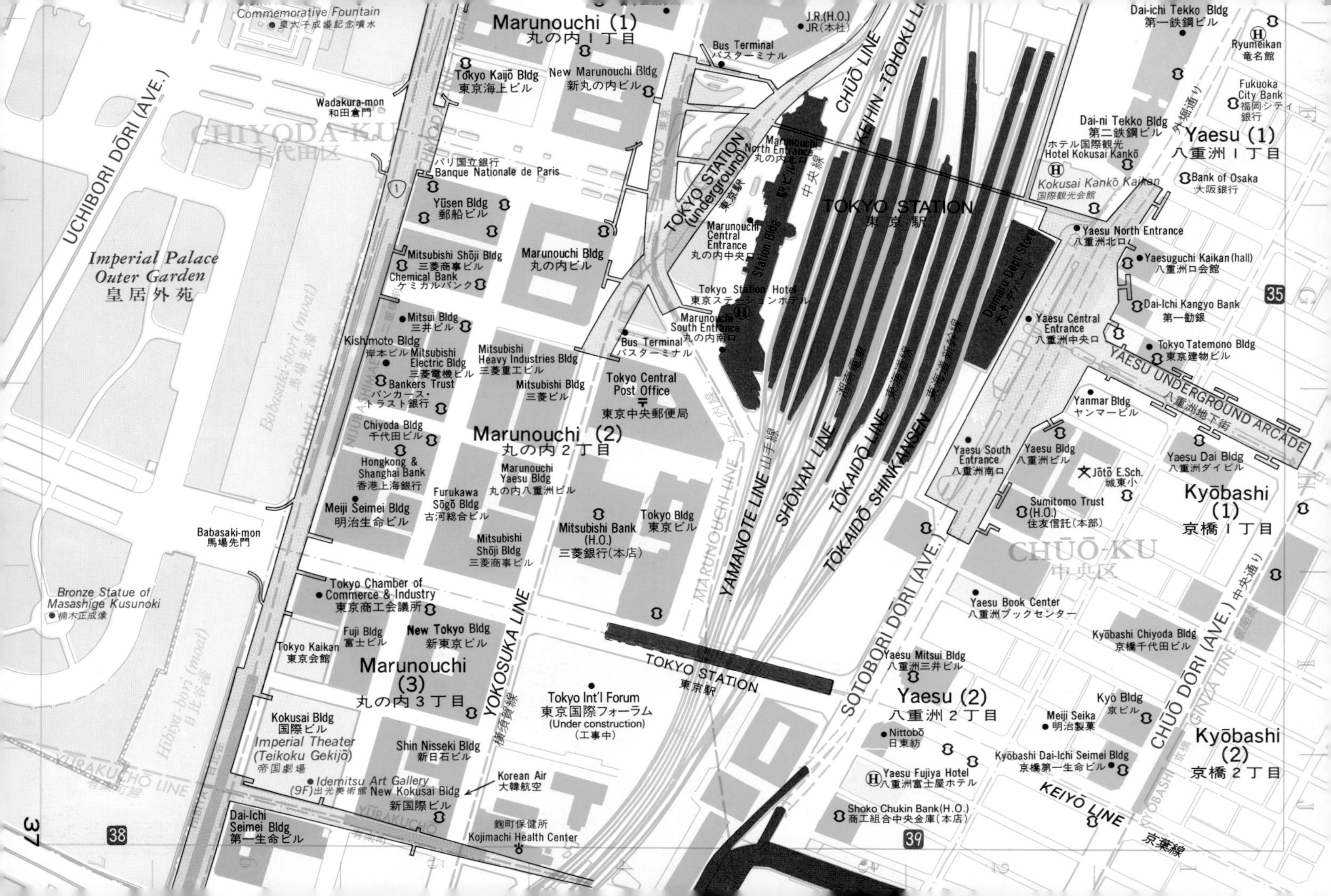

Commemorative Fountain 皇太子成婚記念噴水
Marunouchi (1) 丸の内1丁目
J.R.(H.O.) JR(本社)
Bus Terminal バスターミナル
CHŪŌ LINE
KEIHIN - TŌHOKU LINE
Dai-ichi Tekko Bldg 第一鉄鋼ビル
Ryumeikan 竜名館
Fukuoka City Bank 福岡シティ銀行
Tokyo Kaijō Bldg 東京海上ビル
New Marunouchi Bldg 新丸の内ビル
Wadakura-mon 和田倉門
UCHIBORI DŌRI (AVE.)
CHIYODA-KU 千代田区
Dai-ni Tekko Bldg 第二鉄鋼ビル
Yaesu (1) 八重洲1丁目
Hotel Kokusai Kankō ホテル国際観光
Kokusai Kankō Kaikan 国際観光会館
Bank of Osaka 大阪銀行
パリ国立銀行 Banque Nationale de Paris
TOKYO STATION (underground) 東京駅
Marunouchi North Entrance 丸の内北口
TOKYO STATION 東京駅
Yūsen Bldg 郵船ビル
Imperial Palace Outer Garden 皇居外苑
Mitsubishi Shōji Bldg 三菱商事ビル
Chemical Bank ケミカルバンク
Marunouchi Bldg 丸の内ビル
Marunouchi Central Entrance 丸の内中央口
Station Bldg
Yaesu North Entrance 八重洲北口
Yaesuguchi Kaikan (hall) 八重洲口会館
Daimaru Dept Store 大丸デパート
Tokyo Station Hotel 東京ステーションホテル
35
Dai-Ichi Kangyo Bank 第一勧銀
Mitsui Bldg 三井ビル
Marunouchi South Entrance 丸の内南口
Yaesu Central Entrance 八重洲中央口
Kishimoto Bldg 岸本ビル
Mitsubishi Electric Bldg 三菱電機ビル
Mitsubishi Heavy Industries Bldg 三菱重工ビル
Bus Terminal バスターミナル
Tokyo Tatemono Bldg 東京建物ビル
YAESU UNDERGROUND ARCADE 八重洲地下街
Bankers Trust バンカース・トラスト銀行
Mitsubishi Bldg 三菱ビル
Tokyo Central Post Office 東京中央郵便局
Yanmar Bldg ヤンマービル
Babasaki-bori (moat) 馬場先濠
Chiyoda Bldg 千代田ビル
Marunouchi (2) 丸の内2丁目
Hongkong & Shanghai Bank 香港上海銀行
Marunouchi Yaesu Bldg 丸の内八重洲ビル
YAMANOTE LINE 山手線
SHŌNAN LINE
TŌKAIDŌ LINE
TŌKAIDŌ SHINKANSEN
Yaesu South Entrance 八重洲南口
Yaesu Bldg 八重洲ビル
Yaesu Dai Bldg 八重洲ダイビル
Jōtō E.Sch. 城東小
Kyōbashi (1) 京橋1丁目
Meiji Seimei Bldg 明治生命ビル
Furukawa Sōgō Bldg 古河総合ビル
Mitsubishi Bank (H.O.) 三菱銀行(本店)
Tokyo Bldg 東京ビル
Sumitomo Trust (H.O.) 住友信託(本部)
Babasaki-mon 馬場先門
Mitsubishi Shōji Bldg 三菱商事ビル
MARUNOUCHI LINE
CHŪŌ-KU 中央区
SOTOBORI DŌRI (AVE.)
Bronze Statue of Masashige Kusunoki 楠木正成像
Tokyo Chamber of Commerce & Industry 東京商工会議所
YOKOSUKA LINE 横須賀線
Yaesu Book Center 八重洲ブックセンター
CHŪŌ DŌRI (AVE.) 中央通り
Fuji Bldg 富士ビル
New Tokyo Bldg 新東京ビル
Tokyo Kaikan 東京会館
Kyōbashi Chiyoda Bldg 京橋千代田ビル
Marunouchi (3) 丸の内3丁目
TOKYO STATION 東京駅
Yaesu Mitsui Bldg 八重洲三井ビル
Hibiya-bori (moat) 日比谷濠
Tokyo Int'l Forum 東京国際フォーラム (Under construction) (工事中)
Yaesu (2) 八重洲2丁目
Kyō Bldg 京ビル
Kokusai Bldg 国際ビル
Imperial Theater (Teikoku Gekijō) 帝国劇場
Shin Nisseki Bldg 新日石ビル
Nittobō 日東紡
Meiji Seika 明治製菓
Kyōbashi (2) 京橋2丁目
YŪRAKUCHŌ LINE 有楽町線
Idemitsu Art Gallery (9F) 出光美術館
New Kokusai Bldg 新国際ビル
Korean Air 大韓航空
Kyōbashi Dai-Ichi Seimei Bldg 京橋第一生命ビル
Yaesu Fujiya Hotel 八重洲富士屋ホテル
KEIYŌ LINE 京葉線
Dai-Ichi Seimei Bldg 第一生命ビル
38
麹町保健所 Kojimachi Health Center
Shoko Chukin Bank (H.O.) 商工組合中央金庫(本店)
39

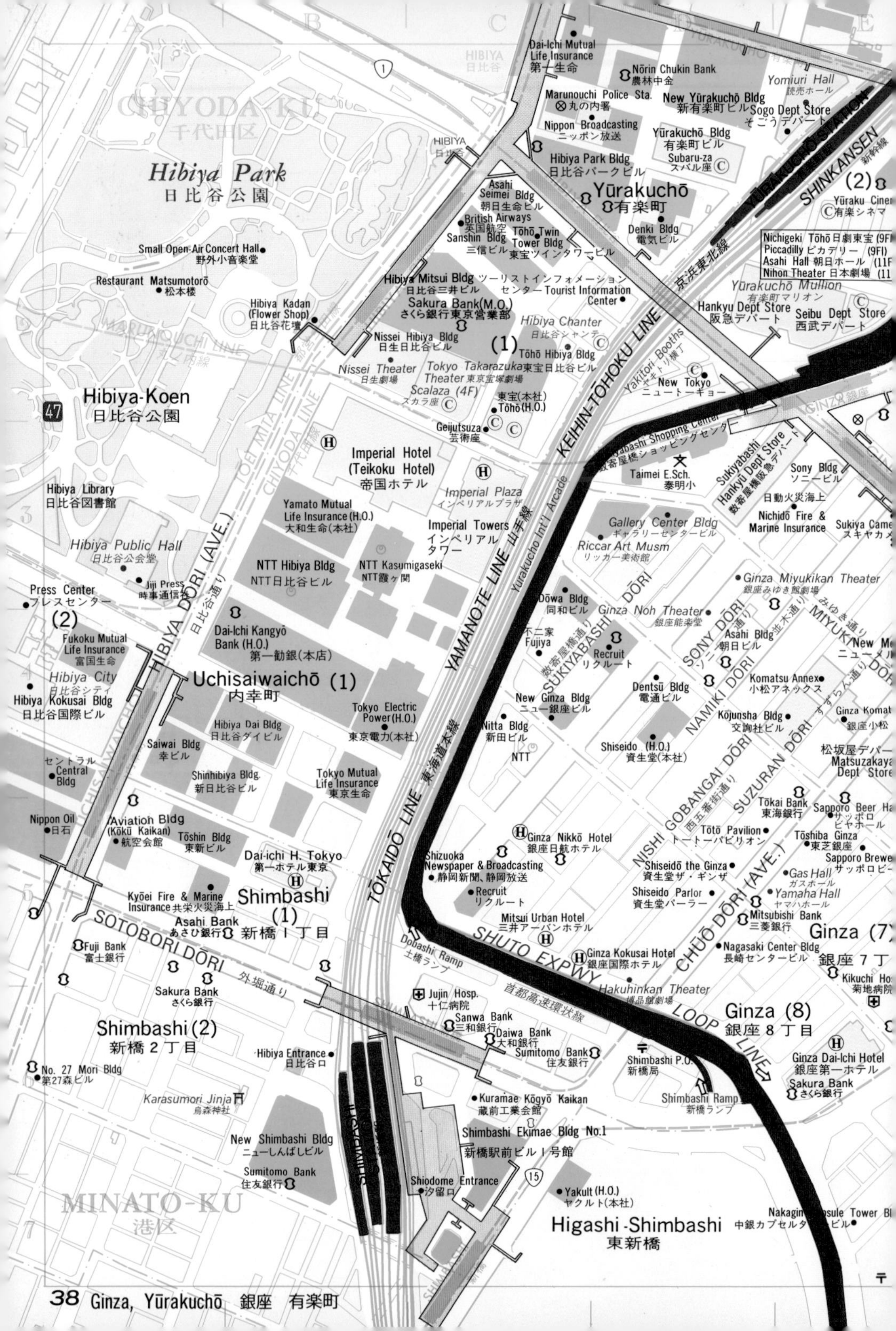
CHIYODA-KU
千代田区
Hibiya Park
日比谷公園
Small Open-Air Concert Hall
野外小音楽堂
Restaurant Matsumotorō
松本楼
Hibiya Kadan (Flower Shop)
日比谷花壇
MARUNOUCHI LINE
丸ノ内線
Hibiya-Koen
日比谷公園
47
Hibiya Library
日比谷図書館
Hibiya Public Hall
日比谷公会堂
Jiji Press
時事通信社
Press Center
プレスセンター
(2)
Fukoku Mutual Life Insurance
富国生命
Hibiya City
日比谷シティ
Hibiya Kokusai Bldg
日比谷国際ビル
セントラル Central Bldg
Nippon Oil
日石
HIBIYA
日比谷
Dai-Ichi Mutual Life Insurance
第一生命
Nōrin Chukin Bank
農林中金
Marunouchi Police Sta.
丸の内署
Nippon Broadcasting
ニッポン放送
New Yūrakuchō Bldg
新有楽町ビル
Sogo Dept Store
そごうデパート
Yomiuri Hall
読売ホール
Yūrakuchō Bldg
有楽町ビル
Subaru-za
スバル座
Hibiya Park Bldg
日比谷パークビル
Yūrakuchō
有楽町
YŪRAKUCHŌ STATION
SHINKANSEN
新幹線
(2)
Yūraku Cine
有楽シネマ
Nichigeki Tōhō 日劇東宝 (9F)
Piccadilly ピカデリー (9F)
Asahi Hall 朝日ホール (11F)
Nihon Theater 日本劇場 (11F)
Asahi Seimei Bldg
朝日生命ビル
British Airways
英国航空
Sanshin Bldg
三信ビル
Tōhō Twin Tower Bldg
東宝ツインタワービル
Denki Bldg
電気ビル
Hibiya Mitsui Bldg
日比谷三井ビル
ツーリストインフォメーションセンター Tourist Information Center
Sakura Bank (M.O.)
さくら銀行東京営業部
Nissei Hibiya Bldg
日生日比谷ビル
(1)
Hibiya Chanter
日比谷シャンテ
Tōhō Hibiya Bldg
東宝日比谷ビル
Nissei Theater
日生劇場
Tokyo Takarazuka Theater
東京宝塚劇場
Scalaza (4F)
スカラ座
東宝(本社)
Tōhō (H.O.)
Geijutsuza
芸術座
Yakitori Booths
ヤキトリ横丁
New Tokyo
ニュートーキョー
Yūrakuchō Mullion
有楽町マリオン
Hankyu Dept Store
阪急デパート
Seibu Dept Store
西武デパート
KEIHIN-TOHOKU LINE
京浜東北線
Sukiyabashi Shopping Center
数寄屋橋ショッピングセンター
Taimei E.Sch.
泰明小
Sukiyabashi Hankyū Dept Store
数寄屋橋阪急デパート
Sony Bldg
ソニービル
日動火災海上
Nichidō Fire & Marine Insurance
Sukiya Camera
スキヤカメラ
Imperial Hotel (Teikoku Hotel)
帝国ホテル
Imperial Plaza
インペリアルプラザ
Imperial Towers
インペリアルタワー
TOEI MITA LINE
CHIYODA LINE
千代田線
Yamato Mutual Life Insurance (H.O.)
大和生命(本社)
NTT Hibiya Bldg
NTT日比谷ビル
NTT Kasumigaseki
NTT霞ヶ関
YAMANOTE LINE
山手線
Yurakucho Int'l Arcade
Gallery Center Bldg
ギャラリーセンタービル
Riccar Art Musm
リッカー美術館
Ginza Miyukikan Theater
銀座みゆき館劇場
HIBIYA DŌRI (AVE.)
日比谷通り
Dai-Ichi Kangyō Bank (H.O.)
第一勧銀(本店)
Dōwa Bldg
同和ビル
Ginza Noh Theater
銀座能楽堂
SUKIYABASHI DŌRI
数寄屋橋通り
不二家 Fujiya
Recruit
リクルート
SONY DŌRI
ソニー通り
Asahi Bldg
朝日ビル
NAMIKI DŌRI
並木通り
MIYUKI DŌRI
みゆき通り
Uchisaiwaichō (1)
内幸町
Hibiya Dai Bldg
日比谷ダイビル
Tokyo Electric Power (H.O.)
東京電力(本社)
Dentsū Bldg
電通ビル
Komatsu Annex
小松アネックス
New Ginza Bldg
ニュー銀座ビル
Nitta Bldg
新田ビル
NTT
Kōjunsha Bldg
交詢社ビル
Shiseido (H.O.)
資生堂(本社)
SUZURAN DŌRI
すずらん通り
Ginza Komatsu
銀座小松
松坂屋デパート
Matsuzakaya Dept Store
Saiwai Bldg
幸ビル
Shinhibiya Bldg.
新日比谷ビル
Tokyo Mutual Life Insurance
東京生命
NISHI GOBANGAI DŌRI
西五番街通り
Tōkai Bank
東海銀行
Sapporo Beer Hall
サッポロビヤホール
Tōtō Pavilion
トートーパビリオン
Tōshiba Ginza
東芝銀座
Sapporo Brewery
サッポロビール
Aviation Bldg (Kōkū Kaikan)
航空会館
Tōshin Bldg
東新ビル
Ginza Nikkō Hotel
銀座日航ホテル
Dai-ichi H. Tokyo
第一ホテル東京
Shizuoka Newspaper & Broadcasting
静岡新聞、静岡放送
Shiseidō the Ginza
資生堂ザ・ギンザ
Gas Hall
ガスホール
Shiseido Parlor
資生堂パーラー
Yamaha Hall
ヤマハホール
CHŪŌ DŌRI (AVE.)
中央通り
Kyōei Fire & Marine Insurance
共栄火災海上
Shimbashi (1)
新橋1丁目
Recruit
リクルート
Mitsubishi Bank
三菱銀行
UCHISAIWAICHO
TŌKAIDŌ LINE
東海道本線
Mitsui Urban Hotel
三井アーバンホテル
Ginza (7)
銀座7丁目
Asahi Bank
あさひ銀行
SOTOBORI DŌRI
外堀通り
Fuji Bank
富士銀行
Dobashi Ramp
土橋ランプ
SHUTO EXPWY
首都高速環状線
Ginza Kokusai Hotel
銀座国際ホテル
Nagasaki Center Bldg
長崎センタービル
Kikuchi Hospital
菊地病院
Sakura Bank
さくら銀行
Jujin Hosp.
十仁病院
Hakuhinkan Theater
博品館劇場
LOOP LINE
Ginza (8)
銀座8丁目
Shimbashi (2)
新橋2丁目
Sanwa Bank
三和銀行
Daiwa Bank
大和銀行
Sumitomo Bank
住友銀行
Hibiya Entrance
日比谷口
Shimbashi P.O.
新橋局
Ginza Dai-Ichi Hotel
銀座第一ホテル
Sakura Bank
さくら銀行
No. 27 Mori Bldg
第27森ビル
Karasumori Jinja
烏森神社
Shimbashi Ramp
新橋ランプ
Kuramae Kōgyō Kaikan
蔵前工業会館
Shimbashi Ekimae Bldg No.1
新橋駅前ビル1号館
New Shimbashi Bldg
ニューしんばしビル
SHIMBASHI
Sumitomo Bank
住友銀行
Shiodome Entrance
汐留口
15
Yakult (H.O.)
ヤクルト(本社)
MINATO-KU
港区
Higashi-Shimbashi
東新橋
Nakagin Capsule Tower Bldg
中銀カプセルタワービル

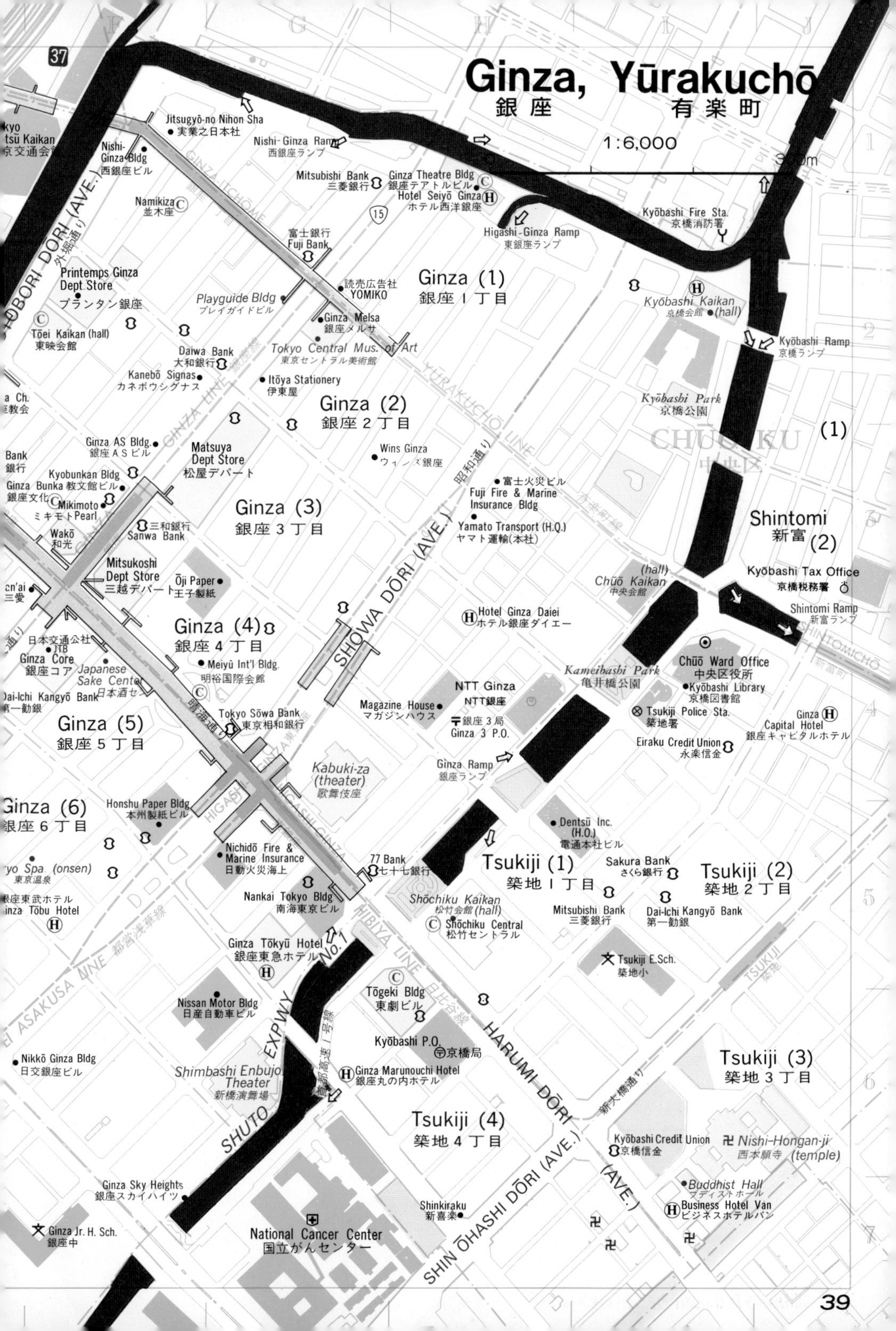

37
Ginza, Yūrakuchō
銀座 有楽町
1:6,000
Jitsugyō-no Nihon Sha
実業之日本社
Nishi-Ginza Ramp
西銀座ランプ
Nishi-Ginza Bldg
西銀座ビル
Mitsubishi Bank
三菱銀行
Ginza Theatre Bldg
銀座テアトルビル
Hotel Seiyō Ginza
ホテル西洋銀座
Namikiza
並木座
15
Higashi-Ginza Ramp
東銀座ランプ
Kyōbashi Fire Sta.
京橋消防署
SOTOBORI DŌRI (AVE.)
外堀通り
GINZA-ITCHŌME
富士銀行
Fuji Bank
Printemps Ginza
Dept Store
プランタン銀座
Playguide Bldg
プレイガイドビル
読売広告社
YOMIKO
Ginza (1)
銀座1丁目
Kyōbashi Kaikan
京橋会館(hall)
Tōei Kaikan (hall)
東映会館
Ginza Melsa
銀座メルサ
Tokyo Central Mus. of Art
東京セントラル美術館
Kyōbashi Ramp
京橋ランプ
Daiwa Bank
大和銀行
Kanebō Signas
カネボウシグナス
Itōya Stationery
伊東屋
GINZA LINE
銀座線
YŪRAKUCHŌ LINE
有楽町線
Kyōbashi Park
京橋公園
Ginza (2)
銀座2丁目
CHŪŌ KU
中央区
(1)
Ginza AS Bldg.
銀座ASビル
Matsuya
Dept Store
松屋デパート
Wins Ginza
ウィンズ銀座
Kyobunkan Bldg
Ginza Bunka 教文館ビル
銀座文化
Mikimoto
ミキモトPearl
昭和通り
富士火災ビル
Fuji Fire & Marine
Insurance Bldg
Ginza (3)
銀座3丁目
三和銀行
Sanwa Bank
Wakō
和光
Yamato Transport (H.Q.)
ヤマト運輸(本社)
Shintomi
新富
(2)
Mitsukoshi
Dept Store
三越デパート
Ōji Paper
王子製紙
SHOWA DŌRI (AVE.)
Chūō Kaikan
中央会館
(hall)
Kyōbashi Tax Office
京橋税務署
Shintomi Ramp
新富ランプ
Hotel Ginza Daiei
ホテル銀座ダイエー
Ginza (4)
銀座4丁目
日本交通公社
JTB
Ginza Core
銀座コア
Japanese
Sake Center
日本酒セン
Meiyū Int'l Bldg.
明裕国際会館
Kameibashi Park
亀井橋公園
Chūō Ward Office
中央区役所
Kyōbashi Library
京橋図書館
SHINTOMICHŌ
新富町
NTT Ginza
NTT銀座
Magazine House
マガジンハウス
銀座3局
Ginza 3 P.O.
Tsukiji Police Sta.
築地署
Ginza
Capital Hotel
銀座キャピタルホテル
晴海通り
Tokyo Sōwa Bank
東京相和銀行
Ginza (5)
銀座5丁目
Eiraku Credit Union
永楽信金
Ginza Ramp
銀座ランプ
Kabuki-za
(theater)
歌舞伎座
Honshu Paper Bldg
本州製紙ビル
HIGASHI GINZA
Ginza (6)
銀座6丁目
Dentsū Inc.
(H.Q.)
電通本社ビル
Nichidō Fire &
Marine Insurance
日動火災海上
77 Bank
七十七銀行
Tsukiji (1)
築地1丁目
Sakura Bank
さくら銀行
Tsukiji (2)
築地2丁目
Nankai Tokyo Bldg
南海東京ビル
Shōchiku Kaikan
松竹会館(hall)
Shōchiku Central
松竹セントラル
Mitsubishi Bank
三菱銀行
Dai-Ichi Kangyō Bank
第一勧銀
Ginza Tōkyū Hotel
銀座東急ホテル
No.1
HIBIYA LINE
日比谷線
Tsukiji E.Sch.
築地小
TSUKIJI
築地
ASAKUSA LINE
都営浅草線
Tōgeki Bldg
東劇ビル
Nissan Motor Bldg
日産自動車ビル
SHUTO EXPWY
首都高速1号線
Kyōbashi P.O.
京橋局
HARUMI DŌRI
Tsukiji (3)
築地3丁目
Nikkō Ginza Bldg
日交銀座ビル
Shimbashi Enbujo
Theater
新橋演舞場
Ginza Marunouchi Hotel
銀座丸の内ホテル
新大橋通り
Tsukiji (4)
築地4丁目
Kyōbashi Credit Union
京橋信金
Nishi-Hongan-ji
西本願寺
(temple)
(AVE.)
SHIN ŌHASHI DŌRI (AVE.)
Ginza Sky Heights
銀座スカイハイツ
Buddhist Hall
ブディストホール
Business Hotel Van
ビジネスホテルバン
Shinkiraku
新喜楽
National Cancer Center
国立がんセンター
Ginza Jr. H. Sch.
銀座中
Printemps Ginza
Tokyo Spa (onsen)
東京温泉
Ginza Tōbu Hotel
Dai-Ichi Kangyō Bank

Shimbashi (4)
新橋 4 丁目
Shimbashi Sumitomo Bldg
新橋住友ビル
Shimbashi (5)
新橋 5 丁目
Shimbashi (6)
新橋 6 丁目
Higashi-Shimbashi (2)
東新橋 2 丁目
TOEI ASAKUSA LINE
Matsuoka Art Musm
松岡美術館
Shiba Post Office
芝局
Sakuragawa E. Sch.
桜川小
Shiba Shinkin (H.O.)
芝信金本店
Shiba Hosp.
芝病院
Atago P.S.
愛宕署
Japan Red Cross (H.Q)
日本赤十字社(本社)
Higashi Nippon Bank
東日本銀行
Shinmei E. Sch.
神明小
Hamamatsuchō (1)
浜松町 1 丁目
World Trade Center Bldg
世界貿易センタービル
HAMAMATSUCHŌ STATION
浜松町駅
Hamamatsuchō (2)
浜松町 2 丁目
Kyū-Shibarikyū Garden
旧芝離宮庭園
Tokyo Seimei Bldg
東京生命ビル
Shiba-daimon (1)
芝大門 1 丁目
Shiba Park Hotel
芝パークホテル
Dai-ichi Kangyo Bank
第一勧銀
Shiba Daijingū
芝大神宮
Asahi Bank
あさひ銀行
Sanwa Bank
三和銀行
Minato-Hamamatsuchō P.O.
港浜松町局
Shiba-daimon (2)
芝大門 2 丁目
Transportation Breau of Tokyo Met.
交通局庁舎
Mitsubishi Bank
三菱銀行
Shōkō Chūkin
DAIMON
Minato Tech. H. Sch.
港工業高校
Jikei Med. Univ. Hosp.
慈恵医大病院
Jikei Med. Univ.
東京慈恵会医大
NTT Shiba
NTT芝
Kyōritsu Coll. of Pharmacy
共立薬科大学
Shiba-Kōen (1)
芝公園 1 丁目
Minato Ward Office
港区役所
Shōwa Denkō
昭和電工
Shiba-kōen (2)
芝公園 2 丁目
Mielperque Tokyo
メルパルク東京
Shiba Swimming Pool
芝プール
abc Hall
abc会館
Welfare Hall
ONARIMON
Onarimon Jr. H. Sch.
御成門中
Minato Library
みなと図書館
Onari-mon
御成門
Niten-mon
二天門
San-gedatsu-mon
三解脱門
TOEI MITA LINE
都営三田線
Atago (2)
愛宕 2 丁目
Seishō-ji
青松寺
NHK Broadcast Musm
NHK放送博物館
Seisoku Gakuin H. Sch.
正則学院高校
Shiba-kōen (3)
芝公園 3 丁目
Tokyo Prince Hotel
東京プリンスホテル
Zōjō-ji
増上寺
Zōjōji Kaikan
増上寺会館
Shiba-kōen (4)
芝公園 4 丁目
Tōshō-gu
東照宮
Shiba Park
Sakura Bank
さくら銀行
Toranomon (3)
虎ノ門 3 丁目
Shiba H. Sch.
芝高校
Konchi-in
金地院
Kinki Bank
近畿銀行
Emb. of Netherlands
オランダ大使館
Tokyo Tower
東京タワー
TV Tokyo
テレビ東京
Bowling Center
ボーリングセンター
Akabane-bashi
赤羽橋
Fuji Bank
富士銀行
Shiba Water Station
芝給水所
KAMIYACHO
神谷町
Toranomon (4)
虎ノ門 4 丁目
Toranomon (5)
虎ノ門 5 丁目
HIBIYA LINE
日比谷線
SAKURADA DŌRI (AVE.)
桜田通
TV Tokyo
テレビ東京
Hachiman Jinja
八幡神社
Reiyūkai Temple
霊友会釈迦殿
Azabudai (1)
麻布台 1 丁目
Noa Bldg
ノアビル
Emb. of Fiji
フィジー大使館
Emb. of Russia
ロシア大使館
Azabudai (2)
麻布台 2 丁目
Radio Nippon
ラジオ日本
Iikura E. Sch.
飯倉小
Higashi-Azabu (1)
東麻布 1 丁目
Higashi-Azabu (2)
東麻布 2 丁目
SHUTO EXPWY CIRCULAR LINE
首都高速都心環状線
Shiba Public Health Center

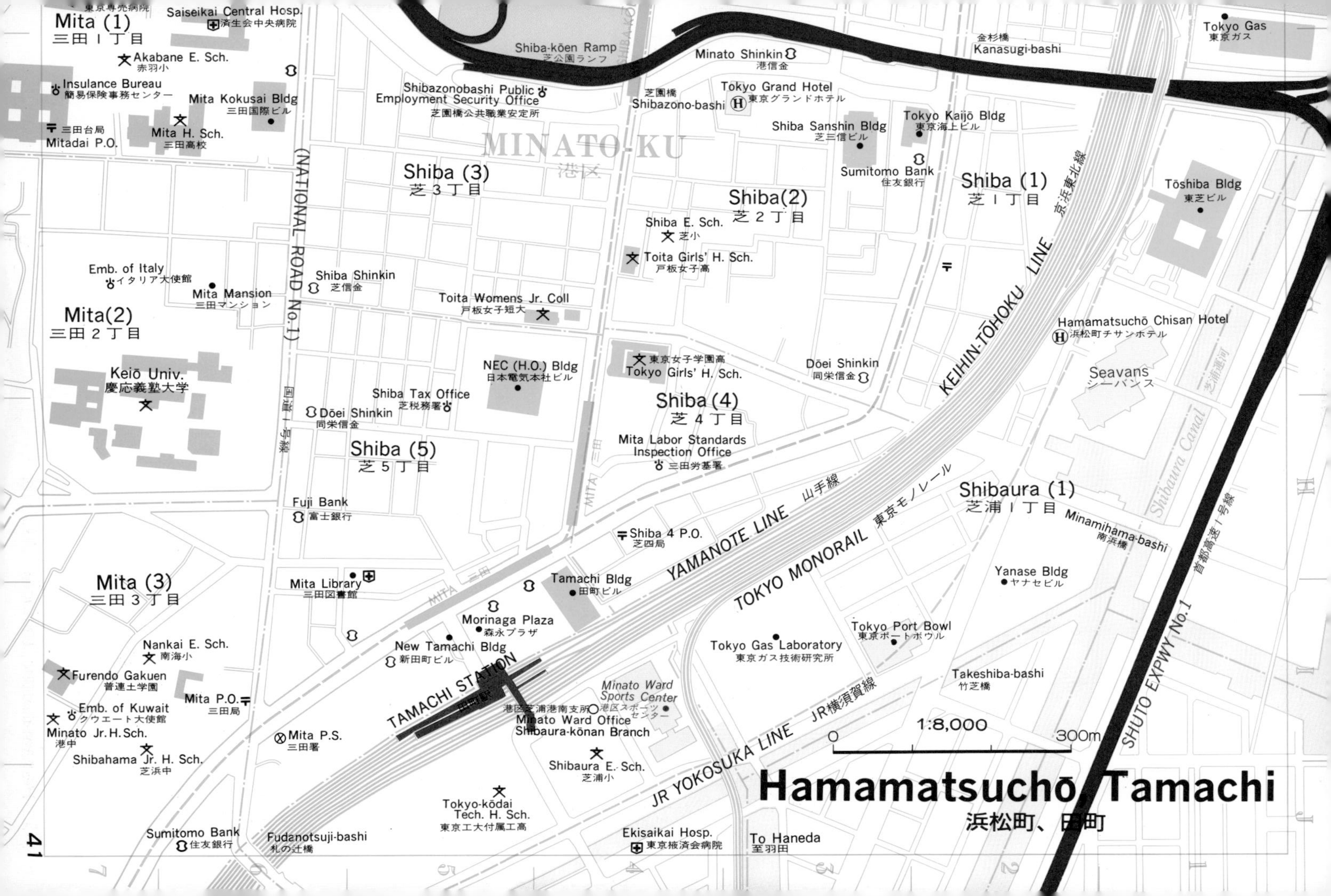
Hamamatsuchō, Tamachi
浜松町、田町
1:8,000
0
300m
Mita (1)
三田１丁目
Saiseikai Central Hosp.
済生会中央病院
Akabane E. Sch.
赤羽小
Insulance Bureau
簡易保険事務センター
Mita Kokusai Bldg
三田国際ビル
Mita H. Sch.
三田高校
三田台局
Mitadai P.O.
Shiba-kōen Ramp
芝公園ランプ
Shibazonobashi Public Employment Security Office
芝園橋公共職業安定所
MINATO-KU
港区
Minato Shinkin
港信金
芝園橋
Shibazono-bashi
Tokyo Grand Hotel
東京グランドホテル
Shiba Sanshin Bldg
芝三信ビル
Tokyo Kaijō Bldg
東京海上ビル
Sumitomo Bank
住友銀行
金杉橋
Kanasugi-bashi
Tokyo Gas
東京ガス
Tōshiba Bldg
東芝ビル
Shiba (1)
芝１丁目
Shiba(2)
芝２丁目
Shiba (3)
芝３丁目
Shiba (4)
芝４丁目
Shiba (5)
芝５丁目
(NATIONAL ROAD No.1)
国道１号線
Shiba E. Sch.
芝小
Toita Girls' H. Sch.
戸板女子高
Emb. of Italy
イタリア大使館
Mita Mansion
三田マンション
Shiba Shinkin
芝信金
Toita Womens Jr. Coll
戸板女子短大
Mita(2)
三田２丁目
Keiō Univ.
慶応義塾大学
NEC (H.O.) Bldg
日本電気本社ビル
東京女子学園高
Tokyo Girls' H. Sch.
Dōei Shinkin
同栄信金
Shiba Tax Office
芝税務署
Mita Labor Standards Inspection Office
三田労基署
KEIHIN-TŌHOKU LINE
京浜東北線
Hamamatsuchō Chisan Hotel
浜松町チサンホテル
Seavans
シーバンス
芝浦運河
Shibaura Canal
Fuji Bank
富士銀行
MITA
三田
Shiba 4 P.O.
芝四局
YAMANOTE LINE
山手線
TOKYO MONORAIL
東京モノレール
Shibaura (1)
芝浦１丁目
Minamihama-bashi
南浜橋
首都高速１号線
SHUTO EXPWY No.1
Yanase Bldg
ヤナセビル
Mita Library
三田図書館
Tamachi Bldg
田町ビル
Mita (3)
三田３丁目
Morinaga Plaza
森永プラザ
New Tamachi Bldg
新田町ビル
Tokyo Port Bowl
東京ポートボウル
Tokyo Gas Laboratory
東京ガス技術研究所
Nankai E. Sch.
南海小
Furendo Gakuen
普連土学園
Mita P.O.
三田局
Emb. of Kuwait
クウエート大使館
Minato Jr.H.Sch.
港中
Shibahama Jr. H. Sch.
芝浜中
Mita P.S.
三田署
TAMACHI STATION
田町駅
港区芝浦港南支所
Minato Ward Office Shibaura-kōnan Branch
Minato Ward Sports Center
港区スポーツセンター
Takeshiba-bashi
竹芝橋
JR YOKOSUKA LINE
JR横須賀線
Shibaura E. Sch.
芝浦小
Tokyo-kōdai Tech. H. Sch.
東京工大付属工高
Sumitomo Bank
住友銀行
Fudanotsuji-bashi
札の辻橋
Ekisaikai Hosp.
東京掖済会病院
To Haneda
至羽田

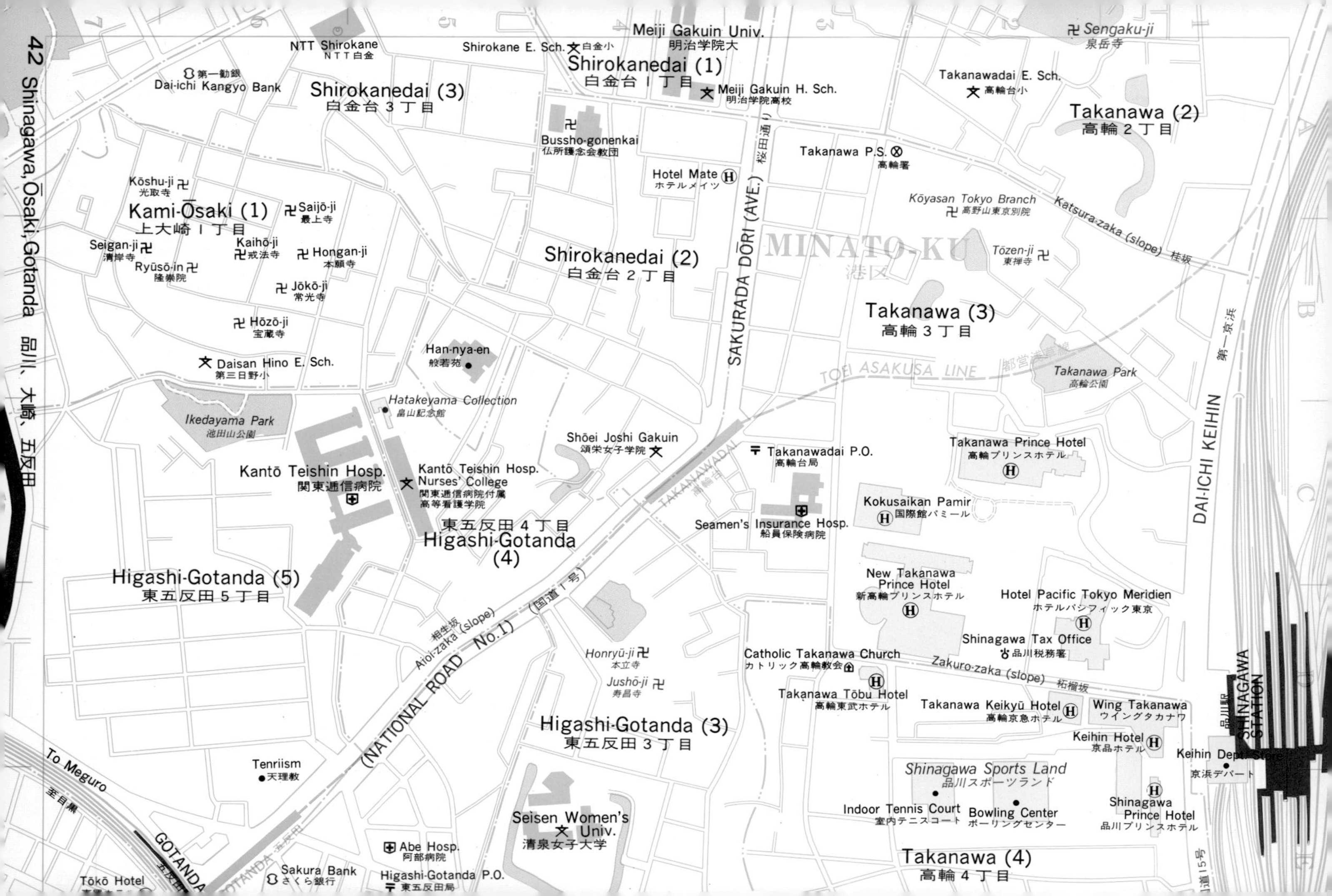
Meiji Gakuin Univ.
明治学院大
NTT Shirokane
NTT白金
Shirokane E. Sch.
白金小
Shirokanedai (1)
白金台1丁目
Sengaku-ji
泉岳寺
Takanawadai E. Sch.
高輪台小
第一勧銀
Dai-ichi Kangyo Bank
Shirokanedai (3)
白金台3丁目
Meiji Gakuin H. Sch.
明治学院高校
Takanawa (2)
高輪2丁目
Bussho-gonenkai
仏所護念会教団
桜田通り
Takanawa P.S.
高輪署
Hotel Mate
ホテルメイツ
Kōshu-ji
光取寺
Kōyasan Tokyo Branch
高野山東京別院
Kami-Ōsaki (1)
上大崎1丁目
Saijō-ji
最上寺
Katsura-zaka (slope)
桂坂
Seigan-ji
清岸寺
Kaihō-ji
戒法寺
Hongan-ji
本願寺
Shirokanedai (2)
白金台2丁目
SAKURADA DŌRI (AVE.)
MINATO-KU
港区
Tōzen-ji
東禅寺
Ryūsō-in
隆崇院
Jōkō-ji
常光寺
Takanawa (3)
高輪3丁目
第一京浜
Hōzō-ji
宝蔵寺
Han-nya-en
般若苑
TOEI ASAKUSA LINE
都営浅草線
Daisan Hino E. Sch.
第三日野小
Takanawa Park
高輪公園
Hatakeyama Collection
畠山記念館
DAI-ICHI KEIHIN
Ikedayama Park
池田山公園
Shōei Joshi Gakuin
頌栄女子学院
Takanawadai P.O.
高輪台局
Takanawa Prince Hotel
高輪プリンスホテル
Kantō Teishin Hosp.
関東逓信病院
Kantō Teishin Hosp. Nurses' College
関東逓信病院付属高等看護学院
TAKANAWADAI
高輪台
Kokusaikan Pamir
国際館パミール
Seamen's Insurance Hosp.
船員保険病院
東五反田4丁目
Higashi-Gotanda (4)
New Takanawa Prince Hotel
新高輪プリンスホテル
Higashi-Gotanda (5)
東五反田5丁目
Hotel Pacific Tokyo Meridien
ホテルパシフィック東京
国道1号
相生坂
Aioi-zaka (slope)
(NATIONAL ROAD No.1)
Shinagawa Tax Office
品川税務署
Honryū-ji
本立寺
Catholic Takanawa Church
カトリック高輪教会
Zakuro-zaka (slope)
柘榴坂
Jushō-ji
寿昌寺
Takanawa Tōbu Hotel
高輪東武ホテル
Takanawa Keikyū Hotel
高輪京急ホテル
Wing Takanawa
ウイングタカナワ
品川駅
SHINAGAWA STATION
Higashi-Gotanda (3)
東五反田3丁目
Keihin Hotel
京品ホテル
Keihin Dept. Store
京浜デパート
Tenriism
天理教
Shinagawa Sports Land
品川スポーツランド
To Meguro
至目黒
Shinagawa Prince Hotel
品川プリンスホテル
Indoor Tennis Court
室内テニスコート
Bowling Center
ボーリングセンター
Seisen Women's Univ.
清泉女子大学
Abe Hosp.
阿部病院
Takanawa (4)
高輪4丁目
GOTANDA
Sakura Bank
さくら銀行
Tōkō Hotel
Higashi-Gotanda P.O.
東五反田局
国道15号

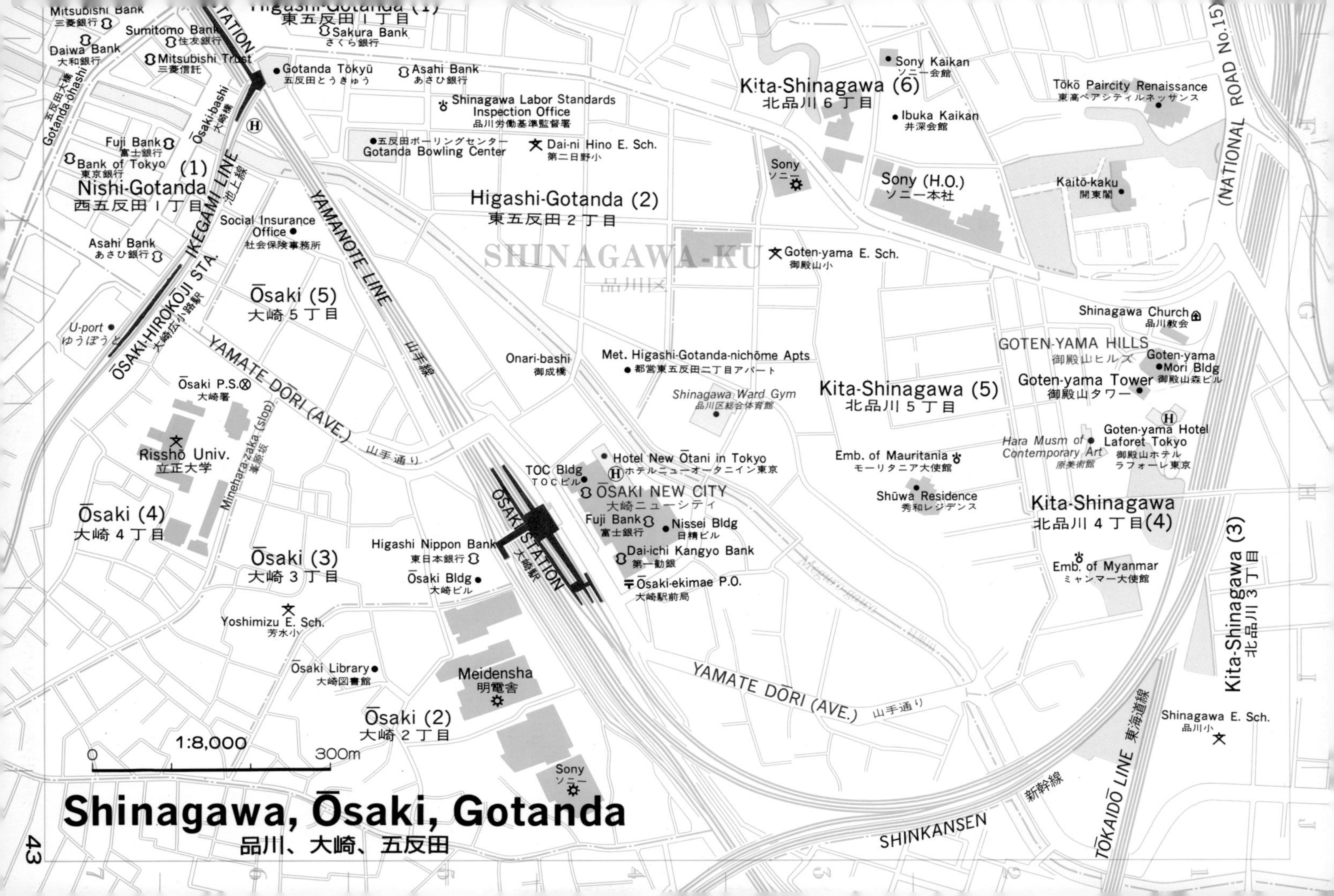
Shinagawa, Ōsaki, Gotanda
品川、大崎、五反田
1:8,000
0
300m
Mitsubishi Bank
三菱銀行
Sumitomo Bank
住友銀行
Daiwa Bank
大和銀行
Mitsubishi Trust
三菱信託
Sakura Bank
さくら銀行
東五反田１丁目
Gotanda Tōkyū
五反田とうきゅう
Asahi Bank
あさひ銀行
Gotanda-ōhashi
五反田大橋
Ōsaki-bashi
大崎橋
Shinagawa Labor Standards Inspection Office
品川労働基準監督署
五反田ボーリングセンター
Gotanda Bowling Center
Dai-ni Hino E. Sch.
第二日野小
Fuji Bank
富士銀行
Bank of Tokyo
東京銀行
(1)
Nishi-Gotanda
西五反田１丁目
IKEGAMI LINE
池上線
YAMANOTE LINE
山手線
Higashi-Gotanda (2)
東五反田２丁目
Social Insurance Office
社会保険事務所
Asahi Bank
あさひ銀行
SHINAGAWA-KU
品川区
Ōsaki (5)
大崎５丁目
ŌSAKI-HIROKOJI STA.
大崎広小路駅
U-port
ゆうぽうと
YAMATE DŌRI (AVE.)
山手通り
Ōsaki P.S.
大崎署
Risshō Univ.
立正大学
Minehara-zaka (slop)
峯原坂
Ōsaki (4)
大崎４丁目
Ōsaki (3)
大崎３丁目
Yoshimizu E. Sch.
芳水小
Ōsaki Library
大崎図書館
Ōsaki (2)
大崎２丁目
Onari-bashi
御成橋
Met. Higashi-Gotanda-nichōme Apts
都営東五反田二丁目アパート
Shinagawa Ward Gym
品川区総合体育館
TOC Bldg
ＴＯＣビル
Hotel New Ōtani in Tokyo
ホテルニューオータニイン東京
ŌSAKI NEW CITY
大崎ニューシティ
Fuji Bank
富士銀行
Nissei Bldg
日精ビル
Dai-ichi Kangyo Bank
第一勧銀
Ōsaki-ekimae P.O.
大崎駅前局
Higashi Nippon Bank
東日本銀行
Ōsaki Bldg
大崎ビル
ŌSAKI STATION
大崎駅
Meidensha
明電舎
Sony
ソニー
Sony Kaikan
ソニー会館
Kita-Shinagawa (6)
北品川６丁目
Ibuka Kaikan
井深会館
Sony
ソニー
Sony (H.O.)
ソニー本社
Goten-yama E. Sch.
御殿山小
Tōkō Paircity Renaissance
東高ペアシティルネッサンス
Kaitō-kaku
開東閣
(NATIONAL ROAD No.15)
Shinagawa Church
品川教会
GOTEN-YAMA HILLS
御殿山ヒルズ
Goten-yama Mori Bldg
御殿山森ビル
Goten-yama Tower
御殿山タワー
Kita-Shinagawa (5)
北品川５丁目
Hara Musm of Contemporary Art
原美術館
Goten-yama Hotel Laforet Tokyo
御殿山ホテルラフォーレ東京
Emb. of Mauritania
モーリタニア大使館
Shūwa Residence
秀和レジデンス
Kita-Shinagawa
北品川４丁目(4)
Emb. of Myanmar
ミャンマー大使館
Kita-Shinagawa (3)
北品川３丁目
Shinagawa E. Sch.
品川小
YAMATE DŌRI (AVE.)
山手通り
SHINKANSEN
新幹線
TŌKAIDŌ LINE
東海道線

Yotsuya, Ichigaya 四谷、市谷

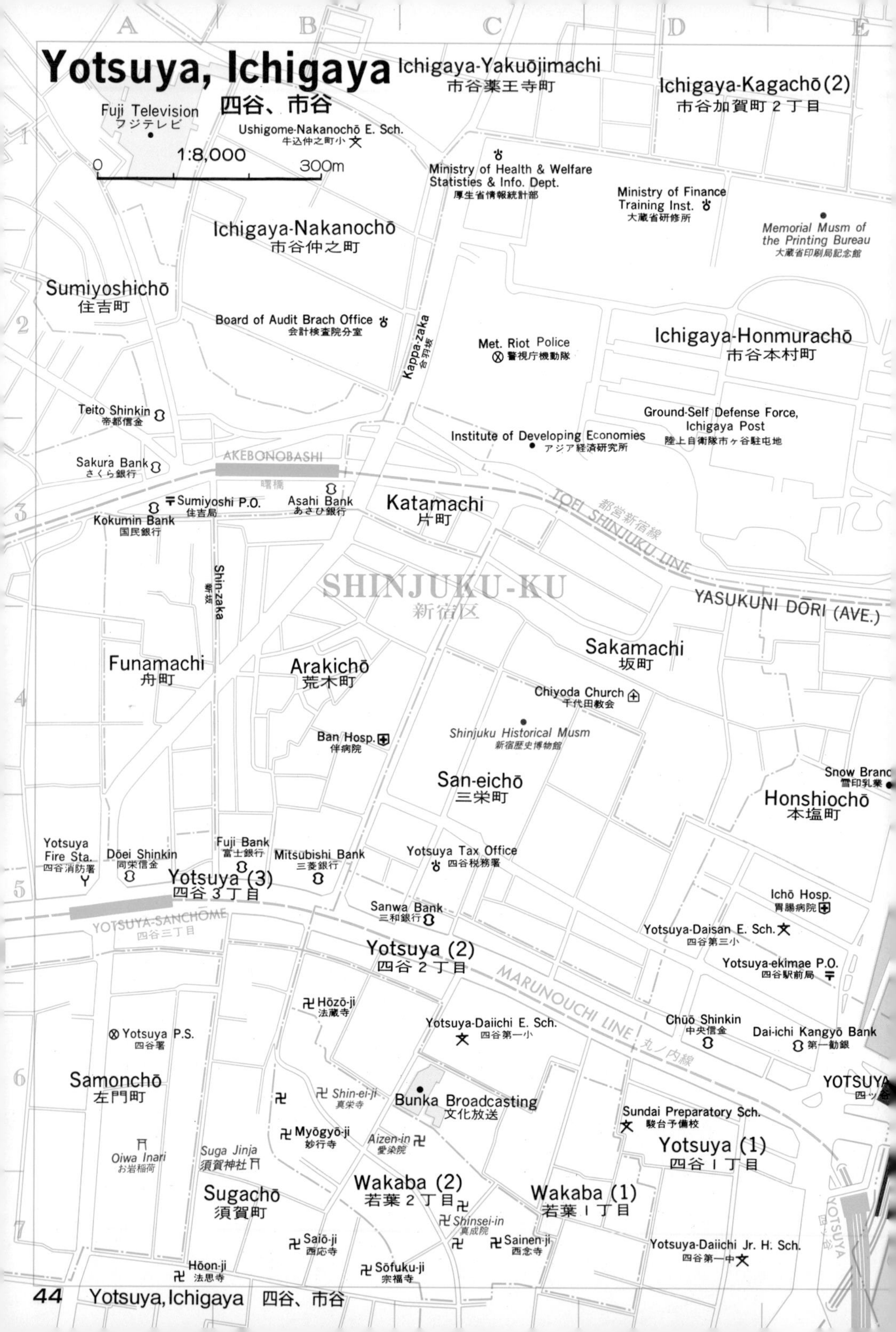

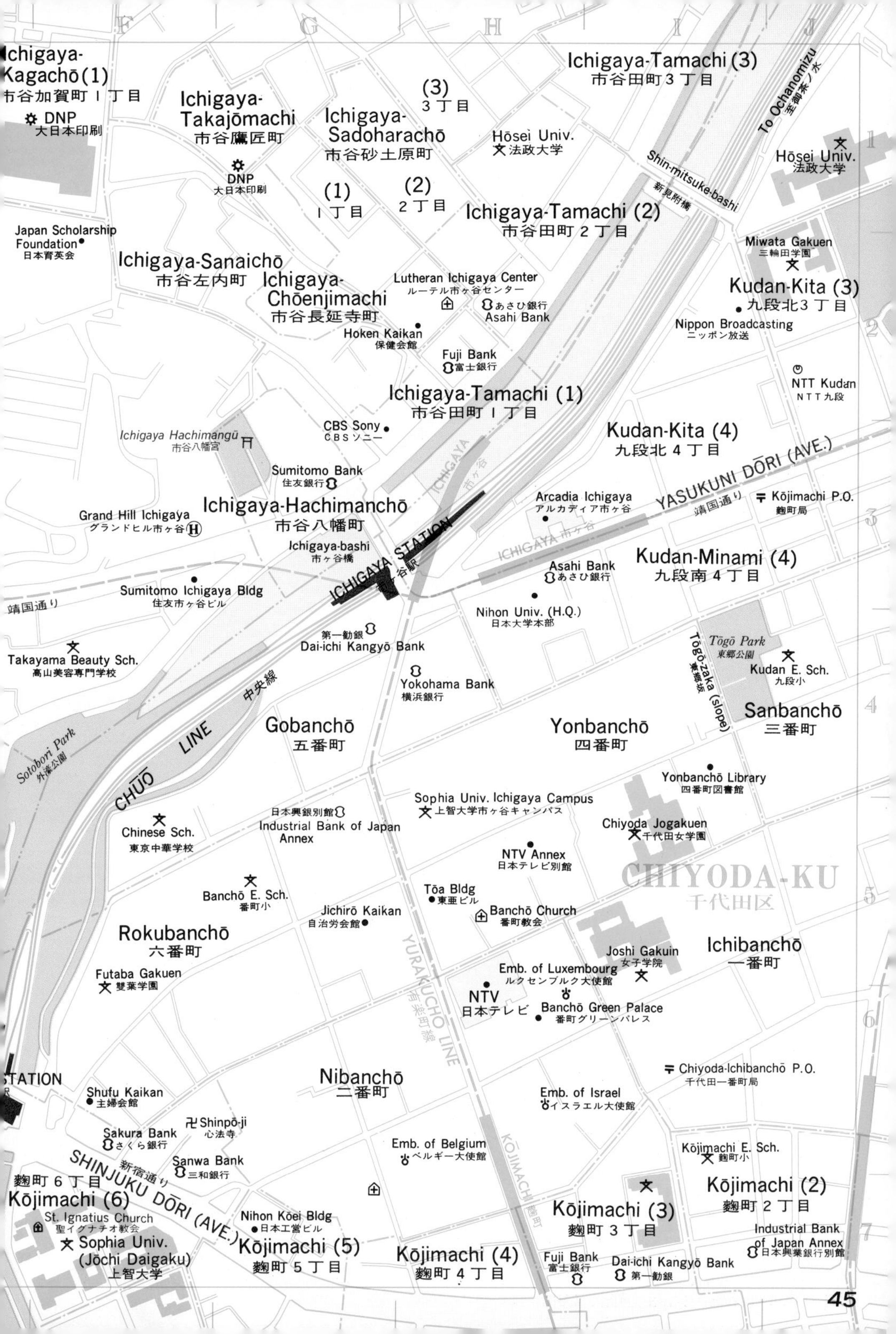

Ichigaya-Kagachō (1)
市谷加賀町1丁目
DNP
大日本印刷
Ichigaya-Takajōmachi
市谷鷹匠町
Ichigaya-Sadoharachō
市谷砂土原町
(3)
3丁目
(1)
1丁目
(2)
2丁目
Ichigaya-Tamachi (3)
市谷田町3丁目
Hōsei Univ.
法政大学
To Ochanomizu
至御茶ノ水
Shin-mitsuke-bashi
新見附橋
Ichigaya-Tamachi (2)
市谷田町2丁目
Japan Scholarship Foundation
日本育英会
Ichigaya-Sanaichō
市谷左内町
Ichigaya-Chōenjimachi
市谷長延寺町
Lutheran Ichigaya Center
ルーテル市ヶ谷センター
あさひ銀行
Asahi Bank
Hoken Kaikan
保健会館
Fuji Bank
富士銀行
Miwata Gakuen
三輪田学園
Kudan-Kita (3)
九段北3丁目
Nippon Broadcasting
ニッポン放送
NTT Kudan
NTT九段
Ichigaya-Tamachi (1)
市谷田町1丁目
CBS Sony
CBSソニー
Ichigaya Hachimangū
市谷八幡宮
Kudan-Kita (4)
九段北4丁目
YASUKUNI DŌRI (AVE.)
靖国通り
Kōjimachi P.O.
麹町局
Sumitomo Bank
住友銀行
Ichigaya-Hachimanchō
市谷八幡町
Grand Hill Ichigaya
グランドヒル市ヶ谷
Arcadia Ichigaya
アルカディア市ヶ谷
ICHIGAYA
市ヶ谷
ICHIGAYA STATION
市ヶ谷駅
Ichigaya-bashi
市ヶ谷橋
Asahi Bank
あさひ銀行
Kudan-Minami (4)
九段南4丁目
Sumitomo Ichigaya Bldg
住友市ヶ谷ビル
靖国通り
Nihon Univ. (H.Q.)
日本大学本部
第一勧銀
Dai-ichi Kangyō Bank
Takayama Beauty Sch.
高山美容専門学校
Yokohama Bank
横浜銀行
Tōgō Park
東郷公園
Tōgō-zaka (slope)
東郷坂
Kudan E. Sch.
九段小
中央線
CHŪŌ LINE
Sotobori Park
外濠公園
Gobanchō
五番町
Yonbanchō
四番町
Sanbanchō
三番町
Yonbanchō Library
四番町図書館
Sophia Univ. Ichigaya Campus
上智大学市ヶ谷キャンパス
日本興銀別館
Industrial Bank of Japan Annex
Chinese Sch.
東京中華学校
Chiyoda Jogakuen
千代田女学園
NTV Annex
日本テレビ別館
CHIYODA-KU
千代田区
Banchō E. Sch.
番町小
Tōa Bldg
東亜ビル
Jichirō Kaikan
自治労会館
Banchō Church
番町教会
Rokubanchō
六番町
Joshi Gakuin
女子学院
Ichibanchō
一番町
Emb. of Luxembourg
ルクセンブルク大使館
Futaba Gakuen
雙葉学園
NTV
日本テレビ
Banchō Green Palace
番町グリーンパレス
YURAKUCHO LINE
有楽町線
Chiyoda-Ichibanchō P.O.
千代田一番町局
STATION
Nibanchō
二番町
Shufu Kaikan
主婦会館
Emb. of Israel
イスラエル大使館
Shinpō-ji
心法寺
Sakura Bank
さくら銀行
Emb. of Belgium
ベルギー大使館
Kōjimachi E. Sch.
麹町小
新宿通り
SHINJUKU DŌRI (AVE.)
Sanwa Bank
三和銀行
麹町6丁目
Kōjimachi (6)
Kōjimachi (2)
麹町2丁目
KŌJIMACHI
麹町
St. Ignatius Church
聖イグナチオ教会
Nihon Kōei Bldg
日本工営ビル
Kōjimachi (3)
麹町3丁目
Industrial Bank of Japan Annex
日本興業銀行別館
Sophia Univ. (Jōchi Daigaku)
上智大学
Kōjimachi (5)
麹町5丁目
Kōjimachi (4)
麹町4丁目
Fuji Bank
富士銀行
Dai-ichi Kangyō Bank
第一勧銀
F
G
H
I
J
1
2
3
4
5
6
7

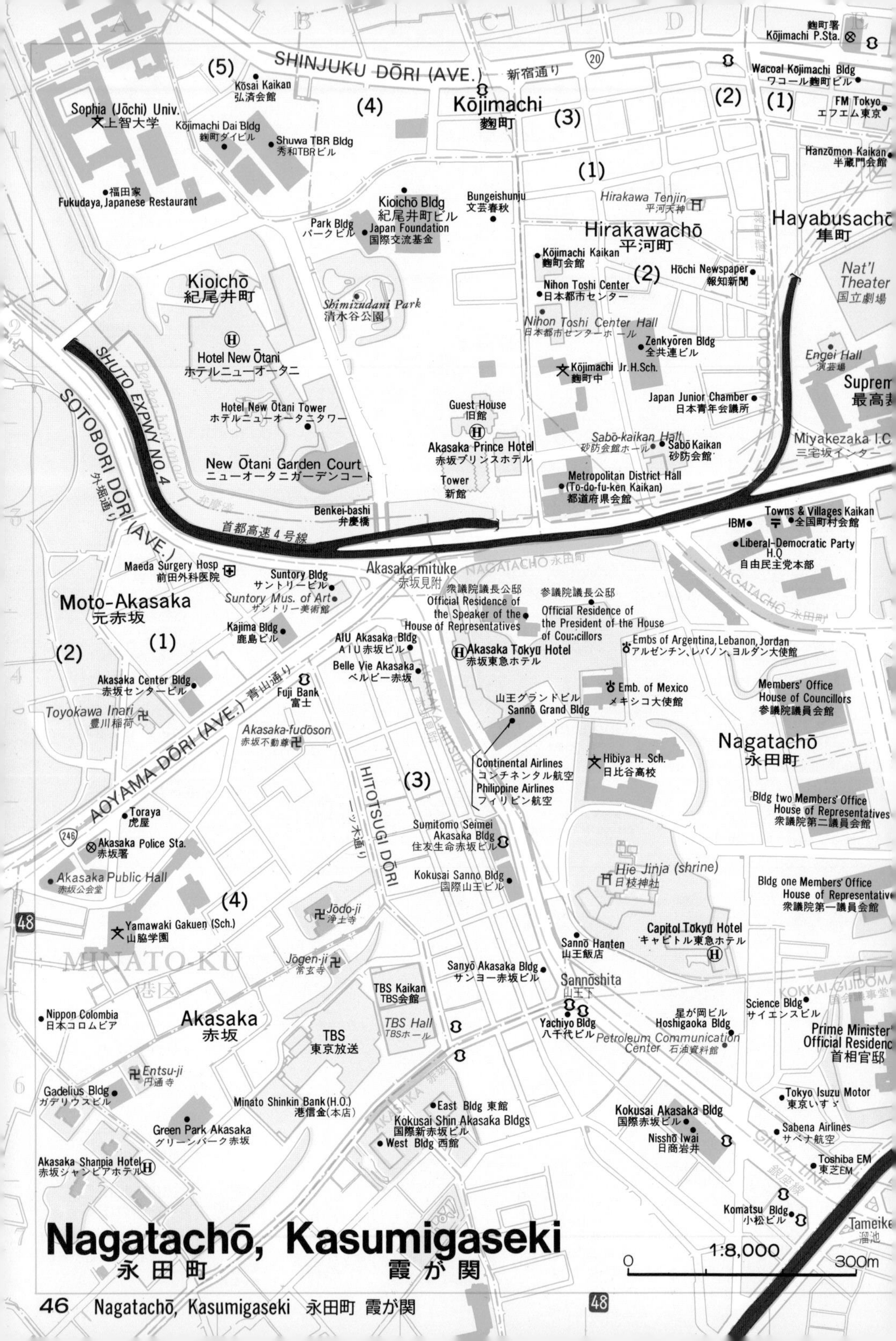
Nagatachō, Kasumigaseki
永田町 霞が関
1:8,000
0
300m
SHINJUKU DŌRI (AVE.)
新宿通り
20
Kōjimachi
麹町
麹町署
Kōjimachi P.Sta.
Wacoal Kōjimachi Bldg
ワコール麹町ビル
FM Tokyo
エフエム東京
Hanzōmon Kaikan
半蔵門会館
Kōsai Kaikan
弘済会館
Sophia (Jōchi) Univ.
上智大学
Kōjimachi Dai Bldg
麹町ダイビル
Shuwa TBR Bldg
秀和TBRビル
福田家
Fukudaya, Japanese Restaurant
Kioichō Bldg
紀尾井町ビル
Japan Foundation
国際交流基金
Park Bldg
パークビル
Bungeishunju
文芸春秋
Hirakawa Tenjin
平河天神
Hirakawachō
平河町
Hayabusachō
隼町
Kōjimachi Kaikan
麹町会館
Hōchi Newspaper
報知新聞
Nat'l Theater
国立劇場
Nihon Toshi Center
日本都市センター
Nihon Toshi Center Hall
日本都市センターホール
Kioichō
紀尾井町
Shimizudani Park
清水谷公園
Hotel New Ōtani
ホテルニューオータニ
Zenkyōren Bldg
全共連ビル
Kōjimachi Jr. H.Sch.
麹町中
Engei Hall
演芸場
Japan Junior Chamber
日本青年会議所
Guest House
旧館
Akasaka Prince Hotel
赤坂プリンスホテル
Hotel New Ōtani Tower
ホテルニューオータニタワー
Sabō-kaikan Hall
砂防会館ホール
Sabō Kaikan
砂防会館
Miyakezaka I.C.
三宅坂インター
New Ōtani Garden Court
ニューオータニガーデンコート
Tower
新館
Metropolitan District Hall
(To-do-fu-ken Kaikan)
都道府県会館
SHUTO EXPWY NO.4
SOTOBORI DŌRI (AVE.)
外堀通り
Benkei-bashi
弁慶橋
首都高速4号線
Towns & Villages Kaikan
全国町村会館
IBM
Liberal-Democratic Party H.Q
自由民主党本部
Maeda Surgery Hosp
前田外科医院
Suntory Bldg
サントリービル
Akasaka-mituke
赤坂見附
NAGATACHŌ 永田町
Moto-Akasaka
元赤坂
Suntory Mus. of Art
サントリー美術館
衆議院議長公邸
Official Residence of the Speaker of the House of Representatives
参議院議長公邸
Official Residence of the President of the House of Councillors
Kajima Bldg
鹿島ビル
AIU Akasaka Bldg
AIU赤坂ビル
Akasaka Tōkyū Hotel
赤坂東急ホテル
Embs of Argentina, Lebanon, Jordan
アルゼンチン、レバノン、ヨルダン大使館
Belle Vie Akasaka
ベルビー赤坂
Akasaka Center Bldg
赤坂センタービル
Fuji Bank
富士
Emb. of Mexico
メキシコ大使館
Members' Office House of Councillors
参議院議員会館
山王グランドビル
Sannō Grand Bldg
Toyokawa Inari
豊川稲荷
AOYAMA DŌRI (AVE.) 青山通り
Akasaka-fudōson
赤坂不動尊
Nagatachō
永田町
Continental Airlines
コンチネンタル航空
Philippine Airlines
フィリピン航空
Hibiya H. Sch.
日比谷高校
HITOTSUGI DŌRI
一ツ木通り
Bldg two Members' Office House of Representatives
衆議院第二議員会館
Toraya
虎屋
246
Akasaka Police Sta.
赤坂署
Sumitomo Seimei Akasaka Bldg
住友生命赤坂ビル
Akasaka Public Hall
赤坂公会堂
Kokusai Sanno Bldg
国際山王ビル
Hie Jinja (shrine)
日枝神社
Bldg one Members' Office House of Representative
衆議院第一議員会館
Jōdo-ji
浄土寺
Yamawaki Gakuen (Sch.)
山脇学園
Capitol Tōkyū Hotel
キャピトル東急ホテル
Sannō Hanten
山王飯店
MINATO-KU
港区
Jōgen-ji
常玄寺
Sanyō Akasaka Bldg
サンヨー赤坂ビル
Sannōshita
山王下
TBS Kaikan
TBS会館
KOKKAI-GIJIDŌMAE
Nippon Colombia
日本コロムビア
Akasaka
赤坂
TBS Hall
TBSホール
星が岡ビル
Hoshigaoka Bldg
Science Bldg
サイエンスビル
Yachiyo Bldg
八千代ビル
TBS
東京放送
Petroleum Communication Center
石油資料館
Prime Minister's Official Residence
首相官邸
Entsu-ji
円通寺
Gadelius Bldg
ガデリウスビル
Minato Shinkin Bank (H.O.)
港信金(本店)
East Bldg 東館
Kokusai Shin Akasaka Bldgs
国際新赤坂ビル
West Bldg 西館
Kokusai Akasaka Bldg
国際赤坂ビル
Tokyo Isuzu Motor
東京いすゞ
Sabena Airlines
サベナ航空
Green Park Akasaka
グリーンパーク赤坂
Nisshō Iwai
日商岩井
Akasaka Shanpia Hotel
赤坂シャンピアホテル
Toshiba EM
東芝EM
GINZA LINE
銀座線
Komatsu Bldg
小松ビル
Tameike
溜池
48

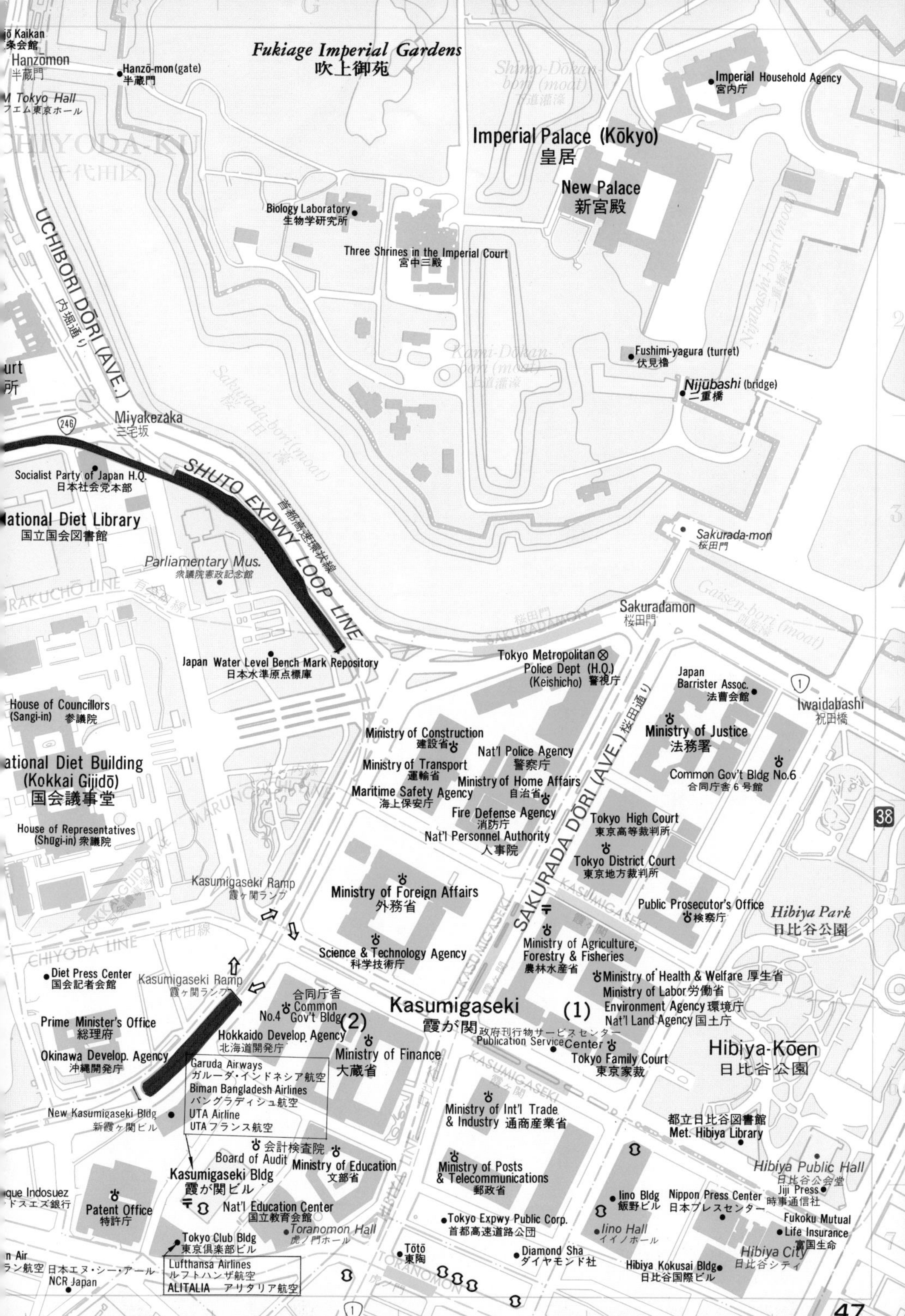

Fukiage Imperial Gardens
吹上御苑
Hanzōmon
半蔵門
Hanzō-mon (gate)
半蔵門
CHIYODA-KU
千代田区
Shimo-Dōkan-bori (moat)
Imperial Household Agency
宮内庁
Imperial Palace (Kōkyo)
皇居
New Palace
新宮殿
Biology Laboratory
生物学研究所
Three Shrines in the Imperial Court
宮中三殿
UCHIBORI DŌRI (AVE.)
内堀通り
Kami-Dōkan-bori (moat)
Nijūbashi-bori (moat)
Fushimi-yagura (turret)
伏見櫓
Nijūbashi (bridge)
二重橋
Sakurada-bori (moat)
Miyakezaka
三宅坂
246
SHUTO EXPWY LOOP LINE
首都高速環状線
Socialist Party of Japan H.Q.
日本社会党本部
National Diet Library
国立国会図書館
Parliamentary Mus.
衆議院憲政記念館
Sakurada-mon
桜田門
YURAKUCHO LINE
Sakuradamon
桜田門
Gaisen-bori (moat)
SAKURADAMON
Japan Water Level Bench Mark Repository
日本水準原点標庫
Tokyo Metropolitan Police Dept (H.Q.) (Keishicho)
警視庁
Japan Barrister Assoc.
法曹会館
Iwaidabashi
祝田橋
House of Councillors (Sangi-in)
参議院
Ministry of Construction
建設省
SAKURADA DŌRI (AVE.)
桜田通り
Ministry of Justice
法務署
Nat'l Police Agency
警察庁
Ministry of Transport
運輸省
Common Gov't Bldg No.6
合同庁舎 6 号館
National Diet Building (Kokkai Gijidō)
国会議事堂
Ministry of Home Affairs
自治省
Maritime Safety Agency
海上保安庁
Fire Defense Agency
消防庁
Tokyo High Court
東京高等裁判所
House of Representatives (Shūgi-in)
衆議院
Nat'l Personnel Authority
人事院
Tokyo District Court
東京地方裁判所
Kasumigaseki Ramp
霞ケ関ランプ
Ministry of Foreign Affairs
外務省
Public Prosecutor's Office
検察庁
Hibiya Park
日比谷公園
CHIYODA LINE
千代田線
Science & Technology Agency
科学技術庁
Ministry of Agriculture, Forestry & Fisheries
農林水産省
Diet Press Center
国会記者会館
Kasumigaseki Ramp
霞ケ関ランプ
Ministry of Health & Welfare 厚生省
Ministry of Labor 労働省
Environment Agency 環境庁
Nat'l Land Agency 国土庁
合同庁舎
No.4 Common Gov't Bldg
(2)
Kasumigaseki
霞が関
(1)
Prime Minister's Office
総理府
Hokkaido Develop. Agency
北海道開発庁
政府刊行物サービスセンター
Publication Service Center
Ministry of Finance
大蔵省
Tokyo Family Court
東京家裁
Hibiya-Kōen
日比谷公園
Okinawa Develop. Agency
沖縄開発庁
Garuda Airways
ガルーダ・インドネシア航空
Biman Bangladesh Airlines
バングラディシュ航空
UTA Airline
UTAフランス航空
KASUMIGASEKI
New Kasumigaseki Bldg
新霞ケ関ビル
Ministry of Int'l Trade & Industry 通商産業省
都立日比谷図書館
Met. Hibiya Library
会計検査院
Board of Audit
Ministry of Education
文部省
Ministry of Posts & Telecommunications
郵政省
Hibiya Public Hall
日比谷公会堂
Kasumigaseki Bldg
霞が関ビル
Jiji Press
時事通信社
Patent Office
特許庁
Nat'l Education Center
国立教育会館
Iino Bldg
飯野ビル
Nippon Press Center
日本プレスセンター
HIBIYA LINE
Tokyo Expwy Public Corp.
首都高速道路公団
Fukoku Mutual Life Insurance
富国生命
Tokyo Club Bldg
東京倶楽部ビル
Toranomon Hall
虎ノ門ホール
Iino Hall
イイノホール
Tōtō
東陶
Diamond Sha
ダイヤモンド社
Hibiya City
日比谷シティ
Hibiya Kokusai Bldg
日比谷国際ビル
日本エヌ・シー・アール
NCR Japan
Lufthansa Airlines
ルフトハンザ航空
ALITALIA アリタリア航空
TORANOMON
虎ノ門
38

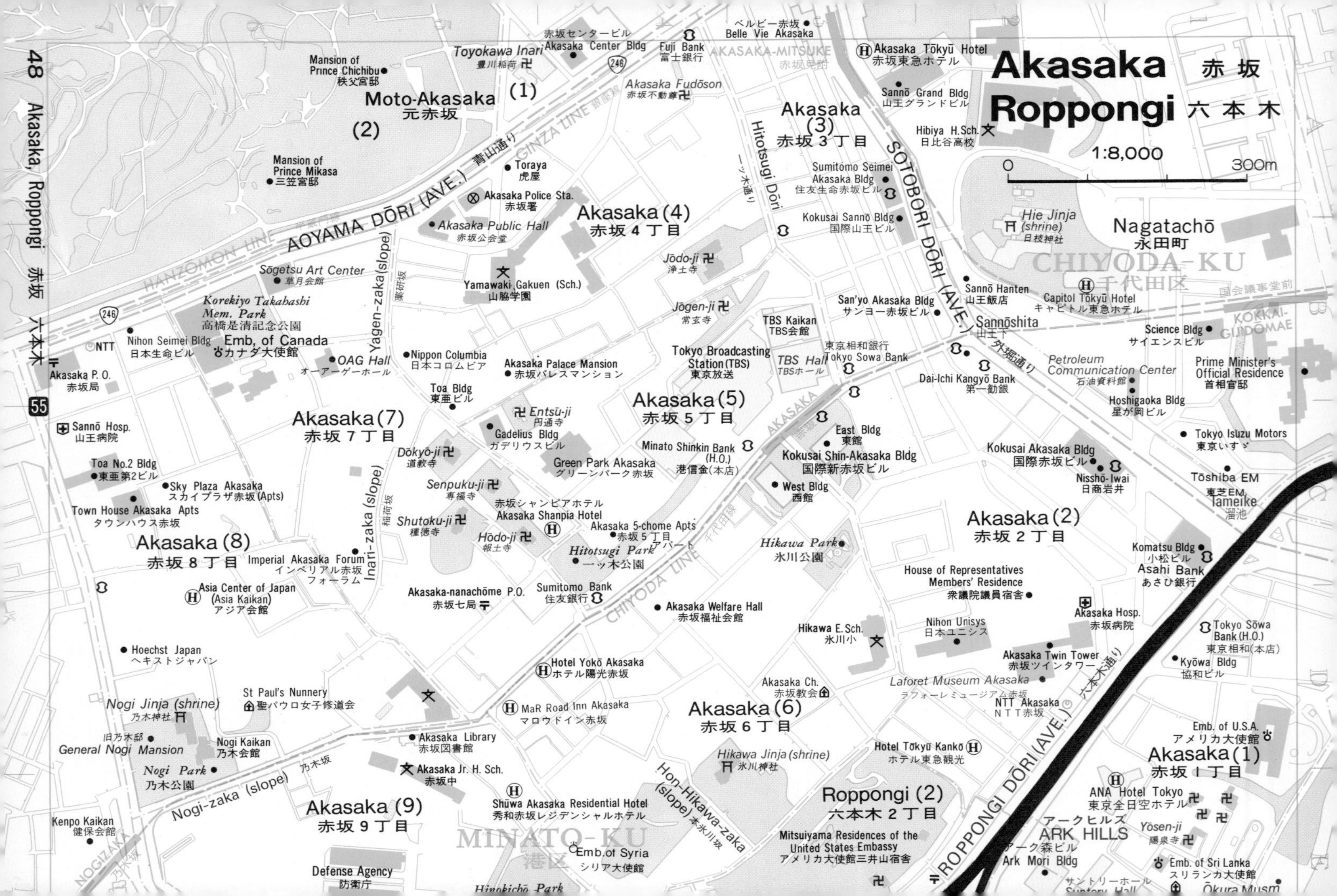

Akasaka 赤坂
Roppongi 六本木
1:8,000
0
300m
Nagatachō
永田町
CHIYODA-KU
千代田区
Hie Jinja (shrine)
日枝神社
Akasaka Tōkyū Hotel
赤坂東急ホテル
Sannō Grand Bldg
山王グランドビル
Hibiya H.Sch.
日比谷高校
Akasaka (3)
赤坂3丁目
SOTOBORI DŌRI (AVE.)
外堀通り
Sumitomo Seimei Akasaka Bldg
住友生命赤坂ビル
Kokusai Sannō Bldg
国際山王ビル
Hitotsugi Dōri
一ッ木通り
Belle Vie Akasaka
ベルビー赤坂
AKASAKA-MITSUKE
赤坂見附
Fuji Bank
富士銀行
Akasaka Center Bldg
赤坂センタービル
Toyokawa Inari
豊川稲荷
Akasaka Fudōson
赤坂不動尊
Moto-Akasaka
元赤坂
(1)
(2)
Mansion of Prince Chichibu
秩父宮邸
Mansion of Prince Mikasa
三笠宮邸
AOYAMA DŌRI (AVE.)
青山通り
GINZA LINE
HANZOMON LINE
Toraya
虎屋
Akasaka Police Sta.
赤坂署
Akasaka Public Hall
赤坂公会堂
Akasaka (4)
赤坂4丁目
Yamawaki Gakuen (Sch.)
山脇学園
Sōgetsu Art Center
草月会館
Korekiyo Takahashi Mem. Park
高橋是清記念公園
Emb. of Canada
カナダ大使館
Nihon Seimei Bldg
日本生命ビル
NTT
Akasaka P. O.
赤坂局
55
OAG Hall
オーアーゲーホール
Yagen-zaka (slope)
薬研坂
Nippon Columbia
日本コロムビア
Akasaka Palace Mansion
赤坂パレスマンション
Toa Bldg
東亜ビル
Jōdo-ji
浄土寺
Jōgen-ji
常玄寺
TBS Kaikan
TBS会館
Tokyo Broadcasting Station (TBS)
東京放送
TBS Hall
TBSホール
東京相和銀行
Tokyo Sowa Bank
San'yo Akasaka Bldg
サンヨー赤坂ビル
Sannō Hanten
山王飯店
Capitol Tōkyū Hotel
キャピトル東急ホテル
Sannōshita
山王下
Science Bldg
サイエンスビル
KOKKAI-GIJIDŌMAE
国会議事堂前
Petroleum Communication Center
石油資料館
Prime Minister's Official Residence
首相官邸
Hoshigaoka Bldg
星が岡ビル
Dai-Ichi Kangyō Bank
第一勧銀
Tokyo Isuzu Motors
東京いすゞ
Tōshiba EM
東芝EM
Tameike
溜池
Kokusai Akasaka Bldg
国際赤坂ビル
Nisshō-Iwai
日商岩井
Akasaka (5)
赤坂5丁目
AKASAKA
East Bldg
東館
Kokusai Shin-Akasaka Bldg
国際新赤坂ビル
West Bldg
西館
Minato Shinkin Bank (H.O.)
港信金(本店)
Entsū-ji
円通寺
Gadelius Bldg
ガデリウスビル
Green Park Akasaka
グリーンパーク赤坂
Akasaka (7)
赤坂7丁目
Dōkyō-ji
道教寺
Senpuku-ji
専福寺
Shutoku-ji
種徳寺
Hōdo-ji
報土寺
赤坂シャンピアホテル
Akasaka Shanpia Hotel
Akasaka 5-chome Apts
赤坂5丁目アパート
Hitotsugi Park
一ッ木公園
Inari-zaka (slope)
稲荷坂
Imperial Akasaka Forum
インペリアル赤坂フォーラム
Akasaka-nanachōme P.O.
赤坂七局
Sumitomo Bank
住友銀行
CHIYODA LINE
Akasaka Welfare Hall
赤坂福祉会館
Hikawa Park
氷川公園
Akasaka (2)
赤坂2丁目
Komatsu Bldg
小松ビル
Asahi Bank
あさひ銀行
House of Representatives Members' Residence
衆議院議員宿舎
Akasaka Hosp.
赤坂病院
Nihon Unisys
日本ユニシス
Hikawa E.Sch.
氷川小
Akasaka Twin Tower
赤坂ツインタワー
Tokyo Sōwa Bank (H.O.)
東京相和(本店)
Kyōwa Bldg
協和ビル
六本木通り
Laforet Museum Akasaka
ラフォーレミュージアム赤坂
NTT Akasaka
NTT赤坂
Akasaka Ch.
赤坂教会
Akasaka (6)
赤坂6丁目
Toa No.2 Bldg
東亜第2ビル
Sky Plaza Akasaka
スカイプラザ赤坂(Apts)
Town House Akasaka Apts
タウンハウス赤坂
Sannō Hosp.
山王病院
Akasaka (8)
赤坂8丁目
Asia Center of Japan (Asia Kaikan)
アジア会館
Hoechst Japan
ヘキストジャパン
Hotel Yokō Akasaka
ホテル陽光赤坂
St Paul's Nunnery
聖パウロ女子修道会
MaR Road Inn Akasaka
マロウドイン赤坂
Nogi Jinja (shrine)
乃木神社
旧乃木邸
General Nogi Mansion
Nogi Kaikan
乃木会館
Nogi Park
乃木公園
Akasaka Library
赤坂図書館
Akasaka Jr. H. Sch.
赤坂中
Nogi-zaka (slope)
乃木坂
Akasaka (9)
赤坂9丁目
Kenpo Kaikan
健保会館
NOGIZAKA
Defense Agency
防衛庁
MINATO-KU
港区
Emb. of Syria
シリア大使館
Shūwa Akasaka Residential Hotel
秀和赤坂レジデンシャルホテル
Hon-Hikawa-zaka (slope)
本氷川坂
Hikawa Jinja (shrine)
氷川神社
Hotel Tōkyū Kankō
ホテル東急観光
Roppongi (2)
六本木2丁目
Mitsuiyama Residences of the United States Embassy
アメリカ大使館三井山宿舎
ROPPONGI DŌRI (AVE.)
アークヒルズ
ARK HILLS
アーク森ビル
Ark Mori Bldg
Emb. of U.S.A.
アメリカ大使館
Akasaka (1)
赤坂1丁目
ANA Hotel Tokyo
東京全日空ホテル
Yōsen-ji
陽泉寺
Emb. of Sri Lanka
スリランカ大使館
サントリーホール
Ōkura Musm
Hinokichō Park

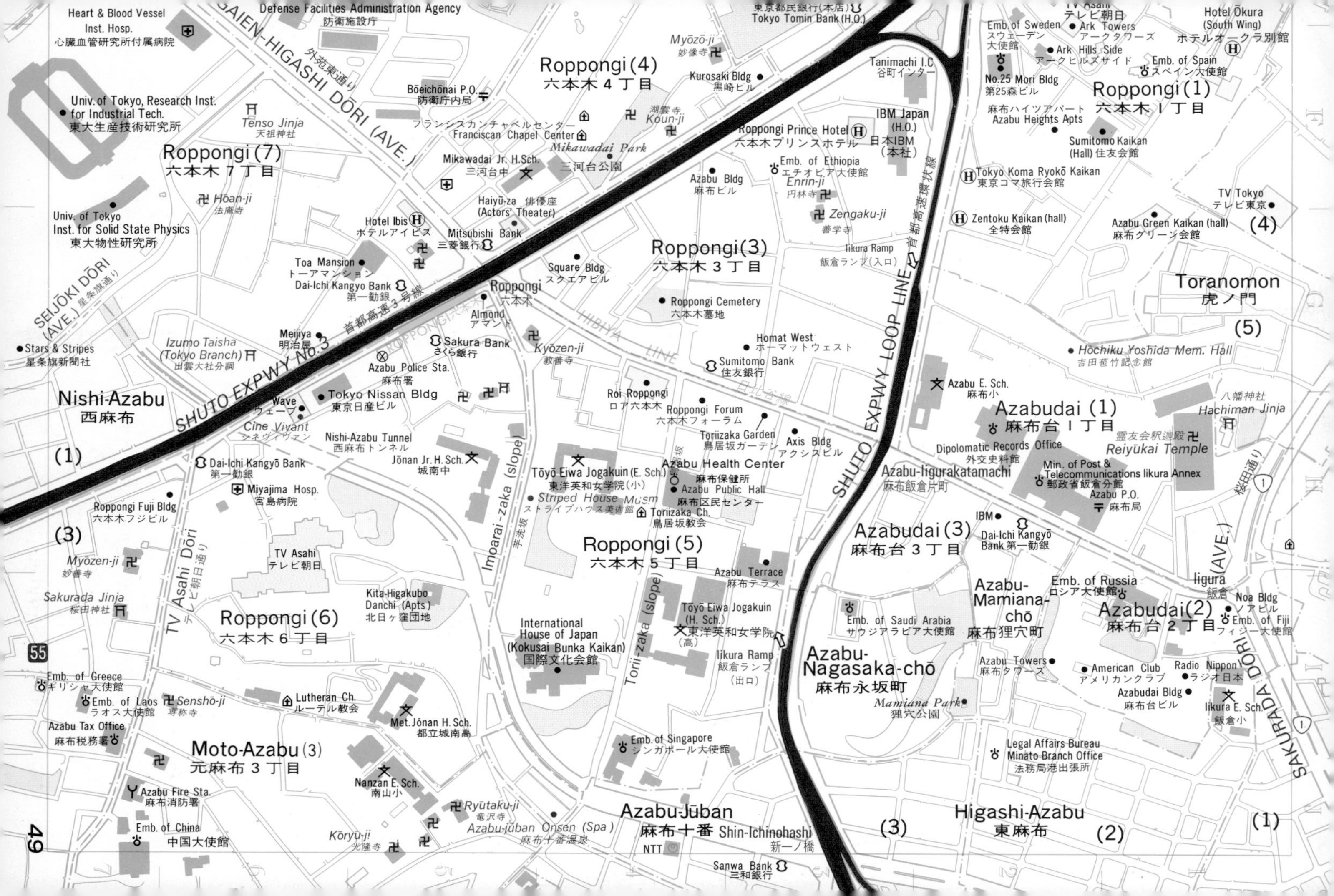
Heart & Blood Vessel Inst. Hosp.
心臓血管研究所付属病院
Defense Facilities Administration Agency
防衛施設庁
GAIEN-HIGASHI DŌRI (AVE.)
外苑東通り
Univ. of Tokyo, Research Inst. for Industrial Tech.
東大生産技術研究所
Tenso Jinja
天祖神社
Roppongi (7)
六本木 7 丁目
Hōan-ji
法庵寺
Univ. of Tokyo Inst. for Solid State Physics
東大物性研究所
SEIJŌKI DŌRI (AVE.)
星条旗通り
Stars & Stripes
星条旗新聞社
Izumo Taisha (Tokyo Branch)
出雲大社分祠
Nishi-Azabu
西麻布
(1)
(3)
Roppongi Fuji Bldg
六本木フジビル
Myozen-ji
妙善寺
Sakurada Jinja
桜田神社
TV Asahi Dōri
テレビ朝日通り
55
Emb. of Greece
ギリシャ大使館
Emb. of Laos
ラオス大使館
Azabu Tax Office
麻布税務署
Azabu Fire Sta.
麻布消防署
Emb. of China
中国大使館
49
Bōeichōnai P.O.
防衛庁内局
フランシスカンチャペルセンター
Franciscan Chapel Center
Mikawadai Jr. H.Sch.
三河台中
Hotel Ibis
ホテルアイビス
Mitsubishi Bank
三菱銀行
Haiyū-za (Actors' Theater)
俳優座
Toa Mansion
トーアマンション
Dai-Ichi Kangyo Bank
第一勧銀
首都高速3号線
SHUTO EXPWY No.3
Meijiya
明治屋
Wave
ウェーブ
Cine Vivant
シネヴィヴァン
Tokyo Nissan Bldg
東京日産ビル
Azabu Police Sta.
麻布署
Sakura Bank
さくら銀行
Almond
アマンド
Roppongi
六本木
Dai-Ichi Kangyō Bank
第一勧銀
Miyajima Hosp.
宮島病院
Nishi-Azabu Tunnel
西麻布トンネル
Jōnan Jr. H. Sch.
城南中
TV Asahi
テレビ朝日
Roppongi (6)
六本木 6 丁目
Kita-Higakubo Danchi (Apts)
北日ヶ窪団地
Lutheran Ch.
ルーテル教会
Met. Jōnan H. Sch.
都立城南高
Moto-Azabu (3)
元麻布 3 丁目
Nanzan E. Sch.
南山小
Ryūtaku-ji
竜沢寺
Kōryū-ji
光隆寺
Azabu-jūban Onsen (Spa)
麻布十番温泉
Roppongi (4)
六本木 4 丁目
Myōzō-ji
妙像寺
Kurosaki Bldg
黒崎ビル
Koun-ji
湖雲寺
Mikawadai Park
三河台公園
Square Bldg
スクエアビル
Kyōzen-ji
教善寺
HIBIYA LINE
日比谷線
ROPPONGI
六本木通り
Imoarai-zaka (slope)
芋洗坂
Tōyō Eiwa Jogakuin (E. Sch.)
東洋英和女学院(小)
Striped House Musm
ストライプハウス美術館
International House of Japan (Kokusai Bunka Kaikan)
国際文化会館
Roppongi (3)
六本木 3 丁目
Roppongi Cemetery
六本木墓地
Homat West
ホーマットウェスト
Sumitomo Bank
住友銀行
Roi Roppongi
ロア六本木
Roppongi Forum
六本木フォーラム
Toriizaka Garden
鳥居坂ガーデン
Axis Bldg
アクシスビル
鳥居坂
Azabu Health Center
麻布保健所
Azabu Public Hall
麻布区民センター
Toriizaka Ch.
鳥居坂教会
Roppongi (5)
六本木 5 丁目
Azabu Terrace
麻布テラス
Torii-zaka (slope)
Tōyō Eiwa Jogakuin (H. Sch.)
東洋英和女学院(高)
Iikura Ramp
飯倉ランプ(出口)
Emb. of Singapore
シンガポール大使館
Azabu-Jūban
麻布十番
Shin-Ichinohashi
新一ノ橋
NTT
Sanwa Bank
三和銀行
東京都民銀行(本店)
Tokyo Tomin Bank (H.O.)
Tanimachi I.C
谷町インター
Roppongi Prince Hotel
六本木プリンスホテル
IBM Japan (H.O.)
日本IBM (本社)
Emb. of Ethiopia
エチオピア大使館
Enrin-ji
円林寺
Azabu Bldg
麻布ビル
Zengaku-ji
善学寺
Iikura Ramp
飯倉ランプ(入口)
首都高速環状線
SHUTO EXPWY LOOP LINE
Azabu E. Sch.
麻布小
Azabu-Iigurakatamachi
麻布飯倉片町
Azabudai (3)
麻布台 3 丁目
Azabu-Nagasaka-chō
麻布永坂町
Emb. of Saudi Arabia
サウジアラビア大使館
Mamiana Park
狸穴公園
(3)
TV Asahi
テレビ朝日
Emb. of Sweden
スウェーデン大使館
Ark Towers
アークタワーズ
Ark Hills Side
アークヒルズサイド
No.25 Mori Bldg
第25森ビル
Hotel Ōkura (South Wing)
ホテルオークラ別館
Emb. of Spain
スペイン大使館
Roppongi (1)
六本木 1 丁目
麻布ハイツアパート
Azabu Heights Apts
Sumitomo Kaikan (Hall)
住友会館
Tokyo Koma Ryokō Kaikan
東京コマ旅行会館
Zentoku Kaikan (hall)
全特会館
TV Tokyo
テレビ東京
Azabu Green Kaikan (hall)
麻布グリーン会館
(4)
Toranomon
虎ノ門
(5)
Hochiku Yoshida Mem. Hall
吉田苞竹記念館
八幡神社
Hachiman Jinja
Azabudai (1)
麻布台 1 丁目
霊友会釈迦殿
Reiyūkai Temple
Dipolomatic Records Office
外交史料館
Min. of Post & Telecommunications Iikura Annex
郵政省飯倉分館
Azabu P.O.
麻布局
桜田通り
IBM
Dai-Ichi Kangyō Bank
第一勧銀
Azabu-Mamiana-chō
麻布狸穴町
Emb. of Russia
ロシア大使館
Iigura
飯倉
(AVE.)
Azabudai (2)
麻布台 2 丁目
Noa Bldg
ノアビル
Emb. of Fiji
フィジー大使館
Azabu Towers
麻布タワーズ
American Club
アメリカンクラブ
Radio Nippon
ラジオ日本
Azabudai Bldg
麻布台ビル
Iikura E. Sch.
飯倉小
SAKURADA DŌRI
Legal Affairs Bureau Minato Branch Office
法務局港出張所
Higashi-Azabu
東麻布
(2)
(1)

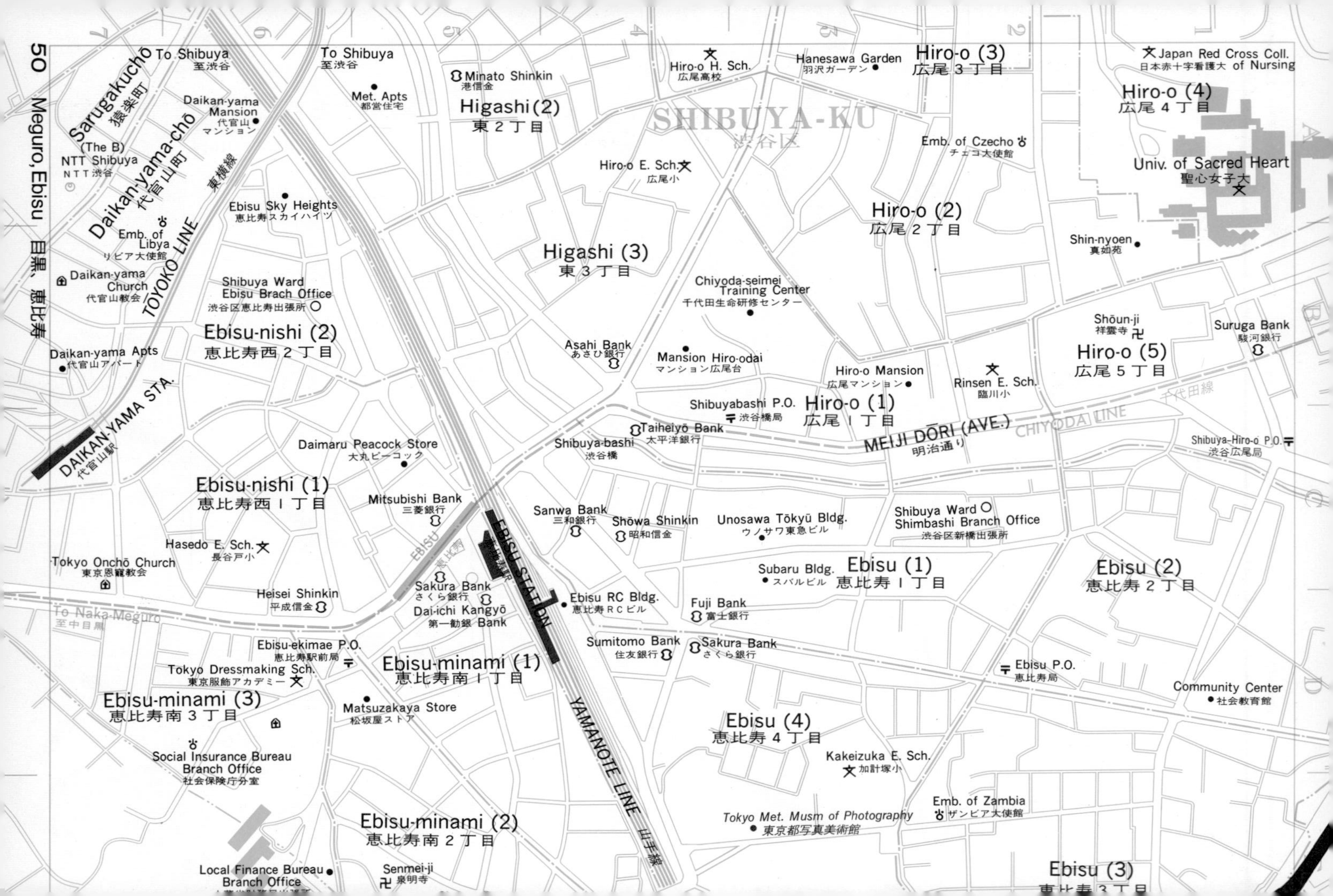

Sarugakuchō
猿楽町
To Shibuya
至渋谷
To Shibuya
至渋谷
Minato Shinkin
港信金
Met. Apts
都営住宅
Higashi (2)
東2丁目
Hiro-o H. Sch.
広尾高校
Hanesawa Garden
羽沢ガーデン
Hiro-o (3)
広尾3丁目
Japan Red Cross Coll. of Nursing
日本赤十字看護大
Hiro-o (4)
広尾4丁目
SHIBUYA-KU
渋谷区
Daikan-yama Mansion
代官山マンション
(The B)
NTT Shibuya
NTT渋谷
Daikan-yama-chō
代官山町
東横線
Emb. of Czecho
チェコ大使館
Univ. of Sacred Heart
聖心女子大
Hiro-o E. Sch.
広尾小
Ebisu Sky Heights
恵比寿スカイハイツ
Emb. of Libya
リビア大使館
TOYOKO LINE
Hiro-o (2)
広尾2丁目
Shin-nyoen
真如苑
Higashi (3)
東3丁目
Daikan-yama Church
代官山教会
Shibuya Ward Ebisu Brach Office
渋谷区恵比寿出張所
Chiyoda-seimei Training Center
千代田生命研修センター
Ebisu-nishi (2)
恵比寿西2丁目
Shōun-ji
祥雲寺
Suruga Bank
駿河銀行
Hiro-o (5)
広尾5丁目
Daikan-yama Apts
代官山アパート
Asahi Bank
あさひ銀行
Mansion Hiro-odai
マンション広尾台
Hiro-o Mansion
広尾マンション
Rinsen E. Sch.
臨川小
千代田線
DAIKAN-YAMA STA.
代官山駅
Shibuyabashi P.O.
渋谷橋局
Hiro-o (1)
広尾1丁目
CHIYODA LINE
Taiheiyō Bank
太平洋銀行
Shibuya-bashi
渋谷橋
MEIJI DŌRI (AVE.)
明治通り
Shibuya-Hiro-o P.O.
渋谷広尾局
Daimaru Peacock Store
大丸ピーコック
Ebisu-nishi (1)
恵比寿西1丁目
Mitsubishi Bank
三菱銀行
Sanwa Bank
三和銀行
Shōwa Shinkin
昭和信金
Unosawa Tōkyū Bldg.
ウノサワ東急ビル
Shibuya Ward Shimbashi Branch Office
渋谷区新橋出張所
Hasedo E. Sch.
長谷戸小
EBISU STATION
恵比寿駅
Tokyo Onchō Church
東京恩寵教会
Subaru Bldg.
スバルビル
Ebisu (1)
恵比寿1丁目
Ebisu (2)
恵比寿2丁目
Sakura Bank
さくら銀行
Ebisu RC Bldg.
恵比寿RCビル
Heisei Shinkin
平成信金
Dai-ichi Kangyō Bank
第一勧銀
Fuji Bank
富士銀行
To Naka-Meguro
至中目黒
Ebisu-ekimae P.O.
恵比寿駅前局
Sumitomo Bank
住友銀行
Sakura Bank
さくら銀行
Tokyo Dressmaking Sch.
東京服飾アカデミー
Ebisu-minami (1)
恵比寿南1丁目
Ebisu P.O.
恵比寿局
Community Center
社会教育館
Ebisu-minami (3)
恵比寿南3丁目
Matsuzakaya Store
松坂屋ストア
Ebisu (4)
恵比寿4丁目
YAMANOTE LINE
山手線
Social Insurance Bureau Branch Office
社会保険庁分室
Kakeizuka E. Sch.
加計塚小
Emb. of Zambia
ザンビア大使館
Tokyo Met. Musm of Photography
東京都写真美術館
Ebisu-minami (2)
恵比寿南2丁目
Local Finance Bureau Branch Office
Senmei-ji
泉明寺
Ebisu (3)

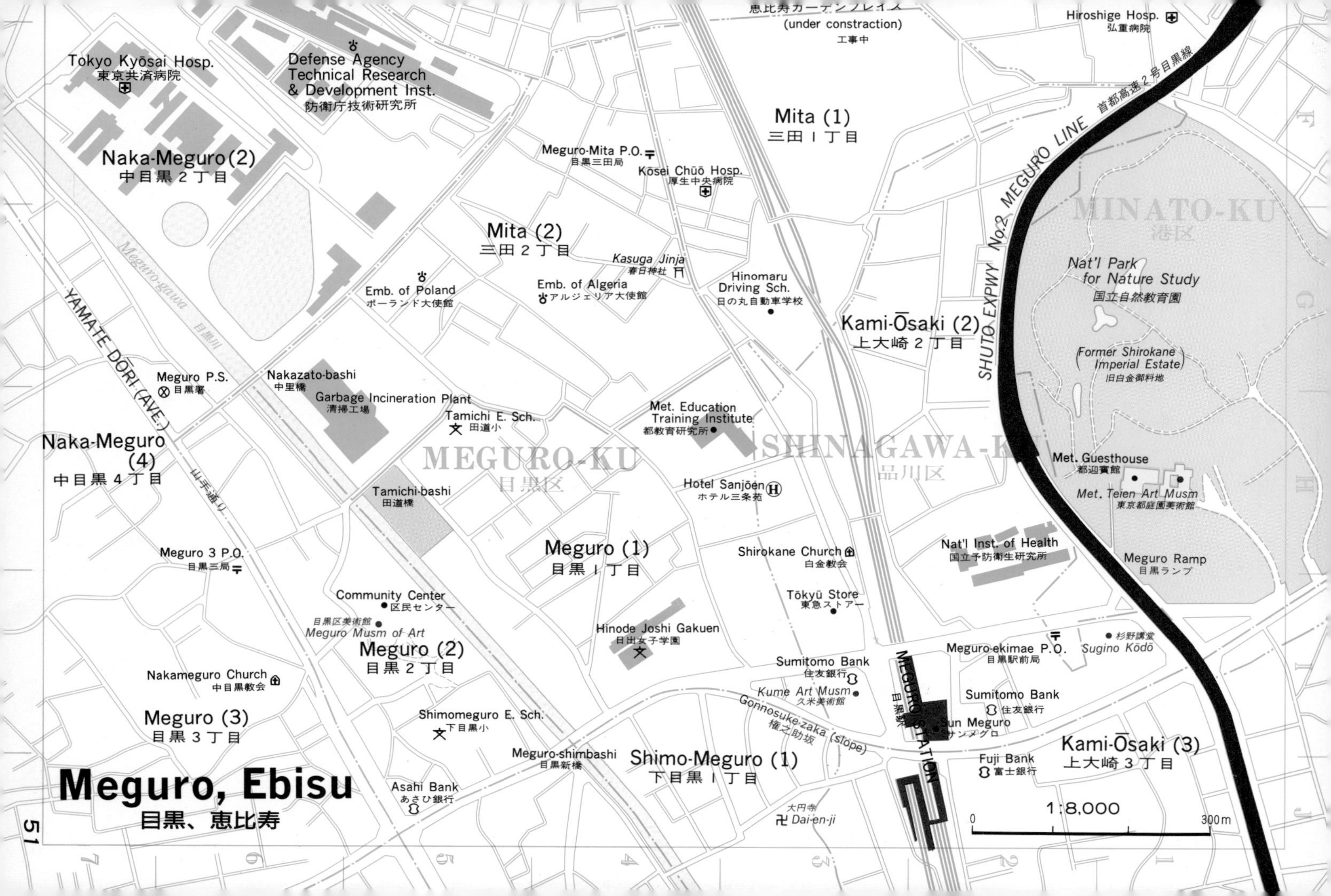
Meguro, Ebisu
目黒、恵比寿
Tokyo Kyōsai Hosp.
東京共済病院
Defense Agency
Technical Research
& Development Inst.
防衛庁技術研究所
Naka-Meguro(2)
中目黒２丁目
(under constraction)
工事中
Hiroshige Hosp.
弘重病院
Mita (1)
三田１丁目
Meguro-Mita P.O.
目黒三田局
Kōsei Chūō Hosp.
厚生中央病院
首都高速２号目黒線
SHUTO EXPWY No.2 MEGURO LINE
MINATO-KU
港区
Nat'l Park
for Nature Study
国立自然教育園
Mita (2)
三田２丁目
Kasuga Jinja
春日神社
Emb. of Algeria
アルジェリア大使館
Emb. of Poland
ポーランド大使館
Hinomaru
Driving Sch.
日の丸自動車学校
Kami-Ōsaki (2)
上大崎２丁目
Former Shirokane
Imperial Estate
旧白金御料地
Meguro-gawa
目黒川
YAMATE DŌRI (AVE.)
山手通り
Meguro P.S.
目黒署
Nakazato-bashi
中里橋
Garbage Incineration Plant
清掃工場
Tamichi E. Sch.
田道小
Met. Education
Training Institute
都教育研究所
Naka-Meguro
(4)
中目黒４丁目
MEGURO-KU
目黒区
SHINAGAWA-KU
品川区
Met. Guesthouse
都迎賓館
Met. Teien Art Musm
東京都庭園美術館
Tamichi-bashi
田道橋
Hotel Sanjōen
ホテル三条苑
Meguro 3 P.O.
目黒三局
Meguro (1)
目黒１丁目
Shirokane Church
白金教会
Nat'l Inst. of Health
国立予防衛生研究所
Meguro Ramp
目黒ランプ
Community Center
区民センター
Tōkyū Store
東急ストアー
目黒区美術館
Meguro Musm of Art
Meguro (2)
目黒２丁目
Hinode Joshi Gakuen
日出女子学園
Sumitomo Bank
住友銀行
Meguro-ekimae P.O.
目黒駅前局
杉野講堂
Sugino Kōdō
Nakameguro Church
中目黒教会
Kume Art Musm
久米美術館
MEGURO STATION
目黒駅
Sumitomo Bank
住友銀行
Gonnosuke-zaka (slope)
権之助坂
Sun Meguro
サンメグロ
Meguro (3)
目黒３丁目
Shimomeguro E. Sch.
下目黒小
Meguro-shimbashi
目黒新橋
Shimo-Meguro (1)
下目黒１丁目
Kami-Ōsaki (3)
上大崎３丁目
Fuji Bank
富士銀行
Asahi Bank
あさひ銀行
大円寺
Dai-en-ji
1:8,000
0
300m

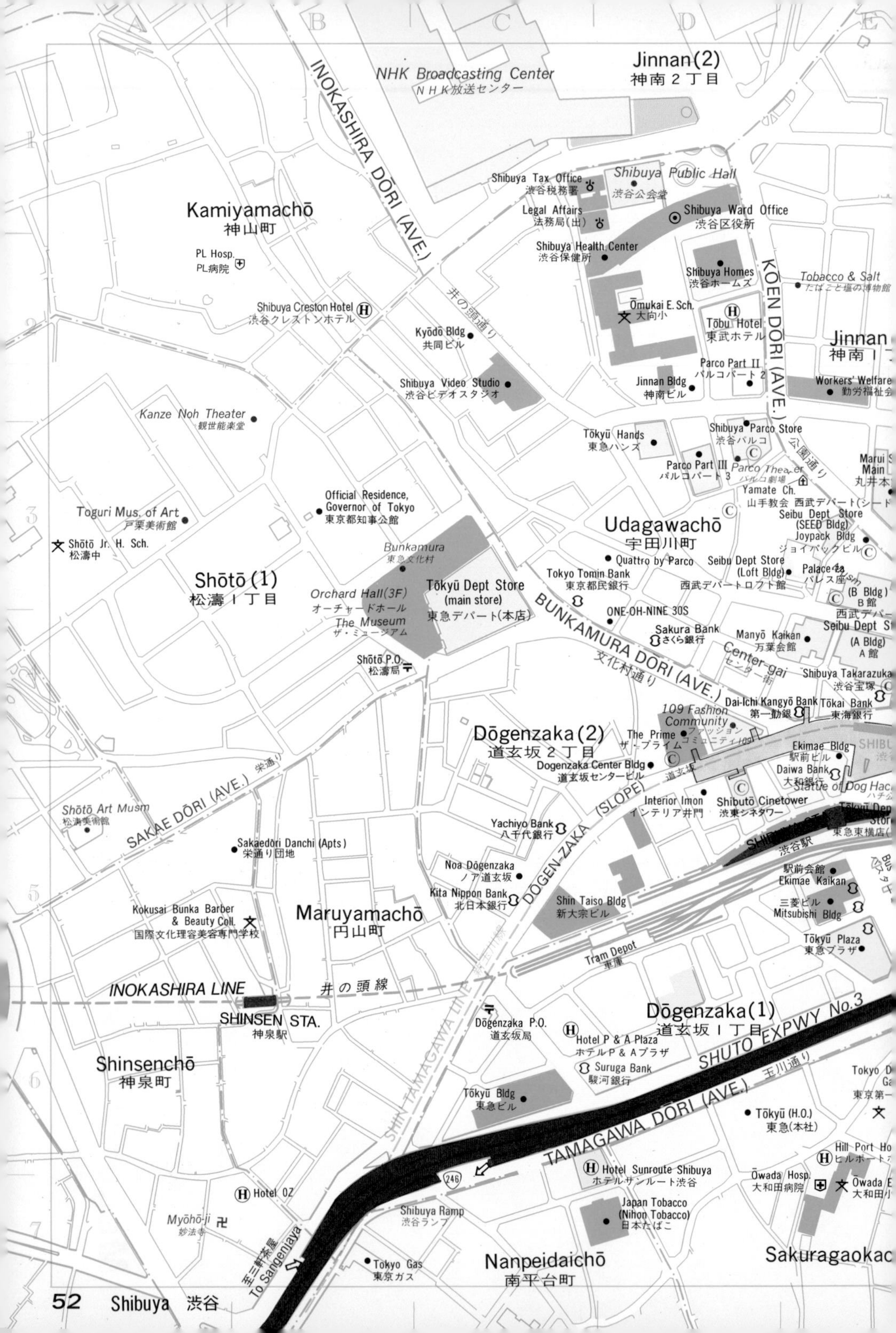
A
B
C
D
E
1
2
3
5
6
7
NHK Broadcasting Center
ＮＨＫ放送センター
Jinnan(2)
神南２丁目
INOKASHIRA DŌRI (AVE.)
Kamiyamachō
神山町
PL Hosp.
PL病院
Shibuya Tax Office
渋谷税務署
Shibuya Public Hall
渋谷公会堂
Legal Affairs
法務局(出)
Shibuya Ward Office
渋谷区役所
Shibuya Health Center
渋谷保健所
Shibuya Homes
渋谷ホームズ
KŌEN DŌRI (AVE.)
Tobacco & Salt
たばこと塩の博物館
Shibuya Creston Hotel
渋谷クレストンホテル
Ōmukai E. Sch.
大向小
Tōbu Hotel
東武ホテル
Jinnan
神南
井の頭通り
Kyōdō Bldg
共同ビル
Parco Part II
パルコパート２
Shibuya Video Studio
渋谷ビデオスタジオ
Jinnan Bldg
神南ビル
Workers' Welfare
勤労福祉会
Kanze Noh Theater
観世能楽堂
Tōkyū Hands
東急ハンズ
Shibuya Parco Store
渋谷パルコ
公園通り
Parco Part III
パルコパート３
Parco Theater
パルコ劇場
Marui
Main
丸井本
Yamate Ch.
山手教会
西武デパート(シード
Seibu Dept Store
(SEED Bldg)
Official Residence,
Governor of Tokyo
東京都知事公館
Toguri Mus. of Art
戸栗美術館
Shōtō Jr. H. Sch.
松濤中
Udagawachō
宇田川町
Joypack Bldg
ジョイパックビル
Bunkamura
東急文化村
Quattro by Parco
Seibu Dept Store
(Loft Bldg)
西武デパートロフト館
Palace Musm
パレス座
Shōtō (1)
松濤１丁目
Orchard Hall(3F)
オーチャードホール
The Museum
ザ・ミュージアム
Tōkyū Dept Store
(main store)
東急デパート(本店)
Tokyo Tomin Bank
東京都民銀行
(B Bldg)
B館
BUNKAMURA DŌRI (AVE.)
ONE-OH-NINE 30S
西武デパ
Seibu Dept St
(A Bldg)
A館
Sakura Bank
さくら銀行
Manyō Kaikan
万葉会館
Shōtō P.O.
松濤局
文化村通り
Center-gai
センター街
Shibuya Takarazuka
渋谷宝塚
Dai-Ichi Kangyō Bank
第一勧銀
Tōkai Bank
東海銀行
109 Fashion Community
ファッションコミュニティ109
Dōgenzaka (2)
道玄坂２丁目
The Prime
ザ・プライム
Ekimae Bldg
駅前ビル
SHIBU
Dogenzaka Center Bldg
道玄坂センタービル
道玄坂
Daiwa Bank
大和銀行
Statue of Dog Hac
ハチ公
栄通り
SAKAE DŌRI (AVE.)
DŌGEN-ZAKA (SLOPE)
Interior Imon
インテリア井門
Shibutō Cinetower
渋東シネタワー
Tōkyū Dept
Store
東急東横店
Shōtō Art Musm
松濤美術館
Yachiyo Bank
八千代銀行
渋谷駅
Sakaedōri Danchi (Apts)
栄通り団地
Noa Dōgenzaka
ノア道玄坂
駅前会館
Ekimae Kaikan
Kita Nippon Bank
北日本銀行
Shin Taiso Bldg
新大宗ビル
三菱ビル
Mitsubishi Bldg
Kokusai Bunka Barber
& Beauty Coll.
国際文化理容美容専門学校
Maruyamachō
円山町
Tōkyū Plaza
東急プラザ
Tram Depot
車庫
INOKASHIRA LINE
井の頭線
SHINSEN STA.
神泉駅
Dōgenzaka P.O.
道玄坂局
Dōgenzaka(1)
道玄坂１丁目
SHUTO EXPWY No.3
Hotel P & A Plaza
ホテルＰ＆Ａプラザ
Shinsenchō
神泉町
Suruga Bank
駿河銀行
玉川通り
SHIN TAMAGAWA LINE
新玉川線
Tōkyū Bldg
東急ビル
TAMAGAWA DŌRI (AVE.)
Tōkyū (H.O.)
東急(本社)
Tokyo
東京第一
Hotel Sunroute Shibuya
ホテルサンルート渋谷
246
Hill Port Ho
ヒルポート
Hotel OZ
Ōwada Hosp.
大和田病院
Ōwada E
大和田小
Myōhō-ji
妙法寺
Shibuya Ramp
渋谷ランプ
Japan Tobacco
(Nihon Tobacco)
日本たばこ
三軒茶屋へ
To Sangenjaya
Tokyo Gas
東京ガス
Nanpeidaichō
南平台町
Sakuragaokac

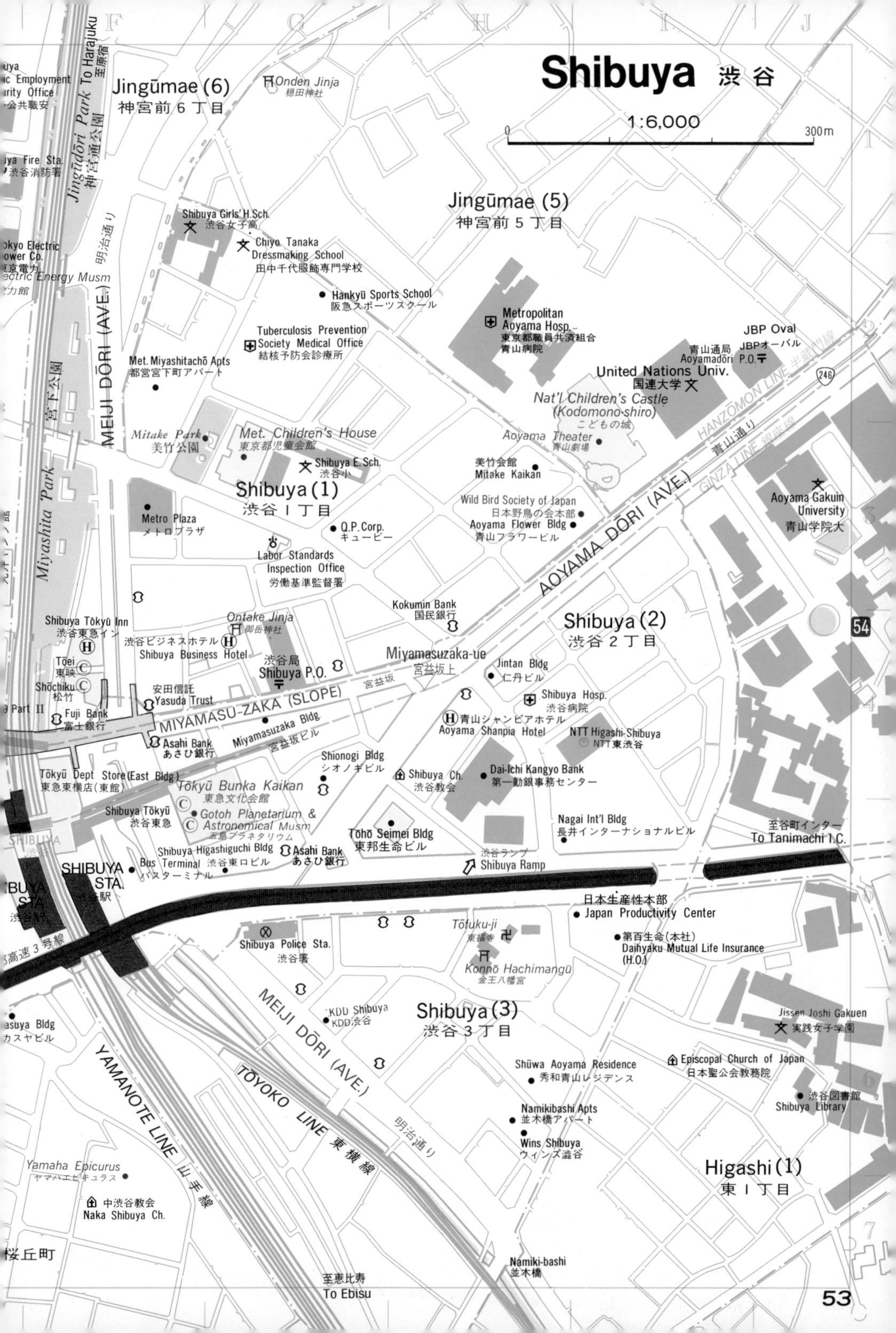
Shibuya 渋谷
1:6,000
0
300m
Jingūmae (6)
神宮前6丁目
Onden Jinja
穏田神社
Jingūmae (5)
神宮前5丁目
To Harajuku
至原宿
Jingūdōri Park
神宮通公園
明治通り
MEIJI DŌRI (AVE.)
Miyashita Park
宮下公園
Shibuya Girls' H.Sch.
渋谷女子高
Chiyo Tanaka Dressmaking School
田中千代服飾専門学校
Hankyū Sports School
阪急スポーツスクール
Metropolitan Aoyama Hosp.
東京都職員共済組合青山病院
Tuberculosis Prevention Society Medical Office
結核予防会診療所
Met. Miyashitachō Apts
都営宮下町アパート
JBP Oval
JBPオーバル
青山通局
Aoyamadōri P.O.
United Nations Univ.
国連大学
Nat'l Children's Castle
(Kodomono-shiro)
こどもの城
Aoyama Theater
青山劇場
HANZŌMON LINE 半蔵門線
GINZA LINE 銀座線
青山通り
246
Mitake Park
美竹公園
Met. Children's House
東京都児童会館
Shibuya E. Sch.
渋谷小
美竹会館
Mitake Kaikan
Shibuya (1)
渋谷1丁目
Metro Plaza
メトロプラザ
Q.P. Corp.
キューピー
Wild Bird Society of Japan
日本野鳥の会本部
Aoyama Flower Bldg
青山フラワービル
Aoyama Gakuin University
青山学院大
Labor Standards Inspection Office
労働基準監督署
AOYAMA DŌRI (AVE.)
Kokumin Bank
国民銀行
Shibuya (2)
渋谷2丁目
54
Shibuya Tōkyū Inn
渋谷東急イン
Ontake Jinja
御岳神社
渋谷ビジネスホテル
Shibuya Business Hotel
渋谷局
Shibuya P.O.
Miyamasuzaka-ue
宮益坂上
Jintan Bldg
仁丹ビル
Toei
東映
Shōchiku
松竹
安田信託
Yasuda Trust
宮益坂
MIYAMASU-ZAKA (SLOPE)
Shibuya Hosp.
渋谷病院
Fuji Bank
富士銀行
Miyamasuzaka Bldg
宮益坂ビル
青山シャンピアホテル
Aoyama Shanpia Hotel
NTT Higashi-Shibuya
NTT東渋谷
Asahi Bank
あさひ銀行
Shionogi Bldg
シオノギビル
Shibuya Ch.
渋谷教会
Dai-Ichi Kangyo Bank
第一勧銀事務センター
Tōkyū Dept Store (East Bldg)
東急東横店(東館)
Tōkyū Bunka Kaikan
東急文化会館
Shibuya Tōkyū
渋谷東急
Gotoh Planetarium & Astronomical Musm
五島プラネタリウム
Nagai Int'l Bldg
長井インターナショナルビル
至谷町インター
To Tanimachi I.C.
Shibuya Higashiguchi Bldg
渋谷東口ビル
Asahi Bank
あさひ銀行
Tōhō Seimei Bldg
東邦生命ビル
渋谷ランプ
Shibuya Ramp
Bus Terminal
バスターミナル
SHIBUYA STA.
渋谷駅
日本生産性本部
Japan Productivity Center
Shibuya Police Sta.
渋谷署
Tōfuku-ji
東福寺
第百生命(本社)
Daihyaku Mutual Life Insurance (H.O.)
Konnō Hachimangū
金王八幡宮
高速3号線
MEIJI DŌRI (AVE.)
KDD Shibuya
KDD渋谷
Shibuya (3)
渋谷3丁目
Jissen Joshi Gakuen
実践女子学園
YAMANOTE LINE 山手線
TŌYOKO LINE 東横線
明治通り
Shūwa Aoyama Residence
秀和青山レジデンス
Episcopal Church of Japan
日本聖公会教務院
渋谷図書館
Shibuya Library
Namikibashi Apts
並木橋アパート
Wins Shibuya
ウィンズ渋谷
Higashi (1)
東1丁目
Yamaha Epicurus
ヤマハエピキュラス
中渋谷教会
Naka Shibuya Ch.
桜丘町
Namiki-bashi
並木橋
至恵比寿
To Ebisu

HARAJUKU STATION
原宿駅
Yoyogi Seminar
代々木ゼミナール(分校)
Seichōno-ie
生長の家
Meiji Jingū (shrine)
明治神宮
Tōgō Jinja (shrine)
東郷神社
Tōgō Mem. Hall
東郷記念館
TAKESHITA DŌRI
竹下通り
Palais France
パレフランス
Boutique Kansai
ブティック寛斎
Rehabilitation Center for the Mentally and Physically Handicapped
心身障害者福祉センター
Harajuku Danchi (Apts)
原宿団地
Myōen-ji
妙円寺
Jingūmae (1)
神宮前 1 丁目
Jingūmae (3)
神宮前 3 丁目
MEIJI DŌRI (AVE.)
明治通り
Kyū Shibuya River Promenade
旧渋谷川遊歩道
Harajuku Jr. H. Sch.
原宿中
原宿クエスト
Harajuku Quest
Ota Mem. Mus. of Art
太田記念美術館
Laforet Harajuku
ラフォーレ原宿
Corp Olympia
コーブオリンピア
Tin Toy Musm
おもちゃの博物館
Jingūmae (4)
神宮前 4 丁目
Jingūmae
神宮前
Harajuku Tower Height
原宿タワーハイツ
Central Apts
セントラルアパート
Japan Int'l Sch.
ジャパン インターナショナル スクール
OMOTE SANDŌ (AVE.)
表参道
Emb. of Portugal
ポルトガル大使館
Nat'l Gymnasium
国立競技場
Jingūmae E. Sch.
神宮前小
Omote-Sandō City House
表参道シティハウス
Harajuku-ekimae P.O.
原宿駅前局
Kiddy Land
キディランド
Kita-Aoyama
北青山 3 丁
Jingūmae (6)
神宮前 6 丁目
Dōjunkai Aoyama Apts
同潤会青山アパート
Jingubashi Bldg
神宮橋ビル
Oriental Bazaar
オリエンタルバザー
Tokyo Central Bldg
東京セントラルビル
Nurse's Agency
看護協会
Kirin Brewery (H.O.)
キリンビール(本社)
Tokyo Union Ch.
東京ユニオン教会
Itō Hosp.
伊藤病院
Zenkō-ji
善光寺
Kyōcera Bldg
京セラビル
Kishi Mem. Hall
岸記念体育会館
長泉寺
Chōsen-ji
Corp Inn Shibuya
コープイン渋谷
Tenriism Shrine
天理教教会
Hanae Mori Bldg
ハナエモリビル
Aoyama Diamond Hall
青山ダイヤモンドホール
Onden Jinja
穏田神社
Jingūmae (5)
神宮前 5 丁目
Fuji Bank
富士銀行
Jingūdōri Park
神宮通公園
Kita-Aoyama Hosp.
北青山病院
SHIBUYA-KU
渋谷区
Natural House
ナチュラルハウス
Sanwa B
三和銀
Shibuya Girls' H. Sch.
渋谷女子高
紀ノ国屋
Kinokuniya International
Spiral
(Wacoal Aoyama Bl
スパイラル
(ワコール青山ビ
Chiyo Tanaka Dressmaking Sch.
東京田中千代服飾専門学校
Met. Aoyama Hosp.
東京都職員共済組合青山病院
JBP Oval
JBPオーバル
Aoyama 5-chome
青山五丁目
Shimada Foreign Books
島田洋書
Minami-Aoyama Kaikan
南青山会館
Nat'l Children's Castle
(Kodomono-shiro)
こどもの城
United Nations Univ.
国連大学
Aoyamadōri P.O.
青山通局
Ohara Bldg
小原ビル
Shibuya (1)
渋谷 1 丁目
Aoyama Theater
青山劇場
Gymnasium
体育館
Tokyo Met. Children's House
東京都児童会館
Shibuya E. Sch.
渋谷小
Aogaku Kaikan Hall
青学会館
YAMANOTE LINE
山手線
Miyashita Park
宮下公園
Metro Plaza
メトロプラザ
HANZOMON LINE
Aoyama Gakuin University
青山学院大学
Chateau Tō
シャトー
52
国民銀行
Kokumin
Ontake Jinja
御岳神社
Shibuya Tōkyū Inn
渋谷東急イン
Shibuya P.O.
渋谷局
Miyamasuzaka-ue
宮益坂上
Jintan Bldg
仁丹ビル
Women's Jr. Coll.
女子短大
Fuji Bank
富士銀行
Shibuya (2)
渋谷 2 丁目
Shibuya (4)
渋谷 4 丁目
SHIBUYA STA.
渋谷駅
Asahi Bank
あさひ銀行
GINZA LINE
銀座線
Aoyama Shanpia Hotel
青山シャンピアホテル
NTT Higashi Shibuya
NTT東渋谷
Junior H. Sch.
中等部
246
High School
高等部
Shionogi Bldg
シオノギビル
Tōkyū Bunka Kaikan
東急文化会館
Tōhō Seimei Bldg
東邦生命ビル
日本コカコーラ(

Prince Chichibu Memorial Rugby Stadium
秩父宮記念ラグビー場
Kita-Aoyama(2)
北青山２丁目
AOYAMA DŌRI (AVE.)
青山通り
Aoyama H. Sch.
青山高
Kōtoku-ji
高徳寺
Nissan Fire & Marine Insurance
日産火災海上
Sumitomo Trust
住友信託
CI Plaza
CIプラザ
C. Itoh (Itochū) (Tokyo H.O.)
伊藤忠(東京本社)
Hazama Bldg
ハザマビル
NTT Aoyama
NTT青山
Asahi Bank
あさひ銀行
Pola Aoyama Bldg
ポーラ青山ビル
Aoyama Twin (New Aoyama Bldg)
新青山ビル
Honda Motor(H.O.)
本田技研(本社)
Hotel President Aoyama
ホテルプレシデント青山
Aoba Park
青葉公園
Emb. of Brazil
Harajuku Ch.
原宿教会
Jihō-ji
持法寺
Kaizō-ji
海蔵寺
Aoyama Sun Crest
青山サンクレスト
Aoyama Bell Commons
青山ベルコモンズ
Aoyama Tower Bldg
青山タワービル
Aoyama E. Sch.
青山小
Baisō-in
梅窓院
Gyokusōzen-ji
玉窓禅寺
Akasaka Health Center
赤坂保健所
Ryusen-ji
竜泉寺
Aoyama Welfare Hall
青山福祉会館
Akasaka H. Sch.
赤坂高
Akasaka Fire Sta.
赤坂消防署
Gaienmae P.O.
外苑前局
Dai-Ichi Kangyō Bank
第一勧銀
Aoyama 3-chome
青山三丁目
Aoyama Metro Hall
青山メトロ会館
第一青山ビル
Daiichi Aoyama Bldg
プラザ
Plaza 246
Japan Traditional Crafts Center
全国伝統的工芸品センター
Tōkyū Store
東急ストア
Aoyama Peacock
青山ピーコック
Minami-Aoyama (2)
南青山２丁目
Sumitomo Seimei Aoyama Bldg
住友生命青山ビル
Aoyama Shopping Center
青山ショッピングセンター
Aoyama Mansion
青山マンション
Aoyama Ch.
青山教会
Aoyama Cemetery (Aoyama Reien)
青山霊園
Kyōwa Bldg
協和ビル
Seinan Welfare Hall
青南福祉会館
Minami-Aoyama(3)
南青山３丁目
Aoyama Funeral Hall
青山葬儀所
MINATO-KU
港区
Science Council of Japan
日本学術会議
Tokyo Aoyama Kaikan (hall)
東京青山会館
Minami-Aoyama(4)
南青山４丁目
CHIYODA LINE
千代田線
Tessenkai Noh Theater
銕仙会能楽研修所
Seinan E. Sch.
青南小
GAIEN-NISHI DŌRI (AVE.)
外苑西通り
Aoyama Park
青山公園
Minami-Aoyama(5)
南青山５丁目
From 1st Bldg
フロムファーストビル
La Collezione
コレッツィオーネビル
Nezu Art Musm
根津美術館
Akasaka Press Center
赤坂プレスセンター
Kensetsu Kyōsai Kaikan
建設共済会館
Nikka Whisky
ニッカウ井スキー
Kyōei Bldg
協栄ビル
Eihei-ji (temple), Tokyo Branch (Chōkoku-ji)
永平寺東京別院(長谷寺)
Nishi-Azabu(2)
西麻布２丁目
Daian-ji
大安寺
Jigan-in
慈眼院
Azabu Daikannon
麻布大観音
Nishi-Azabu P.O.
西麻布局
Emb. of Sudan
スーダン大使館
Minami-Aoyama(6)
南青山６丁目
Fuji Photo Film (H.O.)
富士写真フィルム(本社)
Takagichō Ramp
高樹町ランプ
Nishi-Azabu
西麻布
SHUTO EXPWY No.3
首都高速３号線
Nishiazabu Bldg
西麻布ビル
Harajuku, Aoyama
原宿 青山
1:8,000
0
300m

Shinjuku 新宿
Underground Arcade & Passage
地下街と 地下道路
Kojimaya Confectionery
小島屋乳業製菓
Kashiwagi Bldg
柏木ビル
Shinjuku Health Center
新宿保健所
Naruko Tenjinsha
成子天神社
Jōon-ji
浄音寺
Yodobashi Daiichi E. Sch.
淀橋一小
Tokyo Language Sch.
東京外語専門学校
Shōko Chukin Bank
商工中金
Nishi-Shinjuku (8)
西新宿８丁目
Yamaguchi Bank
山口銀行
ŌME KAIDŌ (AVE.)
青梅街道
Yodobashi Daiichi Kindergarten
淀橋第一幼稚園
Nishi-Shinjuku (7)
西新宿７丁目
太平洋銀行
Taiheiyo Bank
Nishi-shinjuku KB Bldg
西新宿KBビル
Tenriism Central Shr.
天理教中央教会
Kashiwagi Park
柏木公園
Tōhō Ba
東邦銀行
Daikan Plaza Bld
ダイカンプラザビ
Hyōgo Bank
兵庫銀行
Tokyo Cookery Academy
東京調理師専門学校
Tokyo Medical College Hospital
東京医科大学病院
Rōsai Kaikan (hall)
労済会館
MARUNOUCHI LINE
丸ノ内線
Jōen-ji
常円寺
Yamagata Shiawase Bank
山形しあわせ銀行
Jōsen-in
常泉院
Star Hotel Tokyo
スターホテル東京
東京都民銀
Tokyo To Bank
Nishi-Shinjuku (6)
西新宿６丁目
Shinjuku Police Sta.
新宿署
Heiwa Credit Union
平和信組
Shōwa Shinkin Ba
昭和信金
Shinjuku Nomura Bldg
新宿野村ビル (50Fl)
Free Observatory
無料展望ロビー (50Fl)
Nomura Hall
野村ホール (B1)
Tokyo Hilton Int'l
東京ヒルトンインターナショナル
Jōfū-ji
浄風寺
Met. Bureau of Waterworks (Branch Office)
都水道局（支）
Yasuda Kasai-Kaijo Bldg (43Fl)
安田火災海上本社ビル
Tōgō Seiji Art Museum
東郷青児美術館 (42Fl)
Odakyū Hal
小田急ハル
Shinjuku Kokusai Bldg
新宿国際ビル
Waterworks Musm
東京都水道記念館
KITA DŌRI (AVE.)
北通り
Green Tower Bldg
グリーンタワービル
Sanwa Bank
三和銀行
Shinjuku L Tower
新宿Ｌタワー
Shinjuku Mitsui Bldg
新宿三井ビル (55Fl)
Observation Restaurant
展望レストラン (54～55Fl)
Do Sports Plaza
ドゥスポーツプラザ
Shinjuku Daiichi Seimei Bldg
新宿第一生命ビル
Sumitomo Bank
住友銀行
Matsuoka Central B
松岡セントラルビ
Shinjuku Center Bldg
新宿センタービル (54Fl)
Free Observatory
無料展望台 (53Fl)
Asahi Mutual Life Insurance (H.O.)
朝日生命（本社）
Asahi Seimei Hall
朝日生命ホール
Dai-Ichi Kangyō Bank
第一勧銀
Subaru Bldg
スバルビル
Shinjuku Sumitomo Bldg
新宿住友ビル (52Fl)
Free Observatory (51Fl)
無料展望台ロビー
Asahi Culture Center
朝日カルチャーセンター
Sumitomo Hall (B1)
住友ホール
西新宿１丁目
Nishi-Shinjuku (1)
中央通り
CHŪŌ DŌRI (AVE.)
Hotel Century Hyatt
ホテルセンチュリーハイアット
TOCHŌ DŌRI (AVE.)
GIJIDŌ DŌRI (AVE.)
HIGASHI DŌRI (AVE.)
KŌEN DŌRI (AVE.)
Hiroshima Bank
広島銀行
Shinjuku Bldg
新宿ビル
Fuji Bank
富士銀行
West Entra
Meiji Seimei Bldg
明治生命ビル
Yasuda Seimei Bldg
安田生命ビル
Yasuda Seimei Hall
安田生命ホール
Keio Plaza Hotel (47Fl)
京王プラザホテル
Kōgakuin Univ.
工学院大学
Shinjuku P.O.
新宿局
Met. Assembly Hall
都議会議事堂
Plaza Dōri
プラザ通り
Hokkaido Bank
北海道銀行
Highway Bus Terminal
高速バスターミナル
Asahi
Kadoya Hotel
かどやホテル
Yodobashi Camera
ヨドバシカメラ
Mitsubishi Tr
三菱信
Shinjuku Central Park
新宿中央公園
Keiō Plaza Hotel (South Tower)
京王プラザホテル南館
Nishi-Shinjuku (2)
西新宿２丁目
No. 1
Yamanashi Chūō Bank
山梨中央銀行
東洋信託
Tōyō Trust
Industrial Bank of Japan
興銀
東通り
議事堂通り
都庁通り
公園通り
NTT
Sakuraya Camera
カメラのさくらや
Metropolitan Government Office
東京都庁
Shinjuku Monolith
新宿モノリス
San'ei Bldg
サンエービル
People's Finance Corp.
国民金融公庫
国際通り
Kokusai Dōri
Doi Camera
カメラのドイ
Shinjuku Sky Bldg
新宿スカイビル
No. 2
Shinjuku NS Bldg (30Fl)
新宿NSビル
Meihō Bldg
明宝ビル
Sakura Bank
さくら銀行
Kubo Bldg
久保ビル
KDD Bldg (32Fl)
KDDビル
Taihei Bldg
太平ビル
20
Fukutoku Bank
福徳銀行
京王新線
京王線
KDD P.O.
KDD内局
MINAMI DŌRI (AVE.)
南通り
Tokyo Kaijō Bldg
東京海上ビル
Sakakibara Mem. Ho
榊原記念病院
Tsunohazu-bashi (Br.)
角筈橋
Shinjuku Washington Hotel
新宿ワシントンホテル
KEIŌ SHIN-SEN (NEW LINE)
KEIŌ LINE
Yoyogi
代々木
Hotel Sunrout
ホテルサンル

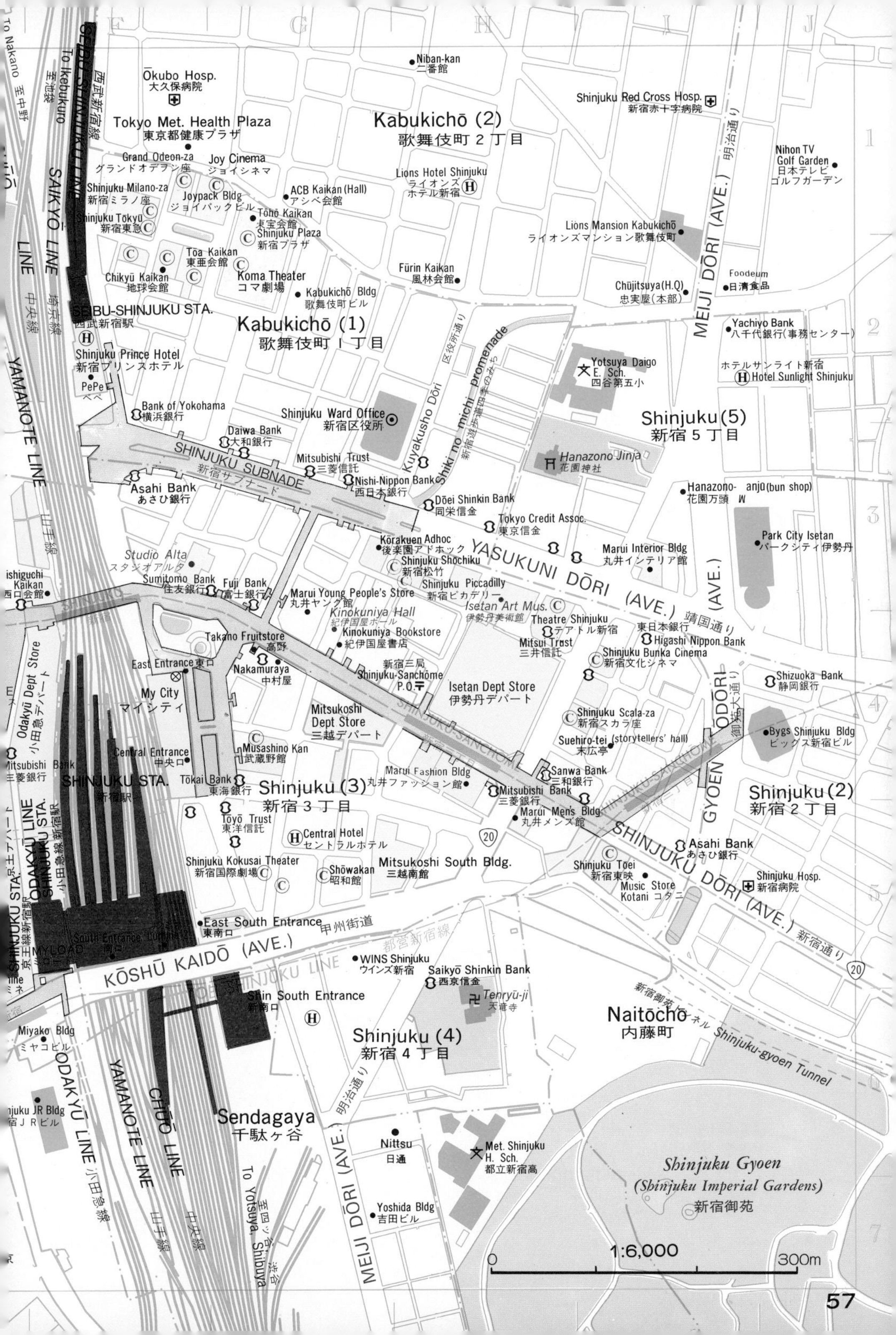

To Nakano 至中野
To Ikebukuro 至池袋
SEIBU-SHINJUKU LINE 西武新宿線
SAIKYŌ LINE 埼京線
CHŪŌ LINE 中央線
YAMANOTE LINE 山手線
Ōkubo Hosp. 大久保病院
Tokyo Met. Health Plaza 東京都健康プラザ
Grand Odeon-za グランドオデヲン座
Joy Cinema ジョイシネマ
Shinjuku Milano-za 新宿ミラノ座
Joypack Bldg ジョイパックビル
Shinjuku Tōkyū 新宿東急
Tōhō Kaikan 東宝会館
Shinjuku Plaza 新宿プラザ
Tōa Kaikan 東亜会館
Koma Theater コマ劇場
Chikyū Kaikan 地球会館
ACB Kaikan (Hall) アシベ会館
Kabukichō Bldg 歌舞伎町ビル
SEIBU-SHINJUKU STA. 西武新宿駅
Shinjuku Prince Hotel 新宿プリンスホテル
PePe ペペ
Kabukichō (1) 歌舞伎町1丁目
Kabukichō (2) 歌舞伎町2丁目
Niban-kan 二番館
Lions Hotel Shinjuku ライオンズホテル新宿
Fūrin Kaikan 風林会館
Shinjuku Red Cross Hosp. 新宿赤十字病院
Nihon TV Golf Garden 日本テレビゴルフガーデン
Lions Mansion Kabukichō ライオンズマンション歌舞伎町
Foodeum 日清食品
Chūjitsuya (H.Q) 忠実屋(本部)
MEIJI DŌRI (AVE.) 明治通り
Yachiyo Bank 八千代銀行(事務センター)
ホテルサンライト新宿 Hotel Sunlight Shinjuku
Yotsuya Daigo E. Sch. 四谷第五小
Shinjuku (5) 新宿5丁目
Hanazono Jinja 花園神社
Hanazono-anjū (bun shop) 花園万頭
Park City Isetan パークシティ伊勢丹
Bank of Yokohama 横浜銀行
Shinjuku Ward Office 新宿区役所
Kuyakusho Dōri 区役所通り
Shiki no michi promenade 新宿遊歩道四季のみち
Daiwa Bank 大和銀行
SHINJUKU SUBNADE 新宿サブナード
Mitsubishi Trust 三菱信託
Nishi-Nippon Bank 西日本銀行
Asahi Bank あさひ銀行
Dōei Shinkin Bank 同栄信金
Tokyo Credit Assoc. 東京信金
Kōrakuen Adhoc 後楽園アドホック
Shinjuku Shochiku 新宿松竹
YASUKUNI DŌRI (AVE.) 靖国通り
Marui Interior Bldg 丸井インテリア館
Studio Alta スタジオアルタ
Sumitomo Bank 住友銀行
Fuji Bank 富士銀行
Marui Young People's Store 丸井ヤング館
Shinjuku Piccadilly 新宿ピカデリー
Isetan Art Mus. 伊勢丹美術館
Theatre Shinjuku テアトル新宿
東日本銀行 Higashi Nippon Bank
Mitsui Trust 三井信託
Shinjuku Bunka Cinema 新宿文化シネマ
Kinokuniya Hall 紀伊國屋ホール
Kinokuniya Bookstore 紀伊國屋書店
Takano Fruitstore 高野
East Entrance 東口
Nakamuraya 中村屋
新宿三局 Shinjuku-Sanchōme P.O.
Isetan Dept Store 伊勢丹デパート
Shizuoka Bank 静岡銀行
Odakyū Dept Store 小田急デパート
My City マイシティ
Mitsukoshi Dept Store 三越デパート
Shinjuku Scala-za 新宿スカラ座
Suehiro-tei (storytellers' hall) 末広亭
GYOEN ŌDŌRI 御苑大通り
Bygs Shinjuku Bldg ビッグス新宿ビル
Musashino Kan 武蔵野館
Central Entrance 中央口
Mitsubishi Bank 三菱銀行
SHINJUKU STA. 新宿駅
Tōkai Bank 東海銀行
Shinjuku (3) 新宿3丁目
Marui Fashion Bldg 丸井ファッション館
Sanwa Bank 三和銀行
Mitsubishi Bank 三菱銀行
Marui Men's Bldg 丸井メンズ館
Shinjuku (2) 新宿2丁目
Tōyō Trust 東洋信託
Central Hotel セントラルホテル
ODAKYŪ LINE
SHINJUKU STA. 小田急線新宿駅
Asahi Bank あさひ銀行
Shinjuku Kokusai Theater 新宿国際劇場
Shōwakan 昭和館
Mitsukoshi South Bldg. 三越南館
Shinjuku Toei 新宿東映
Music Store Kotani コタニ
SHINJUKU DŌRI (AVE.) 新宿通り
Shinjuku Hosp. 新宿病院
East South Entrance 東南口
KŌSHŪ KAIDŌ (AVE.) 甲州街道
都営新宿線
South Entrance 南口
MYLOAD
WINS Shinjuku ウインズ新宿
Saikyō Shinkin Bank 西京信金
Shin South Entrance 新南口
Tenryū-ji 天竜寺
Naitōchō 内藤町
新宿御苑トンネル Shinjuku-gyoen Tunnel
Miyako Bldg ミヤコビル
Shinjuku (4) 新宿4丁目
ODAKYŪ LINE 小田急線
YAMANOTE LINE 山手線
CHŪŌ LINE 中央線
Sendagaya 千駄ヶ谷
MEIJI DŌRI (AVE.) 明治通り
Nittsu 日通
Met. Shinjuku H. Sch. 都立新宿高
Shinjuku Gyoen (Shinjuku Imperial Gardens) 新宿御苑
Yoshida Bldg 吉田ビル
To Yotsuya, Shibuya 至四ッ谷 渋谷
1:6,000
0
300m

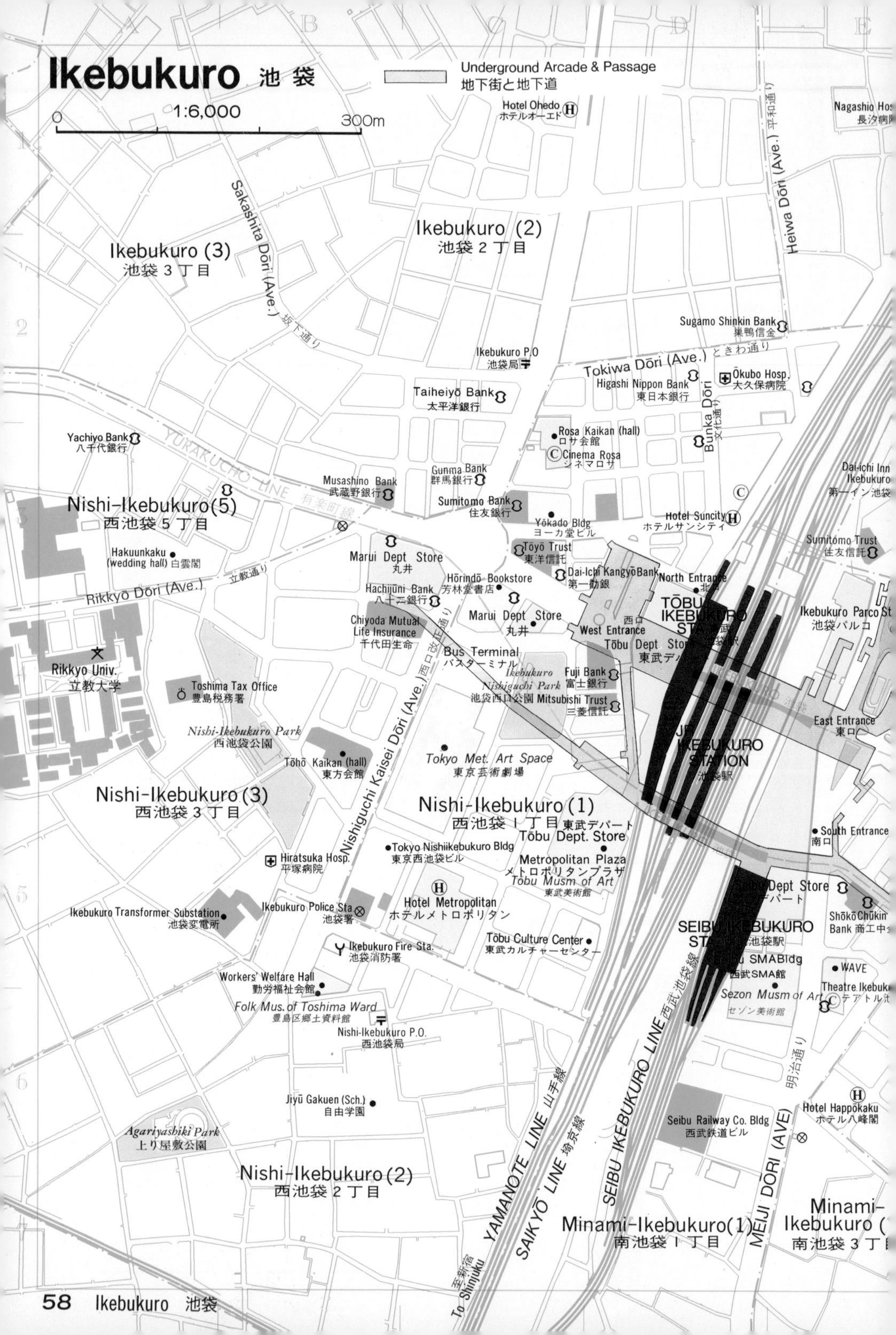
Ikebukuro 池袋
Underground Arcade & Passage
地下街と地下道
1:6,000
0
300m
Ikebukuro (3)
池袋3丁目
Ikebukuro (2)
池袋2丁目
Sakashita Dōri (Ave.) 坂下通り
Heiwa Dōri (Ave.) 平和通り
Hotel Ohedo
ホテルオーエド
Sugamo Shinkin Bank
巣鴨信金
Ikebukuro P.O
池袋局
Tokiwa Dōri (Ave.) ときわ通り
Higashi Nippon Bank
東日本銀行
Ōkubo Hosp.
大久保病院
Taiheiyō Bank
太平洋銀行
Bunka Dōri
文化通り
Rosa Kaikan (hall)
ロサ会館
Cinema Rosa
シネマロサ
Yachiyo Bank
八千代銀行
YURAKUCHO LINE 有楽町線
Gunma Bank
群馬銀行
Musashino Bank
武蔵野銀行
Sumitomo Bank
住友銀行
Nishi-Ikebukuro(5)
西池袋5丁目
Yōkado Bldg
ヨーカ堂ビル
Hotel Suncity
ホテルサンシティ
Tōyō Trust
東洋信託
Hakuunkaku
(wedding hall) 白雲閣
Marui Dept Store
丸井
Dai-Ichi Kangyō Bank
第一勧銀
North Entrance
北口
Sumitomo Trust
住友信託
Rikkyō Dōri (Ave.) 立教通り
Hōrindō Bookstore
芳林堂書店
Hachijūni Bank
八十二銀行
TŌBU IKEBUKURO STA.
Chiyoda Mutual Life Insurance
千代田生命
Marui Dept Store
丸井
West Entrance
西口
Tōbu Dept Store
東武デパート
Ikebukuro Parco
池袋パルコ
Bus Terminal
バスターミナル
Rikkyo Univ.
立教大学
Toshima Tax Office
豊島税務署
Ikebukuro Nishiguchi Park
池袋西口公園
Fuji Bank
富士銀行
Mitsubishi Trust
三菱信託
Nishiguchi Kaisei Dōri (Ave.) 西口改正通り
East Entrance
東口
Nishi-Ikebukuro Park
西池袋公園
Tōhō Kaikan (hall)
東方会館
Tokyo Met. Art Space
東京芸術劇場
JR IKEBUKURO STATION
池袋駅
Nishi-Ikebukuro (3)
西池袋3丁目
Nishi-Ikebukuro (1)
西池袋1丁目
東武デパート
Tōbu Dept. Store
South Entrance
南口
Hiratsuka Hosp.
平塚病院
Tokyo Nishiikebukuro Bldg
東京西池袋ビル
Metropolitan Plaza
メトロポリタンプラザ
Tōbu Musm of Art
東武美術館
Dept Store
デパート
Hotel Metropolitan
ホテルメトロポリタン
Ikebukuro Transformer Substation
池袋変電所
Ikebukuro Police Sta
池袋署
Shōkō Chūkin Bank 商工中
SEIBU IKEBUKURO STA. 池袋駅
Tōbu Culture Center
東武カルチャーセンター
Ikebukuro Fire Sta.
池袋消防署
SMA Bldg
西武SMA館
WAVE
Workers' Welfare Hall
勤労福祉会館
Sezon Musm of Art
セゾン美術館
Theatre Ikebuk
テアトル池
Folk Mus. of Toshima Ward
豊島区郷土資料館
Nishi-Ikebukuro P.O.
西池袋局
明治通り
Jiyū Gakuen (Sch.)
自由学園
YAMANOTE LINE 山手線
SAIKYŌ LINE 埼京線
SEIBU IKEBUKURO LINE 西武池袋線
Hotel Happōkaku
ホテル八峰閣
Seibu Railway Co. Bldg
西武鉄道ビル
Agariyashiki Park
上り屋敷公園
MEIJI DŌRI (AVE)
Nishi-Ikebukuro (2)
西池袋2丁目
Minami-Ikebukuro (1)
南池袋1丁目
Minami-Ikebukuro (
南池袋3丁
To Shinjuku 至新宿
Nagashio Hos
長汐病院
Dai-ichi Inn Ikebukuro
第一イン池袋

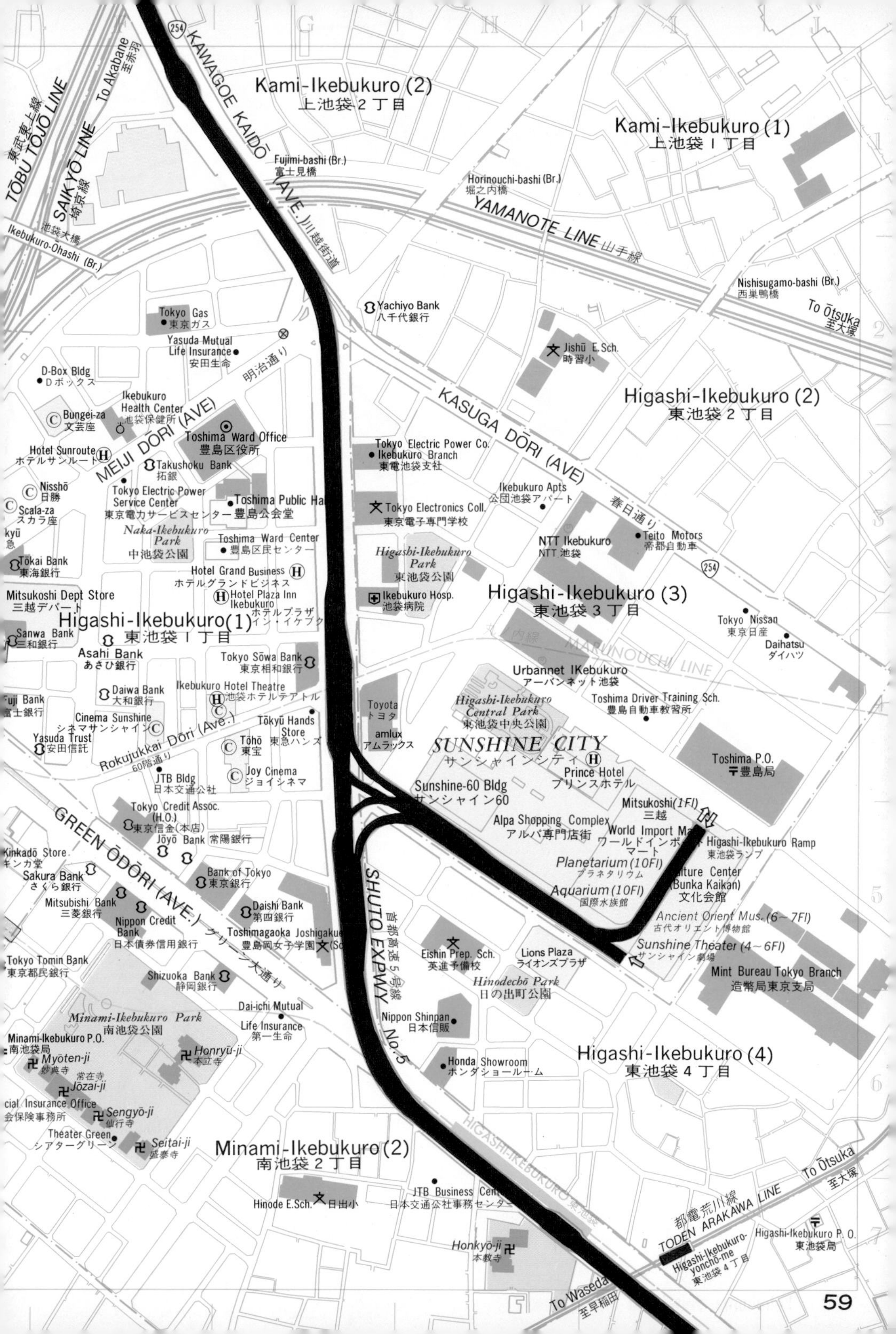

Kami-Ikebukuro (2)
上池袋2丁目
Kami-Ikebukuro (1)
上池袋1丁目
KAWAGOE KAIDŌ (AVE.) 川越街道
TŌBU TŌJŌ LINE
東武東上線
SAIKYŌ LINE
埼京線
To Akabane
至赤羽
Fujimi-bashi (Br.)
富士見橋
Horinouchi-bashi (Br.)
堀之内橋
YAMANOTE LINE 山手線
Ikebukuro-Ohashi (Br.)
池袋大橋
Nishisugamo-bashi (Br.)
西巣鴨橋
To Ōtsuka
至大塚
Yachiyo Bank
八千代銀行
Tokyo Gas
東京ガス
Yasuda Mutual Life Insurance
安田生命
Jishū E.Sch.
時習小
D-Box Bldg
Dボックス
明治通り
KASUGA DŌRI (AVE)
Higashi-Ikebukuro (2)
東池袋2丁目
Ikebukuro Health Center
池袋保健所
Bungei-za
文芸座
MEIJI DŌRI (AVE)
Toshima Ward Office
豊島区役所
Hotel Sunroute
ホテルサンルート
Takushoku Bank
拓銀
Tokyo Electric Power Co. Ikebukuro Branch
東電池袋支社
Nisshō
日勝
Tokyo Electric Power Service Center
東京電力サービスセンター
Toshima Public Hall
豊島公会堂
Ikebukuro Apts
公団池袋アパート
Scala-za
スカラ座
Tokyo Electronics Coll.
東京電子専門学校
春日通り
Naka-Ikebukuro Park
中池袋公園
Toshima Ward Center
豊島区民センター
NTT Ikebukuro
NTT池袋
Teito Motors
帝都自動車
Tōkai Bank
東海銀行
Higashi-Ikebukuro Park
東池袋公園
Hotel Grand Business
ホテルグランドビジネス
Mitsukoshi Dept Store
三越デパート
Hotel Plaza Inn Ikebukuro
ホテルプラザイン・イケブクロ
Ikebukuro Hosp.
池袋病院
Higashi-Ikebukuro (3)
東池袋3丁目
Higashi-Ikebukuro(1)
東池袋1丁目
Sanwa Bank
三和銀行
Tokyo Nissan
東京日産
Daihatsu
ダイハツ
Asahi Bank
あさひ銀行
Tokyo Sōwa Bank
東京相和銀行
MARUNOUCHI LINE
丸ノ内線
Urbannet IKebukuro
アーバンネット池袋
Daiwa Bank
大和銀行
Ikebukuro Hotel Theatre
池袋ホテルテアトル
Toshima Driver Training Sch.
豊島自動車教習所
Fuji Bank
富士銀行
Toyota
トヨタ
Higashi-Ikebukuro Central Park
東池袋中央公園
Cinema Sunshine
シネマサンシャイン
Tōkyū Hands Store
東急ハンズ
Yasuda Trust
安田信託
Rokujukkai Dōri (Ave.)
60階通り
Tōhō
東宝
amlux
アムラックス
SUNSHINE CITY
サンシャインシティ
Prince Hotel
プリンスホテル
Toshima P.O.
豊島局
JTB Bldg
日本交通公社
Joy Cinema
ジョイシネマ
Sunshine-60 Bldg
サンシャイン60
Tokyo Credit Assoc. (H.O.)
東京信金(本店)
Mitsukoshi(1Fl)
三越
Alpa Shopping Complex
アルパ専門店街
World Import Mart
ワールドインポートマート
Higashi-Ikebukuro Ramp
東池袋ランプ
GREEN ŌDŌRI (AVE.)
グリーン大通り
Jōyō Bank
常陽銀行
Kinkadō Store
キンカ堂
Sakura Bank
さくら銀行
Bank of Tokyo
東京銀行
Planetarium (10Fl)
プラネタリウム
Culture Center (Bunka Kaikan)
文化会館
Aquarium (10Fl)
国際水族館
Mitsubishi Bank
三菱銀行
Nippon Credit Bank
日本債券信用銀行
Daishi Bank
第四銀行
SHUTO EXPWY No.5
首都高速5号線
Ancient Orient Mus. (6〜7Fl)
古代オリエント博物館
Toshimagaoka Joshigakuen (Sch.)
豊島岡女子学園
Eishin Prep. Sch.
英進予備校
Lions Plaza
ライオンズプラザ
Sunshine Theater (4〜6Fl)
サンシャイン劇場
Tokyo Tomin Bank
東京都民銀行
Shizuoka Bank
静岡銀行
Hinodechō Park
日の出町公園
Mint Bureau Tokyo Branch
造幣局東京支局
Dai-ichi Mutual Life Insurance
第一生命
Minami-Ikebukuro Park
南池袋公園
Nippon Shinpan
日本信販
Minami-Ikebukuro P.O.
南池袋局
Myōten-ji
妙典寺
Honryū-ji
本立寺
常在寺
Jōzai-ji
Honda Showroom
ホンダショールーム
Higashi-Ikebukuro (4)
東池袋4丁目
Social Insurance Office
社会保険事務所
Sengyō-ji
仙行寺
Theater Green
シアターグリーン
Seitai-ji
盛泰寺
Minami-Ikebukuro(2)
南池袋2丁目
HIGASHI-IKEBUKURO 東池袋
To Ōtsuka
至大塚
Hinode E.Sch.
日出小
JTB Business Center
日本交通公社事務センター
都電荒川線
TODEN ARAKAWA LINE
Higashi-Ikebukuro P.O.
東池袋局
Honkyō-ji
本教寺
Higashi-Ikebukuro-yonchō-me
東池袋4丁目
To Waseda
至早稲田

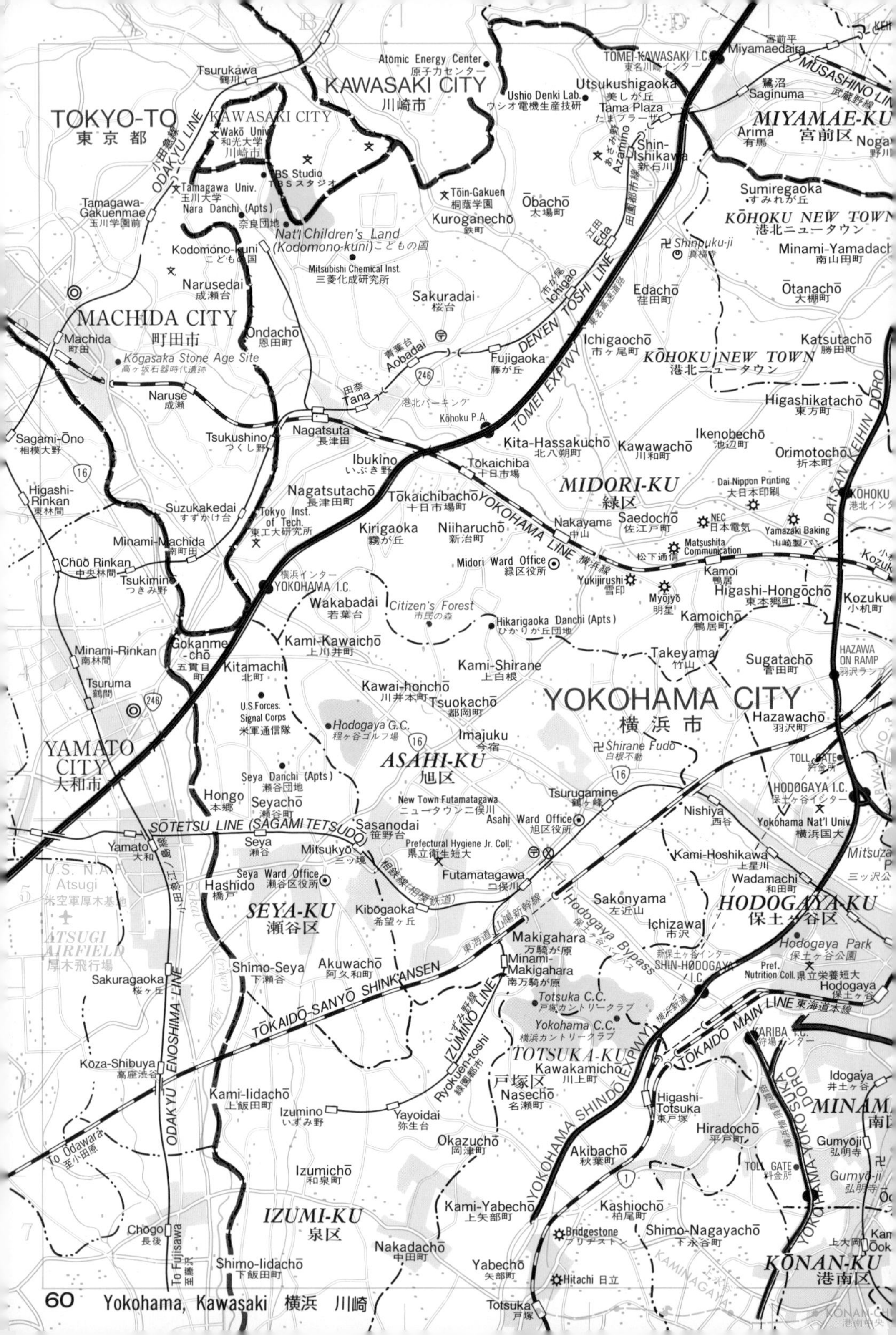
TOKYO-TO
東京都
KAWASAKI CITY
川崎市
MACHIDA CITY
町田市
YAMATO CITY
大和市
YOKOHAMA CITY
横浜市
MIYAMAE-KU
宮前区
MIDORI-KU
緑区
ASAHI-KU
旭区
SEYA-KU
瀬谷区
IZUMI-KU
泉区
TOTSUKA-KU
戸塚区
HODOGAYA-KU
保土ケ谷区
KONAN-KU
港南区
KŌHOKU NEW TOWN
港北ニュータウン
Atomic Energy Center
原子力センター
Tsurukawa
鶴川
Wakō Univ.
和光大学
川崎市
TBS Studio
TBSスタジオ
Tamagawa Univ.
玉川大学
Nara Danchi (Apts)
奈良団地
Tamagawa-Gakuenmae
玉川学園前
Nat'l Children's Land (Kodomono-kuni)
こどもの国
Kodomono-kuni
Tōin-Gakuen
桐蔭学園
Ushio Denki Lab.
ウシオ電機生産技研
Utsukushigaoka
美しが丘
Tama Plaza
たまプラーザ
TOMEI-KAWASAKI I.C.
東名川崎インター
Miyamaedaira
宮前平
Saginuma
鷺沼
MUSASHINO LINE
武蔵野線
Arima
有馬
Azamino
あざみ野
Shin-Ishikawa
新石川
Ōbachō
太場町
Kuroganechō
鉄町
Sumiregaoka
すみれが丘
Shinpuku-ji
真福寺
Minami-Yamadachō
南山田町
Eda
江田
Mitsubishi Chemical Inst.
三菱化成研究所
Narusedai
成瀬台
Ichigao
市が尾
Edachō
荏田町
Ōtanachō
大棚町
Sakuradai
桜台
DEN'EN TOSHI LINE
田園都市線
Ondachō
恩田町
Machida
町田
Kōgasaka Stone Age Site
高ヶ坂石器時代遺跡
Aobadai
青葉台
Fujigaoka
藤が丘
Ichigaochō
市ヶ尾町
Katsutachō
勝田町
Naruse
成瀬
Tana
田奈
港北パーキング
Kōhoku P.A.
TOMEI EXPWY
東名高速道路
Higashikatachō
東方町
Sagami-Ōno
相模大野
Tsukushino
つくし野
Nagatsuta
長津田
Kita-Hassakuchō
北八朔町
Kawawachō
川和町
Ikenobechō
池辺町
Orimotochō
折本町
Ibukino
いぶき野
Tōkaichiba
十日市場
Higashi-Rinkan
東林間
Nagatsutachō
長津田町
Tōkaichibachō
十日市場町
Dai Nippon Printing
大日本印刷
KŌHOKU
Suzukakedai
すずかけ台
Tokyo Inst. of Tech.
東工大研究所
YOKOHAMA LINE
横浜線
Nakayama
中山
Saedochō
佐江戸町
NEC
日本電気
Yamazaki Baking
山崎製パン
Minami-Machida
南町田
Kirigaoka
霧が丘
Niiharuchō
新治町
Matsushita Communication
松下通信
DAI-SAN KEIHIN DŌRO
Chūō Rinkan
中央林間
Tsukimino
つきみ野
Midori Ward Office
緑区役所
Kamoi
鴨居
Kozukue
小机町
横浜インター
YOKOHAMA I.C.
Yukijirushi
雪印
Myōjō
明星
Higashi-Hongōchō
東本郷町
Wakabadai
若葉台
Citizen's Forest
市民の森
Hikarigaoka Danchi (Apts)
ひかりが丘団地
Kamoichō
鴨居町
Gokanme-chō
五貫目町
Kami-Kawaichō
上川井町
Minami-Rinkan
南林間
Kitamachi
北町
Kami-Shirane
上白根
Takeyama
竹山
Sugatachō
菅田町
HAZAWA ON RAMP
羽沢ランプ
Tsuruma
鶴間
Kawai-honchō
川井本町
Tsuokachō
都岡町
U.S.Forces Signal Corps
米軍通信隊
Hazawachō
羽沢町
Hodogaya G.C.
程ヶ谷ゴルフ場
Imajuku
今宿
Shirane Fudō
白根不動
TOLL GATE
料金所
Seya Danchi (Apts)
瀬谷団地
HODOGAYA I.C.
保土ケ谷インター
Hongo
本郷
Seyachō
瀬谷町
New Town Futamatagawa
ニュータウン二俣川
Tsurugamine
鶴ヶ峰
Nishiya
西谷
Yokohama Nat'l Univ.
横浜国大
Asahi Ward Office
旭区役所
SŌTETSU LINE (SAGAMI TETSUDŌ)
相鉄線(相模鉄道)
Sasanodai
笹野台
Yamato
大和
Seya
瀬谷
Mitsukyō
三ッ境
Prefectural Hygiene Jr. Coll.
県立衛生短大
Kami-Hoshikawa
上星川
Mitsuzawa
三ッ沢公
U.S. N.A.F. Atsugi
米空軍厚木基地
Seya Ward Office
瀬谷区役所
Futamatagawa
二俣川
Wadamachi
和田町
Hashido
橋戸
Sakonyama
左近山
Kibōgaoka
希望ヶ丘
Ichizawa
市沢
ATSUGI AIRFIELD
厚木飛行場
Hodogaya Bypass
保土ヶ谷バイパス
Makigahara
万騎が原
Hodogaya Park
保土ケ谷公園
Akuwachō
阿久和町
新保土ケ谷インター
SHIN-HODOGAYA I.C.
Shimo-Seya
下瀬谷
Minami-Makigahara
南万騎が原
Pref. Nutrition Coll.
県立栄養短大
Sakuragaoka
桜ヶ丘
TŌKAIDŌ-SANYŌ SHINKANSEN
東海道山陽新幹線
Hodogaya
保土ケ谷
Totsuka C.C.
戸塚カントリークラブ
Yokohama C.C.
横浜カントリークラブ
IZUMINO LINE
いずみ野線
横浜新道
TŌKAIDŌ MAIN LINE
東海道本線
KARIBA I.C.
狩場インター
Kōza-Shibuya
高座渋谷
Ryokuen-toshi
緑園都市
Kawakamichō
川上町
Idogaya
井土ケ谷
Kami-Iidachō
上飯田町
Nasechō
名瀬町
Higashi-Totsuka
東戸塚
MINAMI-KU
Izumino
いずみ野
Yayoidai
弥生台
Hiradochō
平戸町
Gumyōji
弘明寺
ODAKYU ENOSHIMA LINE
To Odawara
至小田原
Okazuchō
岡津町
Akibachō
秋葉町
YOKOHAMA SHINDŌ (EXPWY)
Izumichō
和泉町
Gumyō-ji
弘明寺
YOKOHAMA-YOKOSUKA DŌRO
横浜横須賀道路
Kami-Yabechō
上矢部町
Kashiochō
柏尾町
Chōgo
長後
Bridgestone
ブリヂストン
Shimo-Nagayachō
下永谷町
上大岡
Nakadachō
中田町
Shimo-Iidachō
下飯田町
Yabechō
矢部町
Hitachi
日立
KAMINAGAYA
To Fujisawa
至藤沢
Totsuka
戸塚
ODAKYU LINE
小田急線
SAKAI RIVER

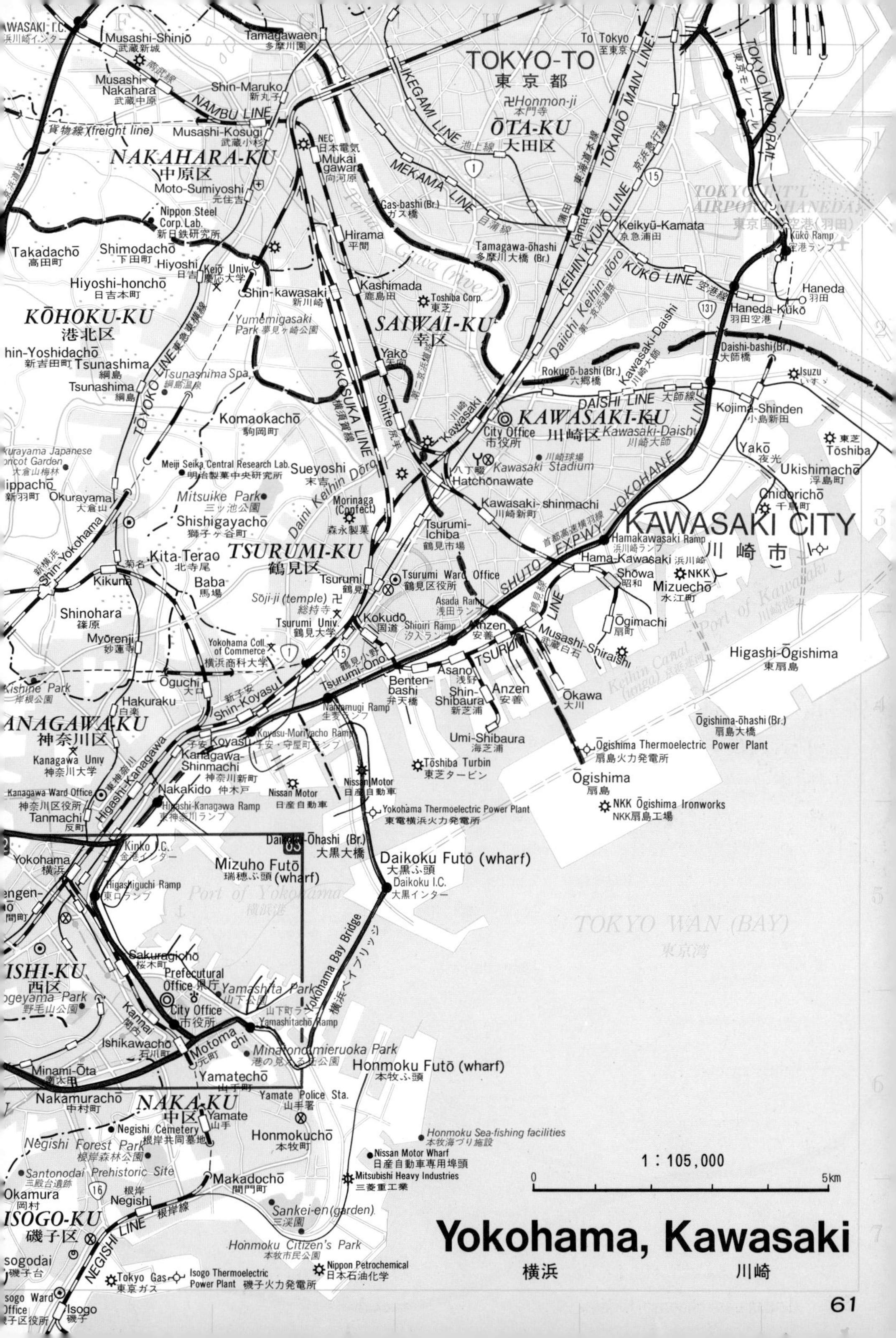

Yokohama, Kawasaki

横浜　川崎

SHUTO EXPWY.
首都高速
Nishiguchi Ramp
西口ランプ
Miyagaya
宮ヶ谷
Mitsuzawa High Town
三ッ沢ハイタウン
Kusunokichō
楠町
Hotel Rich
ホテルリッチ
Mitsukoshi
三越
Tōkyū Hotel
東急ホテル
Kita-Saiwai
北幸
Sōtetsu Bldg
相鉄ビル
Takashimaya
高島屋
Hotel Sunroute Yokohama
ホテルサンルート横浜
MOVIL
Lumine
ルミネ
Sōtetsu Joinas
相鉄ジョイナス
Sengen Jinja
浅間神社
Yokohama Kokusai Hotel
横浜国際ホテル
Daiei
ダイエー
Yokohama Central P.O.
横浜中央局
Kinkō I.C.
金港インター
Onochō
大野町
Central Wholesale Market
中央卸売市場
Kinkōchō
金港町
Yokohama City Air Terminal
横浜シティエアターミナル
Sogō Dept Store
横浜そごうデパート
Sky Bldg
スカイビル
Higashiguchi Ramp
東口ランプ
Sengendai
浅間台
Kyū-Tōkaido
旧東海道
Minami-Saiwai
南幸
Okano
岡野
Okano Park
岡野公園
Hiranuma H. Sch.
平沼高校
Park Heights
パークハイツ
Sengenchō
浅間町
Takashima
高島
Yokohama Golf Dome
横浜ゴルフドーム
Miyatachō
宮田町
NISHI-KU
西区
Hiranumabashi
平沼橋
YOKOSUKA LINE
横須賀線
Takashimachō
高島町
Hiranuma
平沼
New Por
For The 21s
SŌTETSU LINE
相鉄線
TŌKAIDŌ MAIN LINE
東海道本線
Tobe Police Sta.
戸部署
Nishi-Hiranuma-bashi
西平沼橋
Minami-Sengenchō
南浅間町
Sakuragichō
桜木町
Tobechō
戸部町
Midorichō
緑町
Yokohama Musm of Art
横浜美術館
Kōfuku-ji
Tobe
戸部
Tobe-honchō
戸部本町
Tennōchō
天王町
Furukawa-denkō Field
古河電工グラウンド
Chūō
中央
Landmark Towe
ランドマークタワ
Gosho-yamachō
御所山町
Nishi Ward Office
西区役所
Kamonyama Park
掃部山公園
Uchidachō
内田町
Nippon-maru Mem. Park
Owariya-bashi
尾張屋橋
Nishi-Yokohama
西横浜
Hamamatsuchō
浜松町
Nishi Public Hall
西公会堂
Isechō
伊勢町
To Ebina
至海老名
To Hodogaya
至保土ケ谷
Nishimaechō
西前町
Prefectural Youth Center
県立青少年センター
Safety Hea
海上保安本
Kubochō
久保町
Nagasakiya
長崎屋
Baptist Ch.
バプテスト教会
Uehara Ch.
上原教会
Miyazakichō
宮崎町
Iseyama Kōdaijingū
伊勢山皇大神宮
Hanasakichō
花咲町
Fujimioka Gakuen (Sch.)
富士見丘学園
Fujidana-chō
藤棚町
Prefectural Apts
県営アパート
Oimatsuchō
老松町
Narita Fudō
成田不動
Nishi-Tobechō
西戸部町
Nogeyama Zoo
野毛山動物園
City Library
市立図書館
Nogechō
野毛町
Higashi-Kubochō
東久保町
Nogeyama Park
野毛山公園
Miyagawachō
宮川町
Ipponmatsu E. Sch.
一本松小
Yoshidamachi
吉田町
Motokubochō
元久保町
Sakainotani
境之谷
RF Radio Nippon
ラジオ日本
Hinodechō
日ノ出町
Fukutomichō
福富町
Kuboyama Cemetery
久保山墓地
Kasumigaoka
霞ヶ丘
Matsuzakaya Dept Store
松坂屋デパート
Crematorium
斎場
Sakainotani Ch.
境ノ谷教会
Nogeyama Swimming Pool
野毛山プール
Chōjamachi
長者町
Kuboyama Mausoleum
久保山霊堂
Church of the Nazarene
ナザレン教会
Azumagaoka
東ヶ丘
Isezakichō
伊勢佐木町
Fushimichō
伏見町
Hagoromochō
羽衣町
Yokohama-higashi Nat'l Hosp.
国立横浜東病院
Miharudai
三春台
Akamonchō
赤門町
Wakabachō
若葉町
Kantō Gakuin
関東学院
Hatsunechō
初音町
Shimizugaoka Danchi (Apts)
清水ヶ丘団地
Kanoedai
庚台
Sueyoshichō
末吉町
MINAMI-KU
南区
Nishinakachō
西中町
Maesatochō
前里町
Naka P.O.
中局
Isezaki Police Sta.
伊勢佐木署
Odōri Park
大通公園
Shimizugaoka
清水ヶ丘
Koganechō
黄金町
Shimizugaoka Ch.
清水ヶ丘教会
Yamadachō
山田町
Eirakuchō
永楽町
Shimizugaoka H. Sch.
清水ヶ丘高校
Akebonochō
曙町
Maganechō
真金町
Hiechō
日枝町
Minamiōta
南太田
Minami-Yoshidachō
南吉田町
Sannōchō
山王町
Yoshinochō
吉野町
Minami-Otamachi
南太田町
(under construction)
Takanechō
高根町
Chitosechō
Miyoshichō
To Kami-ōoka
至上大岡
Hie Jinja
日枝神社
Shirotaechō
白妙町
Manseichō
万世町
KEIHIN KYŪKŌ LINE
京浜急行線
Futabachō
二葉町
Yokohama Comm. H. Sch.
横浜商業高校
Yokohama City Univ. (Med.)
横浜市立大(医)
Nakamurachō
中村町
Maita Park
蒔田公園
Tax Office
税務署
Yokohama City Univ. Hosp.
市立大病院
Urafunechō
浦舟町

Central Yokohama
横浜中心部
① Bronze Statue of Naosuke Ii 井伊直弼像
② Prefectural Concert Hall 県立音楽堂
③ Prefectural Library 県立図書館
④ Science Museum 文化資料館
⑤ Kanagawa Youth Hostel 神奈川ユースホステル
⑥ Opening Port Mem. Hall 開港記念会館
⑦ Yokohama Archives of History 横浜開港資料館
⑧ Silk Museum シルク博物館
⑨ Yokohama Doll Museum 横浜人形の家
⑩ Yokohama Marine Science Musm 横浜海洋科学博物館
⑪ Yamate Museum 山手資料館
⑫ Iwasaki Museum 岩崎博物館
⑬ Jiro Osaragi Mem. Museum 大仏次郎記念館
⑭ Kanagawa Mus. of Modern Literature 神奈川近代文学館
Mizuho Futō (wharf) 瑞穂ふ頭
Yamanouchichō
山内町
Yamanouchi Futō (wharf)
山内ふ頭
Rinkō Park
臨港パーク
Port of Yokohama
横浜港
Pacifico Yokohama
横浜国際平和会議場
Shinkō Futō (wharf)
新港ふ頭
Yokohama Cosmoworld
よこはまコスモワールド
Grand Pier
(Ōsanbashi Futō)
大さん橋ふ頭
Shinkōchō
新港町
Bankoku-bashi (Br.)
万国橋
Shinkō-bashi (Br.)
新港橋
International
Passenger Terminal
国際船客ターミナルビル
Kaigan-dōri
海岸通
Yūsen Bldg
郵船ビル
Motohamachō
元浜町
Kitanaka-dōri
北仲通
Honchō
本町
Minaminaka-dōri
南仲通
Yokohama Customshouse
横浜税関
Marine Police Sta.
水上署
Kanagawa Pref. Office
神奈川県庁
NHK
Kannai Hall
関内ホール
Silk Center
シルクセンター
Trade Center
産業貿易センター
Yamashita Park
山下公園
Hikawa-maru
氷川丸
Yamashita Futō (wharf)
山下ふ頭
Courthouse
裁判所
Yokohama Port P.O.
横浜港局
Kenmin Hall
県民ホール
Bank of Japan
日本銀行
The Hotel Yokohama
ザ・ホテルヨコハマ
Hotel New Grand
ホテルニューグランド
Nihon-Ōdōri
日本大通
Yamashitachō
山下町
Naka Ward Office
中区役所
Satellite Hotel
サテライトホテル
Star Hotel
スターホテル
Yokohama City Office
横浜市役所
Kagachō Police Sta.
加賀町署
Holiday Inn
ホリディ・イン
Marine Tower
マリンタワー
Yamashitachō Ramp
山下町ランプ
Kannai
関内
Yokohama Park
横浜公園
China Town
(Chūka-gai)
中華街
Seaman's Hall
海員会館
Mielperque Yokohama
メルパルク横浜
TVK
テレビ神奈川
Yokohama Stadium
横浜スタジアム
YMCA
Aster Hotel
アスターホテル
Bund Hotel
バンドホテル
Minato H. Sch. 港高校
Minato Comm. H. Sch. 港商業高校
Shin-Yamashita Ramp
新山下ランプ
Yokohama-kōen Ramp
横浜公園ランプ
Yokohama Central Hosp.
横浜中央病院
Meteorological Observatory
気象台
Motomachi
元町
Okinachō
翁町
Ōgimachi
扇町
Courthouse
裁判所
Foreigners' Cemetery
外人墓地
Minatono-mieruoka Park
港の見える丘公園
Shin-Yamashita
新山下
Kotobukichō
寿町
Yoshihamachō
吉浜町
Ishikawachō
Motomachi Park
元町公園
Yokonama Int'l Sch.
横浜インターナショナルスクール
Matsukagechō
松影町
Ferris Girls' Sch.
フェリス女学院
Suwa-chō
諏訪町
Korean Consulate General
韓国総領事館
Municipal Kōwan Hosp.
市立港湾病院
Yokohama Girls' Comm. H. Sch.
横浜女子商業学園
Yamatechō
山手町
Ishikawachō
石川町
Yamate Hosp.
山手病院
St. Joseph College
セントジョセフカレッジ
Yokohama Girls' H.Sch.
横浜女子高校
Yamate Catholic Ch.
山手カトリック教会
St. Maur Int'l Sch.
サンモール・インターナショナル・スクール
NAKA-KU
NEGISHI LINE
根岸線
Futaba Gakuen
雙葉学園
Ferris Women's Coll.
フェリス女学院大学
Kirin-en Park
キリン園公園
Uchikoshi
打越
Kyōritsu Gakuen (Sch.)
共立学園
Yamate Park
山手公園
To Isogo
至磯子
Chiyozakichō
千代崎町
Kominato Danchi (Apts)
小港団地
1 : 20,000
0
1000m

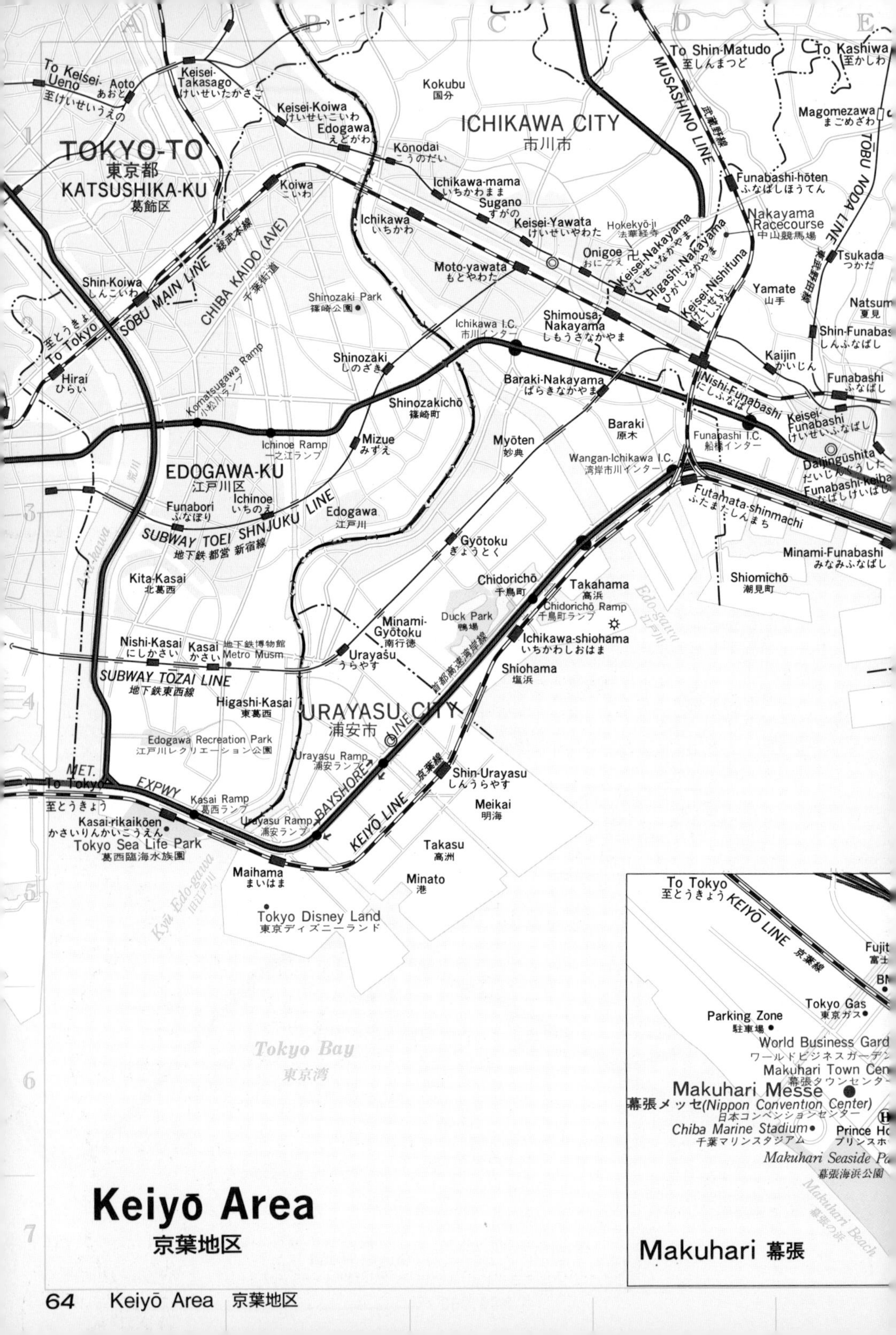

Keiyō Area
京葉地区

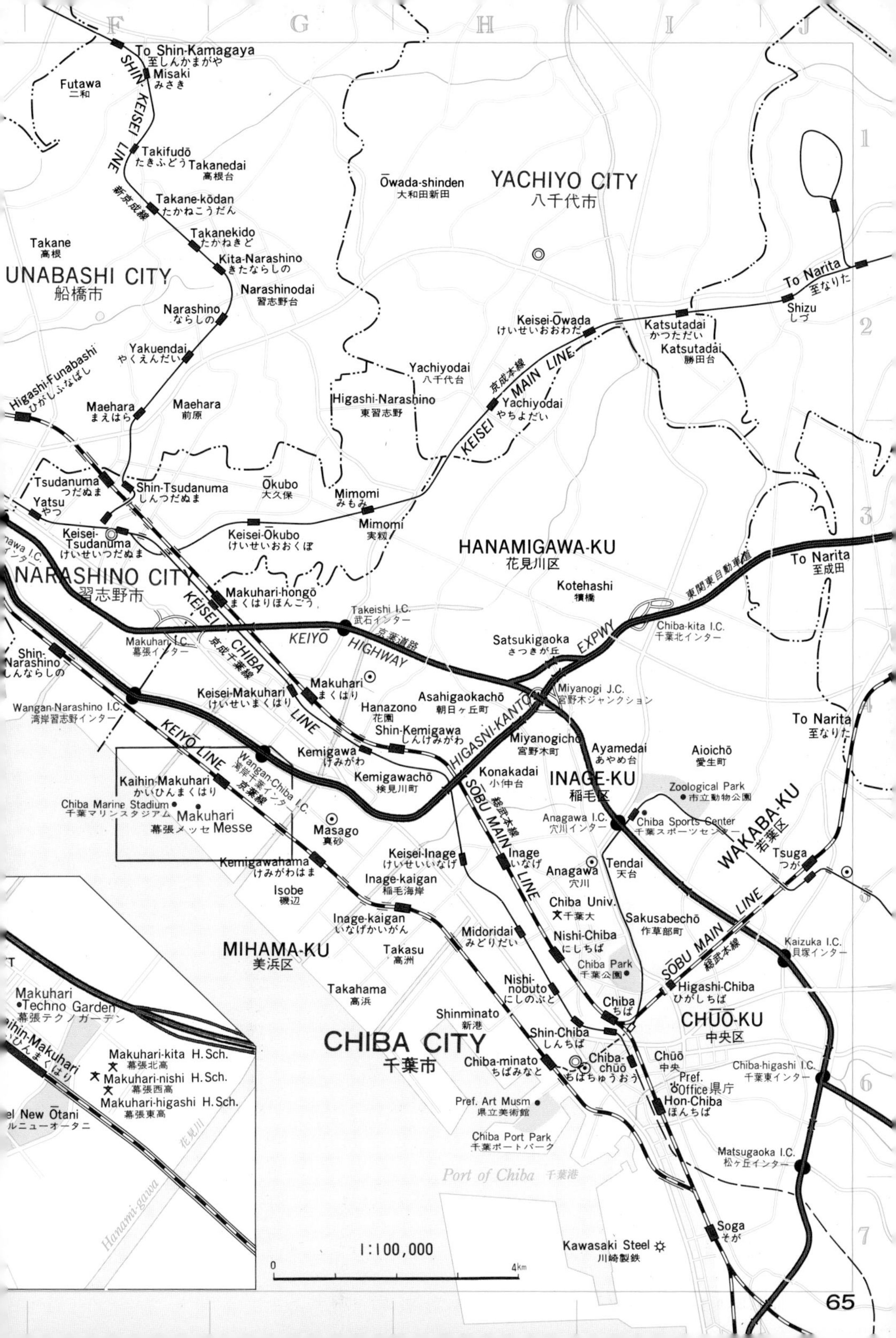
F
G
H
I
J
1
2
3
4
5
6
7
To Shin-Kamagaya
至しんかまがや
Misaki
みさき
Futawa
二和
SHIN KEISEI LINE
新京成線
Takifudō
たきふどう
Takanedai
高根台
Takane-kōdan
たかねこうだん
Takanekido
たかねきど
Kita-Narashino
きたならしの
Takane
高根
UNABASHI CITY
船橋市
Narashinodai
習志野台
Narashino
ならしの
Yakuendai
やくえんだい
Higashi-Funabashi
ひがしふなばし
Maehara
まえはら
Maehara
前原
Ōwada-shinden
大和田新田
YACHIYO CITY
八千代市
To Narita
至なりた
Shizu
しづ
Keisei-Ōwada
けいせいおおわだ
Katsutadai
かつただい
Katsutadai
勝田台
京成本線
KEISEI MAIN LINE
Yachiyodai
八千代台
Higashi-Narashino
東習志野
Yachiyodai
やちよだい
Tsudanuma
つだぬま
Shin-Tsudanuma
しんつだぬま
Ōkubo
大久保
Yatsu
やつ
Mimomi
みもみ
Mimomi
実籾
Keisei-Tsudanuma
けいせいつだぬま
Keisei-Ōkubo
けいせいおおくぼ
HANAMIGAWA-KU
花見川区
To Narita
至成田
NARASHINO CITY
習志野市
Makuhari-hongō
まくはりほんごう
Kotehashi
犢橋
東関東自動車道
KEISEI CHIBA LINE
京成千葉線
Takeishi I.C.
武石インター
KEIYŌ HIGHWAY
京葉道路
Chiba-kita I.C.
千葉北インター
Makuhari I.C.
幕張インター
Satsukigaoka
さつきが丘
EXPWY
Shin-Narashino
しんならしの
Makuhari
まくはり
Miyanogi J.C.
宮野木ジャンクション
Keisei-Makuhari
けいせいまくはり
Wangan-Narashino I.C.
湾岸習志野インター
Hanazono
花園
Asahigaokachō
朝日ヶ丘町
HIGASHI-KANTO
Shin-Kemigawa
しんけみがわ
To Narita
至なりた
Miyanogichō
宮野木町
Ayamedai
あやめ台
Aioichō
愛生町
KEIYŌ LINE
京葉線
Kemigawa
けみがわ
Wangan-Chiba I.C.
湾岸千葉インター
Konakadai
小仲台
INAGE-KU
稲毛区
Zoological Park
市立動物公園
WAKABA-KU
若葉区
Kaihin-Makuhari
かいひんまくはり
Kemigawachō
検見川町
SŌBU MAIN LINE
総武本線
Chiba Marine Stadium
千葉マリンスタジアム
Makuhari
幕張メッセ Messe
Masago
真砂
Anagawa I.C.
穴川インター
Chiba Sports Center
千葉スポーツセンター
Keisei-Inage
けいせいいなげ
Inage
いなげ
Tsuga
つが
Kemigawahama
けみがわはま
Inage-kaigan
稲毛海岸
Anagawa
穴川
Tendai
天台
Isobe
磯辺
Chiba Univ.
千葉大
Inage-kaigan
いなげかいがん
Sakusabechō
作草部町
Midoridai
みどりだい
Nishi-Chiba
にしちば
Kaizuka I.C.
貝塚インター
MIHAMA-KU
美浜区
Takasu
高洲
Chiba Park
千葉公園
Takahama
高浜
Nishi-nobuto
にしのぶと
Higashi-Chiba
ひがしちば
Makuhari
Techno Garden
幕張テクノガーデン
Chiba
ちば
Shinminato
新港
CHŪŌ-KU
中央区
Shin-Chiba
しんちば
Makuhari-kita H. Sch.
幕張北高
Kaihin-Makuhari
かいひんまくはり
CHIBA CITY
千葉市
Chiba-minato
ちばみなと
Chiba-chūō
ちばちゅうおう
Chūō
中央
Chiba-higashi I.C.
千葉東インター
Makuhari-nishi H.Sch.
幕張西高
Pref. Office
県庁
Makuhari-higashi H.Sch.
幕張東高
Pref. Art Musm
県立美術館
Hon-Chiba
ほんちば
New Ōtani
ルニューオータニ
花見川
Chiba Port Park
千葉ポートパーク
Matsugaoka I.C.
松ケ丘インター
Port of Chiba
千葉港
Hanami-gawa
Soga
そが
1:100,000
0
4km
Kawasaki Steel
川崎製鉄

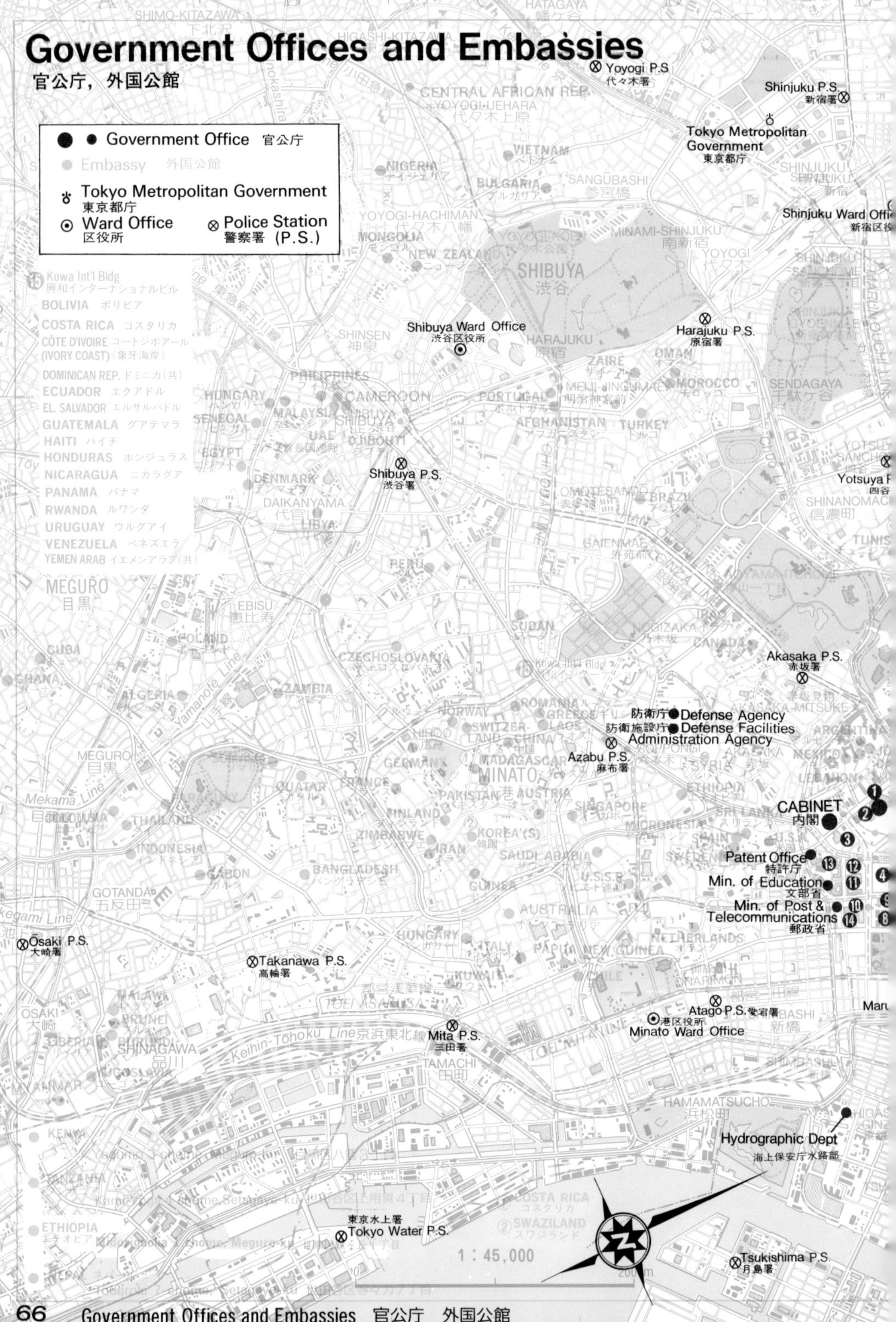
Government Offices and Embassies
官公庁，外国公館
Government Office 官公庁
Embassy 外国公館
Tokyo Metropolitan Government
東京都庁
Ward Office
区役所
Police Station
警察署 (P.S.)
Kowa Int'l Bldg
興和インターナショナルビル
BOLIVIA ボリビア
COSTA RICA コスタリカ
CÔTE D'IVOIRE コートジボアール
(IVORY COAST) (象牙海岸)
DOMINICAN REP. ドミニカ(共)
ECUADOR エクアドル
EL. SALVADOR エルサルバドル
GUATEMALA グアテマラ
HAITI ハイチ
HONDURAS ホンジュラス
NICARAGUA ニカラグア
PANAMA パナマ
RWANDA ルワンダ
URUGUAY ウルグアイ
VENEZUELA ベネズエラ
YEMEN ARAB イエメンアラブ(共)
Yoyogi P.S.
代々木署
Shinjuku P.S.
新宿署
Tokyo Metropolitan Government
東京都庁
Shinjuku Ward Office
新宿区役所
Shibuya Ward Office
渋谷区役所
Harajuku P.S.
原宿署
Shibuya P.S.
渋谷署
Akasaka P.S.
赤坂署
防衛庁 Defense Agency
防衛施設庁 Defense Facilities Administration Agency
Azabu P.S.
麻布署
CABINET
内閣
Patent Office
特許庁
Min. of Education
文部省
Min. of Post & Telecommunications
郵政省
Ōsaki P.S.
大崎署
Takanawa P.S.
高輪署
Mita P.S.
三田署
Atago P.S. 愛宕署
港区役所
Minato Ward Office
Hydrographic Dept
海上保安庁水路部
東京水上署
Tokyo Water P.S.
Tsukishima P.S.
月島署
1：45,000

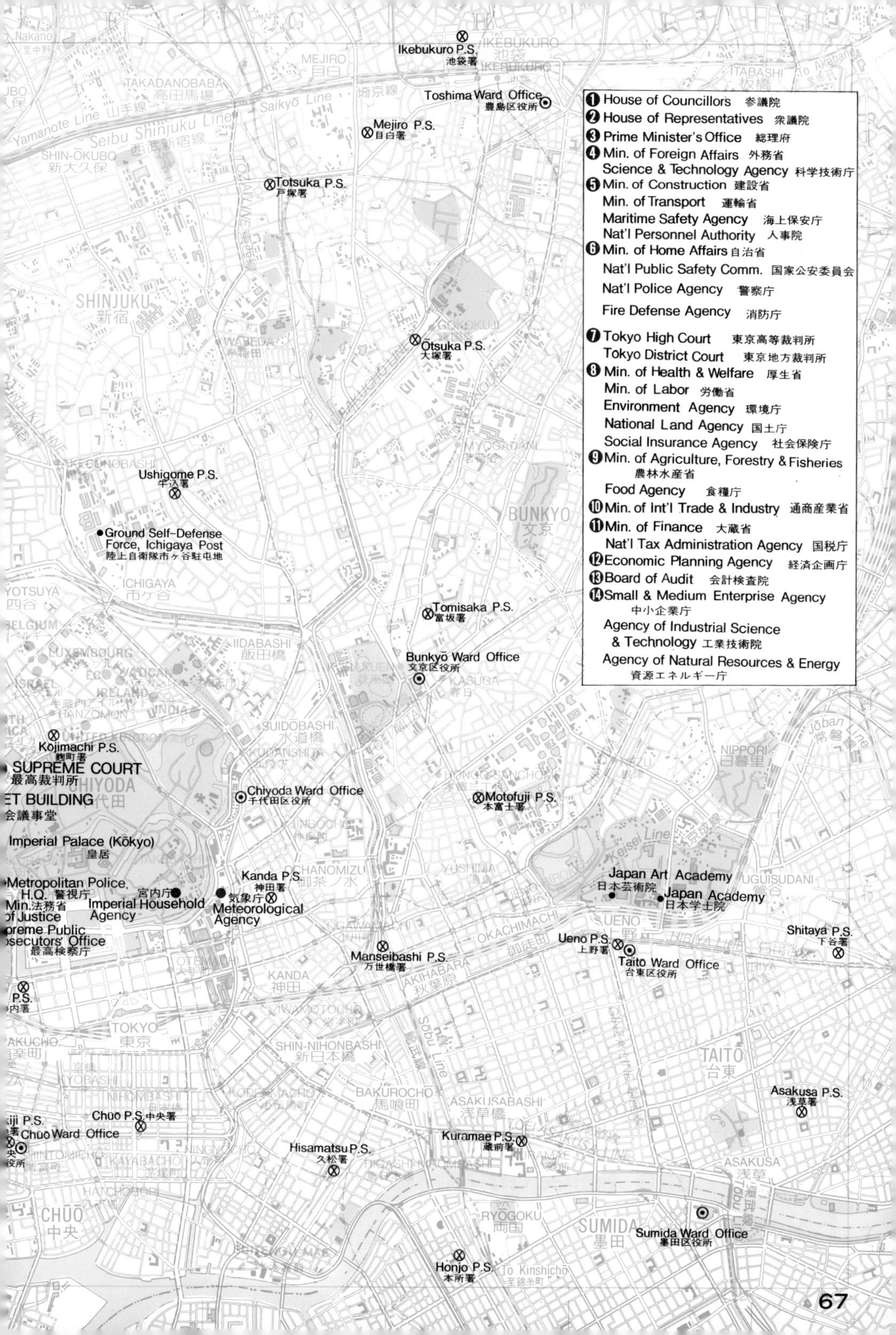
❶ House of Councillors 参議院
❷ House of Representatives 衆議院
❸ Prime Minister's Office 総理府
❹ Min. of Foreign Affairs 外務省
Science & Technology Agency 科学技術庁
❺ Min. of Construction 建設省
Min. of Transport 運輸省
Maritime Safety Agency 海上保安庁
Nat'l Personnel Authority 人事院
❻ Min. of Home Affairs 自治省
Nat'l Public Safety Comm. 国家公安委員会
Nat'l Police Agency 警察庁
Fire Defense Agency 消防庁
❼ Tokyo High Court 東京高等裁判所
Tokyo District Court 東京地方裁判所
❽ Min. of Health & Welfare 厚生省
Min. of Labor 労働省
Environment Agency 環境庁
National Land Agency 国土庁
Social Insurance Agency 社会保険庁
❾ Min. of Agriculture, Forestry & Fisheries 農林水産省
Food Agency 食糧庁
❿ Min. of Int'l Trade & Industry 通商産業省
⓫ Min. of Finance 大蔵省
Nat'l Tax Administration Agency 国税庁
⓬ Economic Planning Agency 経済企画庁
⓭ Board of Audit 会計検査院
⓮ Small & Medium Enterprise Agency 中小企業庁
Agency of Industrial Science & Technology 工業技術院
Agency of Natural Resources & Energy 資源エネルギー庁
Ikebukuro P.S. 池袋署
IKEBUKURO 池袋
MEJIRO 目白
TAKADANOBABA 高田馬場
Saikyō Line 埼京線
Yamanote Line 山手線
Seibu Shinjuku Line 西武新宿線
SHIN-OKUBO 新大久保
Toshima Ward Office 豊島区役所
Mejiro P.S. 目白署
Totsuka P.S. 戸塚署
SHINJUKU 新宿
Ōtsuka P.S. 大塚署
MYOGADANI
BUNKYO 文京
Ushigome P.S. 牛込署
Ground Self-Defense Force, Ichigaya Post 陸上自衛隊市ヶ谷駐屯地
YOTSUYA 四谷
ICHIGAYA 市ケ谷
IIDABASHI 飯田橋
Tomisaka P.S. 富坂署
Bunkyō Ward Office 文京区役所
KASUGA 春日
SUIDOBASHI 水道橋
Kojimachi P.S. 麹町署
SUPREME COURT 最高裁判所
CHIYODA 千代田
Chiyoda Ward Office 千代田区役所
Motofuji P.S. 本富士署
NIPPORI 日暮里
Jōban Line 常磐線
Keisei Line
Imperial Palace (Kōkyo) 皇居
Metropolitan Police H.Q. 警視庁
宮内庁 Imperial Household Agency
気象庁 Meteorological Agency
Kanda P.S. 神田署
OCHANOMIZU 御茶ノ水
YUSHIMA
Japan Art Academy 日本芸術院
Japan Academy 日本学士院
UGUISUDANI
UENO 上野
OKACHIMACHI
Ueno P.S. 上野署
Taito Ward Office 台東区役所
Shitaya P.S. 下谷署
Min. of Justice 法務省
Supreme Public Prosecutors' Office 最高検察庁
Manseibashi P.S. 万世橋署
AKIHABARA 秋葉原
KANDA 神田
TOKYO 東京
SHIN-NIHONBASHI 新日本橋
Sōbu Line 総武線
TAITO 台東
BAKUROCHO 馬喰町
ASAKUSABASHI 浅草橋
Asakusa P.S. 浅草署
Chuo P.S. 中央署
Chuo Ward Office
Hisamatsu P.S. 久松署
Kuramae P.S. 蔵前署
ASAKUSA 浅草
CHUO 中央
RYOGOKU 両国
SUMIDA 墨田
Sumida Ward Office 墨田区役所
Honjo P.S. 本所署
To Kinshichō 至錦糸町

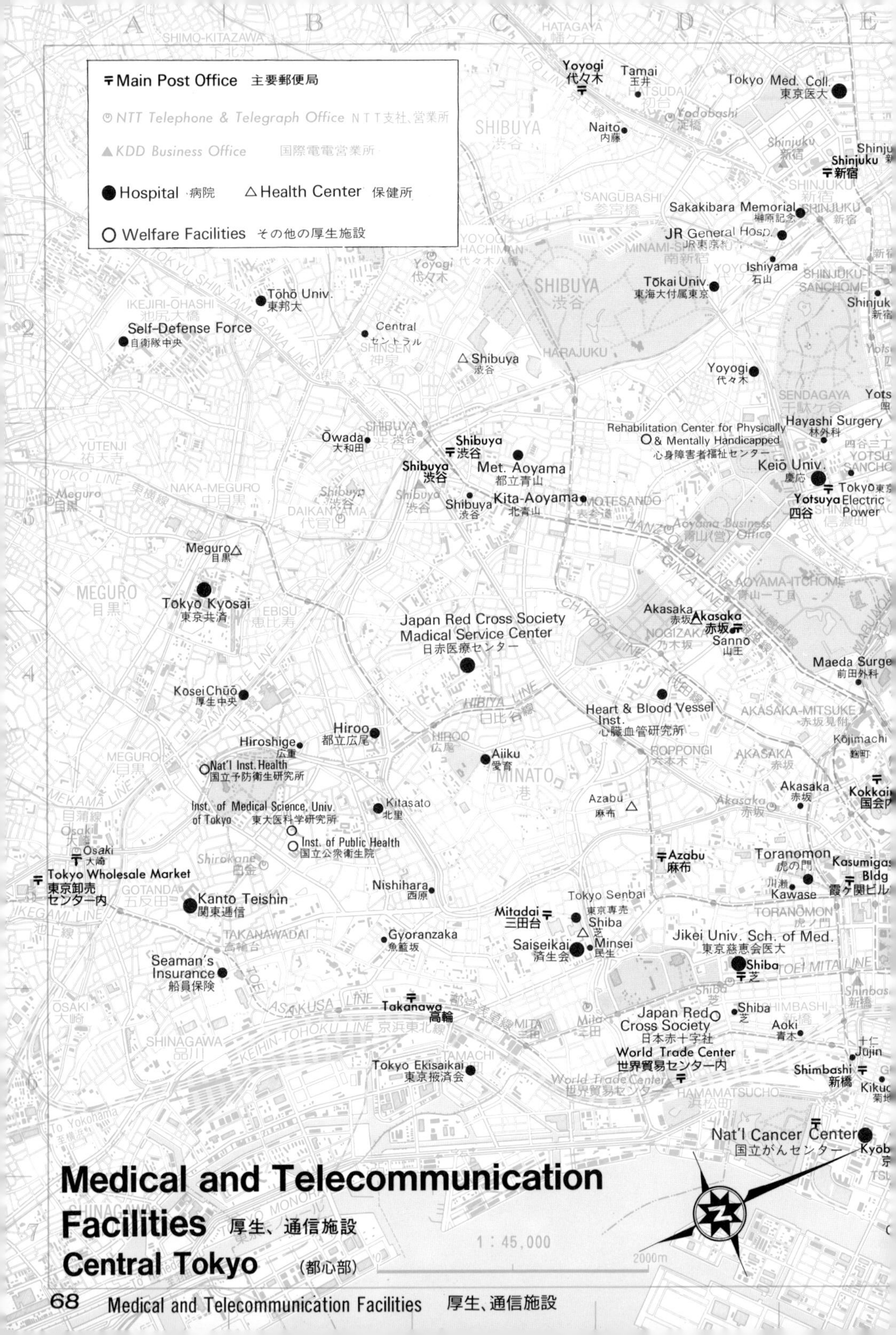

Medical and Telecommunication Facilities 厚生、通信施設

Central Tokyo (都心部)

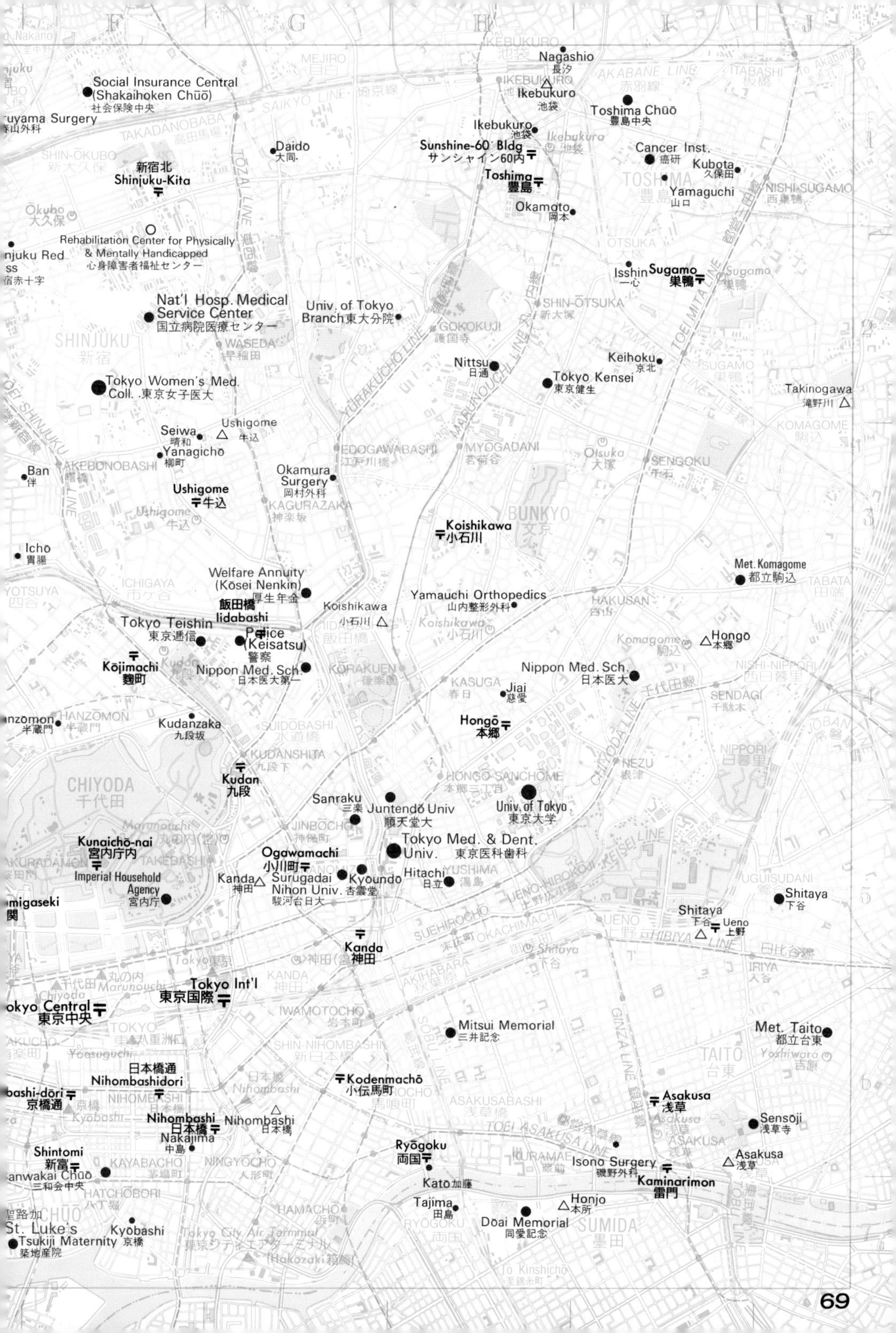
F
G
H
I
J
Nagashio
長汐
Ikebukuro
池袋
Toshima Chūō
豊島中央
Social Insurance Central
(Shakaihoken Chūō)
社会保険中央
Ikebukuro
池袋
Sunshine-60 Bldg
サンシャイン60内
Cancer Inst.
癌研
Kubota
久保田
Daidō
大同
新宿北
Shinjuku-Kita
Toshima
豊島
Yamaguchi
山口
Okamoto
岡本
Rehabilitation Center for Physically
& Mentally Handicapped
心身障害者福祉センター
Isshin
一心
Sugamo
巣鴨
Nat'l Hosp. Medical
Service Center
国立病院医療センター
Univ. of Tokyo
Branch東大分院
SHINJUKU
新宿
Nittsu
日通
Keihoku
京北
Tokyo Women's Med.
Coll. 東京女子医大
Tōkyo Kensei
東京健生
Takinogawa
滝野川
Seiwa
晴和
Ushigome
牛込
Yanagichō
柳町
Ban
伴
Okamura
Surgery
岡村外科
Ushigome
牛込
Koishikawa
小石川
BUNKYO
文京
Icho
胃腸
Met. Komagome
都立駒込
Welfare Annuity
(Kōsei Nenkin)
厚生年金
飯田橋
Iidabashi
Koishikawa
小石川
Yamauchi Orthopedics
山内整形外科
Tokyo Teishin
東京逓信
Police
(Keisatsu)
警察
Hongō
本郷
Kōjimachi
麹町
Nippon Med. Sch.
日本医大第一
Nippon Med. Sch.
日本医大
Jiai
慈愛
Hanzōmon
半蔵門
Kudanzaka
九段坂
Hongō
本郷
Kudan
九段
CHIYODA
千代田
Sanraku
三楽
Juntendō Univ
順天堂大
Univ. of Tokyo
東京大学
Tokyo Med. & Dent.
Univ.
東京医科歯科
Kunaichō-nai
宮内庁内
Imperial Household
Agency
宮内庁
Ogawamachi
小川町
Kanda
神田
Surugadai
Nihon Univ.
駿河台日大
Kyoundo
杏雲堂
Hitachi
日立
Shitaya
下谷
Shitaya
下谷
Ueno
上野
Kasumigaseki
Kanda
神田
Tokyo Int'l
東京国際
Tokyo Central
東京中央
Mitsui Memorial
三井記念
Met. Taito
都立台東
日本橋通
Nihombashidori
Kyobashi-dōri
京橋通
Kodenmachō
小伝馬町
Asakusa
浅草
Nihombashi
日本橋
Nihombashi
日本橋
Nakajima
中島
Sensōji
浅草寺
Shintomi
新富
Sanwakai Chūō
三和会中央
Ryōgoku
両国
Isono Surgery
磯野外科
Asakusa
浅草
Kaminarimon
雷門
Kato 加藤
Tajima
田島
Honjo
本所
St. Luke's
聖路加
Kyobashi
京橋
Doai Memorial
同愛記念
Tsukiji Maternity
築地産院

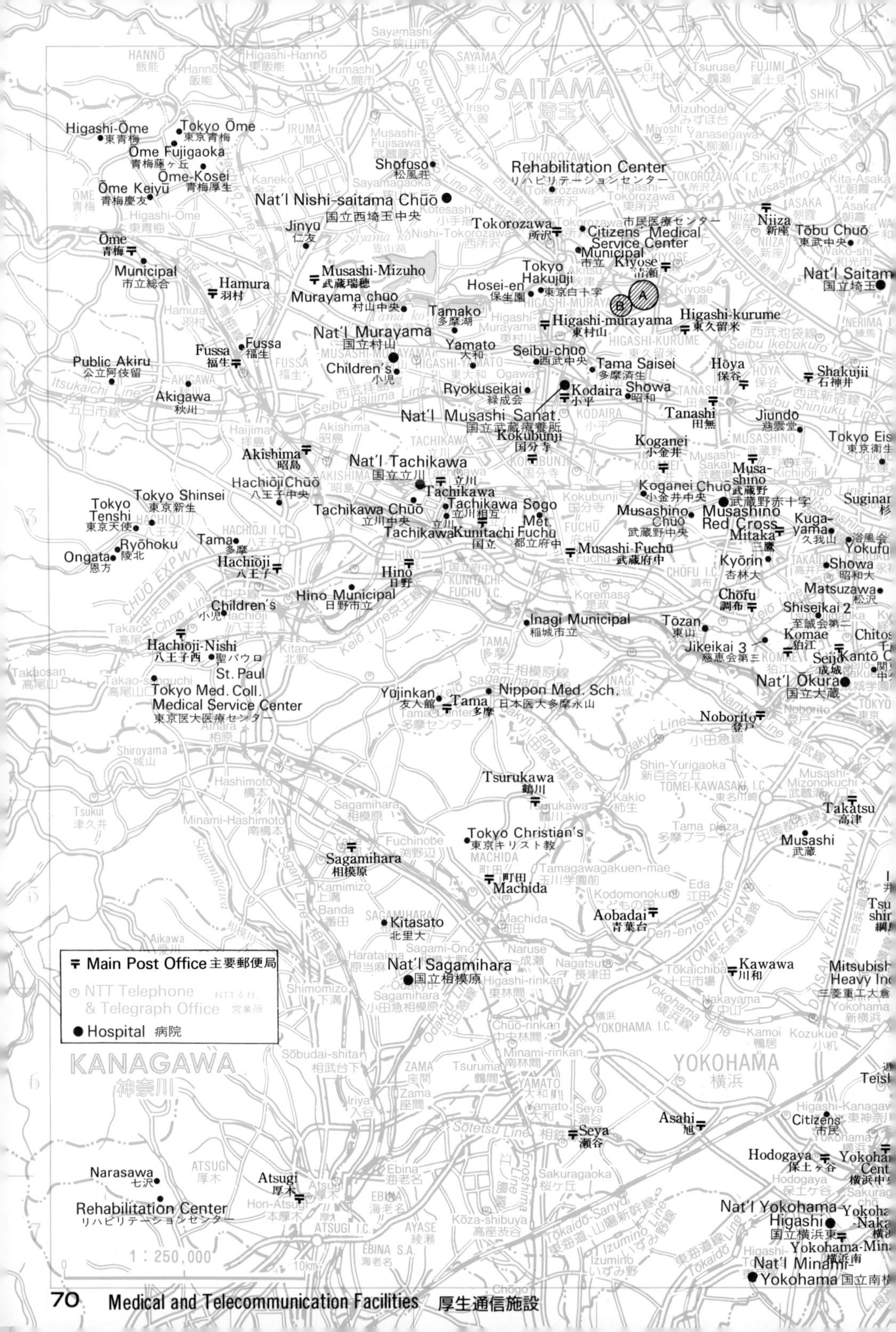

SAITAMA
埼玉
KANAGAWA
神奈川
YOKOHAMA
横浜
Higashi-Ōme
東青梅
Tokyo Ōme
東京青梅
Ōme Fujigaoka
青梅藤ヶ丘
Ōme-Kosei
青梅厚生
Ōme Keiyū
青梅慶友
Ōme
青梅
Municipal
市立総合
Hamura
羽村
Fussa
福生
Public Akiru
公立阿伎留
Akigawa
秋川
Akishima
昭島
Hachiōji Chūō
八王子中央
Tokyo Shinsei
東京新生
Tokyo Tenshi
東京天使
Ryōhoku
陵北
Ongata
恩方
Tama
多摩
Hachiōji
八王子
Children's
小児
Hachiōji-Nishi
八王子西
St. Paul
聖パウロ
Tokyo Med. Coll. Medical Service Center
東京医大医療センター
Shofūso
松風荘
Nat'l Nishi-saitama Chūō
国立西埼玉中央
Jinyū
仁友
Musashi-Mizuho
武蔵瑞穂
Murayama chūō
村山中央
Tamako
多摩湖
Nat'l Murayama
国立村山
Yamato
大和
Children's
小児
Ryokuseikai
緑成会
Nat'l Musashi Sanat.
国立武蔵療養所
Nat'l Tachikawa
国立立川
Tachikawa
立川
Tachikawa Chūō
立川中央
Tachikawa Sogo
立川相互
Kunitachi
国立
Hino
日野
Hino Municipal
日野市立
Rehabilitation Center
リハビリテーションセンター
Tokorozawa
所沢
Citizens' Medical Service Center
市民医療センター
Municipal
市立
Kiyose
清瀬
Tokyo Hakujūji
東京白十字
Hosei-en
保生園
Higashi-murayama
東村山
Higashi-kurume
東久留米
Seibu-chūō
西武中央
Tama Saisei
多摩済生
Kodaira
小平
Showa
昭和
Kokubunji
国分寺
Met. Fuchū
都立府中
Musashi-Fuchū
武蔵府中
Inagi Municipal
稲城市立
Yūjinkan
友人館
Tama
多摩
Nippon Med. Sch.
日本医大多摩永山
Niiza
新座
Tōbu Chūō
東武中央
Nat'l Saitama
国立埼玉
Hōya
保谷
Shakujii
石神井
Tanashi
田無
Jiundo
慈雲堂
Koganei
小金井
Koganei Chūō
小金井中央
Musa-shino
武蔵野
Musashino Red Cross
武蔵野赤十字
Musashino Chūō
武蔵野中央
Mitaka
三鷹
Kuga-yama
久我山
Kyōrin
杏林大
Chōfu
調布
Tōzan
東山
Jikeikai 3
慈恵会第三
Shisejkai 2
至誠会第二
Komae
狛江
Seijō
成城
Nat'l Ōkura
国立大蔵
Noborito
登戸
Showa
昭和大
Matsuzawa
松沢
Tsurukawa
鶴川
Tokyo Christian's
東京キリスト教
Machida
町田
Sagamihara
相模原
Kitasato
北里大
Nat'l Sagamihara
国立相模原
Aobadai
青葉台
Kawawa
川和
Takatsu
高津
Musashi
武蔵
Seya
瀬谷
Asahi
旭
Atsugi
厚木
Narasawa
七沢
Rehabilitation Center
リハビリテーションセンター
Hodogaya
保土ヶ谷
Citizens
市民
Nat'l Yokohama-Higashi
国立横浜東
Nat'l Minami-Yokohama
国立南横浜
Main Post Office 主要郵便局
NTT Telephone & Telegraph Office NTT支社営業所
Hospital 病院
1 : 250,000

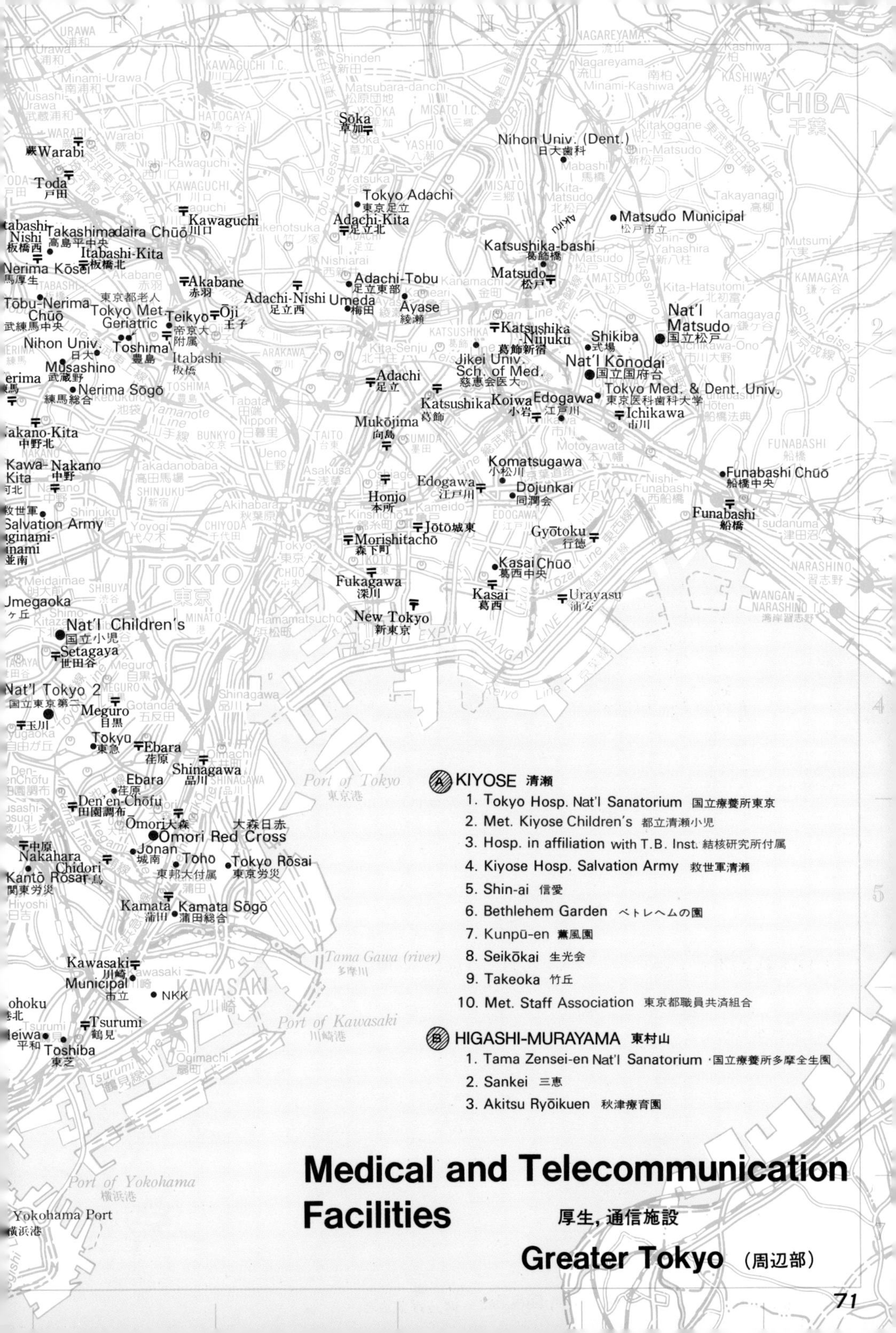
Ⓐ KIYOSE 清瀬
1. Tokyo Hosp. Nat'l Sanatorium 国立療養所東京
2. Met. Kiyose Children's 都立清瀬小児
3. Hosp. in affiliation with T.B. Inst. 結核研究所付属
4. Kiyose Hosp. Salvation Army 救世軍清瀬
5. Shin-ai 信愛
6. Bethlehem Garden ベトレヘムの園
7. Kunpū-en 薫風園
8. Seikōkai 生光会
9. Takeoka 竹丘
10. Met. Staff Association 東京都職員共済組合
Ⓑ HIGASHI-MURAYAMA 東村山
1. Tama Zensei-en Nat'l Sanatorium 国立療養所多摩全生園
2. Sankei 三恵
3. Akitsu Ryōikuen 秋津療育園
Medical and Telecommunication Facilities 厚生, 通信施設
Greater Tokyo (周辺部)

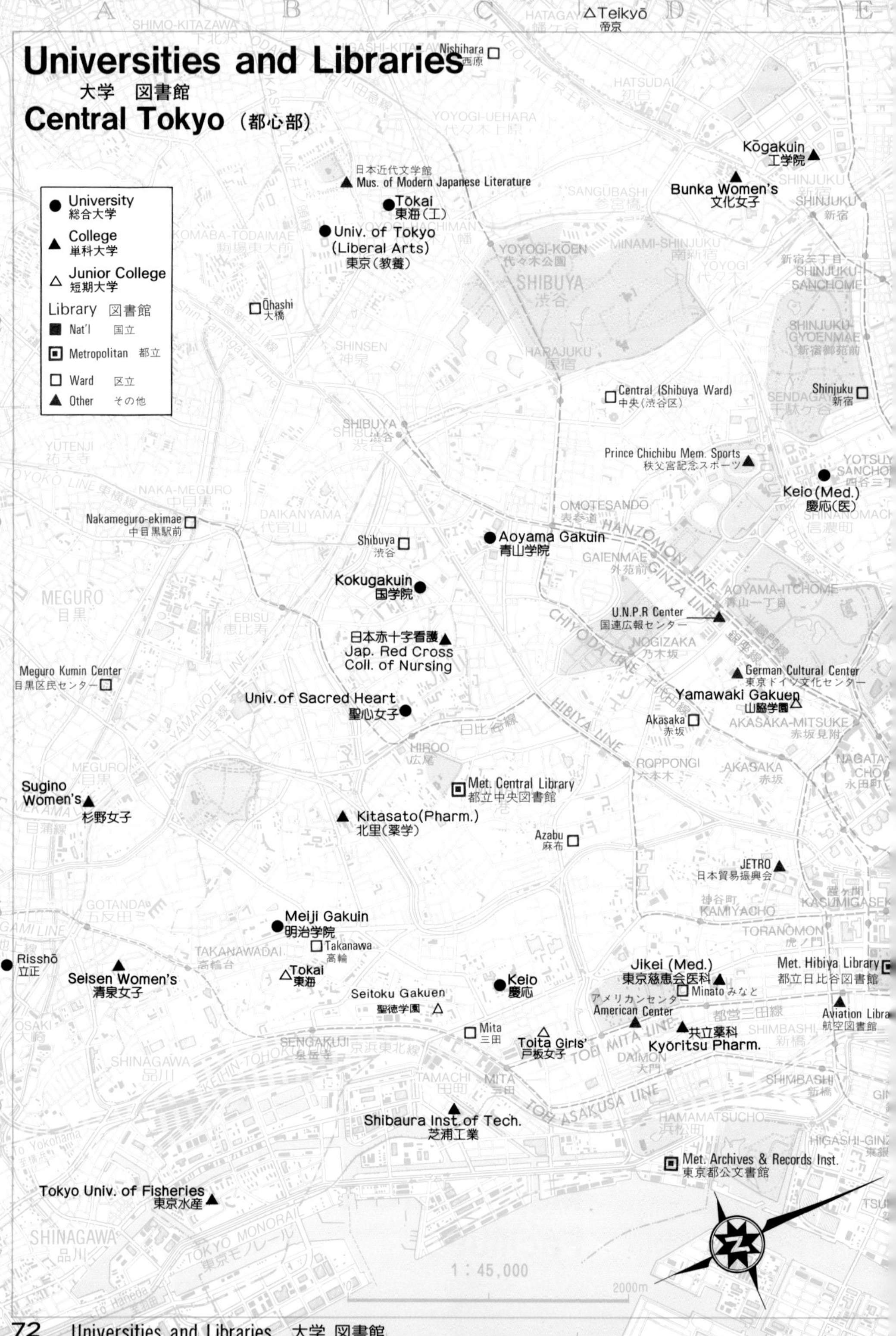

Universities and Libraries
大学 図書館
Central Tokyo (都心部)
University 総合大学
College 単科大学
Junior College 短期大学
Library 図書館
Nat'l 国立
Metropolitan 都立
Ward 区立
Other その他
Teikyō 帝京
Nishihara 西原
Kōgakuin 工学院
Bunka Women's 文化女子
日本近代文学館
Mus. of Modern Japanese Literature
Tokai 東海(工)
Univ. of Tokyo (Liberal Arts) 東京(教養)
Ohashi 大橋
Central (Shibuya Ward) 中央(渋谷区)
Shinjuku 新宿
Prince Chichibu Mem. Sports 秩父宮記念スポーツ
Keio (Med.) 慶応(医)
Nakameguro-ekimae 中目黒駅前
Shibuya 渋谷
Aoyama Gakuin 青山学院
Kokugakuin 国学院
U.N.P.R Center 国連広報センター
日本赤十字看護 Jap. Red Cross Coll. of Nursing
German Cultural Center 東京ドイツ文化センター
Meguro Kumin Center 目黒区民センター
Univ. of Sacred Heart 聖心女子
Yamawaki Gakuen 山脇学園
Akasaka 赤坂
Sugino Women's 杉野女子
Met. Central Library 都立中央図書館
Kitasato (Pharm.) 北里(薬学)
Azabu 麻布
JETRO 日本貿易振興会
Meiji Gakuin 明治学院
Takanawa 高輪
Risshō 立正
Seisen Women's 清泉女子
Tokai 東海
Keio 慶応
Jikei (Med.) 東京慈恵会医科
Minato みなと
Met. Hibiya Library 都立日比谷図書館
Seitoku Gakuen 聖徳学園
アメリカンセンター American Center
共立薬科 Kyōritsu Pharm.
Aviation Libra 航空図書館
Mita 三田
Toita Girls' 戸板女子
Shibaura Inst. of Tech. 芝浦工業
Met. Archives & Records Inst. 東京都公文書館
Tokyo Univ. of Fisheries 東京水産
1 : 45,000
2000m

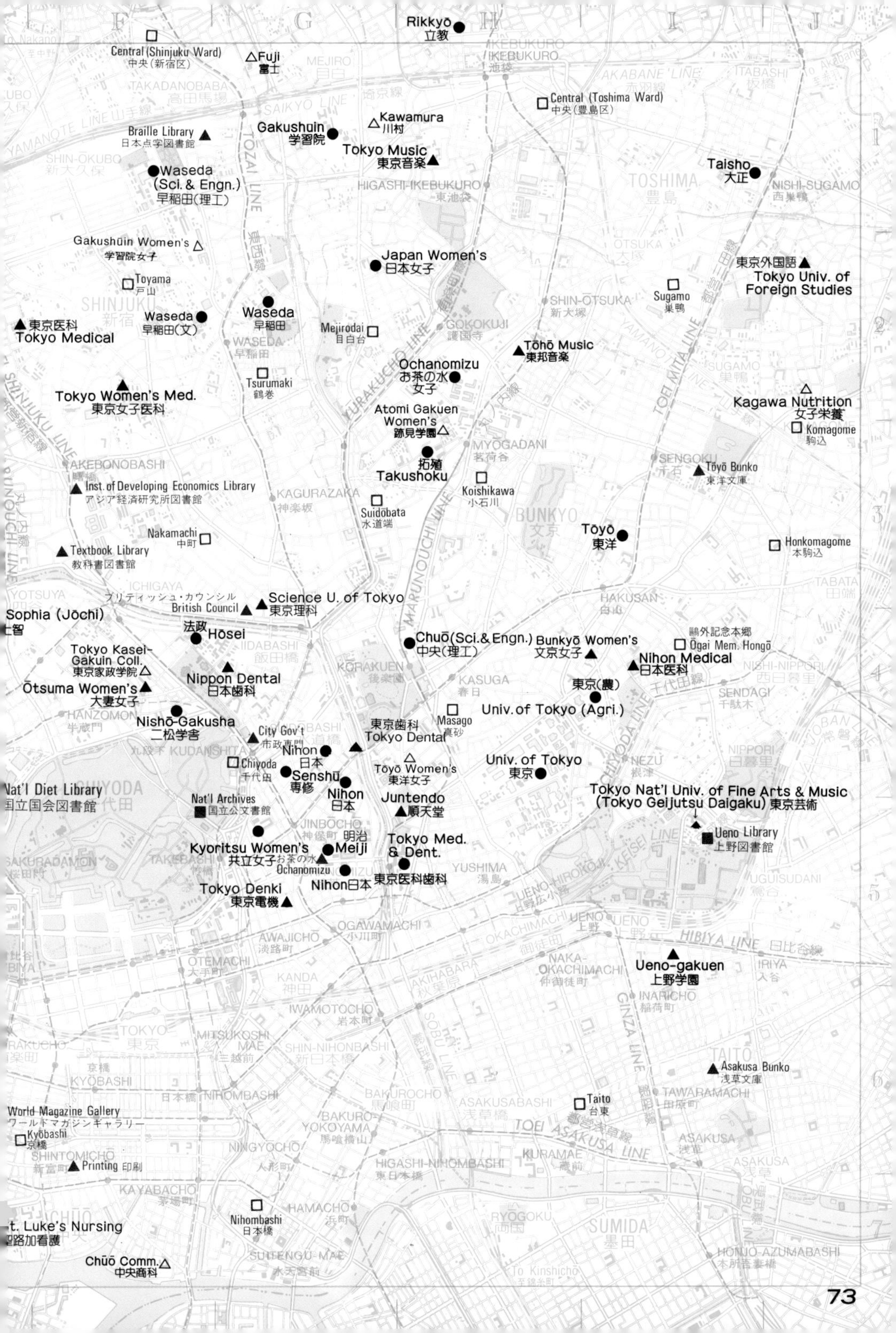
Rikkyō 立教
Central (Shinjuku Ward) 中央(新宿区)
Fuji 富士
Central (Toshima Ward) 中央(豊島区)
Kawamura 川村
Gakushūin 学習院
Braille Library 日本点字図書館
Tokyo Music 東京音楽
Waseda (Sci. & Engn.) 早稲田(理工)
Taisho 大正
Gakushūin Women's 学習院女子
Japan Women's 日本女子
東京外国語 Tokyo Univ. of Foreign Studies
Toyama 戸山
Sugamo 巣鴨
Waseda 早稲田(文)
Waseda 早稲田
東京医科 Tokyo Medical
Mejirodai 目白台
Tōhō Music 東邦音楽
Ochanomizu お茶の水女子
Tsurumaki 鶴巻
Tokyo Women's Med. 東京女子医科
Kagawa Nutrition 女子栄養
Atomi Gakuen Women's 跡見学園
Komagome 駒込
拓殖 Takushoku
Tōyō Bunko 東洋文庫
Koishikawa 小石川
Inst. of Developing Economics Library アジア経済研究所図書館
Suidōbata 水道端
Tōyō 東洋
Nakamachi 中町
Honkomagome 本駒込
Textbook Library 教科書図書館
ブリティッシュ・カウンシル British Council
Science U. of Tokyo 東京理科
Sophia (Jōchi)
法政 Hōsei
Chuō (Sci. & Engn.) 中央(理工)
Bunkyō Women's 文京女子
鷗外記念本郷 Ōgai Mem. Hongō
Tokyo Kasei-Gakuin Coll. 東京家政学院
Nihon Medical 日本医科
Nippon Dental 日本歯科
Ōtsuma Women's 大妻女子
東京(農) Univ. of Tokyo (Agri.)
Nishō-Gakusha 二松学舎
Masago 真砂
City Gov't 市政専門
東京歯科 Tokyo Dental
Nihon 日本
Chiyoda 千代田
Tōyō Women's 東洋女子
Univ. of Tokyo 東京
Senshū 専修
Nihon 日本
Nat'l Diet Library 国立国会図書館
Nat'l Archives 国立公文書館
Juntendo 順天堂
Tokyo Nat'l Univ. of Fine Arts & Music (Tokyo Geijutsu Daigaku) 東京芸術
Ueno Library 上野図書館
明治 Meiji
Kyoritsu Women's 共立女子
お茶の水 Ochanomizu
Tokyo Med. & Dent. 東京医科歯科
Nihon 日本
Tokyo Denki 東京電機
Ueno-gakuen 上野学園
Asakusa Bunko 浅草文庫
World Magazine Gallery ワールドマガジンギャラリー
Kyōbashi 京橋
Taito 台東
Printing 印刷
Nihombashi 日本橋
St. Luke's Nursing 聖路加看護
Chūō Comm. 中央商科
TOSHIMA 豊島
SHINJUKU 新宿
BUNKYO 文京
CHIYODA 千代田
TAITO 台東
SUMIDA 墨田
CHŪŌ
YAMANOTE LINE
TOZAI LINE
YURAKUCHO LINE
MARUNOUCHI LINE
TOEI MITA LINE
CHIYODA LINE
GINZA LINE
HIBIYA LINE
SOBU LINE
TOEI ASAKUSA LINE
SAIKYO LINE
AKABANE LINE
KEISEI LINE
SHINJUKU LINE

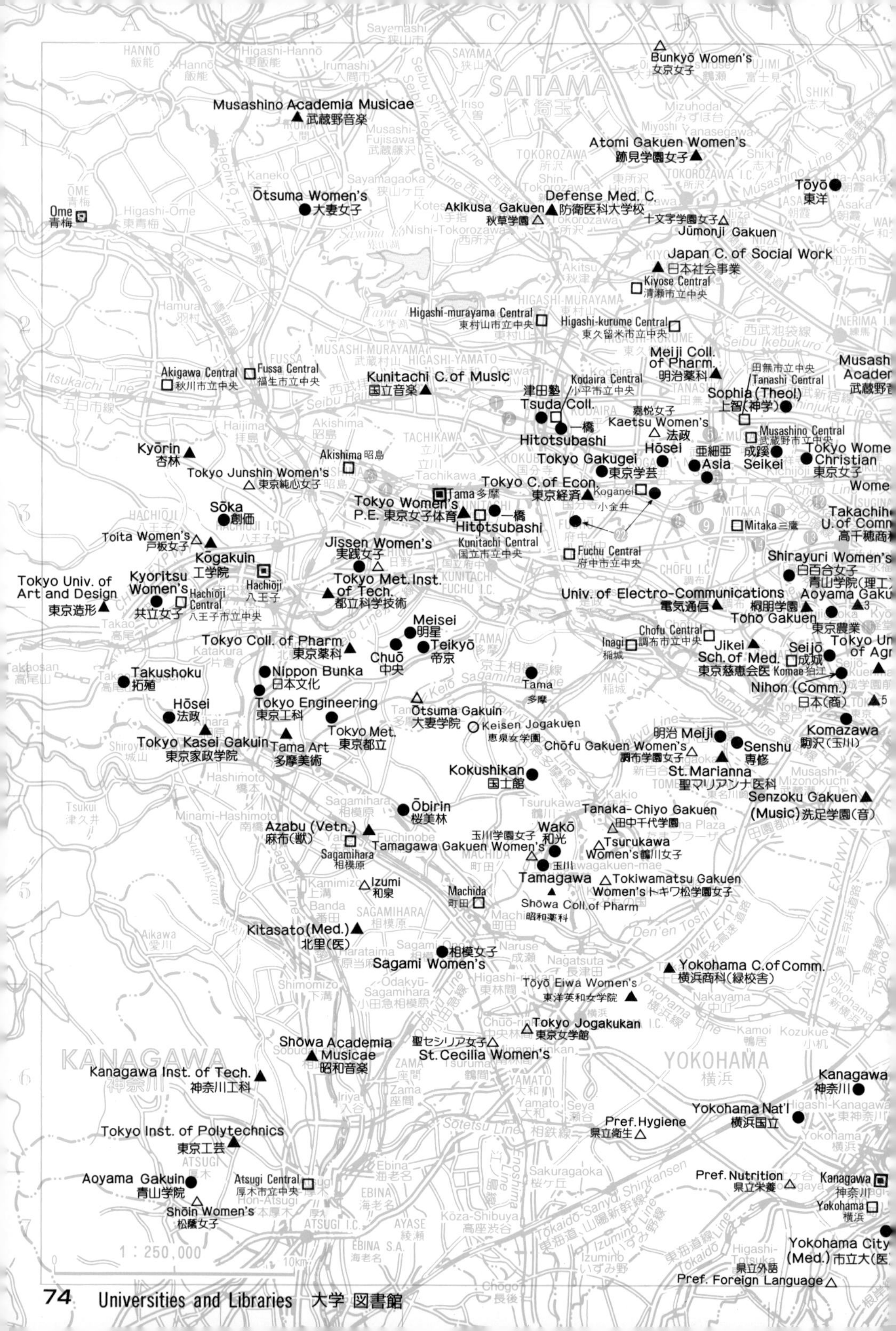
SAITAMA
埼玉
KANAGAWA
神奈川
YOKOHAMA
横浜
Musashino Academia Musicae
武蔵野音楽
Bunkyō Women's
文京女子
Atomi Gakuen Women's
跡見学園女子
Tōyō
東洋
Ōtsuma Women's
大妻女子
Ome
青梅
Defense Med. C.
防衛医科大学校
Akikusa Gakuen
秋草学園
十文字学園女子
Jūmonji Gakuen
Japan C. of Social Work
日本社会事業
Kiyose Central
清瀬市立中央
Higashi-murayama Central
東村山市立中央
Higashi-kurume Central
東久留米市立中央
Akigawa Central
秋川市立中央
Fussa Central
福生市立中央
Kunitachi C. of Music
国立音楽
Kodaira Central
小平市立中央
津田塾
Tsuda Coll.
一橋
Hitotsubashi
Meiji Coll. of Pharm.
明治薬科
田無市立中央
Tanashi Central
Sophia (Theol.)
上智(神学)
嘉悦女子
Kaetsu Women's
法政
Hōsei
亜細亜
Asia
Musashino Central
武蔵野市立中央
成蹊
Seikei
Tokyo Women's Christian
東京女子
Kyōrin
杏林
Akishima
昭島
Tokyo Gakugei
東京学芸
Tokyo Junshin Women's
東京純心女子
Tokyo C. of Econ.
東京経済
Koganei
小金井
Tama 多摩
Tokyo Women's P.E.
東京女子体育
一橋
Hitotsubashi
Sōka
創価
Mitaka 三鷹
Takachiho U. of Comm.
高千穂商科
Toita Women's
戸板女子
Kunitachi Central
国立市立中央
Jissen Women's
実践女子
Fuchu Central
府中市立中央
Kōgakuin
工学院
Hachiōji
八王子
Shirayuri Women's
白百合女子
青山学院(理工)
Aoyama Gakuin
Tokyo Univ. of Art and Design
東京造形
Kyoritsu Women's
共立女子
Hachiōji Central
八王子市立中央
Tokyo Met. Inst. of Tech.
都立科学技術
Univ. of Electro-Communications
電気通信
桐朋学園
Toho Gakuen
東京農業
Meisei
明星
Tokyo Coll. of Pharm.
東京薬科
Chuō
中央
Teikyō
帝京
Chofu Central
調布市立中央
Inagi
稲城
Jikei Sch. of Med.
東京慈恵会医
Seijō
成城
Komae 狛江
Tokyo Univ. of Agr.
Takushoku
拓殖
Nippon Bunka
日本文化
Tama
多摩
Nihon (Comm.)
日本(商)
Tokyo Engineering
東京工科
Ōtsuma Gakuin
大妻学院
Keisen Jogakuen
恵泉女学園
Hōsei
法政
Tokyo Met.
東京都立
明治 Meiji
Senshu
専修
Komazawa
駒沢(玉川)
Tokyo Kasei Gakuin
東京家政学院
Tama Art
多摩美術
Chōfu Gakuen Women's
調布学園女子
St. Marianna
聖マリアンナ医科
Kokushikan
国士舘
Senzoku Gakuen (Music)
洗足学園(音)
Ōbirin
桜美林
Tanaka-Chiyo Gakuen
田中千代学園
Azabu (Vetn.)
麻布(獣)
Sagamihara
相模原
玉川学園女子
Tamagawa Gakuen Women's
Wakō
和光
Tsurukawa Women's
鶴川女子
玉川
Tamagawa
Izumi
和泉
Tokiwamatsu Gakuen Women's
トキワ松学園女子
Machida
町田
Shōwa Coll. of Pharm
昭和薬科
Kitasato (Med.)
北里(医)
相模女子
Sagami Women's
Yokohama C. of Comm.
横浜商科(緑校舎)
Tōyō Eiwa Women's
東洋英和女学院
Tokyo Jogakukan
東京女学館
Shōwa Academia Musicae
昭和音楽
聖セシリア女子
St. Cecilia Women's
Kanagawa Inst. of Tech.
神奈川工科
Kanagawa
神奈川
Yokohama Nat'l
横浜国立
Pref. Hygiene
県立衛生
Tokyo Inst. of Polytechnics
東京工芸
Aoyama Gakuin
青山学院
Shōin Women's
松蔭女子
Atsugi Central
厚木市立中央
Pref. Nutrition
県立栄養
Kanagawa
神奈川
Yokohama
横浜
Yokohama City (Med.)
市立大(医)
県立外語
Pref. Foreign Language
1 : 250,000

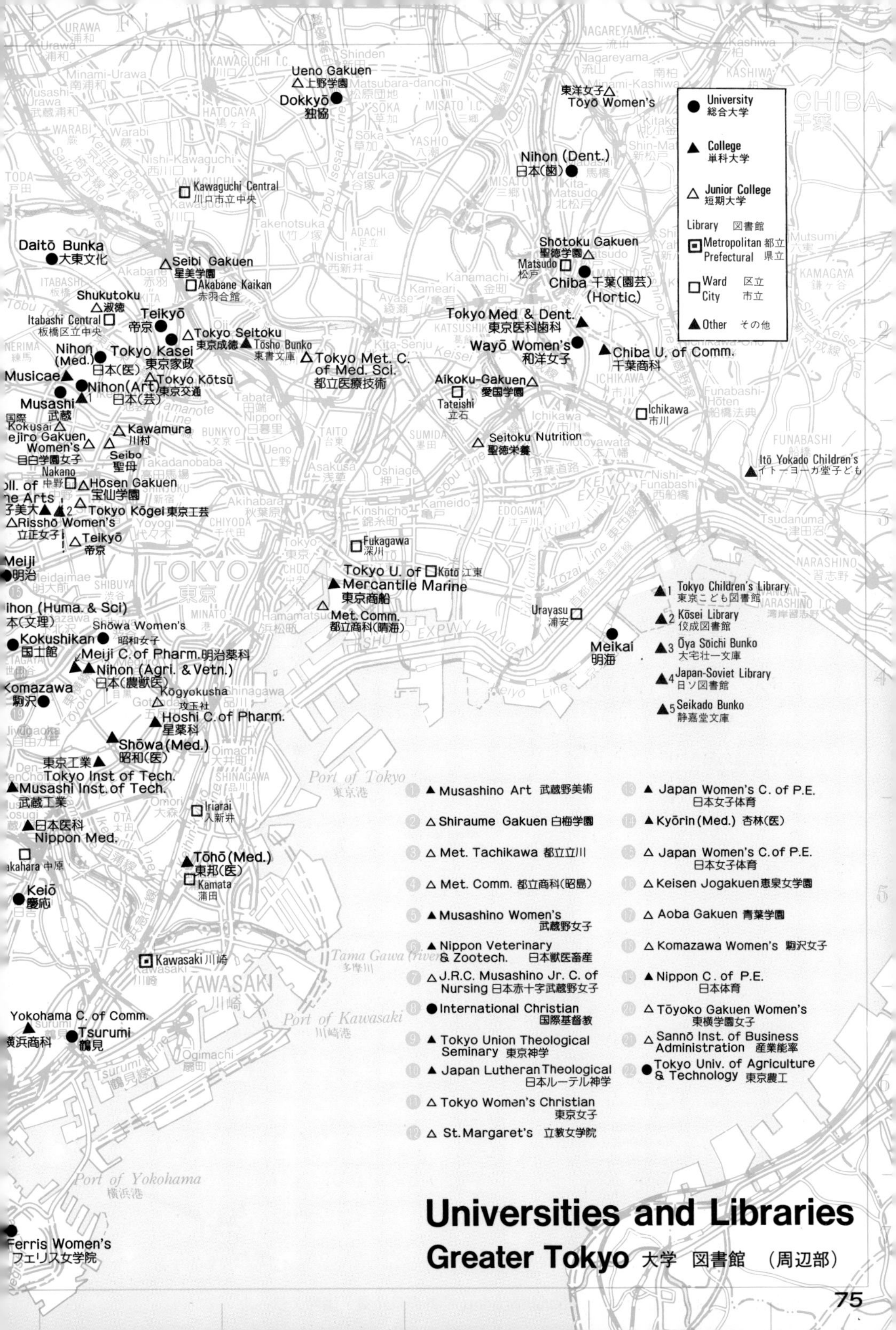

Universities and Libraries
Greater Tokyo 大学 図書館 （周辺部）

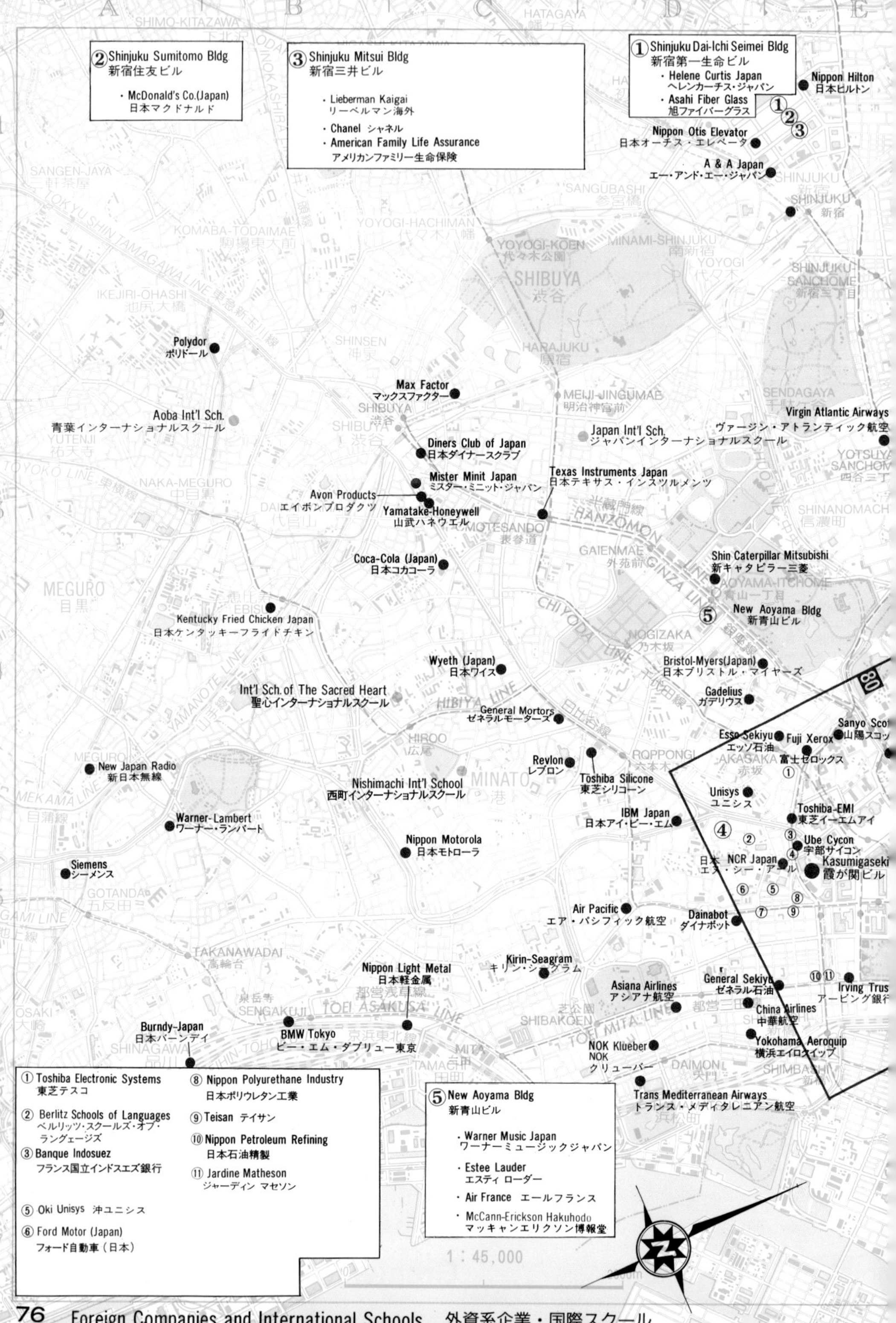
①Shinjuku Dai-Ichi Seimei Bldg 新宿第一生命ビル
・Helene Curtis Japan ヘレンカーチス・ジャパン
・Asahi Fiber Glass 旭ファイバーグラス
②Shinjuku Sumitomo Bldg 新宿住友ビル
・McDonald's Co.(Japan) 日本マクドナルド
③Shinjuku Mitsui Bldg 新宿三井ビル
・Lieberman Kaigai リーベルマン海外
・Chanel シャネル
・American Family Life Assurance アメリカンファミリー生命保険
Nippon Hilton 日本ヒルトン
Nippon Otis Elevator 日本オーチス・エレベータ
A & A Japan エー・アンド・エー・ジャパン
Polydor ポリドール
Max Factor マックスファクター
Aoba Int'l Sch. 青葉インターナショナルスクール
Japan Int'l Sch. ジャパンインターナショナルスクール
Virgin Atlantic Airways ヴァージン・アトランティック航空
Diners Club of Japan 日本ダイナースクラブ
Mister Minit Japan ミスター・ミニット・ジャパン
Avon Products エイボンプロダクツ
Yamatake-Honeywell 山武ハネウエル
Texas Instruments Japan 日本テキサス・インスツルメンツ
Coca-Cola (Japan) 日本コカコーラ
Shin Caterpillar Mitsubishi 新キャタピラー三菱
Kentucky Fried Chicken Japan 日本ケンタッキーフライドチキン
⑤ New Aoyama Bldg 新青山ビル
Wyeth (Japan) 日本ワイス
Bristol-Myers(Japan) 日本ブリストル・マイヤーズ
Int'l Sch. of The Sacred Heart 聖心インターナショナルスクール
Gadelius ガデリウス
General Mortors ゼネラルモーターズ
Esso Sekiyu エッソ石油
Fuji Xerox 富士ゼロックス
Revlon レブロン
Toshiba Silicone 東芝シリコーン
New Japan Radio 新日本無線
Nishimachi Int'l School 西町インターナショナルスクール
Unisys ユニシス
Toshiba-EMI 東芝イーエムアイ
Warner-Lambert ワーナー・ランバート
IBM Japan 日本アイ・ビー・エム
④
Ube Cycon 宇部サイコン
Nippon Motorola 日本モトローラ
NCR Japan 日本エヌ・シー・アール
Kasumigaseki 霞が関ビル
Siemens シーメンス
Air Pacific エア・パシフィック航空
Dainabot ダイナボット
Kirin-Seagram キリン・シーグラム
Nippon Light Metal 日本軽金属
Asiana Airlines アシアナ航空
General Sekiyu ゼネラル石油
China Airlines 中華航空
Burndy-Japan 日本バーンデイ
BMW Tokyo ビー・エム・ダブリュー東京
NOK Klueber NOK クリューバー
Yokohama Aeroquip 横浜エイロクイップ
Trans Mediterranean Airways トランス・メディタレニアン航空
① Toshiba Electronic Systems 東芝テスコ
② Berlitz Schools of Languages ベルリッツ・スクールズ・オブ・ランゲージズ
③ Banque Indosuez フランス国立インドスエズ銀行
⑤ Oki Unisys 沖ユニシス
⑥ Ford Motor (Japan) フォード自動車（日本）
⑧ Nippon Polyurethane Industry 日本ポリウレタン工業
⑨ Teisan テイサン
⑩ Nippon Petroleum Refining 日本石油精製
⑪ Jardine Matheson ジャーディン マセソン
⑤ New Aoyama Bldg 新青山ビル
・Warner Music Japan ワーナーミュージックジャパン
・Estee Lauder エスティ ローダー
・Air France エールフランス
・McCann-Erickson Hakuhodo マッキャンエリクソン博報堂
1：45,000

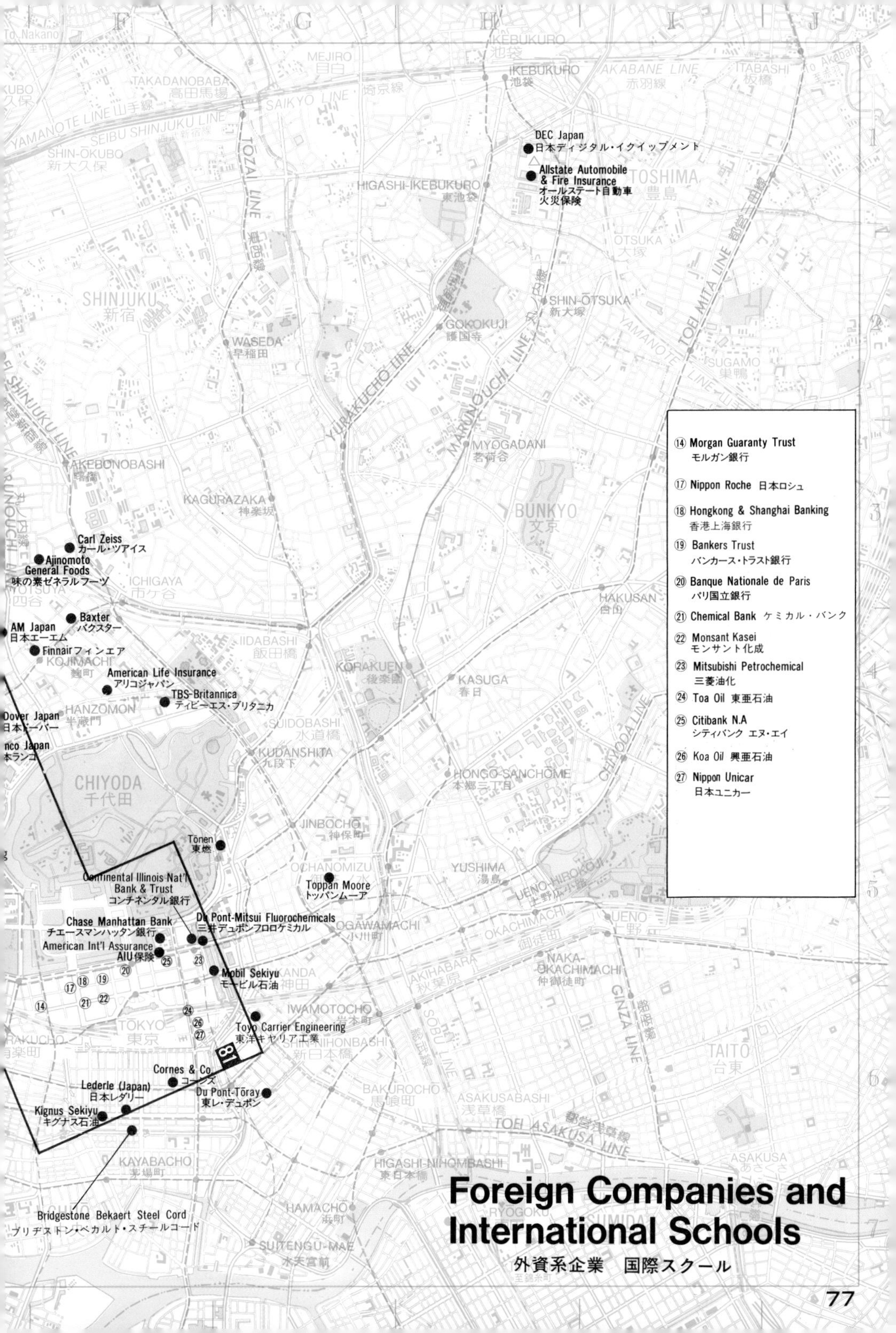

Foreign Companies and International Schools

外資系企業　国際スクール

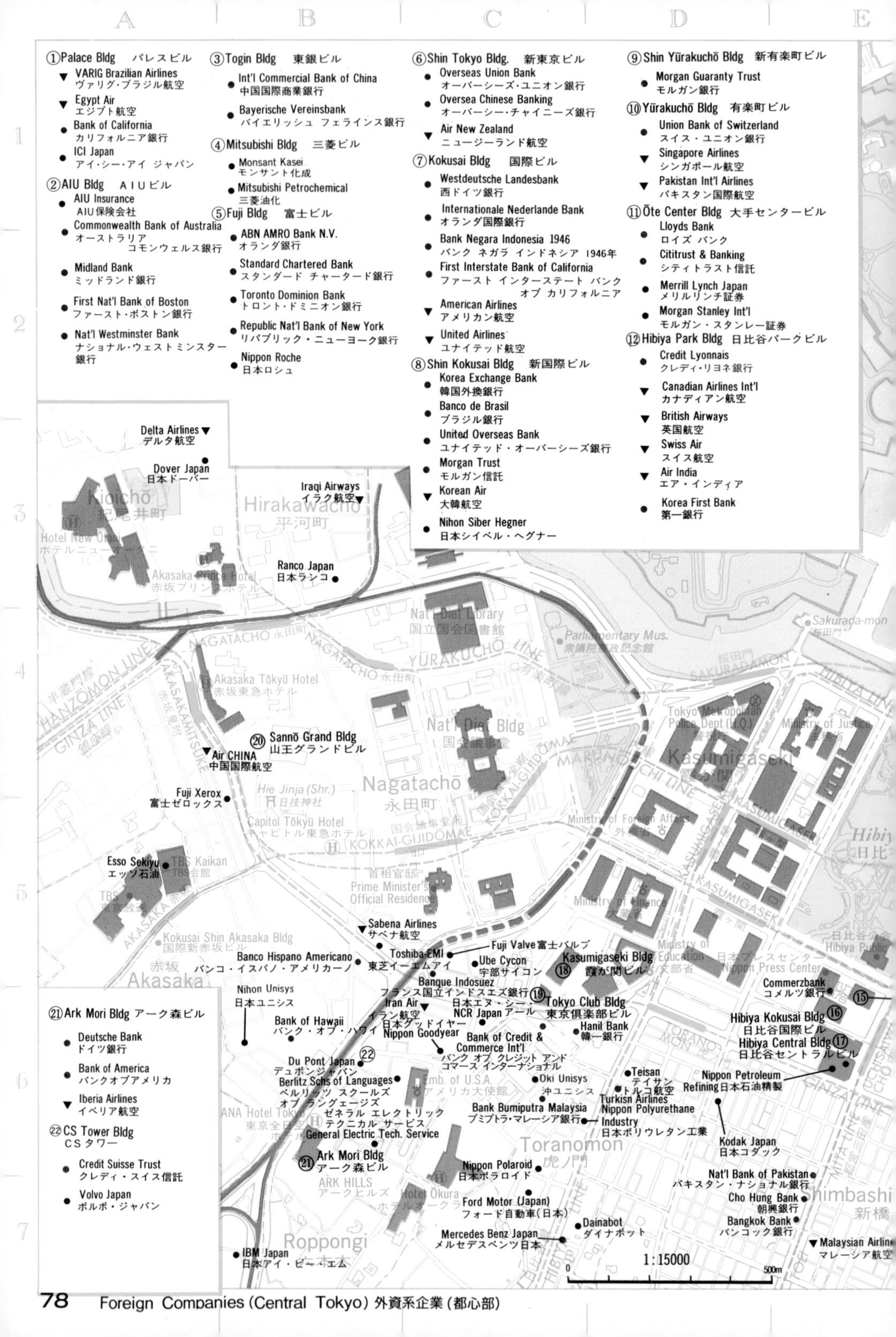
A
B
C
D
E
1
2
3
4
5
6
7
①Palace Bldg パレスビル
VARIG Brazilian Airlines ヴァリグ・ブラジル航空
Egypt Air エジプト航空
Bank of California カリフォルニア銀行
ICI Japan アイ・シー・アイ ジャパン
②AIU Bldg AIUビル
AIU Insurance AIU保険会社
Commonwealth Bank of Australia オーストラリア コモンウェルス銀行
Midland Bank ミッドランド銀行
First Nat'l Bank of Boston ファースト・ボストン銀行
Nat'l Westminster Bank ナショナル・ウェストミンスター銀行
③Togin Bldg 東銀ビル
Int'l Commercial Bank of China 中国国際商業銀行
Bayerische Vereinsbank バイエリッシュ フェラインス銀行
④Mitsubishi Bldg 三菱ビル
Monsant Kasei モンサント化成
Mitsubishi Petrochemical 三菱油化
⑤Fuji Bldg 富士ビル
ABN AMRO Bank N.V. オランダ銀行
Standard Chartered Bank スタンダード チャータード銀行
Toronto Dominion Bank トロント・ドミニオン銀行
Republic Nat'l Bank of New York リパブリック・ニューヨーク銀行
Nippon Roche 日本ロシュ
⑥Shin Tokyo Bldg. 新東京ビル
Overseas Union Bank オーバーシーズ・ユニオン銀行
Oversea Chinese Banking オーバーシー・チャイニーズ銀行
Air New Zealand ニュージーランド航空
⑦Kokusai Bldg 国際ビル
Westdeutsche Landesbank 西ドイツ銀行
Internationale Nederlande Bank オランダ国際銀行
Bank Negara Indonesia 1946 バンク ネガラ インドネシア 1946年
First Interstate Bank of California ファースト インターステート バンク オブ カリフォルニア
American Airlines アメリカン航空
United Airlines ユナイテッド航空
⑧Shin Kokusai Bldg 新国際ビル
Korea Exchange Bank 韓国外換銀行
Banco de Brasil ブラジル銀行
United Overseas Bank ユナイテッド・オーバーシーズ銀行
Morgan Trust モルガン信託
Korean Air 大韓航空
Nihon Siber Hegner 日本シイベル・ヘグナー
⑨Shin Yūrakuchō Bldg 新有楽町ビル
Morgan Guaranty Trust モルガン銀行
⑩Yūrakuchō Bldg 有楽町ビル
Union Bank of Switzerland スイス・ユニオン銀行
Singapore Airlines シンガポール航空
Pakistan Int'l Airlines パキスタン国際航空
⑪Ōte Center Bldg 大手センタービル
Lloyds Bank ロイズ バンク
Cititrust & Banking シティトラスト信託
Merrill Lynch Japan メリルリンチ証券
Morgan Stanley Int'l モルガン・スタンレー証券
⑫Hibiya Park Bldg 日比谷パークビル
Credit Lyonnais クレディ・リヨネ銀行
Canadian Airlines Int'l カナディアン航空
British Airways 英国航空
Swiss Air スイス航空
Air India エア・インディア
Korea First Bank 第一銀行
Delta Airlines デルタ航空
Dover Japan 日本ドーバー
Iraqi Airways イラク航空
Kioichō 紀尾井町
Hirakawachō 平河町
Hotel New Otani ホテルニューオータニ
Akasaka Prince Hotel 赤坂プリンスホテル
Ranco Japan 日本ランコ
Nat'l Diet Library 国立国会図書館
Parliamentary Mus. 衆議院憲政記念館
Sakurada-mon 桜田門
SAKURADAMON
NAGATACHO 永田町
YŪRAKUCHŌ LINE 有楽町線
HANZOMON LINE 半蔵門線
GINZA LINE 銀座線
AKASAKAMITSUKE 赤坂見附
Akasaka Tōkyū Hotel 赤坂東急ホテル
Sannō Grand Bldg 山王グランドビル
Air CHINA 中国国際航空
Nat'l Diet Bldg 国会議事堂
Tokyo Metropolitan Police Dept (H.Q.)
Ministry of Justice
Kasumigaseki 霞が関
MARUNOUCHI LINE
KOKKAI-GIJIDOMAE
Fuji Xerox 富士ゼロックス
Nagatachō 永田町
Hie Jinja (Shr.) 日枝神社
Capitol Tōkyū Hotel キャピトル東急ホテル
Ministry of Foreign Affairs 外務省
KASUMIGASEKI
Hibiya 日比谷
Esso Sekiyu エッソ石油
TBS Kaikan TBS会館
首相官邸 Prime Minister's Official Residence
Ministry of Finance 大蔵省
AKASAKA
Sabena Airlines サベナ航空
Kokusai Shin Akasaka Bldg 国際新赤坂ビル
Banco Hispano Americano バンコ・イスパノ・アメリカーノ
Toshiba-EMI 東芝イーエムアイ
Fuji Valve 富士バルブ
Ube Cycon 宇部サイコン
Kasumigaseki Bldg 霞が関ビル
Ministry of Education 文部省
日本プレスセンター Nippon Press Center
日比谷公会堂 Hibiya Public Hall
赤坂 Akasaka
Banque Indosuez フランス国立インドスエズ銀行
Nihon Unisys 日本ユニシス
Commerzbank コメルツ銀行
Iran Air イラン航空
NCR Japan 日本エヌ・シー・アール
Tokyo Club Bldg 東京倶楽部ビル
Hibiya Kokusai Bldg 日比谷国際ビル
Bank of Hawaii バンク・オブ・ハワイ
日本グッドイヤー Nippon Goodyear
Bank of Credit & Commerce Int'l バンク オブ クレジット アンド コマース インターナショナル
Hanil Bank 韓一銀行
TORANOMON
Hibiya Central Bldg 日比谷セントラルビル
Du Pont Japan デュポンジャパン
Berlitz Schs of Languages ベルリッツ スクールズ オブ ランゲージズ
Emb. of U.S.A. アメリカ大使館
Oki Unisys 沖ユニシス
Teisan テイサン
トルコ航空 Turkish Airlines
Nippon Petroleum Refining 日本石油精製
ANA Hotel Tokyo 東京全日空ホテル
ゼネラル エレクトリック テクニカル サービス General Electric Tech. Service
Bank Bumiputra Malaysia ブミプトラ・マレーシア銀行
Nippon Polyurethane Industry 日本ポリウレタン工業
Toranomon 虎ノ門
Kodak Japan 日本コダック
Ark Mori Bldg アーク森ビル
ARK HILLS アークヒルズ
Nippon Polaroid 日本ポラロイド
Nat'l Bank of Pakistan パキスタン・ナショナル銀行
Cho Hung Bank 朝興銀行
Hotel Okura ホテルオークラ
Ford Motor (Japan) フォード自動車(日本)
Shimbashi 新橋
Dainabot ダイナボット
Bangkok Bank バンコック銀行
Mercedes Benz Japan メルセデスベンツ日本
Malaysian Airlines マレーシア航空
Roppongi 六本木
IBM Japan 日本アイ・ビー・エム
1:15000
0
500m
㉑Ark Mori Bldg アーク森ビル
Deutsche Bank ドイツ銀行
Bank of America バンクオブアメリカ
Iberia Airlines イベリア航空
㉒CS Tower Bldg CSタワー
Credit Suisse Trust クレディ・スイス信託
Volvo Japan ボルボ・ジャパン

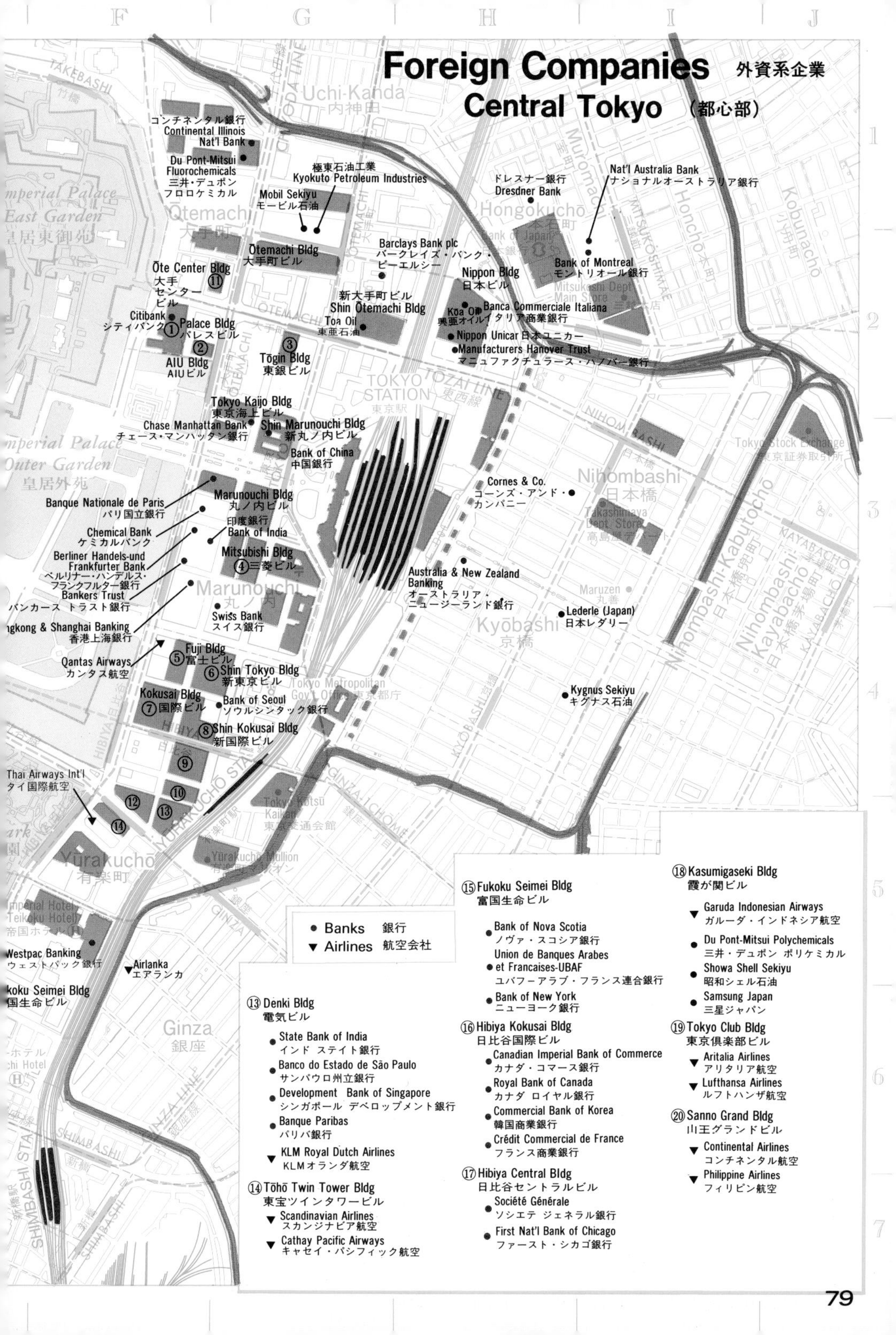

Foreign Companies 外資系企業
Central Tokyo (都心部)
コンチネンタル銀行
Continental Illinois Nat'l Bank
Du Pont-Mitsui Fluorochemicals
三井・デュポン フロロケミカル
極東石油工業
Kyokuto Petroleum Industries
Mobil Sekiyu
モービル石油
Ōtemachi
大手町
Ōtemachi Bldg
大手町ビル
Ōte Center Bldg
大手センタービル
Citibank
シティバンク
Palace Bldg
パレスビル
AIU Bldg
AIUビル
Tōgin Bldg
東銀ビル
Barclays Bank plc
バークレイズ・バンク・ピーエルシー
新大手町ビル
Shin Ōtemachi Bldg
Toa Oil
東亜石油
ドレスナー銀行
Dresdner Bank
Nat'l Australia Bank
ナショナルオーストラリア銀行
Hongokuchō
本石町
Bank of Montreal
モントリオール銀行
Nippon Bldg
日本ビル
Koa Oil
興亜オイル
Banca Commerciale Italiana
イタリア商業銀行
Nippon Unicar 日本ユニカー
Manufacturers Hanover Trust
マニュファクチュラース・ハノバー銀行
TOKYO STATION
東京駅
TŌZAI LINE
東西線
Tokyo Kaijo Bldg
東京海上ビル
Chase Manhattan Bank
チェース・マンハッタン銀行
Shin Marunouchi Bldg
新丸ノ内ビル
Bank of China
中国銀行
Imperial Palace Outer Garden
皇居外苑
Imperial Palace East Garden
皇居東御苑
Marunouchi Bldg
丸ノ内ビル
Banque Nationale de Paris
パリ国立銀行
Chemical Bank
ケミカルバンク
印度銀行
Bank of India
Berliner Handels-und Frankfurter Bank
ベルリナー・ハンデルス・フランクフルター銀行
Bankers Trust
バンカース トラスト銀行
Mitsubishi Bldg
三菱ビル
Marunouchi
丸ノ内
Swiss Bank
スイス銀行
Hongkong & Shanghai Banking
香港上海銀行
Qantas Airways
カンタス航空
Fuji Bldg
富士ビル
Shin Tokyo Bldg
新東京ビル
Kokusai Bldg
国際ビル
Bank of Seoul
ソウルシンタック銀行
Shin Kokusai Bldg
新国際ビル
Tokyo Metropolitan Gov't Office 東京都庁
Cornes & Co.
コーンズ・アンド・カンパニー
Nihombashi
日本橋
Takashimaya Dept. Store
高島屋デパート
Australia & New Zealand Banking
オーストラリア・ニュージーランド銀行
Maruzen
丸善
Lederle (Japan)
日本レダリー
Kyōbashi
京橋
Kygnus Sekiyu
キグナス石油
Tokyo Stock Exchange
東京証券取引所
Mitsukoshi Dept Main Store
Thai Airways Int'l
タイ国際航空
Tokyo Kōtsū Kaikan
東京交通会館
Yūrakuchō
有楽町
Yūrakuchō Mullion
Imperial Hotel
帝国ホテル
Westpac Banking
ウェストパック銀行
Airlanka
エアランカ
Fukoku Seimei Bldg
富国生命ビル
Ginza
銀座
Uchi-Kanda
内神田
Nihombashi-Kabutochō
Nihombashi-Kayabachō
Shimbashi
新橋
● Banks 銀行
▼ Airlines 航空会社
⑬ Denki Bldg
電気ビル
● State Bank of India
インド ステイト銀行
● Banco do Estado de São Paulo
サンパウロ州立銀行
● Development Bank of Singapore
シンガポール デベロップメント銀行
● Banque Paribas
パリバ銀行
▼ KLM Royal Dutch Airlines
KLMオランダ航空
⑭ Tōhō Twin Tower Bldg
東宝ツインタワービル
▼ Scandinavian Airlines
スカンジナビア航空
▼ Cathay Pacific Airways
キャセイ・パシフィック航空
⑮ Fukoku Seimei Bldg
富国生命ビル
● Bank of Nova Scotia
ノヴァ・スコシア銀行
● Union de Banques Arabes et Francaises-UBAF
ユバフーアラブ・フランス連合銀行
● Bank of New York
ニューヨーク銀行
⑯ Hibiya Kokusai Bldg
日比谷国際ビル
● Canadian Imperial Bank of Commerce
カナダ・コマース銀行
● Royal Bank of Canada
カナダ ロイヤル銀行
● Commercial Bank of Korea
韓国商業銀行
● Crédit Commercial de France
フランス商業銀行
⑰ Hibiya Central Bldg
日比谷セントラルビル
● Société Générale
ソシエテ ジェネラル銀行
● First Nat'l Bank of Chicago
ファースト・シカゴ銀行
⑱ Kasumigaseki Bldg
霞が関ビル
▼ Garuda Indonesian Airways
ガルーダ・インドネシア航空
● Du Pont-Mitsui Polychemicals
三井・デュポン ポリケミカル
● Showa Shell Sekiyu
昭和シェル石油
● Samsung Japan
三星ジャパン
⑲ Tokyo Club Bldg
東京倶楽部ビル
▼ Aritalia Airlines
アリタリア航空
▼ Lufthansa Airlines
ルフトハンザ航空
⑳ Sanno Grand Bldg
山王グランドビル
▼ Continental Airlines
コンチネンタル航空
▼ Philippine Airlines
フィリピン航空

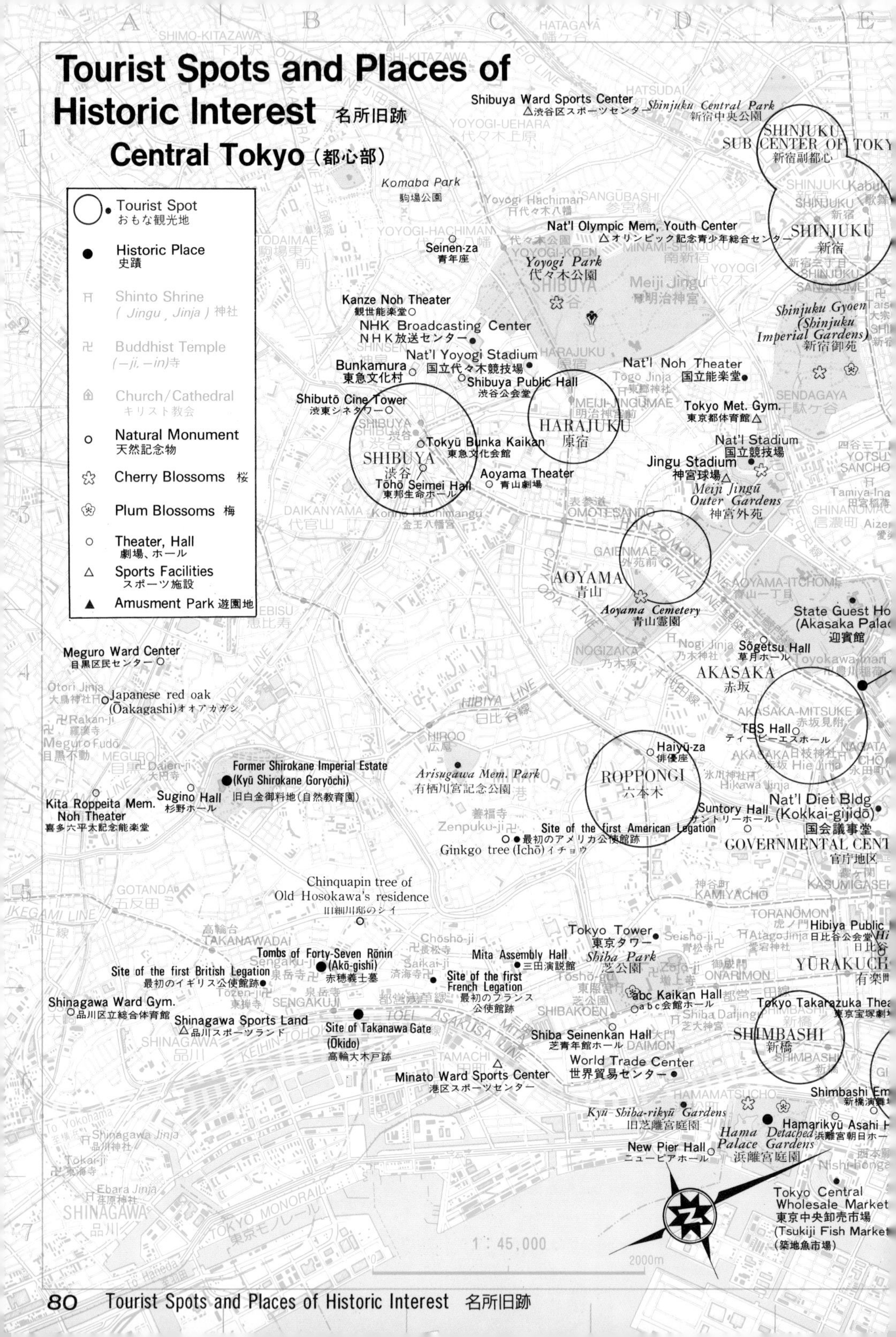

Tourist Spots and Places of Historic Interest 名所旧跡
Central Tokyo（都心部）
Tourist Spot おもな観光地
Historic Place 史蹟
Shinto Shrine (Jingu , Jinja) 神社
Buddhist Temple (−ji, −in)寺
Church/Cathedral キリスト教会
Natural Monument 天然記念物
Cherry Blossoms 桜
Plum Blossoms 梅
Theater, Hall 劇場、ホール
Sports Facilities スポーツ施設
Amusment Park 遊園地
Shibuya Ward Sports Center 渋谷区スポーツセンター
Shinjuku Central Park 新宿中央公園
SHINJUKU SUB CENTER OF TOKY 新宿副都心
SHINJUKU 新宿
Komaba Park 駒場公園
Nat'l Olympic Mem. Youth Center オリンピック記念青少年総合センター
Seinen-za 青年座
Yoyogi Park 代々木公園
Meiji Jingu 明治神宮
Shinjuku Gyoen (Shinjuku Imperial Gardens) 新宿御苑
Kanze Noh Theater 観世能楽堂
NHK Broadcasting Center NHK放送センター
Nat'l Yoyogi Stadium 国立代々木競技場
Bunkamura 東急文化村
Shibuya Public Hall 渋谷公会堂
Nat'l Noh Theater 国立能楽堂
Shibutō Cine Tower 渋東シネタワー
HARAJUKU 原宿
Tokyo Met. Gym. 東京都体育館
Tokyū Bunka Kaikan 東急文化会館
SHIBUYA 渋谷
Nat'l Stadium 国立競技場
Jingu Stadium 神宮球場
Aoyama Theater 青山劇場
Tōhō Seimei Hall 東邦生命ホール
Meiji Jingū Outer Gardens 神宮外苑
AOYAMA 青山
Aoyama Cemetery 青山霊園
State Guest Ho (Akasaka Palac 迎賓館
Sōgetsu Hall 草月ホール
Meguro Ward Center 目黒区民センター
AKASAKA 赤坂
Japanese red oak (Ōakagashi) オオアカガシ
TBS Hall ティービーエスホール
Haiyū-za 俳優座
Former Shirokane Imperial Estate (Kyū Shirokane Goryōchi) 旧白金御料地（自然教育園）
Arisugawa Mem. Park 有栖川宮記念公園
ROPPONGI 六本木
Sugino Hall 杉野ホール
Kita Roppeita Mem. Noh Theater 喜多六平太記念能楽堂
Nat'l Diet Bldg (Kokkai-gijidō) 国会議事堂
Suntory Hall サントリーホール
Site of the first American Legation 最初のアメリカ公使館跡
Ginkgo tree (Ichō) イチョウ
GOVERNMENTAL CENT 官庁地区
Chinquapin tree of Old Hosokawa's residence 旧細川邸のシイ
Tokyo Tower 東京タワー
Hibiya Public 日比谷公会堂
Tombs of Forty-Seven Rōnin (Akō-gishi) 赤穂義士墓
Mita Assembly Hall 三田演説館
Shiba Park 芝公園
YŪRAKUCH 有楽町
Site of the first British Legation 最初のイギリス公使館跡
Site of the first French Legation 最初のフランス公使館跡
abc Kaikan Hall abc会館ホール
Shinagawa Ward Gym. 品川区立総合体育館
Tokyo Takarazuka Thea 東京宝塚劇場
Shinagawa Sports Land 品川スポーツランド
Site of Takanawa Gate (Ōkido) 高輪大木戸跡
Shiba Seinenkan Hall 芝青年館ホール
SHIMBASHI 新橋
World Trade Center 世界貿易センター
Minato Ward Sports Center 港区スポーツセンター
Shimbashi Em 新橋演舞場
Kyū-Shiba-rikyū Gardens 旧芝離宮庭園
Hamarikyū Asahi H 浜離宮朝日ホー
Hama Detached Palace Gardens 浜離宮庭園
New Pier Hall ニューピアホール
Tokyo Central Wholesale Market 東京中央卸売市場 (Tsukiji Fish Market) (築地魚市場)
1 : 45,000
2000m

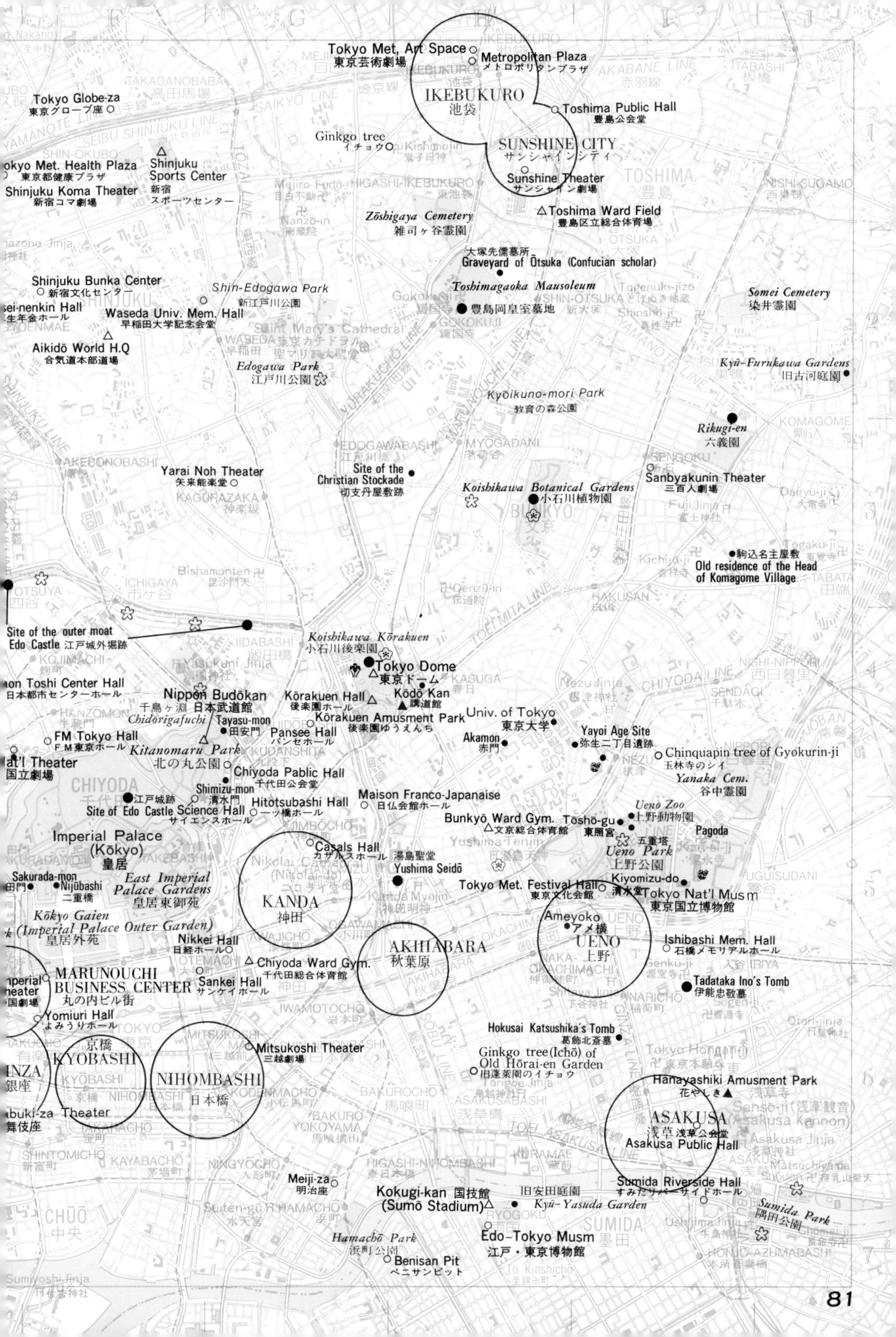

Tokyo Met. Art Space
東京芸術劇場
Metropolitan Plaza
メトロポリタンプラザ
IKEBUKURO
池袋
Toshima Public Hall
豊島公会堂
SUNSHINE CITY
サンシャインシティ
Sunshine Theater
サンシャイン劇場
Tokyo Globe-za
東京グローブ座
Ginkgo tree
イチョウ
Tokyo Met. Health Plaza
東京都健康プラザ
Shinjuku Sports Center
新宿スポーツセンター
Shinjuku Koma Theater
新宿コマ劇場
Toshima Ward Field
豊島区立総合体育場
Zōshigaya Cemetery
雑司ヶ谷霊園
大塚先儒墓所
Graveyard of Ōtsuka (Confucian scholar)
Toshimagaoka Mausoleum
豊島岡皇室墓地
Shinjuku Bunka Center
新宿文化センター
Shin-Edogawa Park
新江戸川公園
Waseda Univ. Mem. Hall
早稲田大学記念会堂
Aikidō World H.Q
合気道本部道場
Somei Cemetery
染井霊園
Edogawa Park
江戸川公園
Kyū-Furukawa Gardens
旧古河庭園
Kyōikuno-mori Park
教育の森公園
Rikugi-en
六義園
Yarai Noh Theater
矢来能楽堂
Site of the Christian Stockade
切支丹屋敷跡
Sanbyakunin Theater
三百人劇場
Koishikawa Botanical Gardens
小石川植物園
駒込名主屋敷
Old residence of the Head of Komagome Village
Site of the outer moat Edo Castle 江戸城外堀跡
Koishikawa Kōrakuen
小石川後楽園
Tokyo Dome
東京ドーム
Kōdō Kan
講道館
Nippon Budōkan
日本武道館
Kōrakuen Hall
後楽園ホール
Kōrakuen Amusment Park
後楽園ゆうえんち
Chidorigafuchi
千鳥ヶ淵
Tayasu-mon
田安門
Univ. of Tokyo
東京大学
Yayoi Age Site
弥生二丁目遺跡
FM Tokyo Hall
FM東京ホール
Pansee Hall
パンセホール
Akamon
赤門
Chinquapin tree of Gyokurin-ji
玉林寺のシイ
Kitanomaru Park
北の丸公園
Chiyoda Public Hall
千代田公会堂
Yanaka Cem.
谷中霊園
Shimizu-mon
清水門
江戸城跡
Site of Edo Castle
Science Hall
サイエンスホール
Hitotsubashi Hall
一ッ橋ホール
Maison Franco-Japanaise
日仏会館ホール
Ueno Zoo
上野動物園
Bunkyō Ward Gym.
文京総合体育館
Toshō-gu
東照宮
五重塔
Pagoda
Imperial Palace
(Kōkyo)
皇居
Casals Hall
カザルスホール
湯島聖堂
Yushima Seidō
Ueno Park
上野公園
Sakurada-mon
Nijūbashi
二重橋
East Imperial Palace Gardens
皇居東御苑
KANDA
神田
Tokyo Met. Festival Hall
東京文化会館
Kiyomizu-do
清水堂
Tokyo Nat'l Musm
東京国立博物館
Kōkyo Gaien
(Imperial Palace Outer Garden)
皇居外苑
Nikkei Hall
日経ホール
Ameyoko
アメ横
UENO
上野
AKIHABARA
秋葉原
Ishibashi Mem. Hall
石橋メモリアルホール
Chiyoda Ward Gym.
千代田総合体育館
MARUNOUCHI BUSINESS CENTER
丸の内ビル街
Sankei Hall
サンケイホール
Tadataka Ino's Tomb
伊能忠敬墓
Yomiuri Hall
よみうりホール
Hokusai Katsushika's Tomb
葛飾北斎墓
Mitsukoshi Theater
三越劇場
京橋
KYOBASHI
NIHOMBASHI
日本橋
Ginkgo tree(Ichō) of Old Hōrai-en Garden
旧蓬莱園のイチョウ
Hanayashiki Amusment Park
花やしき
Senso-ji (浅草観音)
(Asakusa Kannon)
ASAKUSA
浅草
浅草公会堂
Asakusa Public Hall
Meiji-za
明治座
Sumida Riverside Hall
すみだリバーサイドホール
Kokugi-kan 国技館
(Sumō Stadium)
旧安田庭園
Kyū-Yasuda Garden
Sumida Park
隅田公園
Edo-Tokyo Musm
江戸・東京博物館
Hamachō Park
浜町公園
Benisan Pit
ベニサンピット
CHIYODA
千代田
TOSHIMA
豊島
BUNKYO
文京
SUMIDA
墨田
CHŪO
中央

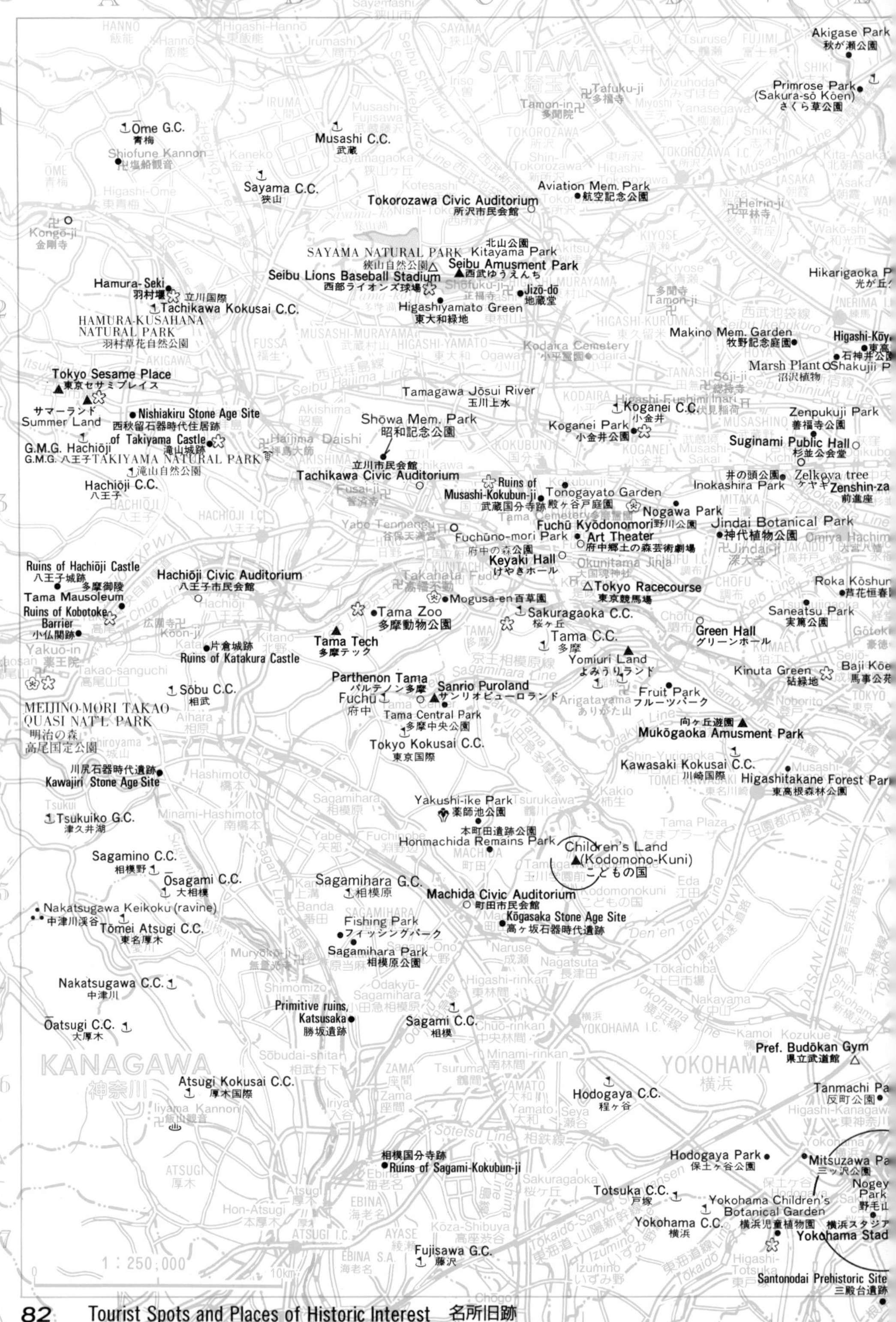

Ōme G.C.
青梅
Shiofune Kannon
塩船観音
Kongō-ji
金剛寺
Musashi C.C.
武蔵
Sayama C.C.
狭山
Tokorozawa Civic Auditorium
所沢市民会館
Aviation Mem. Park
航空記念公園
Tafuku-ji
多福寺
Tamon-in
多聞院
Akigase Park
秋が瀬公園
Primrose Park
(Sakura-sō Kōen)
さくら草公園
Heirin-ji
平林寺
SAYAMA NATURAL PARK
狭山自然公園
北山公園
Kitayama Park
Seibu Amusment Park
西武ゆうえんち
Seibu Lions Baseball Stadium
西部ライオンズ球場
Shōfuku-ji
正福寺
Jizō-dō
地蔵堂
Higashiyamato Green
東大和緑地
Hamura-Seki
羽村堰
立川国際
Tachikawa Kokusai C.C.
HAMURA-KUSAHANA
NATURAL PARK
羽村草花自然公園
Hikarigaoka Park
光が丘公園
Makino Mem. Garden
牧野記念庭園
Higashi-Kōyama
石神井公園
Marsh Plant
沼沢植物
Shakujii Park
Kodaira Cemetery
小平霊園
Tokyo Sesame Place
東京セサミプレイス
サマーランド
Summer Land
Nishiakiru Stone Age Site
西秋留石器時代住居跡
Tamagawa Jōsui River
玉川上水
Sōji-ji
総持寺
Higashi-Fushimi Inari
東伏見稲荷
Koganei C.C.
小金井
Zenpukuji Park
善福寺公園
Shōwa Mem. Park
昭和記念公園
Koganei Park
小金井公園
G.M.G. Hachiōji
G.M.G. 八王子
of Takiyama Castle
滝山城跡
TAKIYAMA NATURAL PARK
滝山自然公園
Haijima Daishi
拝島大師
Suginami Public Hall
杉並公会堂
立川市民会館
Tachikawa Civic Auditorium
井の頭公園
Inokashira Park
Zelkova tree
ケヤキ
Zenshin-za
前進座
Hachiōji C.C.
八王子
Fusai-ji
普済寺
Ruins of
Musashi-Kokubun-ji
武蔵国分寺跡
Tonogayato Garden
殿ヶ谷戸庭園
Nogawa Park
野川公園
Jindai Botanical Park
神代植物公園
Jindai-ji
深大寺
Yabo Tenmangū
谷保天満宮
Fuchūno-mori Park
府中の森公園
Fuchū Kyōdonomori
Art Theater
府中郷土の森芸術劇場
Keyaki Hall
けやきホール
Okunitama Jinja
大国魂神社
Ruins of Hachiōji Castle
八王子城跡
多摩御陵
Tama Mausoleum
Hachiōji Civic Auditorium
八王子市民会館
Takahata Fudō
高幡不動
Tokyo Racecourse
東京競馬場
Roka Kōshun-en
芦花恒春園
Mogusa-en
百草園
Ruins of Kobotoke
Barrier
小仏関跡
Kōon-ji
Tama Zoo
多摩動物公園
Sakuragaoka C.C.
桜ヶ丘
Saneatsu Park
実篤公園
Tama Tech
多摩テック
片倉城跡
Ruins of Katakura Castle
Tama C.C.
多摩
Green Hall
グリーンホール
Yakuō-in
薬王院
Yomiuri Land
よみうりランド
Kinuta Green
砧緑地
Baji Kōen
馬事公苑
Parthenon Tama
パルテノン多摩
Sanrio Puroland
サンリオピューロランド
Fuchū
府中
Fruit Park
フルーツパーク
Sōbu C.C.
相武
Arigatayama
ありがた山
MEIJINO-MORI TAKAO
QUASI NAT'L PARK
明治の森
高尾国定公園
Tama Central Park
多摩中央公園
向ヶ丘遊園
Mukōgaoka Amusment Park
Tokyo Kokusai C.C.
東京国際
Kawasaki Kokusai C.C.
川崎国際
Higashitakane Forest Park
東高根森林公園
川尻石器時代遺跡
Kawajiri Stone Age Site
Tsukuiko G.C.
津久井湖
Yakushi-ike Park
薬師池公園
本町田遺跡公園
Honmachida Remains Park
Children's Land
(Kodomono-Kuni)
こどもの国
Sagamino C.C.
相模野
Ōsagami C.C.
大相模
Sagamihara G.C.
相模原
Machida Civic Auditorium
町田市民会館
Nakatsugawa Keikoku (ravine)
中津川渓谷
Tōmei Atsugi C.C.
東名厚木
Kōgasaka Stone Age Site
高ヶ坂石器時代遺跡
Fishing Park
フィッシングパーク
Sagamihara Park
相模原公園
Muryōkō-ji
無量光寺
Nakatsugawa C.C.
中津川
Primitive ruins,
Katsusaka
勝坂遺跡
Sagami C.C.
相模
Ōatsugi C.C.
大厚木
KANAGAWA
神奈川
Pref. Budōkan Gym
県立武道館
YOKOHAMA
横浜
Atsugi Kokusai C.C.
厚木国際
Hodogaya C.C.
程ヶ谷
Tanmachi Park
反町公園
Iiyama Kannon
飯山観音
相模国分寺跡
Ruins of Sagami-Kokubun-ji
Hodogaya Park
保土ヶ谷公園
Mitsuzawa Park
三ッ沢公園
Nogeyama Park
野毛山
Totsuka C.C.
戸塚
Yokohama Children's
Botanical Garden
横浜児童植物園
Yokohama C.C.
横浜
横浜スタジアム
Yokohama Stadium
Fujisawa G.C.
藤沢
Santonodai Prehistoric Site
三殿台遺跡
1 : 250,000
0
10km

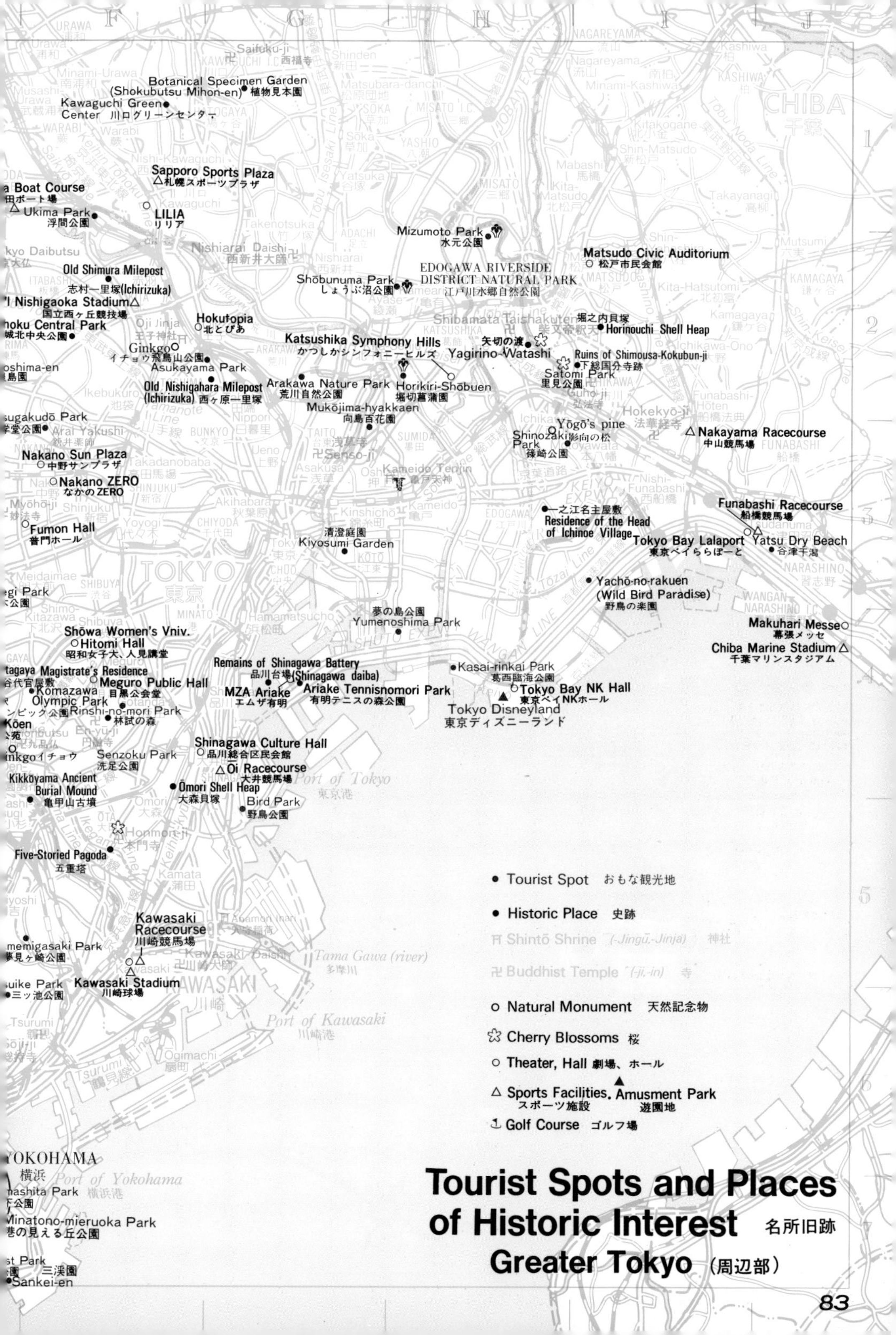

Tourist Spots and Places of Historic Interest 名所旧跡 Greater Tokyo （周辺部）

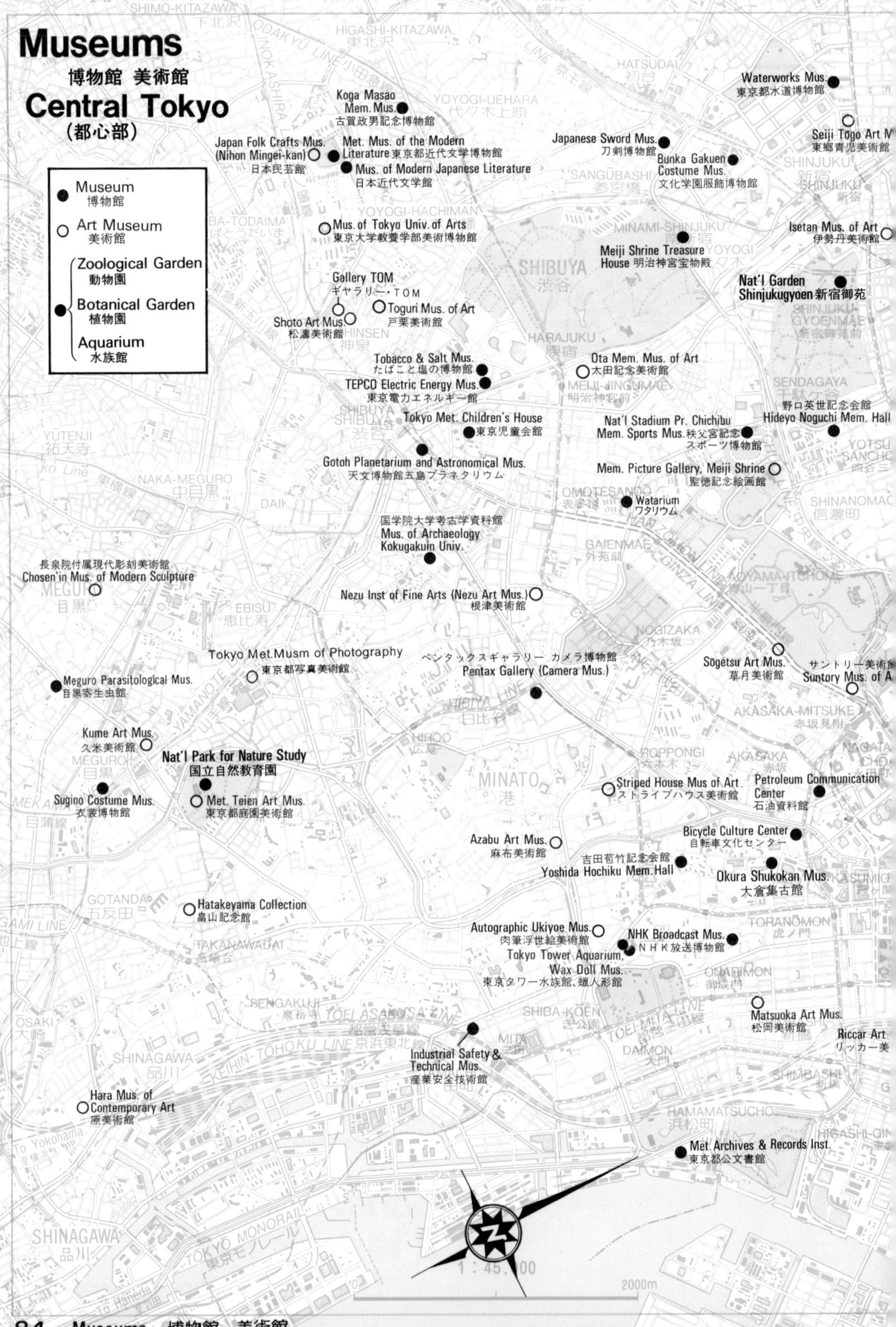

Museums
博物館 美術館
Central Tokyo
(都心部)
Museum
博物館
Art Museum
美術館
Zoological Garden
動物園
Botanical Garden
植物園
Aquarium
水族館
Koga Masao Mem. Mus.
古賀政男記念博物館
Japan Folk Crafts Mus. (Nihon Mingei-kan)
日本民芸館
Met. Mus. of the Modern Literature 東京都近代文学博物館
Mus. of Modern Japanese Literature
日本近代文学館
Mus. of Tokyo Univ. of Arts
東京大学教養学部美術博物館
Gallery TOM
ギャラリー・TOM
Shoto Art Mus.
松濤美術館
Toguri Mus. of Art
戸栗美術館
Tobacco & Salt Mus.
たばこと塩の博物館
TEPCO Electric Energy Mus.
東京電力エネルギー館
Tokyo Met. Children's House
東京児童会館
Gotoh Planetarium and Astronomical Mus.
天文博物館五島プラネタリウム
国学院大学考古学資料館
Mus. of Archaeology Kokugakuin Univ.
長泉院付属現代彫刻美術館
Chosen'in Mus. of Modern Sculpture
Nezu Inst of Fine Arts (Nezu Art Mus.)
根津美術館
Tokyo Met. Musm of Photography
東京都写真美術館
ペンタックスギャラリー カメラ博物館
Pentax Gallery (Camera Mus.)
Meguro Parasitological Mus.
目黒寄生虫館
Kume Art Mus.
久米美術館
Nat'l Park for Nature Study
国立自然教育園
Sugino Costume Mus.
衣裳博物館
Met. Teien Art Mus.
東京都庭園美術館
Hatakeyama Collection
畠山記念館
Hara Mus. of Contemporary Art
原美術館
Waterworks Mus.
東京都水道博物館
Seiji Togo Art M
東郷青児美術館
Japanese Sword Mus.
刀剣博物館
Bunka Gakuen Costume Mus.
文化学園服飾博物館
Meiji Shrine Treasure House 明治神宮宝物殿
Isetan Mus. of Art
伊勢丹美術館
Nat'l Garden Shinjukugyoen 新宿御苑
Ota Mem. Mus. of Art
太田記念美術館
野口英世記念会館
Hideyo Noguchi Mem. Hall
Nat'l Stadium Pr. Chichibu Mem. Sports Mus. 秩父宮記念スポーツ博物館
Mem. Picture Gallery, Meiji Shrine
聖徳記念絵画館
Watarium
ワタリウム
Sogetsu Art Mus.
草月美術館
サントリー美術
Suntory Mus. of A
Striped House Mus of Art
ストライプハウス美術館
Petroleum Communication Center
石油資料館
Azabu Art Mus.
麻布美術館
Bicycle Culture Center
自転車文化センター
吉田苞竹記念会館
Yoshida Hochiku Mem. Hall
Okura Shukokan Mus.
大倉集古館
Autographic Ukiyoe Mus.
肉筆浮世絵美術館
NHK Broadcast Mus.
NHK放送博物館
Tokyo Tower Aquarium, Wax Doll Mus.
東京タワー水族館、蠟人形館
Matsuoka Art Mus.
松岡美術館
Riccar Art
リッカー美
Industrial Safety & Technical Mus.
産業安全技術館
Met. Archives & Records Inst.
東京都公文書館
SHIBUYA
渋谷
HARAJUKU
原宿
MINATO
港
SHINAGAWA
品川
1 : 45,000
2000m

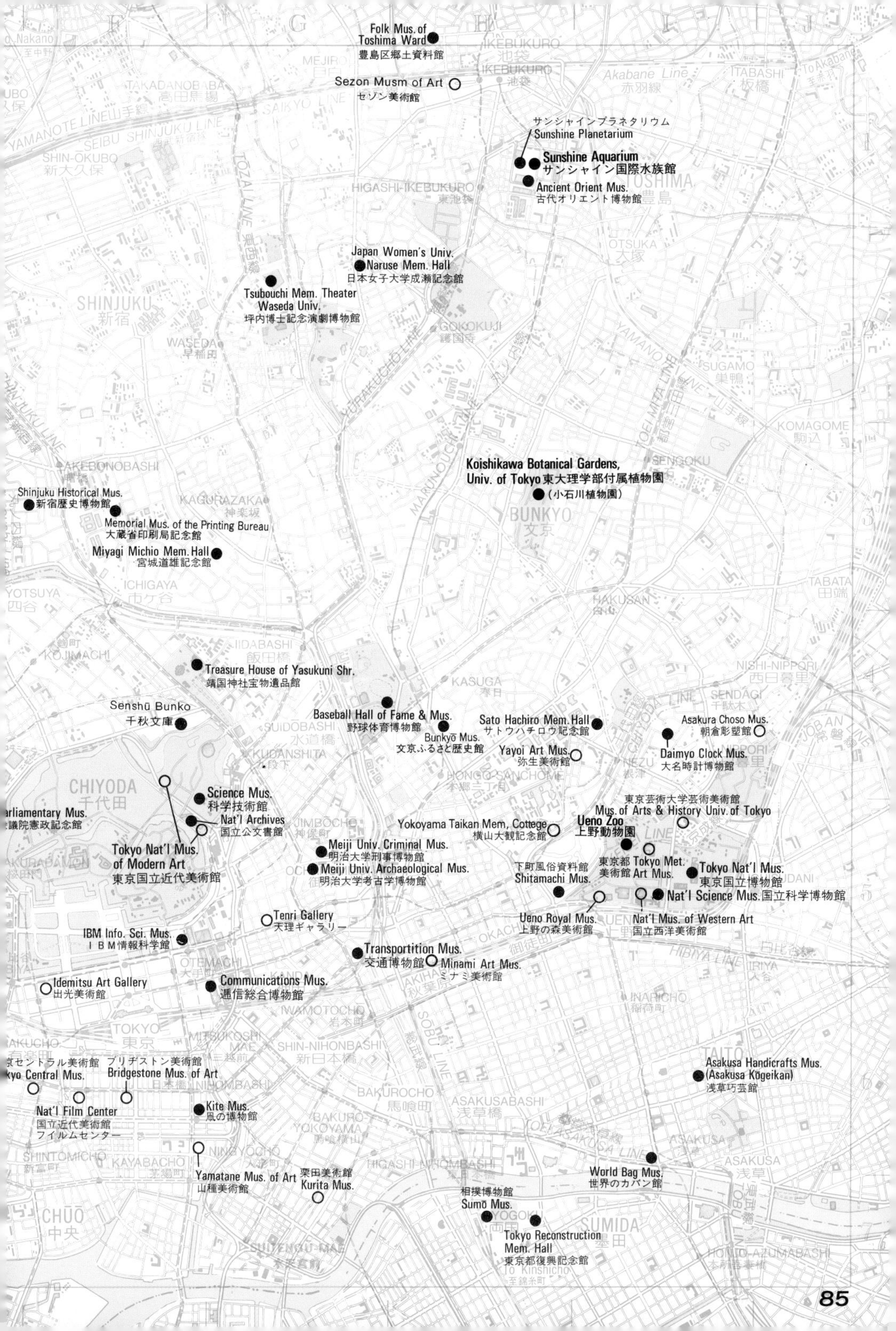
Folk Mus. of Toshima Ward
豊島区郷土資料館
Sezon Musm of Art
セゾン美術館
サンシャインプラネタリウム
Sunshine Planetarium
Sunshine Aquarium
サンシャイン国際水族館
Ancient Orient Mus.
古代オリエント博物館
Japan Women's Univ. Naruse Mem. Hall
日本女子大学成瀬記念館
Tsubouchi Mem. Theater Waseda Univ.
坪内博士記念演劇博物館
Koishikawa Botanical Gardens, Univ. of Tokyo 東大理学部付属植物園
(小石川植物園)
Shinjuku Historical Mus.
新宿歴史博物館
Memorial Mus. of the Printing Bureau
大蔵省印刷局記念館
Miyagi Michio Mem. Hall
宮城道雄記念館
Treasure House of Yasukuni Shr.
靖国神社宝物遺品館
Senshū Bunko
千秋文庫
Baseball Hall of Fame & Mus.
野球体育博物館
Bunkyō Mus.
文京ふるさと歴史館
Sato Hachiro Mem. Hall
サトウハチロウ記念館
Yayoi Art Mus.
弥生美術館
Asakura Choso Mus.
朝倉彫塑館
Daimyo Clock Mus.
大名時計博物館
Science Mus.
科学技術館
Parliamentary Mus.
議院憲政記念館
Nat'l Archives
国立公文書館
Tokyo Nat'l Mus. of Modern Art
東京国立近代美術館
Meiji Univ. Criminal Mus.
明治大学刑事博物館
Meiji Univ. Archaeological Mus.
明治大学考古学博物館
Yokoyama Taikan Mem. Cottege
横山大観記念館
東京芸術大学芸術美術館
Mus. of Arts & History Univ. of Tokyo
Ueno Zoo
上野動物園
下町風俗資料館
Shitamachi Mus.
東京都美術館
Tokyo Met. Art Mus.
Tokyo Nat'l Mus.
東京国立博物館
Nat'l Science Mus. 国立科学博物館
Ueno Royal Mus.
上野の森美術館
Nat'l Mus. of Western Art
国立西洋美術館
Tenri Gallery
天理ギャラリー
IBM Info. Sci. Mus.
IBM情報科学館
Transportition Mus.
交通博物館
Minami Art Mus.
ミナミ美術館
Idemitsu Art Gallery
出光美術館
Communications Mus.
逓信総合博物館
Tokyo Central Mus.
ブリヂストン美術館
Bridgestone Mus. of Art
Nat'l Film Center
国立近代美術館フイルムセンター
Kite Mus.
凧の博物館
Asakusa Handicrafts Mus. (Asakusa Kogeikan)
浅草巧芸館
Yamatane Mus. of Art
山種美術館
栗田美術館
Kurita Mus.
World Bag Mus.
世界のカバン館
相撲博物館
Sumō Mus.
Tokyo Reconstruction Mem. Hall
東京都復興記念館
IKEBUKURO
池袋
TOSHIMA
豊島
SHINJUKU
新宿
BUNKYO
文京
CHIYODA
千代田
TAITO
SUMIDA
墨田
CHŪO
中央
TOKYO
東京

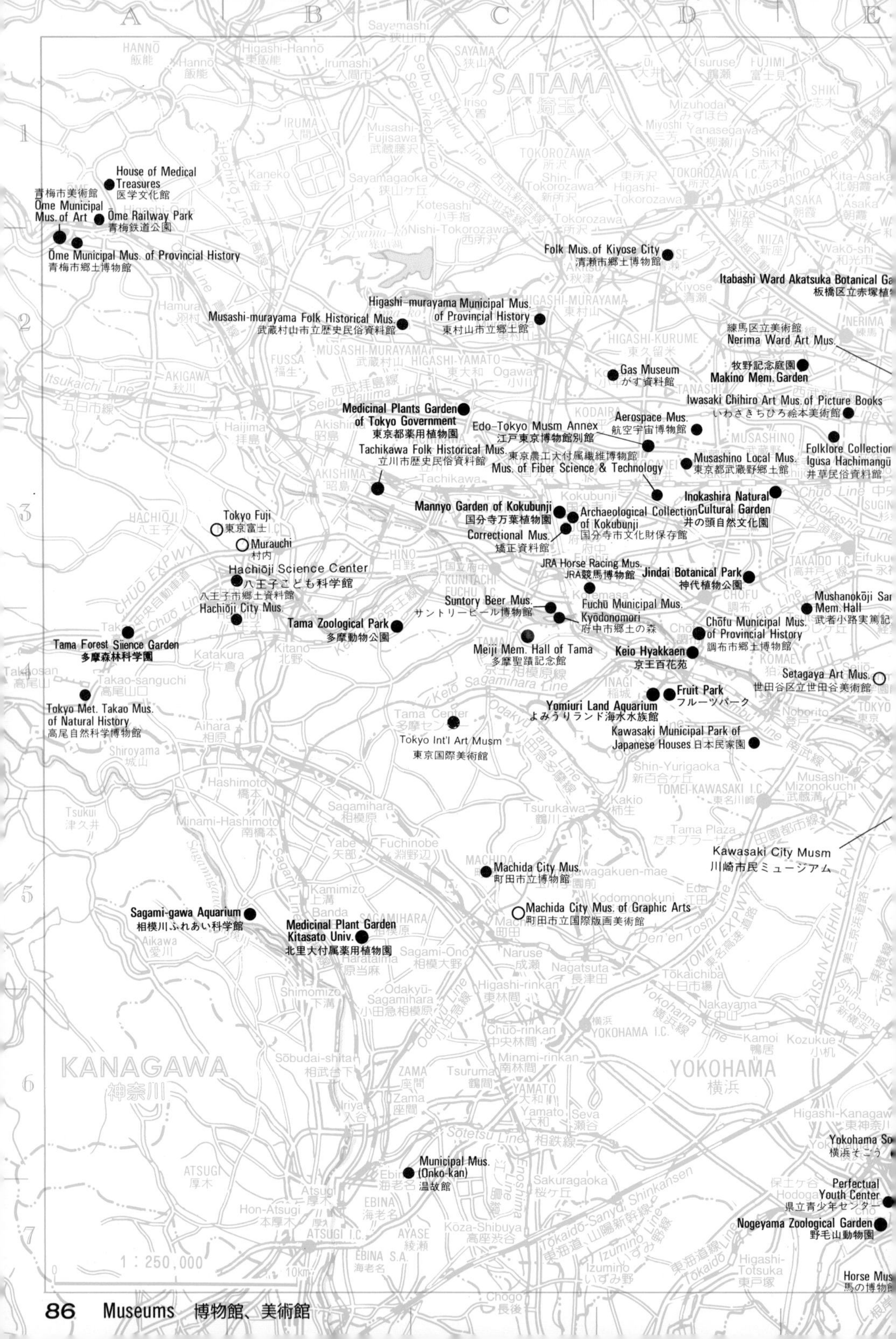
House of Medical Treasures
医学文化館
青梅市美術館
Ōme Municipal Mus. of Art
Ōme Railway Park
青梅鉄道公園
Ōme Municipal Mus. of Provincial History
青梅市郷土博物館
Folk Mus. of Kiyose City
清瀬市郷土博物館
Itabashi Ward Akatsuka Botanical Ga
板橋区立赤塚植
Higashi-murayama Municipal Mus. of Provincial History
東村山市立郷土館
Musashi-murayama Folk Historical Mus.
武蔵村山市立歴史民俗資料館
練馬区立美術館
Nerima Ward Art Mus.
牧野記念庭園
Makino Mem. Garden
Gas Museum
がす資料館
Medicinal Plants Garden of Tokyo Government
東京都薬用植物園
Iwasaki Chihiro Art Mus. of Picture Books
いわさきちひろ絵本美術館
Aerospace Mus.
航空宇宙博物館
Edo-Tokyo Musm Annex
江戸東京博物館別館
Folklore Collection
Igusa Hachimangū
井草民俗資料館
Tachikawa Folk Historical Mus.
立川市歴史民俗資料館
東京農工大付属繊維博物館
Mus. of Fiber Science & Technology
Musashino Local Mus.
東京都武蔵野郷土館
Inokashira Natural Cultural Garden
井の頭自然文化園
Mannyo Garden of Kokubunji
国分寺万葉植物園
Archaeological Collection of Kokubunji
国分寺市文化財保存館
Correctional Mus.
矯正資料館
Tokyo Fuji
東京富士
Murauchi
村内
Hachiōji Science Center
八王子こども科学館
八王子市郷土資料館
Hachiōji City Mus.
JRA Horse Racing Mus.
JRA競馬博物館
Jindai Botanical Park
神代植物公園
Suntory Beer Mus.
サントリービール博物館
Fuchū Municipal Mus.
Kyōdonomori
府中市郷土の森
Mushanokōji San Mem. Hall
武者小路実篤記
Tama Forest Siience Garden
多摩森林科学園
Tama Zoological Park
多摩動物公園
Meiji Mem. Hall of Tama
多摩聖蹟記念館
Chōfu Municipal Mus. of Provincial History
調布市郷土博物館
Keio Hyakkaen
京王百花苑
Setagaya Art Mus.
世田谷区立世田谷美術館
Fruit Park
フルーツパーク
Yomiuri Land Aquarium
よみうりランド海水水族館
Tokyo Met. Takao Mus. of Natural History
高尾自然科学博物館
Tokyo Int'l Art Musm
東京国際美術館
Kawasaki Municipal Park of Japanese Houses 日本民家園
Kawasaki City Musm
川崎市民ミュージアム
Machida City Mus.
町田市立博物館
Machida City Mus. of Graphic Arts
町田市立国際版画美術館
Sagami-gawa Aquarium
相模川ふれあい科学館
Medicinal Plant Garden Kitasato Univ.
北里大付属薬用植物園
KANAGAWA
神奈川
SAITAMA
埼玉
YOKOHAMA
横浜
Yokohama So
横浜そごう
Municipal Mus. (Onko-kan)
温故館
Perfectual Youth Center
県立青少年センター
Nogeyama Zoological Garden
野毛山動物園
Horse Mus
馬の博物館
1:250,000

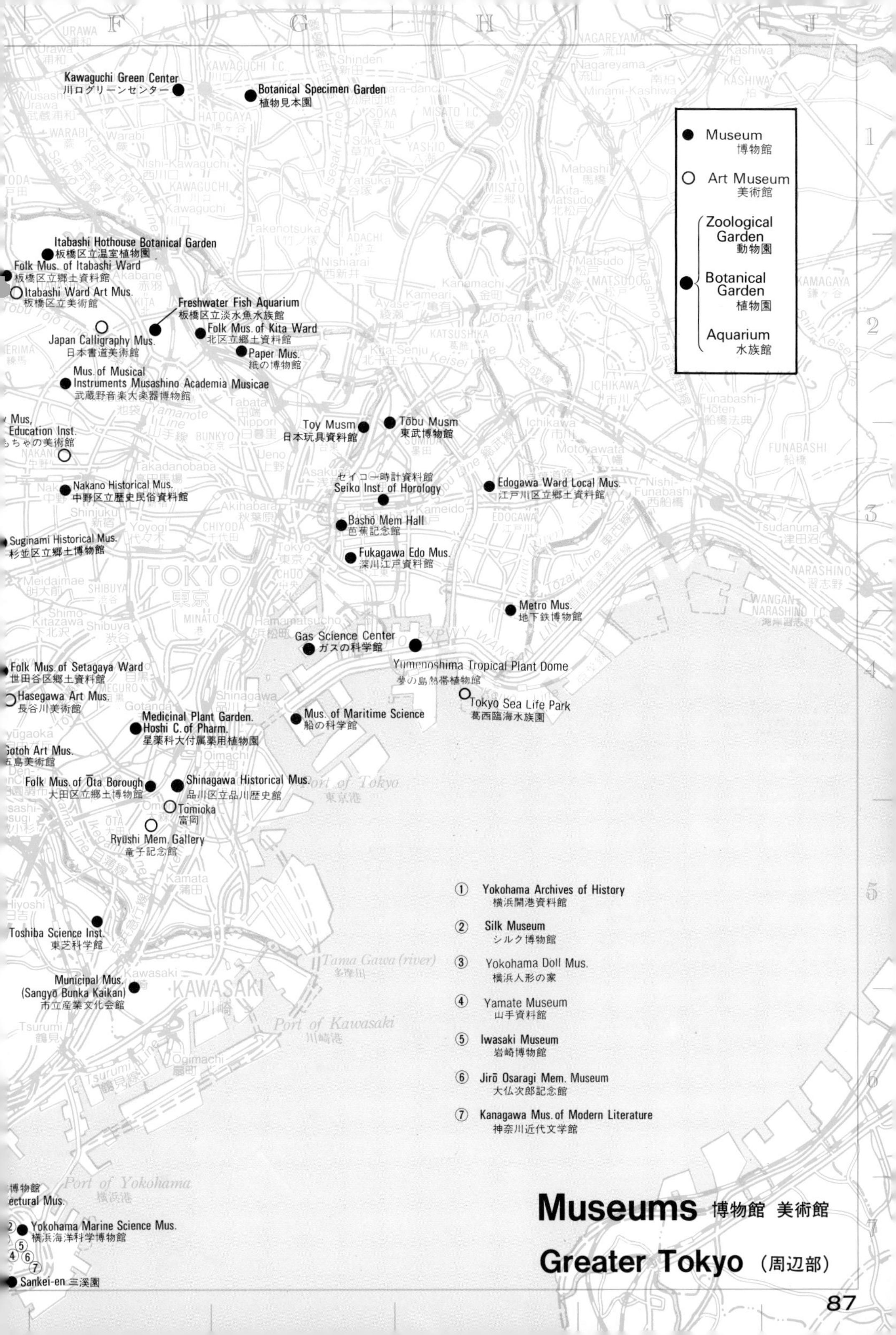
Museum 博物館
Art Museum 美術館
Zoological Garden 動物園
Botanical Garden 植物園
Aquarium 水族館
Kawaguchi Green Center 川ログリーンセンター
Botanical Specimen Garden 植物見本園
Itabashi Hothouse Botanical Garden 板橋区立温室植物園
Folk Mus. of Itabashi Ward 板橋区立郷土資料館
Itabashi Ward Art Mus. 板橋区立美術館
Freshwater Fish Aquarium 板橋区立淡水魚水族館
Japan Calligraphy Mus. 日本書道美術館
Folk Mus. of Kita Ward 北区立郷土資料館
Paper Mus. 紙の博物館
Mus. of Musical Instruments Musashino Academia Musicae 武蔵野音楽大楽器博物館
Toy Musm 日本玩具資料館
Tōbu Musm 東武博物館
Nakano Historical Mus. 中野区立歴史民俗資料館
セイコー時計資料館 Seiko Inst. of Horology
Edogawa Ward Local Mus. 江戸川区立郷土資料館
Bashō Mem Hall 芭蕉記念館
Suginami Historical Mus. 杉並区立郷土博物館
Fukagawa Edo Mus. 深川江戸資料館
Metro Mus. 地下鉄博物館
Gas Science Center ガスの科学館
Yumenoshima Tropical Plant Dome 夢の島熱帯植物館
Folk Mus. of Setagaya Ward 世田谷区郷土資料館
Hasegawa Art Mus. 長谷川美術館
Tokyo Sea Life Park 葛西臨海水族園
Mus. of Maritime Science 船の科学館
Medicinal Plant Garden. Hoshi C. of Pharm. 星薬科大付属薬用植物園
Gotoh Art Mus. 五島美術館
Folk Mus. of Ōta Borough 大田区立郷土博物館
Shinagawa Historical Mus. 品川区立品川歴史館
Tomioka 富岡
Ryūshi Mem. Gallery 竜子記念館
Toshiba Science Inst. 東芝科学館
Municipal Mus. (Sangyō Bunka Kaikan) 市立産業文化会館
Yokohama Marine Science Mus. 横浜海洋科学博物館
Sankei-en 三渓園
TOKYO 東京
KAWASAKI 川崎
Port of Tokyo 東京港
Port of Kawasaki 川崎港
Port of Yokohama 横浜港
Tama Gawa (river) 多摩川
① Yokohama Archives of History 横浜開港資料館
② Silk Museum シルク博物館
③ Yokohama Doll Mus. 横浜人形の家
④ Yamate Museum 山手資料館
⑤ Iwasaki Museum 岩崎博物館
⑥ Jirō Osaragi Mem. Museum 大仏次郎記念館
⑦ Kanagawa Mus. of Modern Literature 神奈川近代文学館

Museums 博物館 美術館

Greater Tokyo (周辺部)

Hotels and Japanese Inns ホテル 旅館
Central Tokyo (都心部)

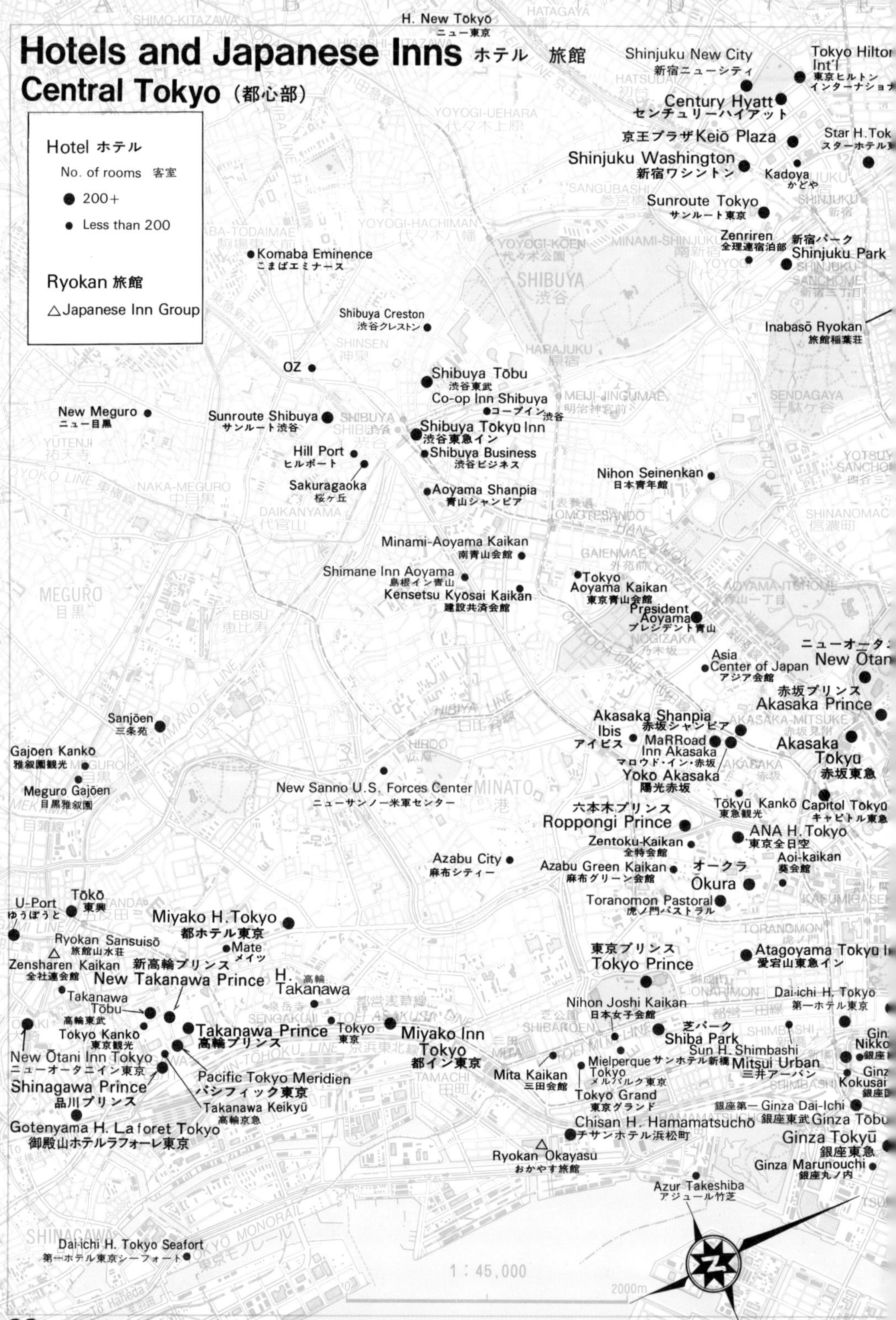

Hotel ホテル
No. of rooms 客室
200+
Less than 200
Ryokan 旅館
△Japanese Inn Group
H. New Tokyo
ニュー東京
Shinjuku New City
新宿ニューシティ
Tokyo Hilton Int'l
東京ヒルトンインターナショナル
Century Hyatt
センチュリーハイアット
京王プラザ Keiō Plaza
Star H. Tokyo
スターホテル東京
Shinjuku Washington
新宿ワシントン
Kadoya
かどや
Sunroute Tokyo
サンルート東京
Zenriren
全理連宿泊部
新宿パーク
Shinjuku Park
Komaba Eminence
こまばエミナース
Shibuya Creston
渋谷クレストン
Inabasō Ryokan
旅館稲葉荘
OZ
Shibuya Tōbu
渋谷東武
Co-op Inn Shibuya
コープイン渋谷
New Meguro
ニュー目黒
Sunroute Shibuya
サンルート渋谷
Shibuya Tōkyū Inn
渋谷東急イン
Hill Port
ヒルポート
Shibuya Business
渋谷ビジネス
Sakuragaoka
桜ヶ丘
Nihon Seinenkan
日本青年館
Aoyama Shanpia
青山シャンピア
Minami-Aoyama Kaikan
南青山会館
Shimane Inn Aoyama
島根イン青山
Tokyo Aoyama Kaikan
東京青山会館
Kensetsu Kyōsai Kaikan
建設共済会館
President Aoyama
プレジデント青山
ニューオータニ
New Otani
Asia Center of Japan
アジア会館
赤坂プリンス
Akasaka Prince
Akasaka Shanpia
赤坂シャンピア
Sanjōen
三条苑
Ibis
アイビス
MaRRoad Inn Akasaka
マロウド・イン・赤坂
Akasaka Tokyū
赤坂東急
Gajōen Kankō
雅叙園観光
Yoko Akasaka
陽光赤坂
Meguro Gajōen
目黒雅叙園
New Sanno U.S. Forces Center
ニューサンノー米軍センター
Tōkyū Kankō
東急観光
Capitol Tokyū
キャピトル東急
六本木プリンス
Roppongi Prince
ANA H. Tokyo
東京全日空
Zentoku-Kaikan
全特会館
Aoi-kaikan
葵会館
Azabu City
麻布シティー
Azabu Green Kaikan
麻布グリーン会館
オークラ
Ōkura
Tōkō
東興
U-Port
ゆうぽうと
Toranomon Pastoral
虎ノ門パストラル
Miyako H. Tokyo
都ホテル東京
Ryokan Sansuisō
旅館山水荘
Mate
メイツ
東京プリンス
Tokyo Prince
Atagoyama Tokyū Inn
愛宕山東急イン
Zensharen Kaikan
全社連会館
新高輪プリンス
New Takanawa Prince
H. Takanawa
高輪
Dai-ichi H. Tokyo
第一ホテル東京
Takanawa Tōbu
高輪東武
Nihon Joshi Kaikan
日本女子会館
Tokyo Kanko
東京観光
Takanawa Prince
高輪プリンス
Tokyo
東京
Miyako Inn Tokyo
都イン東京
芝パーク
Shiba Park
Sun H. Shimbashi
サンホテル新橋
Ginza Nikko
銀座日航
New Ōtani Inn Tokyo
ニューオータニイン東京
Mielperque Tokyo
メルパルク東京
Mitsui Urban
三井アーバン
Ginza Kokusai
銀座国際
Mita Kaikan
三田会館
Pacific Tokyo Meridien
パシフィック東京
Shinagawa Prince
品川プリンス
Tokyo Grand
東京グランド
Takanawa Keikyū
高輪京急
銀座第一 Ginza Dai-Ichi
銀座東武 Ginza Tōbu
Chisan H. Hamamatsuchō
チサンホテル浜松町
Gotenyama H. Laforet Tokyo
御殿山ホテルラフォーレ東京
Ginza Tokyū
銀座東急
Ryokan Okayasu
おかやす旅館
Ginza Marunouchi
銀座丸ノ内
Azur Takeshiba
アジュール竹芝
Dai-ichi H. Tokyo Seafort
第一ホテル東京シーフォート
1 : 45,000
2000m
SHINJUKU
SHIBUYA
渋谷
HARAJUKU
原宿
MEGURO
目黒
EBISU
恵比寿
MINATO
港
SHINAGAWA

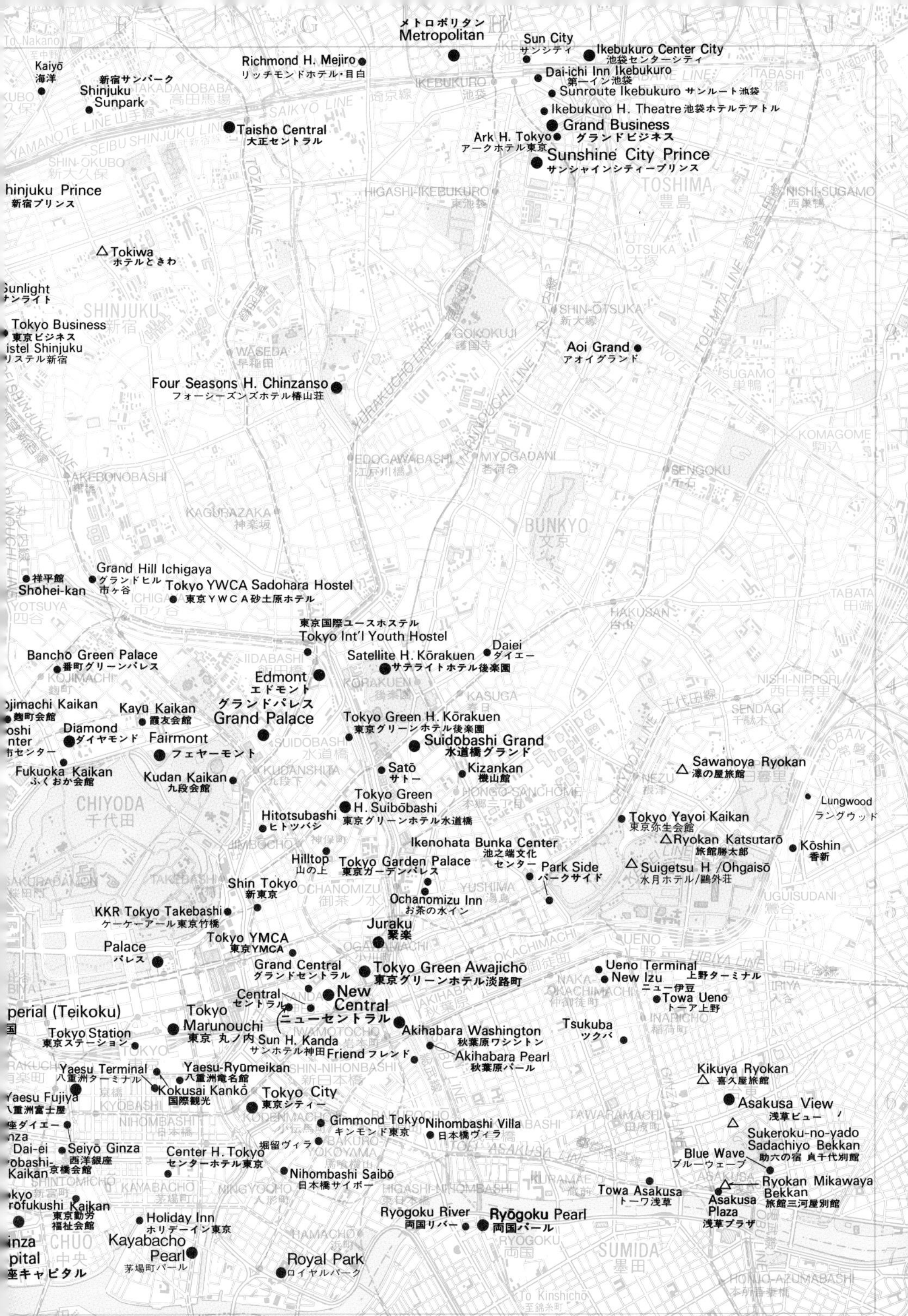

メトロポリタン
Metropolitan
Sun City
サンシティ
Ikebukuro Center City
池袋センターシティ
Richmond H. Mejiro
リッチモンドホテル・目白
Dai-ichi Inn Ikebukuro
第一イン池袋
Sunroute Ikebukuro サンルート池袋
Ikebukuro H. Theatre 池袋ホテルテアトル
Grand Business
グランドビジネス
Ark H. Tokyo
アークホテル東京
Sunshine City Prince
サンシャインシティープリンス
Kaiyō
海洋
新宿サンパーク
Shinjuku
Sunpark
Taisho Central
大正セントラル
hinjuku Prince
新宿プリンス
Tokiwa
ホテルときわ
Tokyo Business
東京ビジネス
Aoi Grand
アオイグランド
Four Seasons H. Chinzanso
フォーシーズンズホテル椿山荘
Grand Hill Ichigaya
グランドヒル
市ヶ谷
祥平館
Shohei-kan
Tokyo YWCA Sadohara Hostel
東京YWCA砂土原ホテル
東京国際ユースホステル
Tokyo Int'l Youth Hostel
Banchō Green Palace
番町グリーンパレス
Satellite H. Kōrakuen
サテライトホテル後楽園
Daiei
ダイエー
Edmont
エドモント
グランドパレス
Grand Palace
Kayū Kaikan
霞友会館
Diamond
ダイヤモンド
Fairmont
フェヤーモント
Tokyo Green H. Kōrakuen
東京グリーンホテル後楽園
Suidōbashi Grand
水道橋グランド
Fukuoka Kaikan
ふくおか会館
Kudan Kaikan
九段会館
Satō
サトー
Kizankan
機山館
Sawanoya Ryokan
澤の屋旅館
Lungwood
ラングウッド
Tokyo Green
H. Suibōbashi
東京グリーンホテル水道橋
Hitotsubashi
ヒトツバシ
Tokyo Yayoi Kaikan
東京弥生会館
Ryokan Katsutarō
旅館勝太郎
Kōshin
香新
Ikenohata Bunka Center
池之端文化
センター
Hilltop
山の上
Tokyo Garden Palace
東京ガーデンパレス
Park Side
パークサイド
Suigetsu H./Ohgaisō
水月ホテル/鷗外荘
Shin Tokyo
新東京
Ochanomizu Inn
お茶の水イン
KKR Tokyo Takebashi
ケーケーアール東京竹橋
Juraku
聚楽
Palace
パレス
Tokyo YMCA
東京YMCA
Grand Central
グランドセントラル
Tokyo Green Awajichō
東京グリーンホテル淡路町
Ueno Terminal
上野ターミナル
New Izu
ニュー伊豆
Towa Ueno
トーア上野
Central
セントラル
New
Central
ニューセントラル
perial (Teikoku)
Tokyo
Marunouchi
東京 丸ノ内
Tokyo Station
東京ステーション
Sun H. Kanda
サンホテル神田
Akihabara Washington
秋葉原ワシントン
Tsukuba
ツクバ
Friend フレンド
Akihabara Pearl
秋葉原パール
Yaesu Terminal
八重洲ターミナル
Yaesu-Ryumeikan
八重洲竜名館
Kokusai Kankō
国際観光
Kikuya Ryokan
喜久屋旅館
Yaesu Fujiya
八重洲富士屋
Tokyo City
東京シティー
Asakusa View
浅草ビュー
Gimmond Tokyo
キンモンド東京
Nihombashi Villa
日本橋ヴィラ
堀留ヴィラ
Sukeroku-no-yado
Sadachiyo Bekkan
助六の宿 貞千代別館
Seiyō Ginza
西洋銀座
Center H. Tokyo
センターホテル東京
Blue Wave
ブルーウェーブ
Nihombashi Saibō
日本橋サイボー
Towa Asakusa
トーワ浅草
Ryokan Mikawaya
Bekkan
旅館三河屋別館
Asakusa
Plaza
浅草プラザ
東京勤労
福祉会館
Holiday Inn
ホリデーイン東京
Ryōgoku River
両国リバー
Ryōgoku Pearl
両国パール
Kayabacho
Pearl
茅場町パール
Royal Park
ロイヤルパーク
pital
座キャピタル
To Nakano
至中野
IKEBUKURO
池袋
TAKADANOBABA
高田馬場
SHIN-OKUBO
新大久保
TOSHIMA
豊島
HIGASHI-IKEBUKURO
東池袋
NISHI-SUGAMO
西巣鴨
OTSUKA
大塚
SHINJUKU
新宿
SHIN-OTSUKA
新大塚
GOKOKUJI
護国寺
WASEDA
早稲田
SUGAMO
巣鴨
KOMAGOME
駒込
EDOGAWABASHI
江戸川橋
MYOGADANI
茗荷谷
SENGOKU
千石
AKEBONOBASHI
KAGURAZAKA
神楽坂
BUNKYO
文京
ICHIGAYA
市ケ谷
YOTSUYA
四谷
HAKUSAN
白山
TABATA
田端
IIDABASHI
飯田橋
KOJIMACHI
麹町
KŌRAKUEN
後楽園
KASUGA
春日
NISHI-NIPPORI
西日暮里
SENDAGI
千駄木
SUIDOBASHI
水道橋
KUDANSHITA
九段下
NEZU
根津
HONGO-SANCHOME
本郷三丁目
CHIYODA
千代田
JIMBOCHO
神保町
TAKEBASHI
OCHANOMIZU
御茶ノ水
YUSHIMA
湯島
UGUISUDANI
鶯谷
OKACHIMACHI
UENO
NAKA-OKACHIMACHI
仲御徒町
IRIYA
入谷
AKIHABARA
秋葉原
INARICHO
稲荷町
IWAMOTOCHO
SHIN-NIHONBASHI
新日本橋
KYOBASHI
NIHOMBASHI
日本橋
KODENMACHO
TAWARAMACHI
田原町
BAKUROCHO
YOKOYAMA
SHINTOMICHO
KAYABACHO
茅場町
NINGYOCHO
人形町
KURAMAE
HIGASHI-NIHOMBASHI
東日本橋
HAMACHO
浜町
RYOGOKU
両国
CHUO
中央
SUMIDA
墨田
To Kinshichō
至錦糸町
HONJO-AZUMABASHI
本所吾妻橋
YAMANOTE LINE 山手線
SEIBU SHINJUKU LINE
SAIKYO LINE
埼京線
TOZAI LINE
YURAKUCHO LINE
MARUNOUCHI LINE
TOEI MITA LINE
CHIYODA LINE
千代田線
JOBAN LINE
HIBIYA LINE
TOEI ASAKUSA LINE

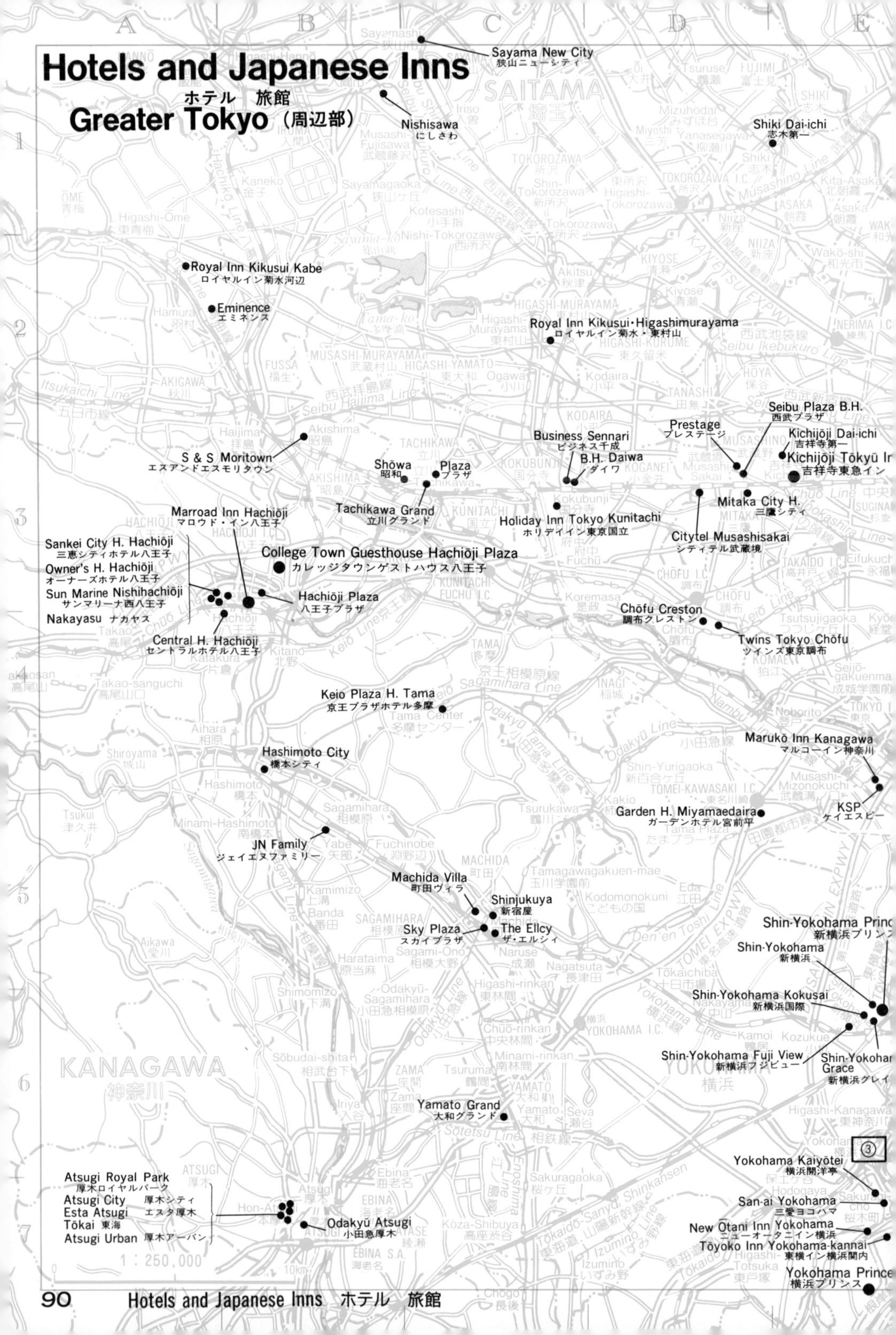

Hotels and Japanese Inns
ホテル 旅館
Greater Tokyo (周辺部)
Sayama New City
狭山ニューシティ
Nishisawa
にしさわ
Shiki Dai-ichi
志木第一
Royal Inn Kikusui Kabe
ロイヤルイン菊水河辺
Eminence
エミネンス
Royal Inn Kikusui·Higashimurayama
ロイヤルイン菊水・東村山
Seibu Plaza B.H.
西武プラザ
Prestage
プレステージ
Kichijōji Dai-ichi
吉祥寺第一
Kichijōji Tōkyū In
吉祥寺東急イン
Business Sennari
ビジネス千成
B.H. Daiwa
ダイワ
S & S Moritown
エスアンドエスモリタウン
Shōwa
昭和
Plaza
プラザ
Tachikawa Grand
立川グランド
Mitaka City H.
三鷹シティ
Holiday Inn Tokyo Kunitachi
ホリデイイン東京国立
Citytel Musashisakai
シティテル武蔵境
Marroad Inn Hachiōji
マロウド・イン八王子
Sankei City H. Hachiōji
三恵シティホテル八王子
Owner's H. Hachiōji
オーナーズホテル八王子
Sun Marine Nishihachiōji
サンマリーナ西八王子
Nakayasu ナカヤス
College Town Guesthouse Hachiōji Plaza
カレッジタウンゲストハウス八王子
Hachiōji Plaza
八王子プラザ
Central H. Hachiōji
セントラルホテル八王子
Chōfu Creston
調布クレストン
Twins Tokyo Chōfu
ツインズ東京調布
Keio Plaza H. Tama
京王プラザホテル多摩
Hashimoto City
橋本シティ
Marukō Inn Kanagawa
マルコーイン神奈川
KSP
ケイエスピー
Garden H. Miyamaedaira
ガーデンホテル宮前平
JN Family
ジェイエヌファミリー
Machida Villa
町田ヴィラ
Shinjukuya
新宿屋
Sky Plaza
スカイプラザ
The Ellcy
ザ・エルシィ
Shin-Yokohama Princ
新横浜プリンス
Shin-Yokohama
新横浜
Shin-Yokohama Kokusai
新横浜国際
Shin-Yokohama Fuji View
新横浜フジビュー
Shin-Yokohar Grace
新横浜グレイ
Yamato Grand
大和グランド
Yokohama Kaiyōtei
横浜開洋亭
San-ai Yokohama
三愛ヨコハマ
New Otani Inn Yokohama
ニューオータニイン横浜
Tōyoko Inn Yokohama-kannai
東横イン横浜関内
Yokohama Prince
横浜プリンス
Atsugi Royal Park
厚木ロイヤルパーク
Atsugi City 厚木シティ
Esta Atsugi エスタ厚木
Tōkai 東海
Atsugi Urban 厚木アーバン
Odakyū Atsugi
小田急厚木
SAITAMA
埼玉
KANAGAWA
神奈川
1 : 250,000

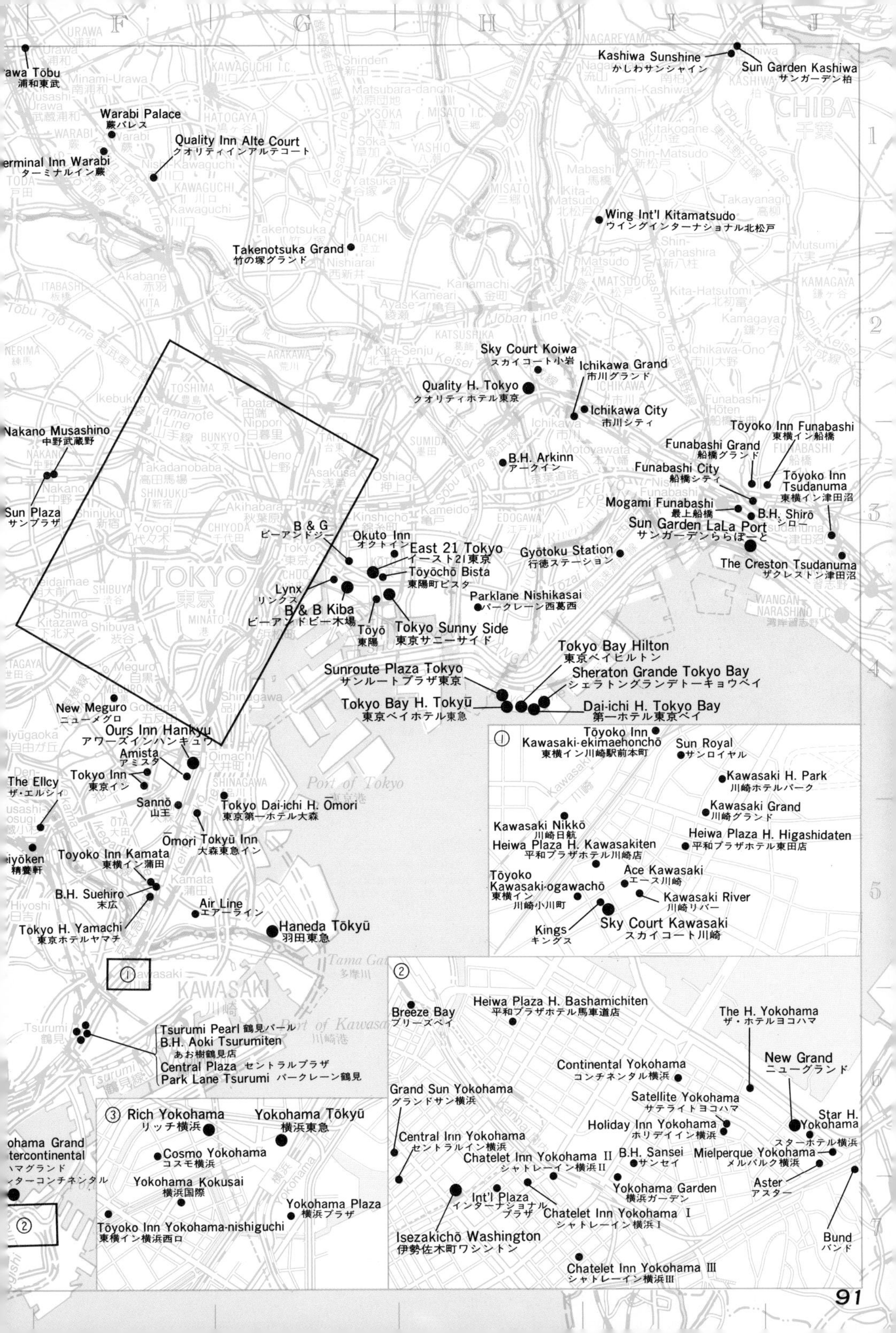

Kashiwa Sunshine
かしわサンシャイン
Sun Garden Kashiwa
サンガーデン柏
Warabi Palace
蕨パレス
Quality Inn Alte Court
クオリティインアルテコート
Terminal Inn Warabi
ターミナルイン蕨
Wing Int'l Kitamatsudo
ウイングインターナショナル北松戸
Takenotsuka Grand
竹の塚グランド
Sky Court Koiwa
スカイコート小岩
Ichikawa Grand
市川グランド
Quality H. Tokyo
クオリティホテル東京
Ichikawa City
市川シティ
Nakano Musashino
中野武蔵野
Tōyoko Inn Funabashi
東横イン船橋
Funabashi Grand
船橋グランド
B.H. Arkinn
アークイン
Funabashi City
船橋シティ
Tōyoko Inn Tsudanuma
東横イン津田沼
Mogami Funabashi
最上船橋
B.H. Shirō
シロー
Sun Plaza
サンプラザ
Sun Garden LaLa Port
サンガーデンららぽーと
B & G
ビーアンドジー
Okuto Inn
オクトイン
East 21 Tokyo
イースト21東京
Gyōtoku Station
行徳ステーション
The Creston Tsudanuma
ザクレストン津田沼
Tōyōchō Bista
東陽町ビスタ
Lynx
リンクス
Parklane Nishikasai
パークレーン西葛西
B & B Kiba
ビーアンドビー木場
Tōyō
東陽
Tokyo Sunny Side
東京サニーサイド
TOKYO
東京
Tokyo Bay Hilton
東京ベイヒルトン
Sunroute Plaza Tokyo
サンルートプラザ東京
Sheraton Grande Tokyo Bay
シェラトングランデトーキョウベイ
Tokyo Bay H. Tokyū
東京ベイホテル東急
Dai-ichi H. Tokyo Bay
第一ホテル東京ベイ
New Meguro
ニューメグロ
Ours Inn Hankyu
アワーズインハンキュウ
Amista
アミスタ
Tokyo Inn
東京イン
The Ellcy
ザ・エルシィ
Sannō
山王
Tokyo Dai-ichi H. Ōmori
東京第一ホテル大森
Ōmori Tokyū Inn
大森東急イン
Toyoko Inn Kamata
東横イン蒲田
B.H. Suehiro
末広
Air Line
エアーライン
Tokyo H. Yamachi
東京ホテルヤマチ
Haneda Tōkyū
羽田東急
Port of Tokyo
KAWASAKI
川崎
Tsurumi Pearl 鶴見パール
B.H. Aoki Tsurumiten
あお樹鶴見店
Central Plaza セントラルプラザ
Park Lane Tsurumi パークレーン鶴見
①
Tōyoko Inn
Kawasaki-ekimaehonchō
東横イン川崎駅前本町
Sun Royal
サンロイヤル
Kawasaki H. Park
川崎ホテルパーク
Kawasaki Grand
川崎グランド
Kawasaki Nikkō
川崎日航
Heiwa Plaza H. Kawasakiten
平和プラザホテル川崎店
Heiwa Plaza H. Higashidaten
平和プラザホテル東田店
Tōyoko
Kawasaki-ogawachō
東横イン
川崎小川町
Ace Kawasaki
エース川崎
Kawasaki River
川崎リバー
Kings
キングス
Sky Court Kawasaki
スカイコート川崎
②
Breeze Bay
ブリーズベイ
Heiwa Plaza H. Bashamichiten
平和プラザホテル馬車道店
The H. Yokohama
ザ・ホテルヨコハマ
New Grand
ニューグランド
Continental Yokohama
コンチネンタル横浜
Grand Sun Yokohama
グランドサン横浜
Satellite Yokohama
サテライトヨコハマ
Star H. Yokohama
スターホテル横浜
Holiday Inn Yokohama
ホリデイイン横浜
Central Inn Yokohama
セントラルイン横浜
Chatelet Inn Yokohama II
シャトレーイン横浜II
B.H. Sansei
サンセイ
Mielperque Yokohama
メルパルク横浜
Aster
アスター
Yokohama Garden
横浜ガーデン
Int'l Plaza
インターナショナルプラザ
Chatelet Inn Yokohama I
シャトレーイン横浜I
Bund
バンド
Isezakichō Washington
伊勢佐木町ワシントン
Chatelet Inn Yokohama III
シャトレーイン横浜III
③
Rich Yokohama
リッチ横浜
Yokohama Tōkyū
横浜東急
Cosmo Yokohama
コスモ横浜
Yokohama Grand Intercontinental
ヨコハマグランドインターコンチネンタル
Yokohama Kokusai
横浜国際
Yokohama Plaza
横浜プラザ
Tōyoko Inn Yokohama-nishiguchi
東横イン横浜西口

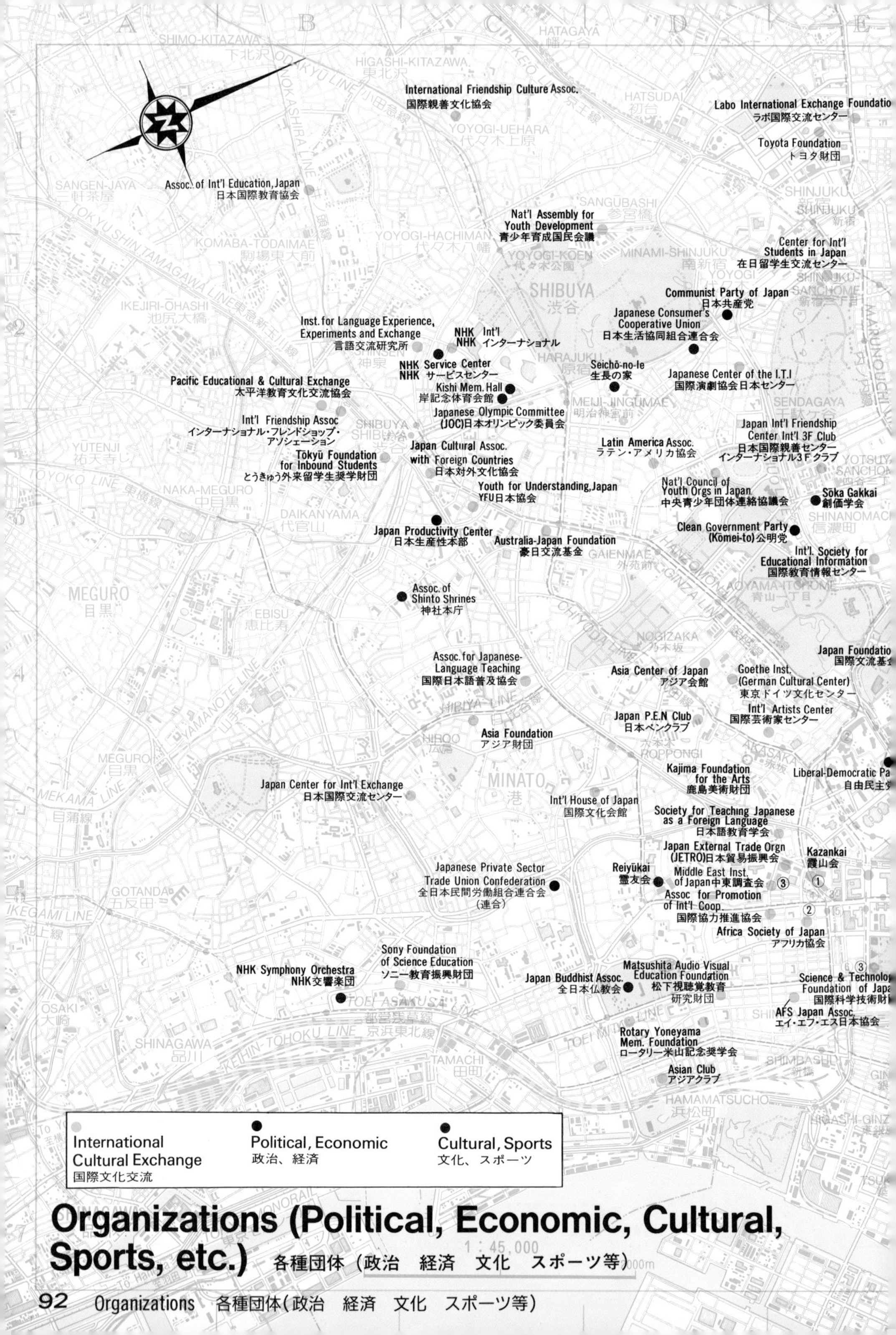

International Friendship Culture Assoc.
国際親善文化協会
Labo International Exchange Foundation
ラボ国際交流センター
Toyota Foundation
トヨタ財団
Assoc. of Int'l Education, Japan
日本国際教育協会
Nat'l Assembly for Youth Development
青少年育成国民会議
Center for Int'l Students in Japan
在日留学生交流センター
Communist Party of Japan
日本共産党
Japanese Consumer's Cooperative Union
日本生活協同組合連合会
Inst. for Language Experience, Experiments and Exchange
言語交流研究所
NHK Int'l
NHK インターナショナル
NHK Service Center
NHK サービスセンター
Seichō-no-Ie
生長の家
Japanese Center of the I.T.I
国際演劇協会日本センター
Pacific Educational & Cultural Exchange
太平洋教育文化交流協会
Kishi Mem. Hall
岸記念体育会館
Japanese Olympic Committee
(JOC)日本オリンピック委員会
Int'l Friendship Assoc
インターナショナル・フレンドショップ・アソシェーション
Japan Int'l Friendship Center Int'l 3F Club
日本国際親善センター
インターナショナル3Fクラブ
Japan Cultural Assoc. with Foreign Countries
日本対外文化協会
Latin America Assoc.
ラテン・アメリカ協会
Tōkyū Foundation for Inbound Students
とうきゅう外来留学生奨学財団
Nat'l Council of Youth Orgs in Japan
中央青少年団体連絡協議会
Sōka Gakkai
創価学会
Youth for Understanding, Japan
YFU日本協会
Japan Productivity Center
日本生産性本部
Clean Government Party
(Komei-to)公明党
Australia-Japan Foundation
豪日交流基金
Int'l Society for Educational Information
国際教育情報センター
Assoc. of Shinto Shrines
神社本庁
Japan Foundation
国際文流基金
Assoc. for Japanese-Language Teaching
国際日本語普及協会
Asia Center of Japan
アジア会館
Goethe Inst. (German Cultural Center)
東京ドイツ文化センター
Int'l Artists Center
国際芸術家センター
Japan P.E.N Club
日本ペンクラブ
Asia Foundation
アジア財団
Kajima Foundation for the Arts
鹿島美術財団
Japan Center for Int'l Exchange
日本国際交流センター
Int'l House of Japan
国際文化会館
Society for Teaching Japanese as a Foreign Language
日本語教育学会
Japan External Trade Orgn
(JETRO)日本貿易振興会
Kazankai
霞山会
Japanese Private Sector Trade Union Confederation
全日本民間労働組合連合会
(連合)
Reiyūkai
霊友会
Middle East Inst. of Japan
中東調査会
Assoc for Promotion of Int'l Coop.
国際協力推進協会
Africa Society of Japan
アフリカ協会
Sony Foundation of Science Education
ソニー教育振興財団
NHK Symphony Orchestra
NHK交響楽団
Japan Buddhist Assoc.
全日本仏教会
Matsushita Audio Visual Education Foundation
松下視聴覚教育研究財団
AFS Japan Assoc.
エイ・エフ・エス日本協会
Rotary Yoneyama Mem. Foundation
ロータリー米山記念奨学会
Asian Club
アジアクラブ
International Cultural Exchange
国際文化交流
Political, Economic
政治、経済
Cultural, Sports
文化、スポーツ
1 : 45,000

Organizations (Political, Economic, Cultural, Sports, etc.) 各種団体（政治　経済　文化　スポーツ等）

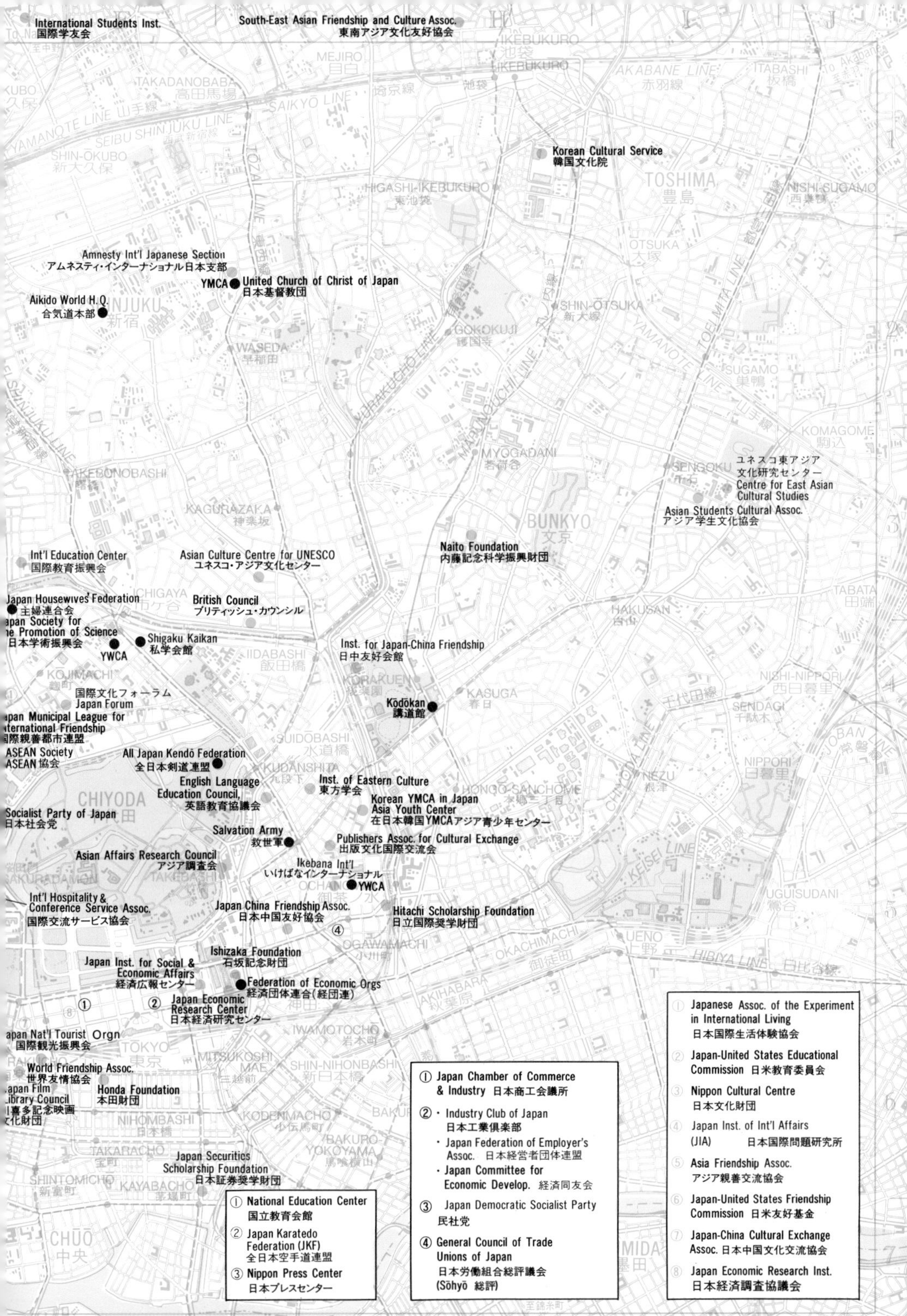
International Students Inst.
国際学友会
South-East Asian Friendship and Culture Assoc.
東南アジア文化友好協会
Korean Cultural Service
韓国文化院
TOSHIMA
豊島
Amnesty Int'l Japanese Section
アムネスティ・インターナショナル日本支部
YMCA
United Church of Christ of Japan
日本基督教団
Aikido World H.Q.
合気道本部
ユネスコ東アジア
文化研究センター
Centre for East Asian
Cultural Studies
Asian Students Cultural Assoc.
アジア学生文化協会
BUNKYO
文京
Naito Foundation
内藤記念科学振興財団
Int'l Education Center
国際教育振興会
Asian Culture Centre for UNESCO
ユネスコ・アジア文化センター
Japan Housewives' Federation
主婦連合会
apan Society for
e Promotion of Science
日本学術振興会
YWCA
Shigaku Kaikan
私学会館
British Council
ブリティッシュ・カウンシル
Inst. for Japan-China Friendship
日中友好会館
国際文化フォーラム
Japan Forum
apan Municipal League for
ternational Friendship
国際親善都市連盟
Kōdōkan
講道館
ASEAN Society
ASEAN 協会
All Japan Kendō Federation
全日本剣道連盟
English Language
Education Council,
英語教育協議会
Inst. of Eastern Culture
東方学会
Korean YMCA in Japan
Asia Youth Center
在日本韓国YMCAアジア青少年センター
CHIYODA
Socialist Party of Japan
日本社会党
Salvation Army
救世軍
Publishers Assoc. for Cultural Exchange
出版文化国際交流会
Asian Affairs Research Council
アジア調査会
Ikebana Int'l
いけばなインターナショナル
YWCA
Int'l Hospitality &
Conference Service Assoc.
国際交流サービス協会
Japan China Friendship Assoc.
日本中国友好協会
Hitachi Scholarship Foundation
日立国際奨学財団
Ishizaka Foundation
石坂記念財団
Japan Inst. for Social &
Economic Affairs
経済広報センター
Federation of Economic Orgs
経済団体連合(経団連)
Japan Economic
Research Center
日本経済研究センター
apan Nat'l Tourist Orgn
国際観光振興会
World Friendship Assoc.
世界友情協会
apan Film
ibrary Council
川喜多記念映画
文化財団
Honda Foundation
本田財団
Japan Securities
Scholarship Foundation
日本証券奨学財団
① National Education Center
国立教育会館
② Japan Karatedo
Federation (JKF)
全日本空手道連盟
③ Nippon Press Center
日本プレスセンター
① Japan Chamber of Commerce
& Industry 日本商工会議所
② ・Industry Club of Japan
日本工業倶楽部
・Japan Federation of Employer's
Assoc. 日本経営者団体連盟
・Japan Committee for
Economic Develop. 経済同友会
③ Japan Democratic Socialist Party
民社党
④ General Council of Trade
Unions of Japan
日本労働組合総評議会
(Sōhyō 総評)
① Japanese Assoc. of the Experiment
in International Living
日本国際生活体験協会
② Japan-United States Educational
Commission 日米教育委員会
③ Nippon Cultural Centre
日本文化財団
④ Japan Inst. of Int'l Affairs
(JIA) 日本国際問題研究所
⑤ Asia Friendship Assoc.
アジア親善交流協会
⑥ Japan-United States Friendship
Commission 日米友好基金
⑦ Japan-China Cultural Exchange
Assoc. 日本中国文化交流協会
⑧ Japan Economic Research Inst.
日本経済調査協議会

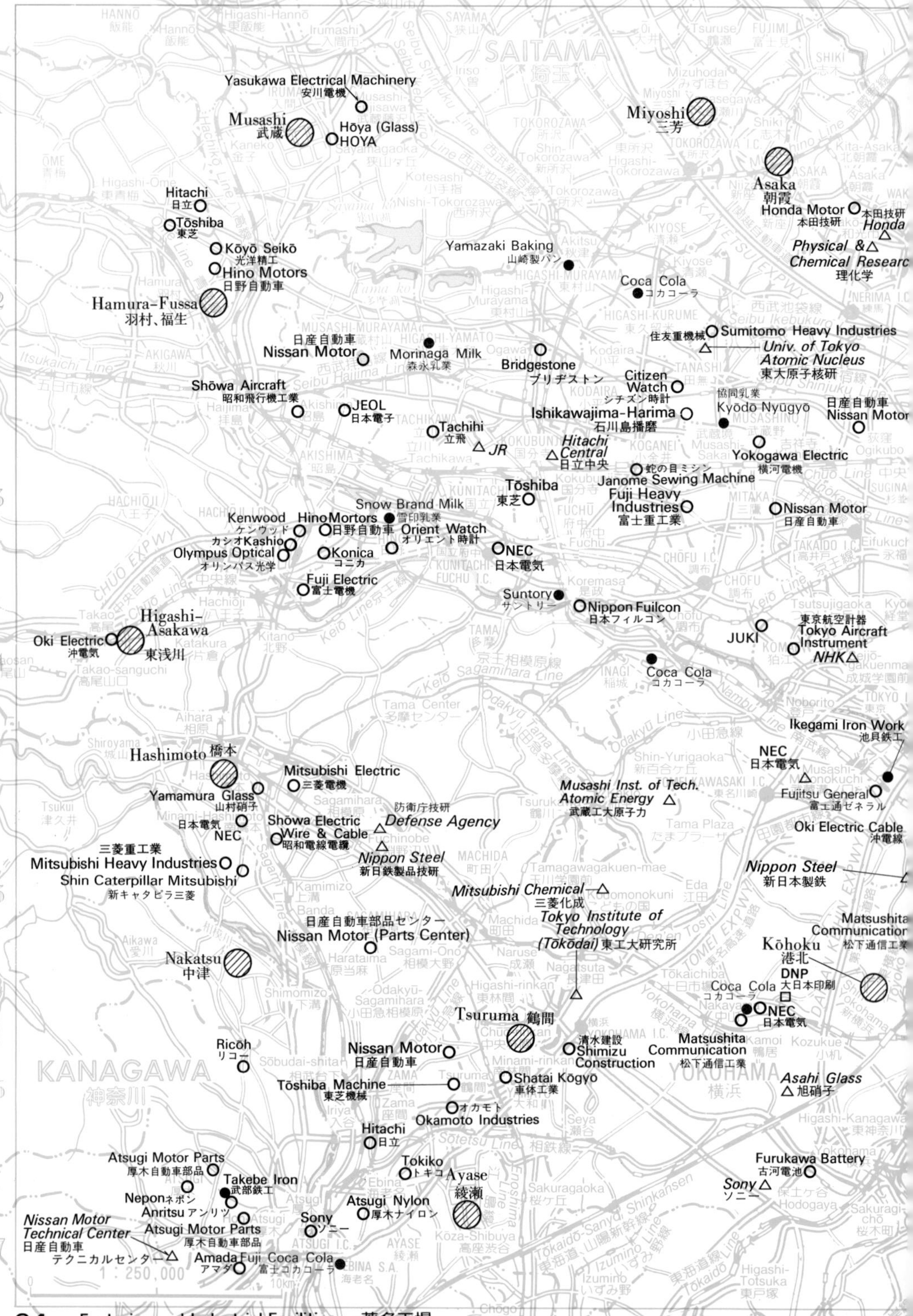

A
B
C
D
E
1
2
3
4
5
6
7
SAITAMA
埼玉
KANAGAWA
神奈川
Yasukawa Electrical Machinery
安川電機
Musashi
武蔵
Hōya (Glass)
HOYA
Miyoshi
三芳
Asaka
朝霞
Honda Motor
本田技研
Honda
Physical & Chemical Researc
理化学
Hitachi
日立
Tōshiba
東芝
Kōyō Seikō
光洋精工
Hino Motors
日野自動車
Hamura-Fussa
羽村、福生
Yamazaki Baking
山崎製パン
Coca Cola
コカコーラ
Sumitomo Heavy Industries
住友重機械
Univ. of Tokyo Atomic Nucleus
東大原子核研
日産自動車
Nissan Motor
Morinaga Milk
森永乳業
Bridgestone
ブリヂストン
Citizen Watch
シチズン時計
協同乳業
Kyōdō Nyūgyō
Ishikawajima-Harima
石川島播磨
日産自動車
Nissan Motor
Shōwa Aircraft
昭和飛行機工業
JEOL
日本電子
Tachihi
立飛
JR
Hitachi Central
日立中央
Yokogawa Electric
横河電機
蛇の目ミシン
Janome Sewing Machine
Tōshiba
東芝
Fuji Heavy Industries
富士重工業
Snow Brand Milk
雪印乳業
Kenwood
ケンウッド
Hino Mortors
日野自動車
Orient Watch
オリエント時計
Nissan Motor
日産自動車
カシオKashio
Olympus Optical
オリンパス光学
Konica
コニカ
NEC
日本電気
Fuji Electric
富士電機
Suntory
サントリー
Nippon Fuilcon
日本フィルコン
Higashi-Asakawa
東浅川
Oki Electric
沖電気
東京航空計器
Tokyo Aircraft Instrument
JUKI
NHK
Coca Cola
コカコーラ
Ikegami Iron Work
池貝鉄工
NEC
日本電気
Hashimoto
橋本
Mitsubishi Electric
三菱電機
Yamamura Glass
山村硝子
防衛庁技研
Defense Agency
Musashi Inst. of Tech. Atomic Energy
武蔵工大原子力
Fujitsu General
富士通ゼネラル
日本電気
NEC
Shōwa Electric Wire & Cable
昭和電線電纜
Nippon Steel
新日鉄製品技研
Oki Electric Cable
沖電線
三菱重工業
Mitsubishi Heavy Industries
Shin Caterpillar Mitsubishi
新キャタピラ三菱
Nippon Steel
新日本製鉄
Mitsubishi Chemical
三菱化成
Tokyo Institute of Technology (Tōkōdai)
東工大研究所
日産自動車部品センター
Nissan Motor (Parts Center)
Matsushita Communication
松下通信工業
Kōhoku
港北
DNP
大日本印刷
Nakatsu
中津
Coca Cola
コカコーラ
NEC
日本電気
Tsuruma
鶴間
Ricōh
リコー
Nissan Motor
日産自動車
清水建設
Shimizu Construction
Matsushita Communication
松下通信工業
Tōshiba Machine
東芝機械
Shatai Kōgyo
車体工業
Asahi Glass
旭硝子
オカモト
Okamoto Industries
Hitachi
日立
Atsugi Motor Parts
厚木自動車部品
Takebe Iron
武部鉄工
Tokiko
トキコ
Ayase
綾瀬
Furukawa Battery
古河電池
Neponネポン
Anritsuアンリツ
Atsugi Nylon
厚木ナイロン
Sony
ソニー
Nissan Motor Technical Center
日産自動車
テクニカルセンター
Atsugi Motor Parts
厚木自動車部品
Sony
ソニー
Amada
アマダ
Fuji Coca Cola
富士コカコーラ
1 : 250,000
10km

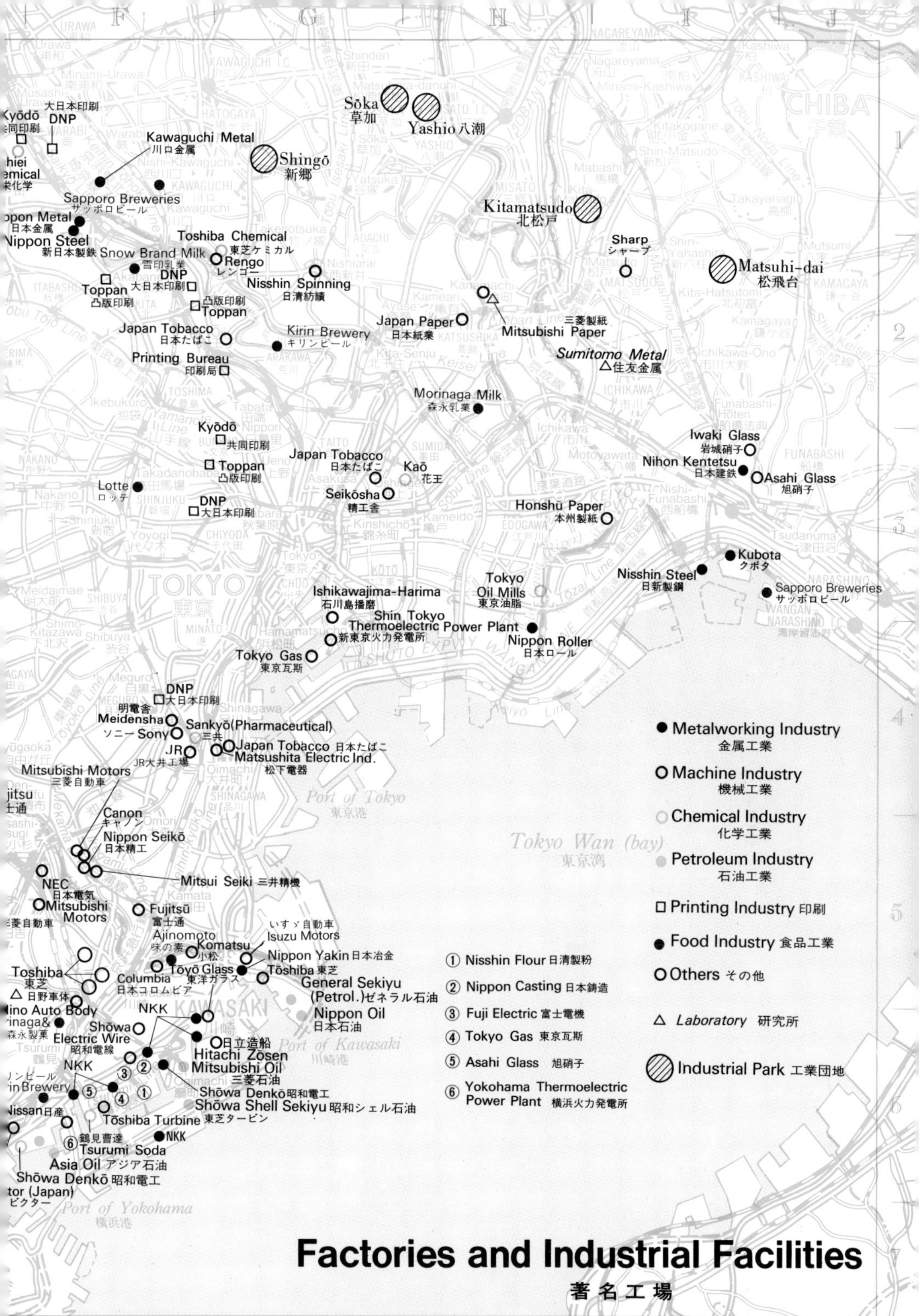

Factories and Industrial Facilities

著名工場

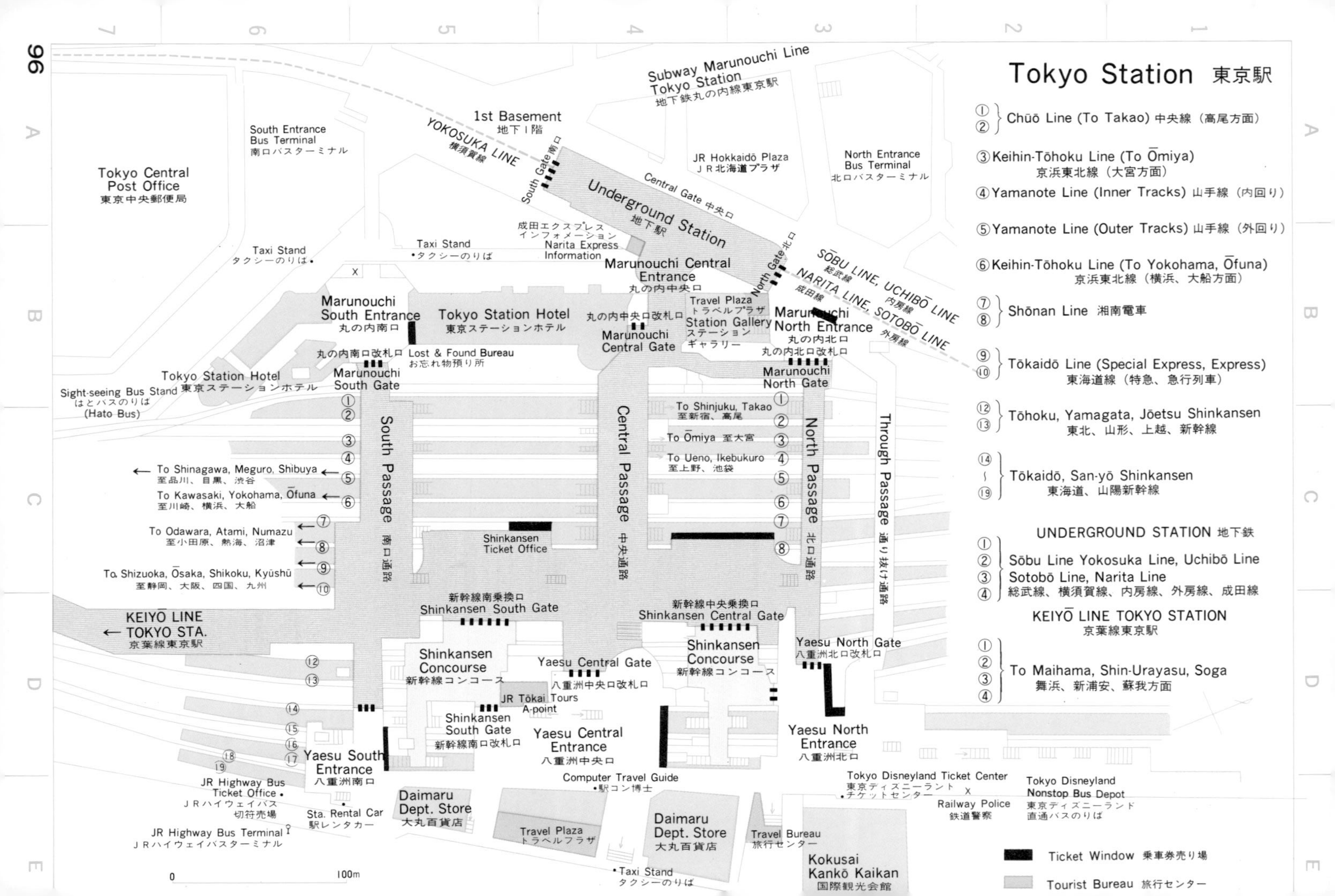
Tokyo Station 東京駅
①② Chūō Line (To Takao) 中央線（高尾方面）
③ Keihin-Tōhoku Line (To Ōmiya) 京浜東北線（大宮方面）
④ Yamanote Line (Inner Tracks) 山手線（内回り）
⑤ Yamanote Line (Outer Tracks) 山手線（外回り）
⑥ Keihin-Tōhoku Line (To Yokohama, Ōfuna) 京浜東北線（横浜、大船方面）
⑦⑧ Shōnan Line 湘南電車
⑨⑩ Tōkaidō Line (Special Express, Express) 東海道線（特急、急行列車）
⑫⑬ Tōhoku, Yamagata, Jōetsu Shinkansen 東北、山形、上越、新幹線
⑭〜⑲ Tōkaidō, San-yō Shinkansen 東海道、山陽新幹線
UNDERGROUND STATION 地下鉄
①②③④ Sōbu Line Yokosuka Line, Uchibō Line Sotobō Line, Narita Line 総武線、横須賀線、内房線、外房線、成田線
KEIYŌ LINE TOKYO STATION 京葉線東京駅
①②③④ To Maihama, Shin-Urayasu, Soga 舞浜、新浦安、蘇我方面
Subway Marunouchi Line Tokyo Station 地下鉄丸の内線東京駅
1st Basement 地下１階
YOKOSUKA LINE 横須賀線
South Gate 南口
Underground Station 地下駅
Central Gate 中央口
North Gate 北口
SŌBU LINE, UCHIBŌ LINE 総武線 内房線
NARITA LINE, SOTOBŌ LINE 成田線 外房線
South Entrance Bus Terminal 南口バスターミナル
JR Hokkaidō Plaza ＪＲ北海道プラザ
North Entrance Bus Terminal 北口バスターミナル
Tokyo Central Post Office 東京中央郵便局
Taxi Stand タクシーのりば
成田エクスプレスインフォメーション Narita Express Information
Marunouchi Central Entrance 丸の内中央口
Travel Plaza トラベルプラザ
Station Gallery ステーションギャラリー
Marunouchi North Entrance 丸の内北口
Marunouchi South Entrance 丸の内南口
Tokyo Station Hotel 東京ステーションホテル
丸の内中央口改札口 Marunouchi Central Gate
丸の内北口改札口 Marunouchi North Gate
丸の内南口改札口 Marunouchi South Gate
Lost & Found Bureau お忘れ物預り所
Sight-seeing Bus Stand はとバスのりば (Hato Bus)
South Passage 南口通路
Central Passage 中央通路
North Passage 北口通路
Through Passage 通り抜け通路
To Shinjuku, Takao 至新宿、高尾
To Ōmiya 至大宮
To Ueno, Ikebukuro 至上野、池袋
To Shinagawa, Meguro, Shibuya 至品川、目黒、渋谷
To Kawasaki, Yokohama, Ōfuna 至川崎、横浜、大船
To Odawara, Atami, Numazu 至小田原、熱海、沼津
To Shizuoka, Ōsaka, Shikoku, Kyūshū 至静岡、大阪、四国、九州
KEIYŌ LINE TOKYO STA. 京葉線東京駅
Shinkansen Ticket Office
新幹線南乗換口 Shinkansen South Gate
新幹線中央乗換口 Shinkansen Central Gate
Shinkansen Concourse 新幹線コンコース
Yaesu Central Gate 八重洲中央口改札口
Yaesu North Gate 八重洲北口改札口
JR Tōkai Tours A-point
Shinkansen South Gate 新幹線南口改札口
Yaesu South Entrance 八重洲南口
Yaesu Central Entrance 八重洲中央口
Yaesu North Entrance 八重洲北口
JR Highway Bus Ticket Office ＪＲハイウェイバス切符売場
JR Highway Bus Terminal ＪＲハイウェイバスターミナル
Sta. Rental Car 駅レンタカー
Daimaru Dept. Store 大丸百貨店
Computer Travel Guide 駅コン博士
Travel Plaza トラベルプラザ
Tokyo Disneyland Ticket Center 東京ディズニーランドチケットセンター
Railway Police 鉄道警察
Tokyo Disneyland Nonstop Bus Depot 東京ディズニーランド直通バスのりば
Travel Bureau 旅行センター
Kokusai Kankō Kaikan 国際観光会館
Taxi Stand タクシーのりば
Ticket Window 乗車券売り場
Tourist Bureau 旅行センター
0 100m

Routes to Airports
空港への交通

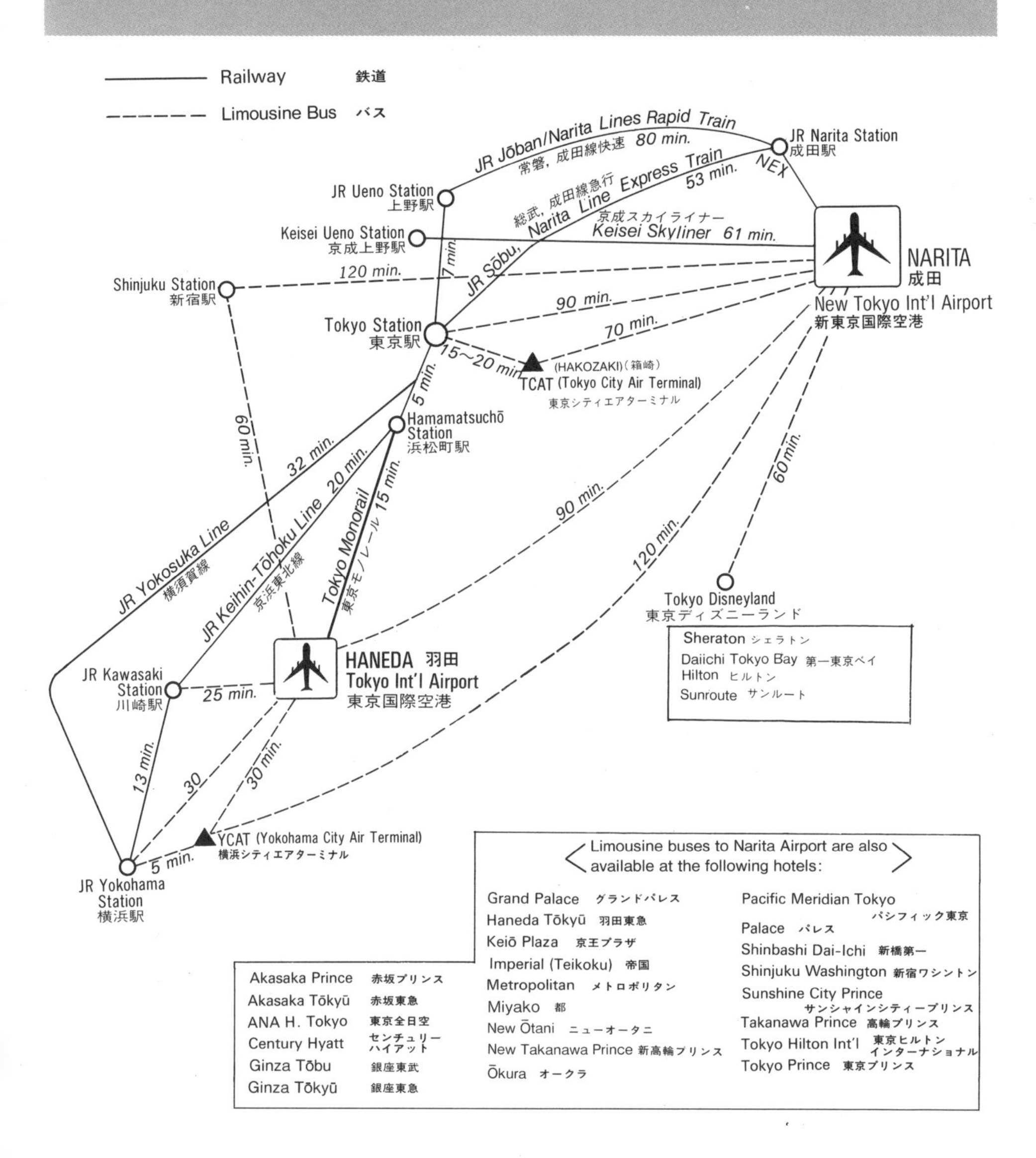

Railway 鉄道
Limousine Bus バス
JR Jōban/Narita Lines Rapid Train
常磐，成田線快速 80 min.
JR Narita Station
成田駅
NEX
総武，成田線急行
JR Sōbu, Narita Line Express Train
53 min.
JR Ueno Station
上野駅
京成スカイライナー
Keisei Skyliner 61 min.
Keisei Ueno Station
京成上野駅
NARITA
成田
New Tokyo Int'l Airport
新東京国際空港
7 min.
Shinjuku Station
新宿駅
120 min.
90 min.
70 min.
Tokyo Station
東京駅
15～20 min.
(HAKOZAKI)（箱崎）
TCAT (Tokyo City Air Terminal)
東京シティエアターミナル
5 min.
Hamamatsuchō Station
浜松町駅
60 min.
32 min.
20 min.
15 min.
90 min.
120 min.
60 min.
JR Yokosuka Line
横須賀線
JR Keihin-Tōhoku Line
京浜東北線
Tokyo Monorail
東京モノレール
Tokyo Disneyland
東京ディズニーランド
Sheraton シェラトン
Daiichi Tokyo Bay 第一東京ベイ
Hilton ヒルトン
Sunroute サンルート
HANEDA 羽田
Tokyo Int'l Airport
東京国際空港
JR Kawasaki Station
川崎駅
25 min.
13 min.
30
30 min.
YCAT (Yokohama City Air Terminal)
横浜シティエアターミナル
5 min.
JR Yokohama Station
横浜駅
Limousine buses to Narita Airport are also available at the following hotels:
Akasaka Prince 赤坂プリンス
Akasaka Tōkyū 赤坂東急
ANA H. Tokyo 東京全日空
Century Hyatt センチュリーハイアット
Ginza Tōbu 銀座東武
Ginza Tōkyū 銀座東急
Grand Palace グランドパレス
Haneda Tōkyū 羽田東急
Keiō Plaza 京王プラザ
Imperial (Teikoku) 帝国
Metropolitan メトロポリタン
Miyako 都
New Ōtani ニューオータニ
New Takanawa Prince 新高輪プリンス
Ōkura オークラ
Pacific Meridian Tokyo パシフィック東京
Palace パレス
Shinbashi Dai-Ichi 新橋第一
Shinjuku Washington 新宿ワシントン
Sunshine City Prince サンシャインシティープリンス
Takanawa Prince 高輪プリンス
Tokyo Hilton Int'l 東京ヒルトンインターナショナル
Tokyo Prince 東京プリンス

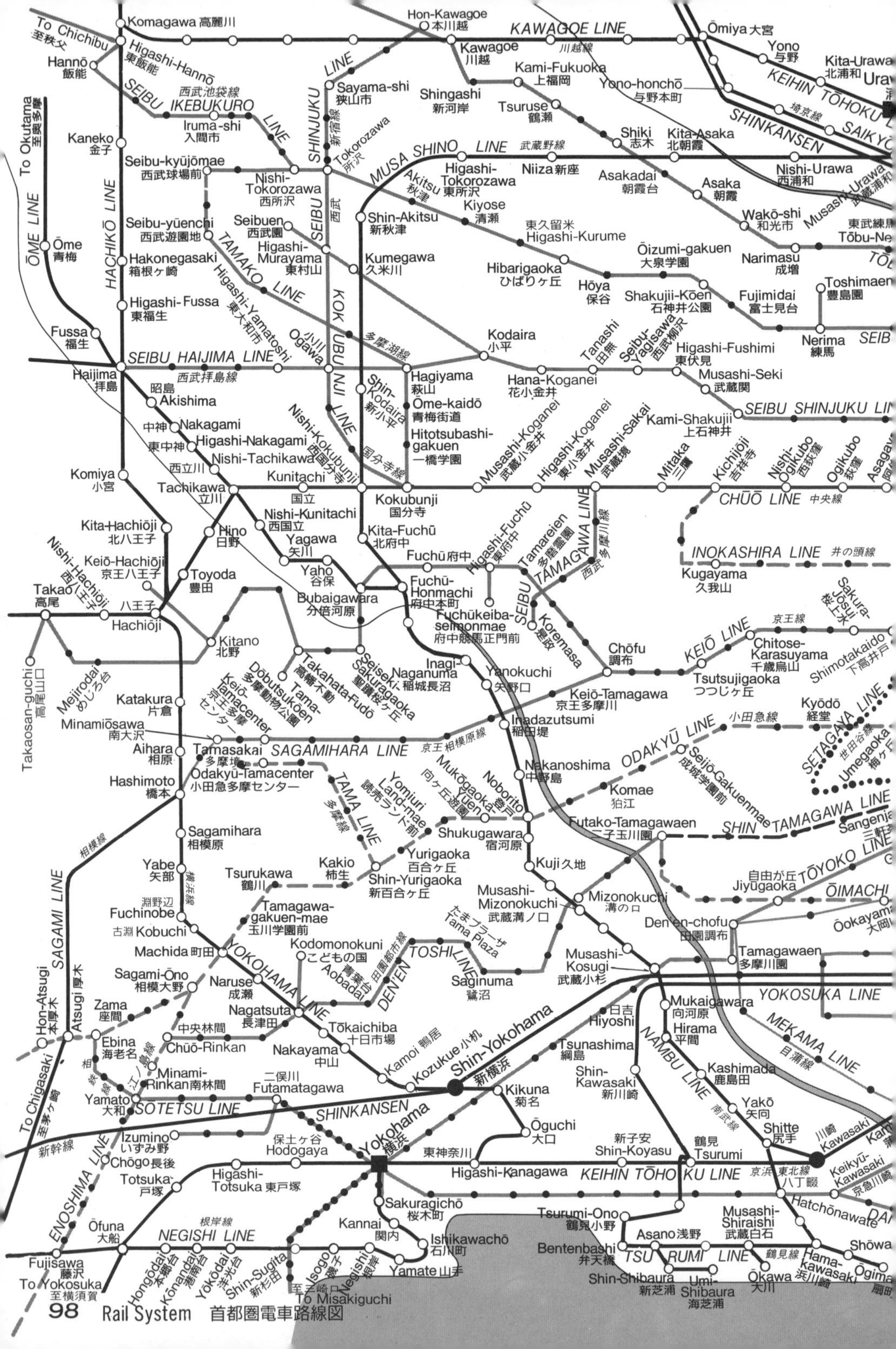

To Chichibu 至秩父
Komagawa 高麗川
Hon-Kawagoe 本川越
KAWAGOE LINE 川越線
Ōmiya 大宮
Yono 与野
Kita-Urawa 北浦和
Hannō 飯能
Higashi-Hannō 東飯能
Kawagoe 川越
KEIHIN TŌHOKU
Kami-Fukuoka 上福岡
Yono-honchō 与野本町
SHINKANSEN
SAIKYŌ
埼京線
Sayama-shi 狭山市
Shingashi 新河岸
SEIBU IKEBUKURO LINE 西武池袋線
Tsuruse 鶴瀬
Iruma-shi 入間市
To Okutama 至奥多摩
Kaneko 金子
SHINJUKU LINE 新宿線
Tokorozawa 所沢
Shiki 志木
Kita-Asaka 北朝霞
MUSA SHINO LINE 武蔵野線
Seibu-kyūjōmae 西武球場前
Nishi-Tokorozawa 西所沢
Higashi-Tokorozawa 東所沢
Niiza 新座
Asakadai 朝霞台
Nishi-Urawa 西浦和
Akitsu 秋津
Asaka 朝霞
Musashi-Urawa 武蔵浦和
HACHIKŌ LINE
Seibu-yūenchi 西武遊園地
Seibuen 西武園
Kiyose 清瀬
Wakō-shi 和光市
ŌME LINE
Ōme 青梅
Hakonegasaki 箱根ヶ崎
TAMAKO LINE
Higashi-Murayama 東村山
SEIBU 西武
Shin-Akitsu 新秋津
Kumegawa 久米川
東久留米 Higashi-Kurume
Ōizumi-gakuen 大泉学園
Narimasu 成増
東武練馬 Tōbu-Nerima
Hibarigaoka ひばりヶ丘
Hōya 保谷
Higashi-Fussa 東福生
Higashi-Yamatoshi 東大和市
KOKUBUNJI LINE
Shakujii-Kōen 石神井公園
Fujimidai 富士見台
Toshimaen 豊島園
Nerima 練馬
Fussa 福生
小川 Ogawa
多摩湖線
Kodaira 小平
Tanashi 田無
Seibu-Yagisawa 西武柳沢
Higashi-Fushimi 東伏見
SEIBU HAIJIMA LINE 西武拝島線
Haijima 拝島
Hagiyama 萩山
Hana-Koganei 花小金井
Musashi-Seki 武蔵関
昭島 Akishima
Shin-Kodaira 新小平
Ōme-kaidō 青梅街道
SEIBU SHINJUKU LINE
中神 Nakagami
Nishi-Kokubunji 西国分寺
Hitotsubashi-gakuen 一橋学園
Musashi-Koganei 武蔵小金井
Higashi-Koganei 東小金井
Musashi-Sakai 武蔵境
Kami-Shakujii 上石神井
東中神 Higashi-Nakagami
Nishi-Tachikawa 西立川
国分寺線
Mitaka 三鷹
Kichijōji 吉祥寺
Nishi-Ogikubo 西荻窪
Ogikubo 荻窪
Asagaya
Komiya 小宮
Tachikawa 立川
Kunitachi 国立
Kokubunji 国分寺
CHŪŌ LINE 中央線
Kita-Hachiōji 北八王子
Nishi-Kunitachi 西国立
Kita-Fuchū 北府中
Nishi-Hachiōji 西八王子
Hino 日野
Yagawa 矢川
Higashi-Fuchū 東府中
Tamareien 多磨霊園
SEIBU TAMAGAWA LINE 西武多摩川線
INOKASHIRA LINE 井の頭線
Keiō-Hachiōji 京王八王子
Toyoda 豊田
Yaho 谷保
Fuchū 府中
Kugayama 久我山
Takao 高尾
八王子 Hachiōji
Bubaigawara 分倍河原
Fuchū-Honmachi 府中本町
Fuchūkeiba-seimonmae 府中競馬正門前
Koremasa 是政
Sakura-Jōsui 桜上水
京王線
Kitano 北野
KEIŌ LINE
Chitose-Karasuyama 千歳烏山
Chōfu 調布
Shimotakaido 下高井戸
Takaosan-guchi 高尾山口
Mejirodai めじろ台
Takahata-Fudō 高幡不動
Seiseki-Sakuragaoka 聖蹟桜ヶ丘
Naganuma 稲城長沼
Inagi
Yanokuchi 矢野口
Tsutsujigaoka つつじヶ丘
Dōbutsukōen 多摩動物公園
Tama-Keiō-Tamacenter 京王多摩センター
Katakura 片倉
Keiō-Tamagawa 京王多摩川
Kyōdō 経堂
Minamiōsawa 南大沢
Inadazutsumi 稲田堤
小田急線
SETAGAYA LINE 世田谷線
Aihara 相原
Tamasakai 多摩境
SAGAMIHARA LINE 京王相模原線
ODAKYŪ LINE
Seijō-Gakuenmae 成城学園前
Umegaoka 梅ヶ丘
Hashimoto 橋本
Odakyū-Tamacenter 小田急多摩センター
TAMA LINE 多摩線
Yomiuri Land-mae 読売ランド前
Mukōgaoka-Yūen 向ヶ丘遊園
Noborito 登戸
Nakanoshima 中野島
Komae 狛江
SHIN TAMAGAWA LINE
Sangenjaya 三軒茶屋
Sagamihara 相模原
Shukugawara 宿河原
Futako-Tamagawaen 二子玉川園
相模線
Yabe 矢部
Kakio 柿生
Yurigaoka 百合ヶ丘
Kuji 久地
TŌYOKO LINE
Tsurukawa 鶴川
Shin-Yurigaoka 新百合ヶ丘
自由が丘 Jiyūgaoka
ŌIMACHI
SAGAMI LINE
横浜線
淵野辺 Fuchinobe
Tamagawa-gakuen-mae 玉川学園前
Musashi-Mizonokuchi 武蔵溝ノ口
Mizonokuchi 溝の口
Den'en-chōfu 田園調布
Ōokayama 大岡山
古淵 Kobuchi
たまプラーザ Tama Plaza
Kodomonokuni こどもの国
Machida 町田
YOKOHAMA LINE
田園都市線
TOSHI LINE
Musashi-Kosugi 武蔵小杉
Tamagawaen 多摩川園
Sagami-Ōno 相模大野
Naruse 成瀬
Aobadai 青葉台
DEN'EN
Saginuma 鷺沼
Hon-Atsugi 本厚木
Atsugi 厚木
Zama 座間
Nagatsuta 長津田
日吉 Hiyoshi
Mukaigawara 向河原
YOKOSUKA LINE
中央林間
Chūō-Rinkan
Tōkaichiba 十日市場
Shin-Yokohama 新横浜
Hirama 平間
MEKAMA LINE 目蒲線
Ebina 海老名
相鉄線
江ノ島線
Nakayama 中山
Kamoi 鴨居
Kozukue 小机
Tsunashima 綱島
NAMBU LINE 南武線
Minami-Rinkan 南林間
Shin-Kawasaki 新川崎
Kashimada 鹿島田
二俣川 Futamatagawa
Kikuna 菊名
To Chigasaki 至茅ヶ崎
Yamato 大和
SOTETSU LINE
SHINKANSEN
Yakō 矢向
Ōguchi 大口
新子安 Shin-Koyasu
鶴見 Tsurumi
Shitte 尻手
川崎 Kawasaki
新幹線
Izumino いずみ野
保土ケ谷 Hodogaya
Yokohama 横浜
東神奈川 Higashi-Kanagawa
KEIHIN TŌHOKU LINE 京浜東北線
八丁畷
Keikyū-Kawasaki 京急川崎
ENOSHIMA LINE
Chōgo 長後
Totsuka 戸塚
Higashi-Totsuka 東戸塚
Sakuragichō 桜木町
Tsurumi-Ono 鶴見小野
Musashi-Shiraishi 武蔵白石
Hatchōnawate
Kannai 関内
Ishikawachō 石川町
Asano 浅野
Ōfuna 大船
根岸線 NEGISHI LINE
Bentenbashi 弁天橋
TSURUMI LINE 鶴見線
Shōwa
Hama-kawasaki 浜川崎
Ōgima 扇町
Fujisawa 藤沢
To Yokosuka 至横須賀
Hongōdai 本郷台
Kōnandai 港南台
Yōkōdai 洋光台
Shin-Sugita 新杉田
Isogo 磯子
Negishi 根岸
Yamate 山手
Shin-Shibaura 新芝浦
Umi-Shibaura 海芝浦
Ōkawa 大川
至三崎口 To Misakiguchi

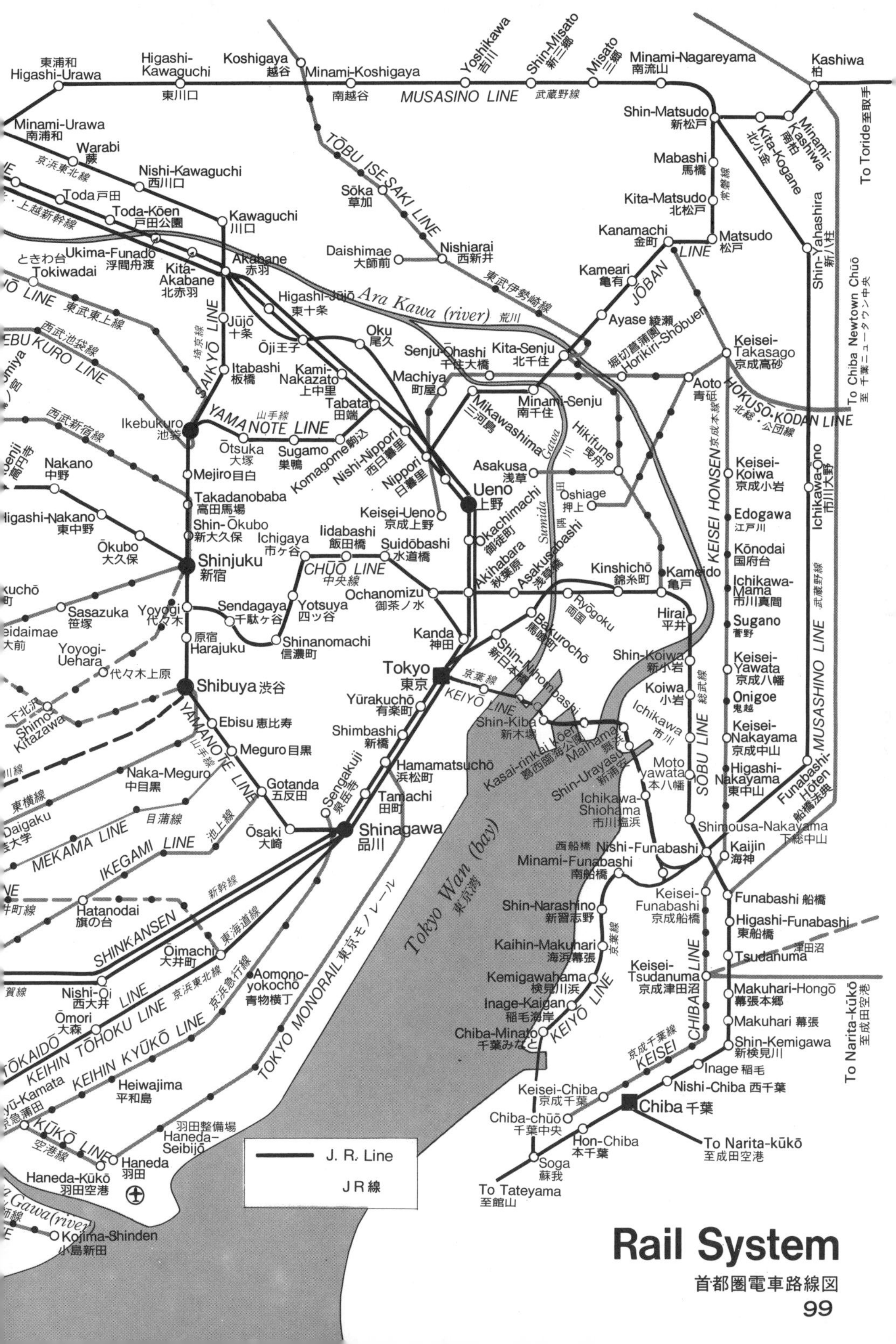
東浦和
Higashi-Urawa
Higashi-Kawaguchi
東川口
Koshigaya
越谷
Minami-Koshigaya
南越谷
Yoshikawa
吉川
Shin-Misato
新三郷
Misato
三郷
Minami-Nagareyama
南流山
Kashiwa
柏
MUSASINO LINE
武蔵野線
Minami-Urawa
南浦和
Warabi
蕨
京浜東北線
Nishi-Kawaguchi
西川口
Toda 戸田
Toda-Kōen
戸田公園
上越新幹線
Kawaguchi
川口
Ukima-Funado
浮間舟渡
ときわ台
Tokiwadai
Kita-Akabane
北赤羽
Akabane
赤羽
TŌBU ISESAKI LINE
Sōka
草加
Daishimae
大師前
Nishiarai
西新井
東武伊勢崎線
Shin-Matsudo
新松戸
Mabashi
馬橋
常磐線
Kita-Matsudo
北松戸
Kanamachi
金町
Matsudo
松戸
Kita-Kogane
北小金
Minami-Kashiwa
南柏
To Toride 至取手
Shin-Yahashira
新八柱
JŌBAN LINE
Kameari
亀有
Ayase 綾瀬
Horikiri-Shōbuen
堀切菖蒲園
Keisei-Takasago
京成高砂
To Chiba Newtown Chūō
至 千葉ニュータウン中央
HOKUSŌ·KŌDAN LINE
北総・公団線
Higashi-Jūjō
東十条
Ara Kawa (river)
荒川
東武東上線
西武池袋線
Jūjō
十条
Ōji 王子
Oku
尾久
Senju-Ōhashi
千住大橋
Kita-Senju
北千住
埼京線
SAIKYŌ LINE
Itabashi
板橋
Kami-Nakazato
上中里
Machiya
町屋
Minami-Senju
南千住
Aoto
青砥
京成本線
Tabata
田端
Mikawashima
三河島
Hikifune
曳舟
西武新宿線
Ikebukuro
池袋
山手線
YAMANOTE LINE
Ōtsuka
大塚
Sugamo
巣鴨
Komagome 駒込
Nishi-Nippori
西日暮里
Nippori
日暮里
Asakusa
浅草
Sumida Gawa
隅田川
Keisei-Koiwa
京成小岩
Ichikawa-Ōno
市川大野
Nakano
中野
Mejiro 目白
Takadanobaba
高田馬場
Ueno
上野
Oshiage
押上
KEISEI HONSEN
Edogawa
江戸川
Higashi-Nakano
東中野
Shin-Ōkubo
新大久保
Keisei-Ueno
京成上野
Okachimachi
御徒町
Kōnodai
国府台
Ōkubo
大久保
Ichigaya
市ヶ谷
Iidabashi
飯田橋
Suidōbashi
水道橋
Shinjuku
新宿
CHŪŌ LINE
中央線
Akihabara
秋葉原
Asakusabashi
浅草橋
Kinshichō
錦糸町
Kameido
亀戸
Ichikawa-Mama
市川真間
武蔵野線
Sasazuka
笹塚
Yoyogi
代々木
Sendagaya
千駄ヶ谷
Yotsuya
四ツ谷
Ochanomizu
御茶ノ水
Ryōgoku
両国
Hirai
平井
Sugano
菅野
Yoyogi-Uehara
代々木上原
原宿
Harajuku
Shinanomachi
信濃町
Kanda
神田
Bakurochō
馬喰町
Shin-Nihombashi
新日本橋
Shin-Koiwa
新小岩
Keisei-Yawata
京成八幡
MUSASHINO LINE
Tokyo
東京
京葉線
KEIYŌ LINE
Koiwa
小岩
Onigoe
鬼越
Shibuya 渋谷
下北沢
Shimo-Kitazawa
Yūrakuchō
有楽町
Shin-Kiba
新木場
総武線
Ichikawa
市川
Keisei-Nakayama
京成中山
Ebisu 恵比寿
Shimbashi
新橋
Kasai-rinkai Kōen
葛西臨海公園
Maihama
舞浜
Higashi-Nakayama
東中山
Meguro 目黒
Sengakuji
泉岳寺
Hamamatsuchō
浜松町
Shin-Urayasu
新浦安
Moto yawata
本八幡
SŌBU LINE
Funabashi-Hōten
船橋法典
Naka-Meguro
中目黒
Gotanda
五反田
Tamachi
田町
Ichikawa-Shiohama
市川塩浜
東横線
目蒲線
Daigaku
MEKAMA LINE
Ōsaki
大崎
Shinagawa
品川
Shimousa-Nakayama
下総中山
池上線
IKEGAMI LINE
西船橋 Nishi-Funabashi
Kaijin
海神
Minami-Funabashi
南船橋
Tokyo Wan (bay)
東京湾
新幹線
Hatanodai
旗の台
Keisei-Funabashi
京成船橋
Funabashi 船橋
Shin-Narashino
新習志野
Higashi-Funabashi
東船橋
SHINKANSEN
東海道線
Ōimachi
大井町
東京モノレール
Kaihin-Makuhari
海浜幕張
京葉線
津田沼
Tsudanuma
Keisei-Tsudanuma
京成津田沼
Nishi-Ōi
西大井
京浜東北線
京浜急行線
Aomono-yokochō
青物横丁
Kemigawahama
検見川浜
Makuhari-Hongō
幕張本郷
To Narita-kūkō
至成田空港
Ōmori
大森
Inage-Kaigan
稲毛海岸
Makuhari 幕張
TŌKAIDŌ LINE
KEIHIN TŌHOKU LINE
KEIHIN KYŪKŌ LINE
TOKYO MONORAIL
Chiba-Minato
千葉みなと
KEIYŌ LINE
京成千葉線
KEISEI CHIBA LINE
Shin-Kemigawa
新検見川
Inage 稲毛
Heiwajima
平和島
Nishi-Chiba 西千葉
Keisei-Chiba
京成千葉
Chiba 千葉
Chiba-chūō
千葉中央
羽田整備場
Haneda-Seibijō
KŪKŌ LINE
空港線
Hon-Chiba
本千葉
To Narita-kūkō
至成田空港
Haneda
羽田
Haneda-Kūkō
羽田空港
Soga
蘇我
J. R. Line
JR線
To Tateyama
至館山
Kojima-Shinden
小島新田
Rail System
首都圏電車路線図

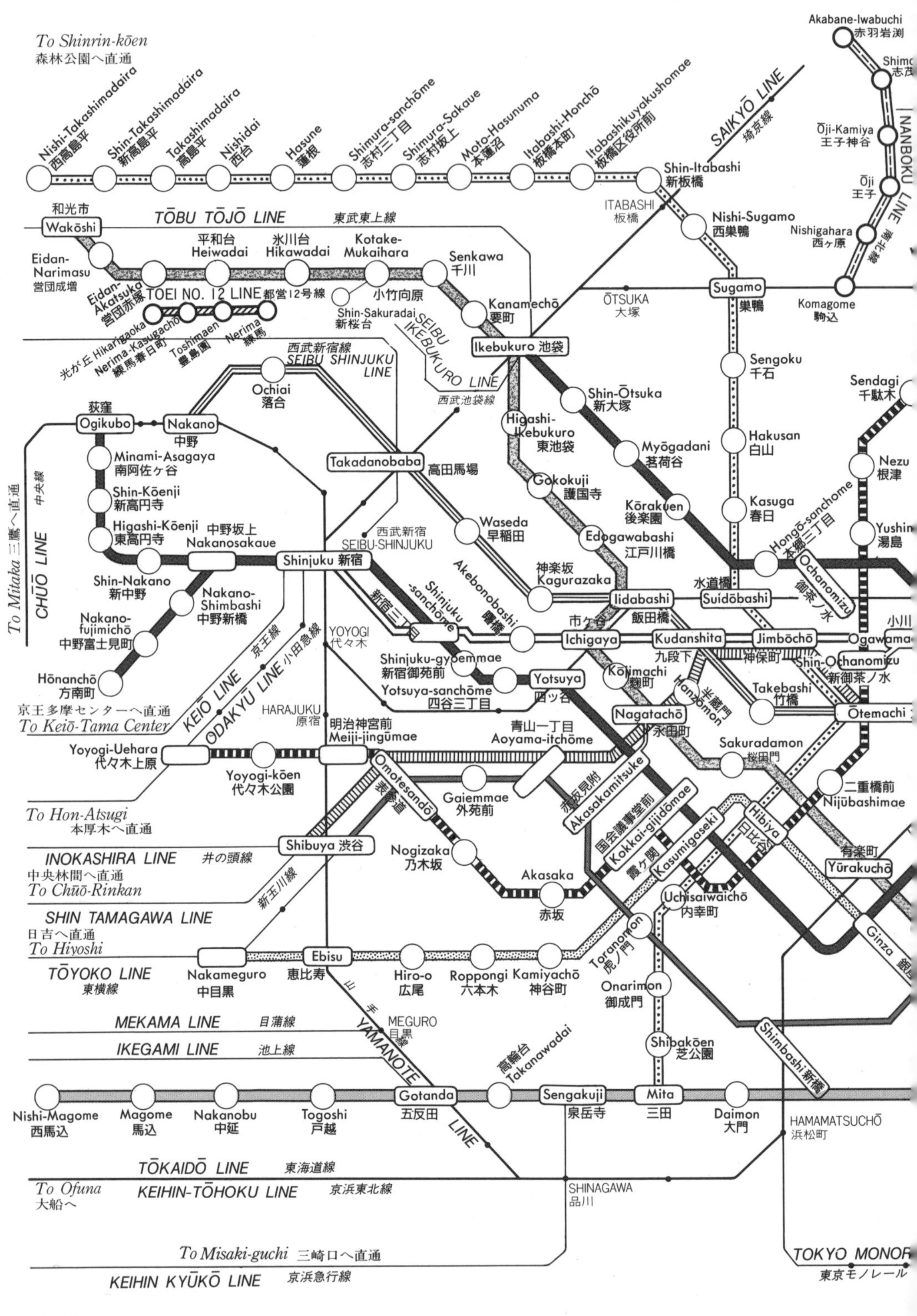

To Shinrin-kōen
森林公園へ直通
Nishi-Takashimadaira
西高島平
Shin-Takashimadaira
新高島平
Takashimadaira
高島平
Nishidai
西台
Hasune
蓮根
Shimura-sanchōme
志村三丁目
Shimura-Sakaue
志村坂上
Moto-Hasunuma
本蓮沼
Itabashi-Honchō
板橋本町
Itabashikuyakushomae
板橋区役所前
Shin-Itabashi
新板橋
SAIKYŌ LINE
埼京線
Akabane-Iwabuchi
赤羽岩渕
Ōji-Kamiya
王子神谷
Ōji
王子
Nishigahara
西ヶ原
Komagome
駒込
NANBOKU LINE
ITABASHI
板橋
Nishi-Sugamo
西巣鴨
和光市
Wakōshi
TŌBU TŌJŌ LINE
東武東上線
Eidan-Narimasu
営団成増
Eidan-Akatsuka
営団赤塚
平和台
Heiwadai
氷川台
Hikawadai
Kotake-Mukaihara
小竹向原
Senkawa
千川
TOEI NO. 12 LINE
都営12号線
Shin-Sakuradai
新桜台
光が丘 Hikarigaoka
Nerima-Kasugachō
練馬春日町
Toshimaen
豊島園
Nerima
練馬
Kanamechō
要町
SEIBU IKEBUKURO LINE
西武池袋線
ŌTSUKA
大塚
Sugamo
巣鴨
Ikebukuro 池袋
西武新宿線
SEIBU SHINJUKU LINE
Ochiai
落合
Sengoku
千石
Sendagi
千駄木
Shin-Ōtsuka
新大塚
Higashi-Ikebukuro
東池袋
荻窪
Ogikubo
Nakano
中野
Minami-Asagaya
南阿佐ヶ谷
Shin-Kōenji
新高円寺
Higashi-Kōenji
東高円寺
Myōgadani
茗荷谷
Hakusan
白山
Nezu
根津
Takadanobaba
高田馬場
Gokokuji
護国寺
Kōrakuen
後楽園
Kasuga
春日
Hongō-sanchome
本郷三丁目
Yushima
湯島
中央線
To Mitaka 三鷹へ直通
CHŪŌ LINE
中野坂上
Nakanosakaue
西武新宿
SEIBU-SHINJUKU
Shinjuku 新宿
Waseda
早稲田
Edogawabashi
江戸川橋
Shin-Nakano
新中野
Nakano-Shimbashi
中野新橋
Akebonobashi
曙橋
神楽坂
Kagurazaka
水道橋
Suidōbashi
Ochanomizu
御茶ノ水
Iidabashi
飯田橋
Nakano-fujimichō
中野富士見町
Shinjuku-sanchōme
新宿三丁目
YOYOGI
代々木
市ヶ谷
Ichigaya
Kudanshita
九段下
Jimbōchō
神保町
小川町
Ogawamachi
Shin-Ochanomizu
新御茶ノ水
Hōnanchō
方南町
京王線
KEIŌ LINE
小田急線
ODAKYŪ LINE
Shinjuku-gyoemmae
新宿御苑前
Yotsuya
四ツ谷
Kōjimachi
麹町
Hanzōmon
半蔵門
Takebashi
竹橋
Ōtemachi
Yotsuya-sanchōme
四谷三丁目
京王多摩センターへ直通
To Keiō-Tama Center
HARAJUKU
原宿
明治神宮前
Meiji-jingūmae
青山一丁目
Aoyama-itchōme
Nagatachō
永田町
Sakuradamon
桜田門
Yoyogi-Uehara
代々木上原
Yoyogi-kōen
代々木公園
Omotesandō
表参道
Gaiemmae
外苑前
赤坂見附
Akasakamitsuke
国会議事堂前
Kokkai-gijidōmae
霞ケ関
Kasumigaseki
Hibiya
日比谷
二重橋前
Nijūbashimae
To Hon-Atsugi
本厚木へ直通
Shibuya 渋谷
INOKASHIRA LINE
井の頭線
中央林間へ直通
To Chūō-Rinkan
Nogizaka
乃木坂
Akasaka
赤坂
有楽町
Yūrakuchō
SHIN TAMAGAWA LINE
新玉川線
日吉へ直通
To Hiyoshi
Uchisaiwaichō
内幸町
Toranomon
虎ノ門
Ginza
TŌYOKO LINE
東横線
Nakameguro
中目黒
Ebisu
恵比寿
Hiro-o
広尾
Roppongi
六本木
Kamiyachō
神谷町
Onarimon
御成門
山手
YAMANOTE LINE
MEGURO
目黒
MEKAMA LINE
目蒲線
IKEGAMI LINE
池上線
高輪台
Takanawadai
Shibakōen
芝公園
Shimbashi 新橋
Nishi-Magome
西馬込
Magome
馬込
Nakanobu
中延
Togoshi
戸越
Gotanda
五反田
Sengakuji
泉岳寺
Mita
三田
Daimon
大門
HAMAMATSUCHŌ
浜松町
TŌKAIDŌ LINE
東海道線
To Ofuna
大船へ
KEIHIN-TŌHOKU LINE
京浜東北線
SHINAGAWA
品川
To Misaki-guchi 三崎口へ直通
KEIHIN KYŪKŌ LINE
京浜急行線
TOKYO MONOR
東京モノレール

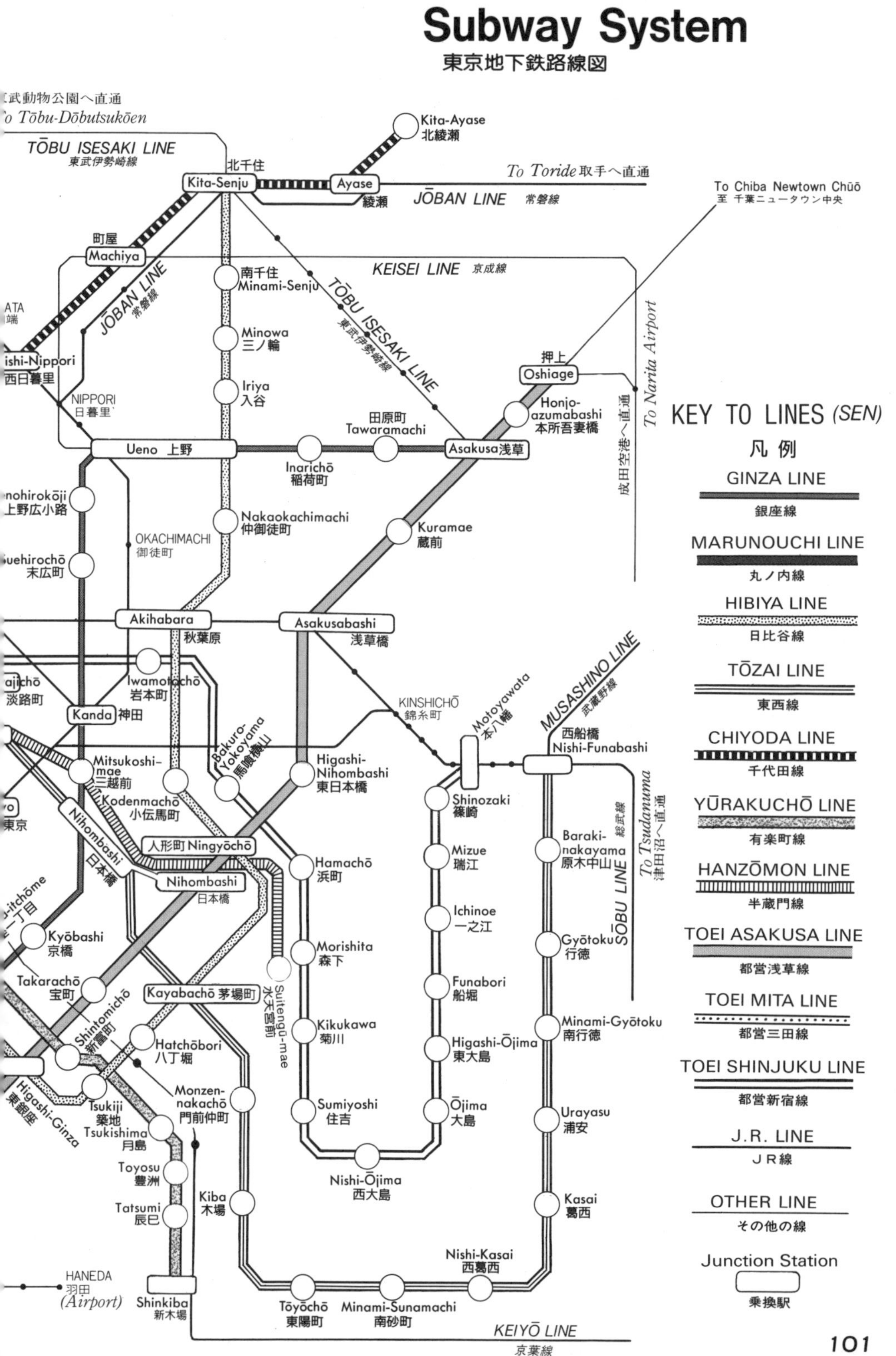
Subway System
東京地下鉄路線図
To Tōbu-Dōbutsukōen
TŌBU ISESAKI LINE
東武伊勢崎線
北千住
Kita-Senju
Ayase
綾瀬
Kita-Ayase
北綾瀬
To Toride 取手へ直通
JŌBAN LINE
常磐線
To Chiba Newtown Chūō
至 千葉ニュータウン中央
町屋
Machiya
JŌBAN LINE
常磐線
南千住
Minami-Senju
KEISEI LINE
京成線
TŌBU ISESAKI LINE
東武伊勢崎線
Minowa
三ノ輪
Iriya
入谷
Nishi-Nippori
西日暮里
NIPPORI
日暮里
押上
Oshiage
Honjo-azumabashi
本所吾妻橋
To Narita Airport
成田空港へ直通
田原町
Tawaramachi
Ueno 上野
Inarichō
稲荷町
Asakusa浅草
KEY TO LINES (SEN)
凡例
GINZA LINE
銀座線
MARUNOUCHI LINE
丸ノ内線
HIBIYA LINE
日比谷線
TŌZAI LINE
東西線
CHIYODA LINE
千代田線
YŪRAKUCHŌ LINE
有楽町線
HANZŌMON LINE
半蔵門線
TOEI ASAKUSA LINE
都営浅草線
TOEI MITA LINE
都営三田線
TOEI SHINJUKU LINE
都営新宿線
J.R. LINE
JR線
OTHER LINE
その他の線
Junction Station
乗換駅
上野広小路
末広町
OKACHIMACHI
御徒町
Nakaokachimachi
仲御徒町
Kuramae
蔵前
Akihabara
秋葉原
Asakusabashi
浅草橋
Iwamotochō
岩本町
淡路町
Kanda
神田
KINSHICHŌ
錦糸町
Motoyawata
本八幡
MUSASHINO LINE
武蔵野線
西船橋
Nishi-Funabashi
Bakuro-Yokoyama
馬喰横山
Mitsukoshi-mae
三越前
Kodenmachō
小伝馬町
Higashi-Nihombashi
東日本橋
Shinozaki
篠崎
Baraki-nakayama
原木中山
To Tsudanuma
津田沼へ直通
SŌBU LINE
総武線
東京
Nihombashi
日本橋
人形町 Ningyōchō
Nihombashi
日本橋
Hamachō
浜町
Mizue
瑞江
Ichinoe
一之江
Kyōbashi
京橋
Morishita
森下
Gyōtoku
行徳
Takarachō
宝町
Kayabachō 茅場町
Suitengū-mae
水天宮前
Funabori
船堀
Shintomichō
新富町
Hatchōbori
八丁堀
Kikukawa
菊川
Minami-Gyōtoku
南行徳
Higashi-Ōjima
東大島
Higashi-Ginza
東銀座
Tsukiji
築地
Monzen-nakachō
門前仲町
Tsukishima
月島
Sumiyoshi
住吉
Ōjima
大島
Urayasu
浦安
Toyosu
豊洲
Nishi-Ōjima
西大島
Tatsumi
辰巳
Kiba
木場
Kasai
葛西
HANEDA
羽田
(Airport)
Shinkiba
新木場
Nishi-Kasai
西葛西
Tōyōchō
東陽町
Minami-Sunamachi
南砂町
KEIYŌ LINE
京葉線

Map of Japan 日本全図

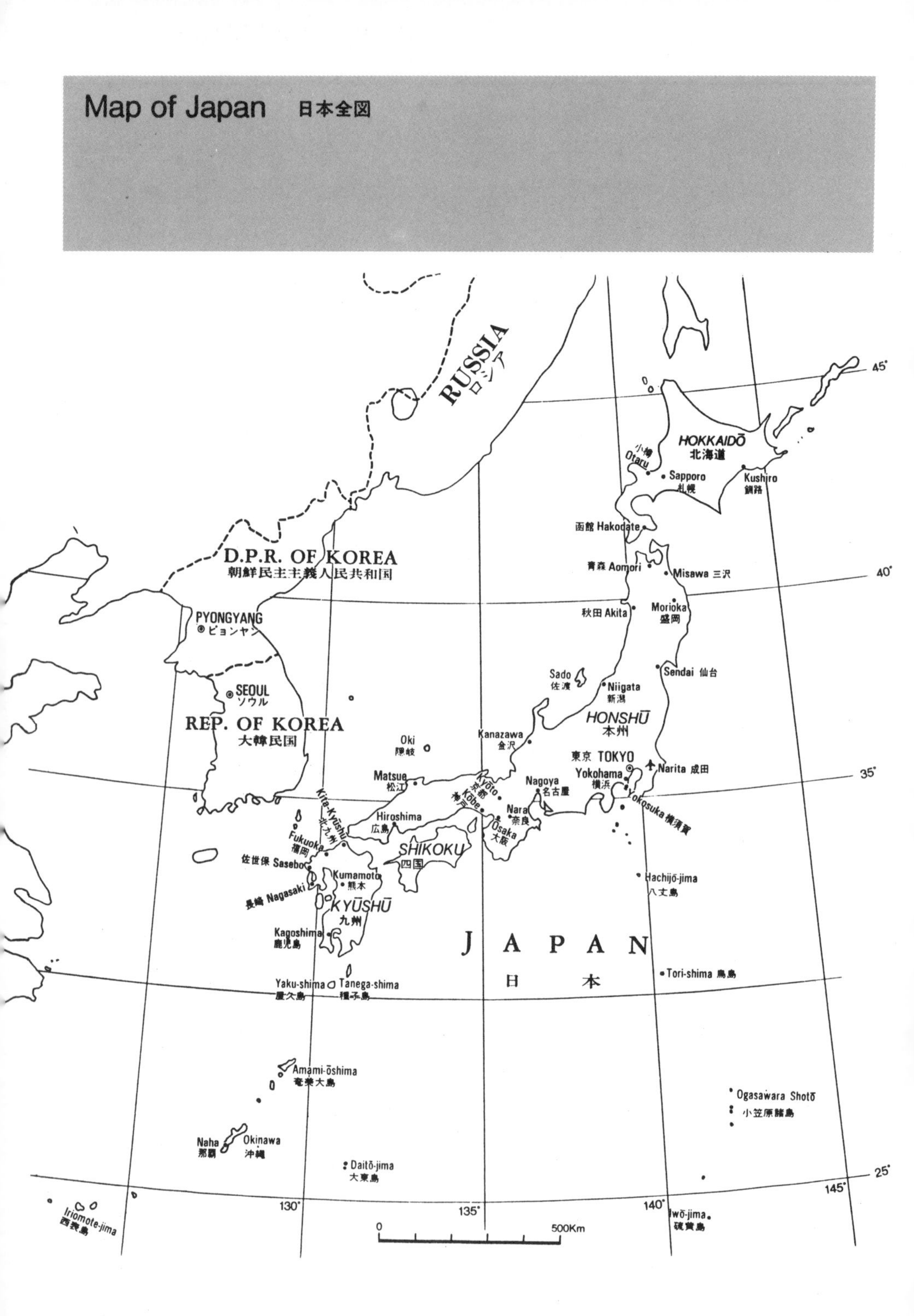

INDEX
索　引（ABC順）

Please refer to the Useful Telephone Numbers section for government offices, embassies, airlines, hotels and inns.
官公庁、外国公館、航空会社、ホテル／旅館は、各種電話番号のページをご参照下さい。

Japanese Index
各種機関、著名企業、博物館などの五十音順索引

この索引は、英語からでは検索しにくいと思われる各種機関、著名企業、博物館などを、五十音順で収載したものです。地名、駅名等は、ABC 順の索引をご参照下さい。また、官公庁、外国公館、航空会社、ホテル／旅館は、各種電話番号のページをご参照下さい。

さ

し

は

ひ

ふ

へ

ほ

Government Offices
官公庁

Agency for Cultural Affairs 文化庁	3581-4211		
Agency of Natural Resources & Energy 資源エネルギー庁	3501-1511		
Board of Audit 会計検査院	3581-3251	47	G6
Defense Agency 防衛庁	3408-5211	48	E6
Defense Facilities Administration Agency 防衛施設庁	3408-5211	49	E6
Economic Planning Agency 経済企画庁	3581-0261		
Environment Agency 環境庁	3581-3351	47	I 6
Fair Trade Commission 公正取引委員会	3581-5471		
Fire Defense Agency 消防庁	3581-5311	47	H5
Fisheries Agency 水産庁	3502-8111		
Food Agency 食糧庁	3502-8111		
Foreign Service Training Institute 外務省研修所	3943-5481	25	H7
Forestry Agency 林野庁	3502-8111		
Hokkaido Development Agency 北海道開発庁	3581-9111	47	G6
House of Councillors 参議院	3581-3111	47	F4
House of Represetatives 衆議院	3581-5111	47	F5
Imperial Household Agency 宮内庁	3213-1111	47	I 1
Institute of Public Health 国立公衆衛生院	3441-7111	28	E1
Japan Academy 日本学士院	3822-2101	67	I 5
Japan Art Academy 日本芸術院	3821-7191	16	E1
Management & Coordination Agency 総務庁	3581-6361		
Maritime Safety Agency 海上保安庁	3591-6361	47	H4
Meteorological Agency 気象庁	3212-8341	36	A6
Metropolitan Police Dept. 警視庁	3581-4321	47	H4
Ministry of Agriculture Forestry & Fisheries 農林水産省	3502-8111	47	H5
Ministry of Construction 建設省	3580-4311	47	H4
Ministry of Education 文部省	3581-4211	47	G6
Ministry of Finance 大蔵省	3581-4111	47	G6
Ministry of Foreign Affairs 外務省	3580-3311	47	G5
Ministry of Health & Welfare 厚生省	3503-1711	47	I 5
Ministry of Home Affairs 自治省	3581-5311	47	H4
Ministry of Int'l Trade & Industry 通商産業省	3501-1511	47	H6
Ministry of Justice 法務省	3580-4111	47	I 4
Ministry of Labor 労働省	3593-1211	47	I 6
Minisury of Posts & Telecommunications 郵政省	3504-4411	47	H6
Ministry of Transport 運輸省	3580-3111	47	H4
National Diet 国会議事堂		47	F4
National Diet Library 国立国会図書館	3581-2331	47	F3
National Institute of Health 国立予防衛生研究所	3444-2181	28	C2
National Land Agency 国土庁	3593-3311	47	I 6
National Personnel Authority 人事院	3581-5311	47	H5
National Police Agency 警察庁	3581-0141	47	H4
National Public Safety Commission 国家公安委員会	3581-0141		
National Tax Administration Agency 国税庁	3581-4161		
Okinawa Development Agency 沖縄開発庁	3581-2361	47	F6
Patent Office 特許庁	3581-1101	47	F7
Prime Minister's Office 総理府	3581-2361	47	F6
Prime Minister's Official Residence 内閣総理大臣官邸	3581-0101	46	E6
Printing Bureau 大蔵省印刷局	3582-4411	21	J3
Public Prosecutor's Office 検察庁	3592-5611	47	I 5
Science & Technology Agency 科学技術庁	3581-5271	47	G5
Science Council of Japan 日本学術会議	3403-6291	21	G3
Small & Medium Enterprise Agency 中小企業庁	3501-1511		
Social Insurance Agency 社会保険庁	3503-1711		
Supreme Court 最高裁判所	3264-8111	46	E2
Tokyo Customshouse 東京税関	3472-7000	29	I 3
Tokyo District Court 東京地方裁判所	3581-5411	47	I 5
Tokyo High Court 東京高等裁判所	3581-5411	47	I 5
Tokyo Regional Immigration Bureau 東京入国管理局	3213-8111	36	B5
Tokyo Metropolitan Government 東京都庁	5321-1111	56	A5
Yokohama Customshouse 横浜税関	(045) 201-4981	63	G4

Embassies
外国公館

Afghanistan アフガニスタン 3407-7900
Algeria アルジェリア 3711-2661 *66* A4
Argentina アルゼンチン 5420-7101 *46* D4
Australia オーストラリア 5232-4111 *66* D6
Austria オーストリア 3451-8281 *21* H5
Bangladesh バングラデシュ 3442-1501 *29* E1
Belgium ベルギー 3262-0191 *23* H6
Bolivia ボリビア 3499-5441 *66* C4
Brazil ブラジル 3404-5211 *55* F1
Britain (see United Kingdom) 3265-5511 *23* J6
Brunei ブルネイ 3447-7997 *66* A6
Bulgaria ブルガリア 3465-1021 *20* A2
Burundi ブルンジ 3443-7321
Cameroon カメルーン 3496-1125 *66* B2
Canada カナダ 3408-2101 *48* B6
Central African Rep. 中央アフリカ 3485-7591 *66* C1
Chile チリ 3452-7561 *21* J5
China 中華人民共和国 3403-3380 *49* J7
Colombia コロンビア 3440-6451 *66* A5
Costa Rica コスタリカ 3486-1812 *66* C4
Côte d'Ivoire コートジボアール 3499-7021 *66* C4
Cuba キューバ 3716-3112 *29* F4
Czechoslovakia チェコスロバキア 3400-8122 *21* E6
Denmark デンマーク 3496-3001 *20* C6
Djibouti ジブティ 3496-6135
Dominican Rep. ドミニカ 3499-6020 *66* C4
EC-Delegation 駐日EC委員会 3239-0441 *67* F4
Ecuador エクアドル 3499-2800 *66* C4
Egypt エジプト 3770-8022 *20* C6
El Salvador エルサルバドル 3499-4461 *66* C4
Ethiopia エチオピア 3718-1003 *49* F3
Fiji フィジー 3587-2038 *49* I1
Finland フィンランド 3442-2231 *21* G6
France フランス 3473-0171 *21* G6
Gabon ガボン 3448-9540 *29* F4
Germany ドイツ連邦共和国 3473-0151 *21* G6
Ghana ガーナ 3710-8831 *21* F4
Greece ギリシア 3403-0871 *49* I7
Guatemala グアテマラ 3400-1830 *66* C4
Guinea ギニア 3769-0451 *21* H6
Haiti ハイチ 3486-7070 *66* C4
Honduras ホンジュラス 3409-1150 *66* C4
Hungary ハンガリー 3798-8801 *20* B6
Iceland アイスランド 3531-8776
India インド 3262-2391 *23* J4
Indonesia インドネシア 3441-4201 *28* D3
Iran イラン 3446-8011 *21* H6
Iraq イラク 3423-1727 *66* D4
Ireland アイルランド 3263-0695 *67* F4
Israel イスラエル 3264-0911 *23* I6
Italy イタリア 3453-5291 *21* I6
Jordan ヨルダン 3580-5856 *46* D4
Kenya ケニア 3723-4006
Korea (South) 大韓民国 3452-7611 *21* H6
Kuwait クウェート 3455-0361 *21* I7
Laos ラオス 5411-2291 *49* I7
Lebanon レバノン 3580-1227 *46* D4
Liberia リベリア 3441-7138 *66* C4
Libya リビア 3477-0701 *66* B3
Luxembourg ルクセンブルク 3265-9621 *67* F4
Madagascar マダガスカル 3446-7252 *66* C4
Malaysia マレーシア 3476-3840 *20* B6
Mauritania モーリタニア 3449-3822
Mexico メキシコ 3581-1131 *46* D7
Micronesia ミクロネシア 3585-5456
Monaco モナコ 3211-4994
Mongolia モンゴル 3469-2088 *20* A4
Morocco モロッコ 3478-3271 *21* D1
Myanmar ミャンマー 3441-9291 *29* F5
Nepal ネパール 3705-5558 *66* A7
Netherlands オランダ 5401-0411 *21* J4
New Zealand ニュージーランド 3467-2271 *20* A4
Nicaragua ニカラグア 3499-0400 *66* C4
Niger ニジェール 3505-6371
Nigeria ナイジェリア 3468-5531 *66* B1
Norway ノルウェー 3440-2611 *21* F5
Oman オマーン 3402-0877 *20* D1
Pakistan パキスタン 3454-4861 *21* G5
Panama パナマ 3499-3741 *66* C4
Papua New Guinea パプア・ニューギニア 3454-7801 *66* C5
Paraguay パラグアイ 5570-4307 *66* A5
Peru ペルー 3406-4240 *20* E5
Philippines フィリピン 3496-2731 *20* B5
Poland ポーランド 3711-5224 *66* A4
Portugal ポルトガル 3400-7907 *66* C2
Qatar カタール 3446-7561 *66* B4
Romania ルーマニア 3479-0311 *66* C4
Russia ロシア 3583-4224 *49* I1
Rwanda ルワンダ 3486-7800 *66* C4
Saudi Arabia サウジアラビア 3589-5241 *49* I3

Senegal	セネガル	3464-8451	*20* B6
Seychelles	セイシェル	3561-8002	
Singapore	シンガポール	3586-9111	*49* I4
South Africa	南アフリカ	3265-3366	*67* E4
Spain	スペイン	3583-8531	*49* E1
Sri Lanka	スリランカ	3585-7431	*48* E1
Sudan	スーダン	3406-0811	*21* E4
Swaziland	スワジランド	3864-2075	
Sweden	スウェーデン	5562-5050	*49* F1
Switzerland	スイス	3473-0121	*21* F5
Syria	シリア	3586-8977	*48* E4
Tanzania	タンザニア	3425-4531	*66* A6
Thailand	タイ	3441-7352	*28* D3
Tonga	トンガ	3502-2371	
Tunisia	チュニジア	3353-4111	*66* E5
Turkey	トルコ	3470-5131	*20* D2
U.A.E.	アラブ首長国連邦	5489-0804	*66* C4
United Kingdom	イギリス	3265-5511	*23* J6
Uruguay	ウルグアイ	3486-1888	*66* C4
U.S.A.	アメリカ合衆国	3224-5000	*48* D1
Vatican City	ローマ法王庁	3263-6851	*23* I5
Venezuela	ベネズエラ	3409-1501	*66* C4
Viet Nam	ベトナム	3466-3311	*20* A2
Western Samoa	西サモア	3211-7604	
Yemen	イエメン	3499-7151	*66* C4
Yugoslavia	ユーゴスラビア	3447-3571	*29* F5
Zaire	ザイール	3423-3981	*20* D1
Zambia	ザンビア	3445-1041	*66* B4
Zimbabwe	ジンバブエ	3280-0331	*21* G6

Airlines
航空会社

Aeroflot Russia Airlines (SU) アエロフロート・ロシア航空		3434-9671	
Air CHINA (CA) 中国国際航空		3505-2021	
Air France (AF) エールフランス		3475-2211	
Air India (AI) エア・インディア		3214-1981	
Airlanka (UL) エアランカ		3573-4261	
Air New Zealand (TE) ニュージーランド航空		3284-1291	
Air Pacific (FJ) エア・パシフィック航空		3582-1461	
Alitalia Airlines (AZ) アリタリア航空		3580-2181	*47* F7
All Nippon Airways (NH)	Int'l 国際	3272-1212	
全日空	Domestic 国内	5489-8800	
American Airlines (AA) アメリカン航空		3214-2111	
Asiana Airlines (OZ) アシアナ航空		5472-8400	
Biman Bangladesh Airlines (BG) バングラディシュ航空		3593-1252	*47* F6
British Airways (BA) 英国航空		3593-8811	*38* C1
Canadian Airlines Int'l (CP) カナディアン航空		3281-7426	
Cathay Pacific Airways (CX) キャセイ・パシフィック航空		3504-1531	
China Airlines (CI) 中華航空		3436-0841	
Continental Airlines Int'l コンチネンタル航空		3592-0646	
Delta Air Lines (DL) デルタ航空		5275-7000	
Egypt Air (MS) エジプト航空		3211-4521	*36* D6
Finnair (AY) フィンランド航空		3222-1691	
Garuda Indonesian Airways (GA) ガルーダ・インドネシア航空		3593-1181	*47* F6
Iberia Airlines (IB) イベリア航空		3582-3831	
Iran Air (IR) イラン航空		3586-2101	*47* E7
Iraqi Aiways (IA) イラク航空		3264-5503	*46* C5
Japan Airlines (JL)	Int'l 国際	3457-1181	
日本航空	Domestic 国内	3456-2111	
Japan Air System (JD) 日本エアシステム		3273-7773	
Japan Asia Aiways (EG) 日本アジア航空		3284-2674	
KLM Royal Dutch Airlines (KL) KLMオランダ航空		3211-5322	
Korean Air (KE) 大韓航空		3216-5168	*37* J5
Lufthansa German Airlines (LH) ルフトハンザ・ドイツ航空		3580-2111	*47* F7
Malaysian Airline (MH) マレーシア航空		3432-8501	*78* E7
Nothwest Airlines (NW) ノースウエスト・オリエント航空		3532-7100	
Pakistan Int'l Airlines (PK) パキスタン国際航空		3216-4641	
Philippine Airlines (PR) フィリピン航空		3593-2421	*46* C4
Qantas Airways (QF) カンタス・オーストラリア航空		3211-4482	
Sabena Belgian World Airlines (SN) サベナベルギー航空		3585-6552	*46* E6
Scandinavian Airlines (SK) スカンジナビア航空		3503-8101	
Singapore Airlines (SQ) シンガポール航空		3213-3431	
Swiss Air Transport (SR) スイス航空		3212-1016	
Thai Ariways Int'l (TG) タイ国際航空		3503-3311	
United Airlines (UA) ユナイテッド航空		3240-8800	
Varig Brazilian Airlines (RG) ヴァリグ・ブラジル航空		3212-1953	*36* D6
Virgin Atlantic Airlines (VS) ヴァージンアトランティック航空		5269-2865	

Hotel and Inns

ホテル，旅館

Name	Japanese	Phone	Map
Akasaka Prince Hotel	赤坂プリンスホテル	3234-1111	*46* C3
Akasaka Shanpia Hotel	赤坂シャンピアホテル	3586-0811	*48* C5
Akasaka Tōkyū Hotel	赤坂東急ホテル	3580-2311	*46* C4
Akihabara Washington Hotel	秋葉原ワシントンホテル	3255-3311	*33* I 4
ANA Hotel Tokyo	東京全日空ホテル	3505-1111	*20* E1
Aoi Grand Hotel	アオイグランドホテル	3946-2721	*89* I 2
Aoi Kaikan	葵会館	3582-9721	*88* E5
Aoyama Shanpia Hotel	青山シャンピアホテル	3407-2111	*53* H4
Asakusa Plaza Hotel	浅草プラザホテル	3845-2621	*89* I 7
Asakusa View Hotel	浅草ビューホテル	3847-1111	*31* F2
Asia Center of Japan (Hotel Asia Kaikan)	ホテルアジア会館	3402-6111	*48* C6
Aster Hotel	アスターホテル	(045) 651-0141	*63* G5
Atagoyama Tōkyū Inn	愛宕山東急イン	3431-0109	*88* E5
Azabu City Hotel	麻布シティーホテル	3453-4311	*88* C5
Azabu Green Kaikan	麻布グリーン会館	3583-6861	*49* G1
Banchō Green Palace	番町グリーンパレス	3265-9251	*89* F4
B & G Center	B&Gセンター	3630-2711	*91* G5
Bund Hotel	バンドホテル	(045) 621-1101	*63* H5
Business Hotel Mate	ビジネスホテルメイツ	3443-4161	*88* B5
Business Hotel Park Kawasaki	ビジネスホテルパーク川崎	(044) 211-5885	*91* I 4
Business Hotel Silver Inn	ビジネスホテルシルバーイン	3251-2791	*33* I 1
Business Hotel Suehiro	ビジネスホテル末広	3734-6561	*91* F5
Capitol Tōkyū Hotel	キャピトル東急ホテル	3581-4511	*46* D5
Center Hotel Tokyo	センターホテル東京	3667-2711	*89* F6
Central Hotel (Uchi-kanda)	セントラルホテル	3256-6251	*33* H6
Chisan Hotel Gotanda	チサンホテル五反田	3785-3211	
Co-op Inn Shibuya	コープ・イン・渋谷	3486-6600	*88* C2
Daiichi Hotel Tokyo	第一ホテル東京	3501-4411	*38* B5
Daiichi Hotel Tokyo Bay	第一ホテル東京ベイ	(0473) 55-3333	*91* H4
Diamond Hotel	ダイヤモンドホテル	3263-2211	*23* I 6
Escal Yokohama Int'l Seamen's Hall	(エスカル)横浜海員会館	(045) 681-2141	*63* G5
Fairmont Hotel	フェヤーモントホテル	3262-1151	*89* F4
Four Seasons Hotel Chinzansō	フォーシーズンズホテル椿山荘	3943-2222	*89* G2
Fuji View Hotel	フジビューホテル	(045) 473-0021	*90* E6
Fukuoka Kaikan	ふくおか会館	3265-3171	*89* F4
Gajōen Kankō Hotel	雅叙園観光ホテル	3491-0111	*28* C3
Ginza Capital Hotel	銀座キャピタルホテル	3543-8211	*39* J4
Ginza Dai-Ichi Hotel	銀座第一ホテル	3542-5311	*38* E6
Ginza International Hotel	銀座国際ホテル	3574-1121	*38* D5
Ginza Marunouchi Hotel	銀座丸ノ内ホテル	3543-5431	*39* G6
Ginza Nikkō Hotel	銀座日航ホテル	3571-4911	*38* C5
Ginza Tōbu Hotel	銀座東武ホテル	3546-0111	*39* F5
Ginza Tōkyū Hotel	銀座東急ホテル	3541-2411	*39* G5
Gotenyama Hills Hotel Laforet Tokyo	御殿山ヒルズホテルラフォーレ東京	5488-3911	
Grand Central Hotel	グランドセントラルホテル	3256-3211	*33* G6
Grand Hill Ichigaya	グランドヒル市ヶ谷	3268-0111	*89* F3
Haneda Tōkyū Hotel	羽田東急ホテル	3747-0311	*91* G5
Heiwa Plaza Hotel	平和プラザホテル	(044) 222-3131	*91* I 5
Hill Port Hotel	ヒルポートホテル	3462-5171	*52* E6
Hilltop (Yamanoue) Hotel	山の上ホテル	3293-2311	*32* D3
Holiday Inn Tokyo	ホリディ・イン東京	3553-6161	*89* F7
Holiday Inn Yokohama	ホリディ・イン横浜	(045) 681-3311	*63* G5
Hotel Asia Kaikan (*see* Asia Center of Japan)			
Hotel Century Hyatt	ホテルセンチュリーハイアット	3349-0111	*56* A4
Hotel Continental Yokohama	ホテルコンチネンタル横浜	(045) 681-4111	*91* I 6
Hotel East21 Tokyo	ホテルイースト21東京	5683-5683	
Hotel Edmont	ホテルエドモント	3237-1111	*89* G4
Hotel Friend	ホテルフレンド	3866-2244	*89* G6
Hotel Ginza Dai-ei	ホテル銀座ダイエー	3545-1111	*39* H4
Hotel Grand Business	ホテルグランドビジネス	3984-5121	*59* G3
Hotel Grand Palace	ホテルグランドパレス	3264-1111	*16* A4
Hotel Hitotsubashi	ホテルヒトツバシ	3261-9886	*32* C5
Hotel Ibis	ホテルアイビス	3403-4411	*49* G5
Hotel Kayū Kaikan	ホテル霞友会館	3230-1111	*89* F4
Hotel Kizankan	ホテル機山館	3812-1211	*89* H4
Hotel Daiei	ホテルダイエー	3813-6271	*89* H4
Hotel Kokusai Kankō	ホテル国際観光	3215-3281	*37* F2
Hotel Kōshin	ホテル香新	3876-2601	*89* J5
Hotel Lynx	ホテルリンクス	3630-4111	*91* G3
Hotel Metropolitan	ホテルメトロポリタン	3980-1111	*58* C5
Hotel Mita Kaikan	ホテル三田会館	3453-6601	*88* C6
Hotel New Grand	ホテルニューグランド	(045) 681-1841	*63* H5

Hotel New Meguro ホテルニューメグロ 3719-8121 *91* F 4
Hotel New Ōtani ホテルニューオータニ 3265-1111 *46* B 2
Hotel New Tokyo ホテルニュー東京 3469-5211
Hotel New Washington ホテルニューワシントン 3460-1701 *88* C 2
Hotel Ōkura ホテルオークラ 3582-0111 *21* J 3
Hotel OZ ホテルOZ 3463-0202 *52* B 7
Hotel Pacific Meridien Tokyo ホテルパシフィック東京 3445-6711 *29* F 3
Hotel Park Side ホテルパークサイド 3836-5711 *89* H5
Hotel President Aoyama ホテルプレシデント青山 3497-0111 *21* F 2
Hotel Rich Yokohama ホテルリッチ横浜 (045) 312-2111 *62* C1
Hotel Satoh ホテルサトー 3815-1133 *32* B1
Hotel Seaside Edogawa ホテルシーサイド江戸川 3804-1180
Hotel Seiyō Ginza ホテル西洋銀座 3535-1111 *39* H1
Hotel Sun City Ikebukuro ホテルサンシティ池袋 3986-1101 *58* D3
Hotel Sunlite Shinjuku ホテルサンライト新宿 3356-0391 *57* I 2
Holel Sunroute Plaza Tokyo ホテルサンルートプラザ東京 (0475) 55-1111 *91* H4
Hotel Sunroute Shibuya ホテルサンルート渋谷 3464-6411 *52* D6
Hotel Sunroute Tokyo ホテルサンルート東京 3375-3211 *56* E 7
Hotel Sunroute Yokohama ホテルサンルート横浜 (045) 314-3111 *62* B1
Hotel Takanawa ホテル高輪 5488-1000 *88* B 5
Hotel Tokiwa ホテルときわ 3202-4321 *89* F 2
Hotel Tokyo ホテル東京 3447-5771 *88* B 6
Hotel Kaiyō ホテル海洋 3368-1121 *89* F 1
Hotel Tōkyū Kankō ホテル東急観光 3582-0451 *48* D2
Hotel Tōyō ホテル東陽 3615-1041 *91* G3
Hotel Yaesu Ryūmeikan ホテル八重洲竜名館 3271-0971 *37* F 1
Hotel Yōkō Akasaka ホテル陽光赤坂 3586-4050 *48* D4
Hotel Yokohama, The ザ・ホテルヨコハマ (045) 662-1321 *63* G5
Ikebukuro Hotel Theatre 池袋ホテルテアトル 3988-2251 *59* G4
Ikenohata Bunka Center 池之端文化センター 3822-0151 *89* H5
Imperial Hotel (Teikoku Hotel) 帝国ホテル 3504-1111 *38* B3
Inabasō Ryokan 旅館稲葉荘 3341-9581 *88* E 2
Isezakichō Washington Hotel 伊勢佐木町ワシントンホテル (045) 243-1111 *91* H7
Kadoya Hotel かどやホテル 3346-2561 *56* D5
Kawasaki Grand Hotel 川崎グランドホテル (044) 244-2111 *91* I 5
Kawasaki Nikkō Hotel 川崎日航ホテル (044) 244-5941 *91* H5
Kayabachō Pearl Hotel 茅場町パールホテル 3553-2211 *89* F 7
Keiō Plaza (Inter-Continental) Hotel 京王プラザホテル 3344-0111 *56* C5
Kenpo Kaikan 健保会館 3403-0531 *48* E 7
Kensetsu Kyōsai Kaikan 建設共済会館 3400-4020 *55* F 5
Kichijōji Tōkyū Inn 吉祥寺東急イン (0422) 47-0109 *90* E 3
Kikuya Ryokan 喜久屋旅館 3841-6404 *89* I 6
Kōjimachi Kaikan 麹町会館 3265-5361 *89* E 4
Komaba Eminence こまばエミナース 3485-1411 *88* B 2
Kudan Kaikan Hotel 九段会館 3261-5521 *32* A 5
Kyōbashi Kaikan 京橋会館 3564-0888 *39* I 2
Lions Hotel Shinjuku ライオンズホテル新宿 3208-5111 *57* H1
Marroad Inn Akasaka マロウド・イン赤坂 3585-7611 *48* D5
Marunouchi Hotel (*see* Tokyo or Ginza)
Minami Aoyama Kaikan 南青山会館 3406-1365 *54* E 5
Mitsui Urban Hotel Ginza 三井アーバンホテル銀座 3572-4131 *38* C5
Miyako Hotel Tokyo 都ホテル東京 3447-3111 *29* E 1
Miyako Inn Tokyo 都イン東京 3454-3111 *29* G1
New Central Hotel ニューセントラルホテル 3256-2171 *33* G5
New Meguro ニュー目黒 3713-8131 *88* A 2
New Ōtani Inn Tokyo ニューオータニイン東京 3779-9111 *88* A 6
New Ōtani Inn Yokohama ニューオータニイン横浜 (045) 252-1311 *90* E 7
New Sanno U.S. Forces Center, The ニューサンノー米軍センター 3440-7871 *88* B 4
New Takanawa Prince Hotel 新高輪プリンスホテル 3442-1111 *29* F 3
Nihon Seinenkan Hotel 日本青年館ホテル 3401-0101 *88* D3
Omori Tōkyū Inn 大森東急イン 3768-0109 *91* F 5
Ours Inn Hankyū アワーズインハンキュウ 3775-6121 *91* F 4
Palace Hotel パレスホテル 3211-5211 *36* D6
Roppongi Prince Hotel 六本木プリンスホテル 3587-1111 *49* F 3
Royal Park Hotel ロイヤルパークホテル 3667-1111 *89* G7
Ryokan Katsutarō 旅館勝太郎 3821-9808 *26* D7
Ryokan Mikawaya Bekkan 旅館三河屋別館 3843-2345 *31* H4
Ryokan Okayasu おかやす旅館 3452-5091 *88* C6
Ryokan Sansuisō 旅館山水荘 3441-7475 *88* A 5
Ryōgoku Pearl Hotel 両国パールホテル 3625-8080 *89* H7
Ryōgoku River Hotel 両国リバーホテル 3634-1711 *89* H7
Satellite Hotel Kōrakuen サテライトホテル後楽園 3814-0202 *89* G4
Satellite Hotel Yokohama サテライトホテルヨコハマ (045) 641-0202 *63* G5
Sawanoya Ryokan 澤の屋旅館 3822-2251 *26* C6
Sheraton Grande Tokyo Bay Hotel シェラトングランデトーキョウベイホテル (0473) 55-5555 *91* H4
Shiba Park Hotel 芝パークホテル 3433-4141 *88* D6
Shiba Yayoi Kaikan 芝弥生会館 3434-6841 *88* D6
Shibuya Business Hotel 渋谷ビジネスホテル 3409-9300 *53* G4
Shibuya Tōbu Hotel 渋谷東武ホテル 3476-0111 *52* D2
Shibuya Tōkyū Inn 渋谷東急イン 3498-0109 *53* F 4
Shinagawa Prince Hotel 品川プリンスホテル 3440-1111 *29* F 4
Shinjuku New City Hotel 新宿ニューシティホテル 3375-6511 *88* D1
Shinjuku Park Hotel 新宿パークホテル 3356-0241 *88* E 2
Shinjuku Prince Hotel 新宿プリンスホテル 3205-1111 *57* F 2
Shinjuku Sunpark Hotel 新宿サンパークホテル 3362-7101 *89* F 1
Shinjuku Washington Hotel 新宿ワシントンホテル 3343-3111 *56* B7
Shin Tokyo Hotel 新東京ホテル 3291-6111 *32* D6
Shin Yokohama Hotel 新横浜ホテル (045) 471-6011 *90* E 6

Shin Yokohama Kokusai Hotel (045) 473-1311 *90* E 6
新横浜国際ホテル

Star Hotel Tokyo スターホテル東京 3361-1111 *56* E 2

Star Hotel Yokohama (045) 651-3111 *63* H5
スターホテル横浜

Suidōbashi Grand Hotel 3816-2101 *89* H4
水道橋グランドホテル

Suigetsu Hotel／Ohgaisō 3822-4611 *26* D7
水月ホテル／鷗外荘

Sukeroku-no-yado Sadachiyo Bekkan 3842-6431 *89* I 6
助六の宿 貞千代別館

Sun Plaza Hotel サンプラザホテル 3388-1151 *91* F 3

Sunshine City Prince Hotel 3988-1111 *59* I 4
サンシャインシティプリンスホテル

Taishō Central Hotel 大正セントラルホテル 3232-0101 *89* G1

Takanawa Prince Hotel 高輪プリンスホテル 3447-1111 *29* F 3

Takanawa Tōbu Hotel 高輪東武ホテル 3447-0111 *88* A6

Teikoku Hotel (*see* Imperial Hotel) 3504-1111 *38* B3

Tōkō Hotel 東興ホテル 3494-1050 *88* A5

Tokyo-to Kinrō Fukushi Kaikan 3552-9131 *89* F 7
東京都勤労福祉会館

Tokyo Aoyama Kaikan 東京青山会館 3403-1541 *55* G4

Tokyo Bay Hilton 東京ベイヒルトン (0473) 55-5000 *91* H4

Tokyo Bay Hotel Tokyū 東京ベイホテル東急 (0473) 55-2411

Tokyo City Hotel 東京シティーホテル 3270-7671 *34* C3

Tokyo Garden Palace 東京ガーデンパレス 3813-6211 *33* F 1

Tokyo Grand Hotel 東京グランドホテル 3456-2222 *88* D6

Tokyo Green Hotel Awajichō 3255-4161 *33* G4
東京グリーンホテル淡路町

Tokyo Green Hotel Kōrakuen 3816-4161 *32* A1
東京グリーンホテル後楽園

Tokyo Green Hotel Suidōbashi 3295-4161 *32* C6
東京グリーンホテル水道橋

Tokyo Hilton International 3344-5111 *56* A3
東京ヒルトンインターナショナル

Tokyo Hotel Urashima 東京ホテル浦島 3533-3111 *19* F 5

Tokyo Int'l Youth Hostel 3235-1107 *89* G4
東京国際ユースホステル

Tokyo Koma Ryokō Kaikan 3585-1046 *49* F 2
東京コマ旅行会館

Tokyo Kōsei Nenkin Kaikan Hotel 3356-1111 *89* E 2
東京厚生年金会館ホテル

Tokyo Marunouchi Hotel 東京丸ノ内ホテル 3215-2151 *36* E 3

Tokyo Ochanomizu Hotel Juraku 3251-7222 *33* G3
東京お茶の水ホテル聚楽

Tokyo Prince Hotel 東京プリンスホテル 3432-1111 *18* A4

Tokyo Station Hotel 3231-2511 *37* G3
東京ステーションホテル

Tokyo Sunny Side Hotel 3649-1221 *91* G3
東京サニーサイドホテル

Tokyo Yayoi Kaikan 東京弥生会館 3823-0841 *89* I 5

Tokyo YMCA Hotel 東京YMCAホテル 3293-1911 *33* F 6

Tokyo YWCA Hostel 3293-5421 *32* E 3
東京YWCAホステル

Tokyo YWCA Sadohara Hostel 3268-7313 *89* F 3
東京YWCA砂土原ホステル

Toranomon Pastoral 虎ノ門パストラル 3432-7261 *88* D5

Toshi Center Hotel 都市センターホテル 3265-8211 *46* C2

Tukuba Hotel ツクバホテル 3834-2556 *89* I 6

Ueno Terminal Hotel 上野ターミナルホテル 3831-1110 *30* D4

U-Port (Yūbin Nenkin Kaikan) ゆうぽうと 3490-5111 *28* D4

Yaesu Fujiya Hotel 八重洲富士屋ホテル 3273-2111 *37* J 3

Yamanoue Hotel 山の上ホテル (*see* Hilltop Hotel)

YMCA Asia Youth Center 3233-0631 *93* G4
YMCAアジア青少年センター

Yokohama Grand Intercontinental Hotel (045) 223-2222 *91* E 7
ヨコハマグランドインターコンチネンタルホテル

Yokohama Kokusai Hotel (045) 311-1311 *62* B1
横浜国際ホテル

Yokohama Plaza Hotel (045) 461-1771 *91* G7
ヨコハマプラザホテル

Yokohama Prince Hotel (045) 751-1111 *90* E 7
横浜プリンスホテル

Yokohama Tōkyū Hotel (045) 311-1682 *62* C1
横浜東急ホテル

Zenriren Kaikan (Hotel) 全理連宿泊部 3379-4181 *88* D2

Zensharen Kaikan 全社連会館 3445-0800 *88* A5

Zentoku Kaikan 全特会館 3585-2261 *49* G2

Others
その他

Police　警察への急報　110
Fire and Ambulance（calls answered in Japanese）　火事・救急車　119
Telephone：電話
　Long Distance Calls（operator-assisted）　市外通話　100
　Collect /Credit Calls　コレクト/クレジット通話　106
　Number Inquiries　電話番号案内　5295-1010（English）or 104
　Repair Service　電話の故障　113
International Telephone：国際電話
　Booking（operator-assisted calls）申し込み　0051
　Inquiries（operator-assisted calls）　問い合わせ　0057
Domestic Telegram：国内電報　115
International Telegram：国際電報　3344-5151
Time 時報　117
Weather　天気予報　（045）319-8100 and （0425）52-2511 Ext. 4181（English）,or 177
Tourist Information Centers：ツーリスト・インフォメーション・センター
　Tokyo（Yurakucho）　東京（有楽町）　3502-1461
　Asakusa 浅草　3842-5566
　New Tokyo International Airport（Narita）　新東京国際空港(成田）　（0476）32-8711
　Yokohama　横浜　（045）641-5824
Japan Travel-Phones（toll free）：旅行相談
　Eastern Japan　東日本　0120-222800
　Western Japan　西日本　0120-444800
Teletourist Service（English tape）　観光案内（英語）　3503-2911
　〃　（French tape）　〃　（仏語）　3503-2926
Flight Information：フライト案内
　Narita　成田　（0476）32-2800
　Haneda　羽田　3747-8010
Airport Baggage Service（ABC）　空港荷物サービス　3545-1131
Airport Limousine Bus Information　空港リムジンバス案内　3665-7251
Keisei Skyliner（Ueno-Narita）　京成スカイライナー（上野─成田）　3831-0131
Railway Information Center（Japan Railways）　鉄道案内（JR）　3212-4441
JAF（car breakdown service）　日本自動車連盟(車故障サービス）　3463-0111
Japan Travel Bureau　日本交通公社　3276-7777
Hospital Information　病院案内　3212-2323
American Pharmacy（English spoken）　アメリカン・ファーマシー　3271-4034
Tokyo English Life Line（TELL）　東京イングリッシュ・ライフ・ライン　3264-4347
Tokyo Regional Immigration Bureau　東京入国管理局　3213-8111
Foreign Residents' Advisory Center（Tokyo）　東京都庁外国人相談センター　5320-7744
Tokyo International Post Office　東京国際郵便局　3241-4891

Useful Phrases

道のたずね方

Occassionally the romaji phrases differ slightly in translation from the literal Japanese.

GENERAL

Excuse me.
すみません。
Sumimasen.

Thank you.
ありがとう。
Arigatō.

train
電車/列車
densha/ressha

subway
地下鉄
chikatetsu

station
駅
eki

bus
バス
basu

bus stop
バス停
basu-tei

ticket
切符
kippu

entrance
入口
iriguchi

exit
出口
deguchi

straight
まっすぐ
massugu

turn
まがる
magaru

right
右
migi

left
左
hidari

stop
止まる
tomaru

back
うしろ
ushiro

How much?
料金は、いくら？
Ikura?

I want to go to (place name).
私は、(場所名)に行きたい。
Watashi wa, (place name) ni ikitai.

Where is the toilet?
トイレはどこですか?
Toile wa, doko desu ka?

Is there anyone here who speaks English?
英語のできる人はいますか?
Eigo no dekiru hito wa, imasu ka?

Please telephone (number/name).
(電話番号/人・機関名)に、電話をかけて下さい。
(number/name) ni, denwa o kakete kudasai.

ASKING THE WAY

Is this (place name)?
ここは(場所名)ですか？
Koko wa, (place name) desu ka?

Where is (place name)?
(場所名)は、どこですか？
(place name) wa, doko desu ka?

Where is (place name) on this map?
(場所名)は、この地図のどこにありますか？
(place name) wa, kono chizu no, doko ni arimasu ka?

How long will it take to go to (place name)?
(場所名)に行くには、どのくらい時間がかかりますか？
(place name) ni iku ni wa, dono kurai jikan ga kakarimasu ka?

TAKING A TAXI

(destination), please.
(行き先)まで、行って下さい。
(destination) made, itte kudasai.

Please stop here.
ここで、止めて下さい。
Koko de, tomete kudasai.

How much is it?
料金は、いくらですか？
Ikura desu ka?

TAKING A TRAIN/SUBWAY

Which line should I take to go to (station name)?
(駅名)に行くには、何線ですか？
(station name) wa, nanisen desu ka ?

Which train should I take to go to (station name)?
(駅名)に行くには、どの電車に乗ればよいですか？
(station name) wa, dono densha ni noreba yoi desu ka?

Where do I buy a ticket?
切符は、どこで買えますか？
Kippu wa, doko de kaemasu ka?

How much is a ticket to (station name)?
(駅名)まで、料金はいくらですか？
(station name) made, ikura desu ka?

What is the platform number for (station name)?
(駅名)行きは、何番線ですか？
(station name)-iki wa, nanbansen desu ka?

Is this the right platform for (station name)?
(駅名)行きは、このホームですか？
(station name)-iki wa, kono hōmu desu ka?

Is this the right train to (station name)?
この電車は、(駅名)に行きますか？
Kore wa, (station name) ni ikimasu ka?

Does this train stop at (station name)?
この電車は、(駅名)に停まりますか？
Kore wa, (station name) ni tomarimasu ka?

How many more stops to (station name)?
(駅名)は、いくつ目ですか？
(station name) wa, ikutsume desu ka?

Where should I change trains to go to (station name)?
(駅名)に行くには、どこで乗り換えですか？
(station name) wa, doko de norikae desu ka?

Please let me know when we arrive at (station name).
(駅名)に着いたら、教えて下さい。
(station name) ni tsuitara, oshiete kudasai.

What time is the next train to (station name)?
次の(駅名)行きの電車は、何時ですか？
Tsugi no (station name)-iki wa, nanji desu ka?

本書の基図は(株)人文社版使用。
京葉地区－「この地図の作成に当たっては、建設省国土地理院発行の20万分の1地勢図を使用しました。(測量法第30条に基づく成果使用承認　平5　関使、第69号)」

The New Tokyo Bilingual Atlas 新東京二ヵ国語地図

1993年8月5日　第1刷発行

定価はカバーに表示してあります

編著者　株式会社 アイリス社
〒182 東京都調布市富士見町1丁目39－30
電話　(0424)82－7360

発行者　野間佐和子
発行所　株式会社 講談社
〒112-01 東京都文京区音羽2丁目12－21
電話　編集部 (03) 5395－3575
販売部 (03) 5395－3622
製作部 (03) 5395－3615
印刷所　凸版印刷株式会社
製本所　株式会社 国宝社

ISBN 4-06-206590-8　(国A)

1：500,000
0 5 10 15Km
Nagatoro 長瀞
Yorii 寄居
GYŌDA 行田
KAZO 加須
上越新幹線 Jōetsu Shinkansen
Kisai 騎西
Fukiage 吹上
Namegawa 滑川
Minano 皆野
Ogawa 小川
Higashi-chichibu 東秩父
HIGASHI-MATSUYAMA 東松山
KONOSU 鴻巣
Shōbu 菖蒲
Yoshida 吉田
Ranzan 嵐山
SAITAMA-KEN 埼玉県
Takasaki Line 高崎線
KITAMOTO 北本
Ina 伊奈
Ryōkami 両神
Ogano 小鹿野
Tamagawa 玉川
CHICHIBU 秩父
Yokoze 横瀬
Tokigawa 都幾川
OKEGAWA 桶川
Hachikō Line 八高線
Hatoyama 鳩山
Mitsumineguchi 三峰口
Kawajima 川島
AGEO 上尾
Ōtaki 大滝
Ogose 越生
SAKADO 坂戸
Shōmaru-tōge 正丸峠
Bukō-san 1295 武甲山
Moroyama 毛呂山
Mitsumine-san 三峰山
KAWAGOE 川越
TSURUGASHIMA 鶴ヶ島
川越線 Kawagoe Line
Ōmiya 大宮
Seibu Chichibu Line 西武秩父線
KAMETSU EXPWY 関越自動車道
HIDAKA 日高
KAMI-FUKUOKA 上福岡
YONO 与野
Naguri 名栗
CHICHIBU-TAMA NAT'L PARK 秩父多摩国立公園
SAYAMA 狭山
FUJIMI 富士見
Kumotori-yama 雲取山 2017
HANNŌ 飯能
Ara kawa
Ōi 大井
SHIKI 志木
Miyoshi 三芳
IRUMA 入間
青梅線 Ōme Line
Tabayama 丹波山
Okutama 奥多摩
ŌME 青梅
TOKOROZAWA 所沢
NIIZA 新座
ASAKA 朝霞
Tama Gawa 多摩川
Mizuho 瑞穂
KIYOSE 清瀬
WAKŌ 和光
Ōtake-san 大岳山 1266
HAMURA 羽村
MUSASHI-MURAYAMA 武蔵村山
HIGASHI-MURAYAMA 東村山
HIGASHI-KURUME 東久留米
Okutama-ko 奥多摩湖
Kosuge 小菅
Hinode 日の出
AKIGAWA 秋川
FUSSA 福生
YOKOTA 横田
HIGASHI-YAMATO 東大和
TANASHI 田無
HŌYA 保谷
Hinohara 檜原
Itsukaichi 五日市
KODAIRA 小平
TACHIKAWA 立川
国立
KOGANEI 小金井
MUSASHINO 武蔵野
AKISHIMA 昭島
KUNITACHI
KOKUBUNJI 国分寺
MITAKA 三鷹
MEIJINOMORI-TAKAO QUASI-NAT'L PARK 明治の森高尾国定公園
HACHIŌJI 八王子
中央自動車道 CHUO EXPWY
FUCHŪ 府中
CHŌFU 調布
YAMANASHI-KEN 山梨県
小田急線 Odakyū Line
Ōgiyama 1138 扇山
Uenohara 上野原
Sagamiko 相模湖
TAMA 多摩
CHŌFU 調布
KOMAE 狛江
599 Takao-san 高尾山
INAGI 稲城
Fujino 藤野
Sagami-ko 相模湖
Shiroyama 城山
TAMA NEW TOWN 多摩ニュータウン
Chūō Honsen 中央本線
Nambu Line
ŌTSUKI 大月
Tsukui 津久井
MACHIDA 町田
Akiyama 秋山
相模原 SAGAMIHARA
Sagami Gawa 相模川
KŌHOKU NEW TOWN 港北ニュータウン
TSURU 都留
Dōshi 道志
Aikawa 愛川
相模線 Sagami Line
Shin-Yokohama 新横浜
Yokohama Line 横浜線
ZAMA 座間
YAMATO 大和
Tanzawa-yama 丹沢山 1567
Kiyokawa 清川
TOMEI EXPWY 東名高速道路
TANZAWA-ŌYAMA QUASI-NAT'L PARK 丹沢大山国定公園
ATSUGI 厚木
ATSUGI 厚木
Yamana-ko 山中湖
1252 Ōyama 大山
AYASE 綾瀬
Tōkaidō Shinkansen
KANAGAWA-KEN 神奈川県
EBINA 海老名
ISEHARA 伊勢原
Keihin Kyūkō Line 京急本線
FUJI-HAKONE-IZU NAT'L PARK 富士箱根伊豆国立公園
HADANO 秦野
Odakyū Line 小田急線
東海道新幹線
Samukawa 寒川
Tōkaidō Honsen 東海道本線
Oyama 小山
Matsuda 松田
Yamakita 山北
Kaisei 開成
HIRATSUKA 平塚
FUJISAWA 藤沢
Ōfuna 大船
KAMAKURA 鎌倉
MINAMI-ASHIGARA 南足柄
Ōi 大井
Nakai 中井
CHIGASAKI 茅ヶ崎
GOTEMBA 御殿場
Oiso 大磯
Ninomiya 二宮
Kōzu 国府津
Enoshima 江ノ島
ZUSHI 逗子
Gotemba Line 御殿場線
Hakone 箱根
Sagami Wan (Bay) 相模湾
Hayama 葉山
ODAWARA 小田原
Hakone-yama 箱根山 1438
Ashino-ko 芦ノ湖
Miura